Schooling and the Making of Citizens in the Long Nineteenth Century

Routledge Research in Education

For a full list of titles in this series please visit www.routledge.com

27. Science, Society and Sustainability
Education and Empowerment for an Uncertain World
Edited by Donald Gray, Laura Colucci-Gray and Elena Camino

28. The Social Psychology of the Classroom
Elisha Babad

29. Cross-Cultural Perspectives on Policy and Practice
Decolonizing Community Contexts
Edited by Jennifer Lavia and Michele Moore

30. Education and Climate Change
Living and Learning in Interesting Times
Edited by Fumiyo Kagawa and David Selby

31. Education and Poverty in Affluent Countries
Edited by Carlo Raffo, Alan Dyson, Helen Gunter, Dave Hall, Lisa Jones and Afroditi Kalambouka

32. What's So Important About Music Education?
J. Scott Goble

33. Educational Transitions
Moving Stories from Around the World
Edited by Divya Jindal-Snape

34. Globalization, the Nation-State and the Citizen
Dilemmas and Directions for Civics and Citizenship Education
Edited by Alan Reid, Judith Gill and Alan Sears

35. Collaboration in Education
Edited by Judith J. Slater and Ruth Ravid

36. Trust and Betrayal in Educational Administration and Leadership
Edited by Eugenie A. Samier and Michèle Schmidt

37. Teaching and Learning with Technology
Beyond Constructivism
Edited by Concetta M. Stewart, Catherine C. Schifter and Melissa E. Markaridian Selverian

38. Gender Inclusive Engineering Education
Julie Mills, Mary Ayre and Judith Gill

39. Intercultural and Multicultural Education
Enhancing Global Interconnectedness
Edited by Carl A. Grant and Agostino Portera

40. Systemization in Foreign Language Teaching
Monitoring Content Progression
Wilfried Decoo

41. **Inclusive Education in the Middle East**
Eman Gaad

42. **Critical Issues in Peace and Education**
Edited by Peter Pericles Trifonas and Bryan Wright

43. **Children's Drawing and Writing**
The Remarkable in the Unremarkable
Diane Mavers

44. **Citizenship, Education and Social Conflict**
Israeli Political Education in Global Perspective
Edited by Hanan A. Alexander, Halleli Pinson and Yossi Yonah

45. **Emerging Teachers and Globalisation**
Gerry Czerniawski

46. **Social Studies as New Literacies for Living in a Global Society**
Relational Cosmopolitanism in the Classroom
Mark Baildon and James S. Damico

47. **Education Policy, Space and the City**
Markets and the (In)visibility of Race
Kalervo N. Gulson

48. **Memory and Pedagogy**
Edited by Claudia Mitchell, Teresa Strong-Wilson, Kathleen Pithouse and Susann Allnutt

49. **Universities and Global Diversity**
Preparing Educators for Tomorrow
Edited by Beverly Lindsay and Wanda J. Blanchett

50. **Equity and Excellence in Education**
Towards Maximal Learning Opportunities for All Students
Edited by Kris Van den Branden, Piet Van Avermaet and Mieke Van Houtte

51. **Global Pathways to Abolishing Physical Punishment**
Realizing Children's Rights
Edited by Joan E. Durrant and Anne B. Smith

52. **From Testing to Productive Student Learning**
Implementing Formative Assessment in Confucian-Heritage Settings
David Carless

53. **Changing Schools in an Era of Globalization**
Edited by John C. K. Lee and Brian J. Caldwell

54. **Boys and Their Schooling**
The Experience of Becoming Someone Else
John Whelen

55. **Education and Sustainability**
Learning Across the Diaspora, Indigenous, and Minority Divide
Seonaigh MacPherson

56. **International Case Studies of Dyslexia**
Edited by Peggy L. Anderson and Regine Meier-Hedde

57. **Schooling and the Making of Citizens in the Long Nineteenth Century**
Comparative Visions
Edited by Daniel Tröhler, Thomas S. Popkewitz and David F. Labaree

Schooling and the Making of Citizens in the Long Nineteenth Century

Comparative Visions

Edited by Daniel Tröhler,
Thomas S. Popkewitz,
and David F. Labaree

LONDON AND NEW YORK

First published 2011
by Routledge
711 Third Avenue, New York, NY 10017

Simultaneously published in the UK
by Routledge
2 Park Square, Milton Park, Abingdon, Oxfordshire OX14 4RN

Routledge is an imprint of the Taylor and Francis Group, an informa business

First issued in paperback 2015

© 2011 Taylor & Francis

The right of the Daniel Tröhler, Thomas S. Popkewitz, and David F. Labaree to be as the authors of the editorial material, and of the authors for their individual chapters, has been asserted by them in accordance with sections 77 and 78 of the Copyright, Designs and Patents Act 1988.

Typeset in Sabon by IBT Global.

All rights reserved. No part of this book may be reprinted or reproduced or utilised in any form or by any electronic, mechanical, or other means, now known or hereafter invented, including photocopying and recording, or in any information storage or retrieval system, without permission in writing from the publishers.

Trademark Notice: Product or corporate names may be trademarks or registered trademarks, and are used only for identification and explanation without intent to infringe.

Library of Congress Cataloging-in-Publication Data

Schooling and the making of citizens in the long nineteenth century : comparative visions / edited by Daniel Tröhler, Thomas S. Popkewitz, and David F. Labaree.
  p. cm. — (Routledge research in education ; 57)
  Includes bibliographical references and index.
  1. Education—History—century—Cross-cultural studies. 2. Education—Aims and objectives—Cross-cultural studies. 3. Citizenship—Cross-cultural studies. I. Tröhler, Daniel. II. Popkewitz, Thomas S. III. Labaree, David F., 1947–
  LA126.S32 2011
  370'.9034—dc22
  2010044447

ISBN 978-0-415-88900-1 (hbk)
ISBN 978-1-138-18480-0 (pbk)
ISBN 978-0-203-81805-3 (ebk)

Contents

Preface   xi

1 Introduction: Children, Citizens, and Promised Lands: Comparative History of Political Cultures and Schooling in the Long 19th Century   1
DANIEL TRÖHLER, THOMAS S. POPKEWITZ, AND DAVID F. LABAREE

PART I
Christian Souls, Enlightenment Ideals, and Pedagogical Forms

2 New Wine into Old Bottles: Luther's Table of Duties as a Vehicle of Changing Civic Virtues in 18th- and 19th-Century Sweden   31
DANIEL LINDMARK

3 From Imaginations to Realities: The Transformation of Enlightenment Pedagogical Illusions of the Dutch Republic into Late 19th-Century Realities of the Dutch Monarchy   50
JEROEN J. H. DEKKER

4 Republican Deliveries for the Modernization of Secondary Education in Portugal in the 19th Century: From Alexandre Herculano, Ramalho Ortigão, and Bernardino Machado to Jaime Moniz   70
JORGE RAMOS DO Ó

5 Republicanism and Education from Enlightenment to Liberalism: Discourses and Realities in the Education of the Citizen in Spain   94
ANTONIO VIÑAO

6   Republicanism, National Identity, and the Scottish
    Enlightenment   111
    DAVID HAMILTON

PART II
Organizing Schooling as Rationalizing Moral Codes

7   Republicanism "Out-of-Place": Readings on the Circulation of
    Republicanism in Education in 19th-Century Argentina   131
    INÉS DUSSEL

8   Classical Republicanism, Local Democracy, and Education:
    The Emergence of the Public School of the Republic of Zurich,
    1770–1870   153
    DANIEL TRÖHLER

9   Citizens and Consumers: Changing Visions of Virtue and
    Opportunity in U.S. Education, 1841–1954   177
    DAVID F. LABAREE

10 France—Schools in Defense of Modern Democracy: Tradition
    and Change in French Educational Republicanism from
    Condorcet to Quinet and Ferry   193
    FRITZ OSTERWALDER

PART III
Curriculum, Science, and the Fabrication of the Virtuous Citizen

11 From Virtue as the Pursuit of Happiness to Pursuing the
    Unvirtuous: Republicanism, Cosmopolitanism, and Reform
    Protestantism in American Progressive Education   219
    THOMAS S. POPKEWITZ

12 Literacy, Nation, Schooling: Reading (in) Australia   240
    BILL GREEN AND PHILLIP CORMACK

13 *Historia Magistra Civis*: Citizenship Education and Notions of
   Republicanism in Dutch History Textbooks Around 1800   262
   WILLEKE LOS

14 The Masters of Republicanism? Teachers and Schools in Rural
   and Urban Zurich in the 18th and the Long 19th Centuries   282
   ANDREA DE VINCENTI AND NORBERT GRUBE

Contributors   303
Index   307

Preface

The modern school is an enterprise that begins to take shape in the 18th century and emerges at the end of the 20th century as a globalized institution. To understand the emergence of the modern school and its particular traditions of teaching, curriculum, and learning, the book explores the major processes that made this institution possible and necessary, the creation of republican government, and the construction of the child as a future citizen. Historically, republican forms of government depended on conceptions of civic virtue, citizenship, and eventually democratic participation. That participation, however, was not natural to the individual but something that had to be produced. The making of the citizen through education was recognized in the founding of the American and French Republics at the end of the 18th century as well as in other European republics and emerging nation states in the early 19th century. Schools were central sites in this transformation of politics and the development of modern societies.

The central focus of this book is a comparative history that explores the social, cultural, and political complexities of the formation of the modern nation through examining the debates about education. The pathways to modern schooling in the different nations revolved around the power of existing mentalities; that is, the taken-for-granted and historically derived assumptions that linked individuality to collectively shared convictions. The technologies of teaching and curriculum, for example, were not born from one model or ideal of the citizen but arose from different historical practices and sometimes competing visions about the social order, the relation of the individual to collective norms and values, and the intersection of images of the individual with those of religion, social sciences, and philosophy. Further, these mentalities and technologies inscribed in the schools entailed principles about the character of the child that differentiated and divided. If we are going to be able to understand contemporary reforms of schooling that seek to change society by changing the child, we need to understand the historical characteristics and assumptions embedded in the modern school that enabled it both to produce the citizen and to differentiate the child.

In the 18th century, the singular focus on political stability in Europe and North America was challenged by a focus on progress. In this debate education became a crucial element while the idea of the republic became more and more dominant. Toward the end of the century, the American and the French revolutions brought this convergence to a head. The new republics brought a new kind of knowledge producing the conduct necessary for government. The Republican preoccupation with civic virtue—overcoming one's self-interest to take up the common interest—required the education of individuals capable of self-guided rational action for the public good.

We begin with the broad question about nation, citizen, and republicanism to locate the formation of the modern school. Our use of republicanism is to focus on the cultural norms, values, and dispositions about the participation of the citizen that the modern state required. Notions of republicanism circulated widely in Europe with the Renaissance and Reformation of the 16th and 17th centuries and with the secularizing processes associated with the Enlightenments that followed in Europe and North America.

The ideas of the individual were reassembled and reformulated in the 19th century in accordance with or in rejection of new ideas about social order and progress, science as a practice to intervene in human affairs, notions of individuality and human agency in processes of change, and comparative systems of reason through which the enlightened individual was differentiated from that of the Other. The new ideas and social technologies about child rearing and learning had an impact on education through new ways of thinking about the child with a moldable soul, who would learn to act as a self-motivated, self-responsible individual in the name of the common good. The pedagogy of the school embodied these changes as it was reconstituted at the level of transforming the self and organizing the problems of personal life. This transformation in seemingly secular projects of making the citizen, as multiple chapters in this book illustrate, were not merely shedding the past for the new but realigning prior technologies of pedagogy, such as found in Jesuit and Lutheran modes of instruction.

The various chapters argue that the political culture associated with republicanism was intertwined with salvation themes that were secularized in the new forms of government. In the northern European and North American contexts, this entailed the Protestant visions of the soul that combined with political themes to provide a solution to the central problem of order in modern society. In a capitalist economy, where individual entrepreneurs and consumers act as independent agents in their own interest, and in a post-traditional state, where individual members of society operate without the direct controls of monarch and lord, there is no single force that maintains social order and orients individuals toward the public good. However, the citizen constitutes an independent political actor who is imbued with civic virtue, and the soul constitutes an independent spiritual actor who is imbued with God's grace; together they form the possibility of creating a society of self-regulating individuals who pursue the public good of their own volition. But for this mechanism to work, there needs to be an institution that promotes systematic internalization of political and moral principles within the individual psyche, and that institution is the modern public school. One country after another invented or adopted the modern school as the new model of socialization, which was grounded in republican and Protestant principles even in countries where the monarchy and the Catholic Church remained in control.

This process started—if we dare to talk about starting points—in the 17th century with the rise of capitalism in the relative calm than ensued from the Peace of Westphalia in 1648 and the death of Oliver Cromwell in 1658. We call this uneven movement of different events that came together in the modern school as "the long 19th century." The different historical trajectories "ended" in the establishment of modern school systems in the 19th century, as schooling came to be understood as a key institution to secure the making of the citizen and the progress of nations. Contemporary discussions of universal human rights, the value of social inclusion and minority rights, as well as the cultural processes embedded in the new internationalism all are historically embedded in prior republican notions.

It is within this way of thinking of history as the movement of different trajectories that has become important to focus on the formation of the modern school in the late 18th century through the 1930s. For some, that might seem too broad. But we chose these dates for historical and practical reasons. Historically, if we use the markers of the American Revolution to the Great Depression, the formation of the modern school encompasses, for example, a continuous development and (re)visioning of republican ideas and state formation. To provide appropriate historical interpretation, the comparative approach of this book required flexibility to allow the various historians to locate their studies of the formation of the school in the context of republicanism in their target countries. For example, Swiss historical discussions would focus on relationships of Reformation, Enlightenment, and Republicanism in the formation of schooling. Argentinean discussions of republicanism and schooling would have a more recent set of historical trajectories through which to consider the relation of schooling and the modern self in pedagogy.

Building on this background, the book does not ask about the impact of schooling in modernization, nor does it seek to examine the impact that ideologies have on the development of school systems. Instead, it asks how modern school systems arose in the confluence of different historical trajectories through which the modern citizen is made possible as an actor and agent. In order to understand what can be called republicanism and schooling, for example, we need not only to compare the different republics in the 18th century and their developments in the 19th century, but we need also to compare those counties to one's that, at least in formal governmental structures, are definitely non-republican nations, such as England, Australia, Germany, Portugal, Spain, Scandinavia, and South American nations such as Argentina, because the processes related to republicanism in education have different sets of assemblages and connections even in the absence of formal republican governments.

The historians who contribute to this book examine a range of different sources and archival materials to explore the complex intersections of social, political, religious, cultural, and economic processes. The studies focus on schooling as it arises under different historical conditions in Northern, Central, and Southern Europe; North and South America; and Australia. One might ask at this point, why choose these countries and not others? While of course other countries and geographical spaces could easily be included, the choice of historical conditions was not one of a sampling. The selection of nations was practical, that is, they included historians who were willing to take up the historical methods that underlie this study of schooling and what are often lacking in the history of education.

We think of the contributions of this book to the study of schooling and the history of education as three.

First, it brings together major American, European, Australian, and Latin American writers to explore the emergence and implications of the modern school within a broader historical and comparative approach than typical. It does this by connecting the development of schooling with political theories of citizenship, enlightenment notions of progress and "reason," and at points capitalist, and anti-capitalist discourses of the 18th and 19th centuries. The book generates a differentiated picture in the history of education between ideas and practice and between national and international development. It places previously traditional homogenous and linear histories in a comparative field to understand the various distinctions and overlays that make possible the modern school.

Second, the chapters provide unique and challenging perspectives to the commonsense understanding of the historical development of the school and the problem of educational change as solely a national phenomenon. It does this by engaging in a conversation that interrelates historical studies of education with social, cultural, and political theories of knowledge. In this sense, the book engages U.S. traditions of historical research in education through its comparative perspective.

Third, although different understandings of public/civic virtues play an important role within the (recovered) concepts of historical and contemporary debates about the nation and citizen, these debates tend to marginalize education. Oddly, although political tracts about the making of the citizen of the republic through education were central to the formation of 18th-century republics, contemporary scholarship on political formation largely ignores schooling. If it appears at all, it is as footnotes, as authors focus on more exotic political and social-economic changes while paying little or no attention to the processes of the making of the citizen who was the agent of these changes. The studies in this book provide strong evidence of how popular educational discourses and concepts of schooling were embedded in the different concepts of republicanism.

Preface xv

The chapters in this book were originally papers presented at an international conference in Zurich in March 2007, which was sponsored by Pestalozzianum Research Institute for the History of Education Zurich (University of Applied Sciences Zurich: Teacher's College) and the Swiss National Science Foundation. It was organized by the three editors, with Daniel Tröhler as the host. The title of the conference was "Republican and Non-Republican Imaginations: Comparative Visions and Developments of Schooling from the 18th Century to 1930."

The book has profited from the help of many persons. In particular we wish to thank Chris Kruger (Madison-Wisconsin) and Ragnhild Barbu (Luxembourg) for their help in the manuscript preparation and Diana Goncalves Morgado (Luxembourg) for the Index.

Daniel Tröhler, University of Luxembourg
Thomas S. Popkewitz, University of Wisconsin–Madison
David F. Labaree, Stanford University
4 October 2010

1 Introduction
Children, Citizens, and Promised Lands: Comparative History of Political Cultures and Schooling in the Long 19th Century

Daniel Tröhler, Thomas S. Popkewitz, and David F. Labaree

This book emerges out of a long-term effort to understand schooling as a set of cultural and institutional practices concerned with the making of society by making the child as a future citizen. The aim of the national studies in the volume is to engage in a comparative discussion with historians of education and scholars of contemporary schooling about the formation of the school and its pedagogy through overlapping political, religious, institutional, and social practices in different geographical spaces, particularly Europe, the Americas, and Australia. Each nation tends to write its own history of schooling as a generic account of the modern school, but it is clear that these national developments are part of a global phenomenon that formed as part of the long 19th century to profoundly shape contemporary school and society—the intersection between the rise of schooling and the formation of the nation-state, which emerged from different and uneven historical practices between the late 18th century and the start of the 20th century. Among the themes we explore in this volume are salvation, the political cultures of the republicanism, the making of the citizen required for new forms of government, and the sciences of people that provided the basis of the new pedagogies of the new (progressive) schools.

Walter Benjamin (1955/1985) suggests that modern historiography entails an *emptying of time*, the depiction of a universal, boundless human progress with ideas of infinite perfectibility, an additive method whose illusions are of a seemingly continuous movement from the past to the present, and a rejection of theory. To write history, however, is to rethink the possibility of history as a reliable representation of the past. The past is not the point that culminates in the present from which people "learn" about their domestication and that provides a temporal index for their future. Instead, in line with Benjamin, we argue that history is the critical engagement of the present by making its production of collective memories available for scrutiny and revision.

The rethinking of the history of education has implications for more than the writing of the history of schooling. As Quentin Skinner (1998) said, one of the big advantages of history is not only the acquisition of knowledge but also the acquisition of self-awareness: "To learn from the past—and we cannot otherwise learn at all— . . . is to learn the key to self-awareness" (p. 67). Doing history is essentially the discovery of one's own standpoint. From a historiographic point of view, the critical question to be discussed, therefore, is not how we explain the differences of civic culture and citizenship against the background of an alleged ideal development, but rather why and how that kind of history is framed as a history of triumph or decline.

In an important sense, historical studies provide a way to explore the limits of the vision of the modern school as the repository of the general good and as society's mechanism for promoting moral health and social regeneration. The collective sense of the chapters in this book is to rethink the historical understanding of how schools were formed and to enable alternative ways of thinking and acting about the social role of schooling.

POLITICAL CULTURES AND THE COMPARATIVE STUDY OF CONTEMPORARY SCHOOLING

Policymakers and researchers today tend to assume that schools are responsible for developing the civic culture and the democratic participatory norms necessary for republican forms of government. Particularly in recent decades, researchers of citizenship education have argued, both nationally and internationally, that the schools need to improve not only instruction in school subjects but even more instruction for democracy. Especially in the wake of the two major political events in 1989, the Chinese government's crackdown on the protests in Tiananmen Square and the fall of the Iron Curtain in Europe, the idea emerged in Western societies that peace and progress on earth depend on an improved form of citizenship education.

It might be called the irony of fate that the missionary zeal of democratizing other countries by means of education also affected the West in seeking a new political consensus. Whereas some in the West prematurely declared "the end of ideology" (Bell, 1962) and "the end of history" (Fukuyama, 1989), others were concerned about the political culture and the quality of citizenship. These worries about the dangers of the lack of a viable civic culture were expressed over the decades in comparative studies of political cultures in the 1960s (Almond & Verba, 1963), the 1990s comparative study of civic education in six countries (Hahn, 1998; Mellor, 1998), and the International Association of the Evaluation of Educational Achievement (IAEEA) study of the relation of civic education and citizenship identity in 28 countries (Torney-Purta et al., 2001). The development of civic culture was also given psychological resonance in moral education through the work of Lawrence Kohlberg in the 1960s, the national call for educational reform (see the 1983 U.S. *A Nation at Risk* report and the 2001 *No Child Left Behind Act*, and *UNESCO's "Education for All"* (Jomiten, Thailand, 1990, and Dakar, Senegal, 2000), and the introduction of a British national curriculum on citizenship in the 1990s (see *Oxford Review of Education* during this decade).[1]

The findings of these studies provided the public with a lot of facts and correlations about trust and efficacy connected to something called "political culture" but left unexamined the specific historically grown cultural visions of the (ideal) state, the (ideal) citizen, and thus the (ideal) education of the child (which is the object of civic education). French political education, for instance, emphasizes national identity and the importance of national symbols more strongly than, for example, in England; and the English concepts of civic education emphasize the role of community, whereas the French neglect the same concept and accentuate the rational citizen (Osier/Starkey, 2001). Against this background, input and output factors turn out to be ultimately incompatible, and the results to a large degree are unexplainable. For example, the German test results did not correlate at all with the enormous German effort in citizenship education.

These failings show the limits of quantitative empirical comparative research: "Whether they are rooted in culture, history, or some aspects of schooling is not evident," the authors say; the results appear to be some sort of a "combination of all those factors," which cannot be operationalized by empirical research (Hahn, 1999, pp. 246f). The problem is that what works in one political culture with its "distinct set of values" cannot simply be adopted in another with "differing traditions, values and meanings" (p. 231). Accordingly, as recent research showed, it is hardly possible to transfer the successful Finnish educational policy model, for example, to Germany because the Finnish political culture perceives schooling as a common and corporate national project, whereas the German political culture understands schooling as matter of the political parties (Overesch, 2007). Consequently, the German *Bürger* means and therefore *is* something completely other than the French *citoyen*, the U.S. citizen, and the Spanish *ciudadano*.

The distinctions are not simply a question of different languages but of different cultural ascriptions. Even the German *Bürger* is something completely different from the Swiss *Bürger*, the Austrian *Bürger*, or the *Bürger* in the former German Democratic Republic. This becomes evident in the analysis of how some governmental activities are carried out in different countries. When in the early 1960s postal codes were introduced, for example, the four governments distributed their postal code directories to their citizens (*Bürger*). All of these directories had short forewords (one to five paragraphs). Whereas the two German countries used a sober official language to instruct their citizens, the Austrian and Swiss tried to be much more careful, using a friendly tone trying to convince citizens to participate in the new postal code system. Both started with an excuse, explaining the exigencies and describing what the implementation was *not* about. They tried to avoid the impression that the booklet might be interpreted as an authoritative prescription, and they tried to present it as an operating manual useful for all citizens. Both addressed themselves to the customers of the post; in Austria it was the "Dear esteemed postal costumer," and in Switzerland the "Honored post users"—whereas in both German directories there was no personal address at all. The West German foreword (it was the shortest one with only one paragraph) explained that the codes were developed strictly by technical criteria and tried this way to create respect for the new system, whereas the Eastern Germans expressed confidence that their citizens would help the state have an efficient post system. The Austrian foreword ended by thanking postal customers for their understanding and cooperation, and the Swiss thanked their citizens for being kind enough to use the codes and thus express their confidence that together the citizens and the postal system would be able to reach their common goal (Schelbert, 1983).

The Swiss *Bürger*—somewhat comparable to the U.S. citizen—represents a concept of being fundamentally responsible for the common good and the opposite of a subject, whereas the German *Bürger* has always been compatible with the status of subject. Therefore, the *Bürger's* reference group is not the state but the private family. The difference can be seen in the famous request by President John F. Kennedy: "Ask not what the country can do for you, ask what you can do for your country." The ideology behind this request is the perception of a citizen participating in the common good, a virtuous citizen identifying him or herself with the nation. The opposite is true for the German *Bürger*, as we can see in the politics of Bismarck, the first chancellor of the German Empire at the end of the 19th century. The broad acceptance of his social legislation as part of an encompassing welfare state, starting with the health insurance bill in 1883, indicated how the German *Bürger* expected as a matter of course broad protection from the state, rather than feeling responsible to provide this protection him or herself. And it is revealing as well that in Germany Bismarck successfully used the welfare state to prevent workers from being attracted to socialism and thus mobilized to political participation, whereas in contrast the introduction of universal health insurance by President Barack Obama was labeled socialistic in the United States—exactly what Bismarck wanted to prevent with similar means.

Where studies of political culture have been explored historically, it has been by examining the shared and universalizing technologies through which schools and nationalism overlap. As John Meyer and others have suggested, the organization of education has been a shared technology expressing the rationalized visions of different nation-states (Hüfner, Meyer, & Naumann, 1987; Meyer & Ramirez, 2000; Meyer & Rowan, 1977). This research is important for illuminating general trends. Yet at the same time, the different national starting points for this vision, the cultural idiosyncrasies and differential effects of this technology—and even the different visions that transformed an apparently identical technology into something culturally different—all require scrutiny. A comparative analysis of the nation-states in the long 19th century might conclude that their structures of nationalism are similar, but this does not tell us anything about the culturally inscribed principles that ordered assumptions, expectations, and actions of the individual nations. The deep hate, for example, of Germans toward British athletes and sport fans (Eisenberg, 1999) is not explainable on the basis of nationalism and physical exercise instruction but on the basis of cultural identities that have framed national institutions such as politics and the curriculum and the practices of schooling. Similarly, consider the fact that John Dewey's pragmatism was disparaged in German philosophy in the beginning of the 20th century as "dollar-philosophy" and "kitchen-utilitarianism," whereas it was well received and discussed for instance in Geneva (Tröhler, 2005).

The central focus of this book, therefore, is a comparative history that explores the social, cultural, and political complexities of modernity—more precisely of modernities—by examining debates about education, their effects in organizing mass schooling, and the backlash of mass schooling on the debates. We use the term "modern" here to refer to varied historical practices that come together in the long 19th century that combined to make the language of schooling and its institutional forms. The book engages the cultural and institutional dynamics through which certain central conceptions of society and individuality appear[2] and come to occupy a sacred position in the practices of change within which the "modern school" is located.

Therefore, the political cultures are not merely that of the creation of the explicit curriculum for "citizen education." Histories of the formation of school subjects in the late 19th and early 20th centuries direct attention to French art education (Nesbit, 2000), British mother-tongue education (Hunter, 1988), and American music education (Gustafson, 2009), for example, as practices concerned with the cultural making of the citizen, which permeated notions of child development, content selection, and pedagogical principles—practices that ordered schooling rather than embodying an explicit concept of civic education. For instance, the psychological shift in the pedagogy of U.S. art education focused on participation and the inner development of children in order to head off European-style fascism and its associated "authoritarian personality" (Freedman & Popkewitz, 1988).

Thus, our concern is not only with institutional, legal, and organizational qualities of schools but with the language of schooling as a cultural set of principles about what is known and how that knowing is to occur. The ideological languages or systems of reason are important to consider in the history of schooling as they embody cultural and political values and norms that generate principles about individual "belonging" to collective sites such as the nation (Popkewitz, 2008; Tröhler, 2011).

CULTURE, POLITICS, AND EDUCATION

The analysis of the mutual relation between political/cultural systems and educational practices is by no means a new project but stands rather at the outset of the phenomenon we discuss in this book. This discussion began shortly before the beginning of the long 19th century and was later overlapped by both the nationalism of the 18th and 19th centuries and the emerging global theories of the last 20 or 30 years. Shortly before the middle of the 18th century, it was the eminent French philosopher Montesquieu who in his magnum opus, *The Spirit of Laws* (1748), reminded the public of Aristotle's distinction between different forms of government and their idiosyncratic practices of education.[3] The following reconstruction of Montesquieu's considerations serves to frame the fundamental question of the following chapters about cultures, children, and citizens, and the vision of schooling as the route to the Promised Land(s).

The whole fourth book in Montesquieu's *The Spirit of Laws* deals with the thesis "That the Laws of Education Ought to Be in Relation to the Principles of Government." The notion of the "law" was by no means a legal term but referred to cultural idiosyncrasies and practices, and the notion of "principles" referred to what would be called today a distinctive political system. Montesquieu discerns three: monarchy, despotism, and the republic. The republic is able to take democratic or aristocratic forms, and the distinction between monarchy and despotism depends on whether or not the monarch governs "by fixed and established laws" (*The Spirit of Laws*, book 2, Chapter 1).

In accordance with sensationism,[4] the then dominant theory of cognition in France, Montesquieu starts his fourth book of *The Spirit of Laws* by saying: "The laws of education are the first impressions we receive; and as they prepare us for civil life, every private family ought to be governed by the plan of that great household which comprehends them all"—the "great household" being the state or the type of government (republic, monarchy, or despotism).[5] "The laws of education will be therefore different in each species of government: in monarchies they will have honor for their object; in republics, virtue; in despotic governments, fear" (book 4, Chapter 1). In other words, the citizen of a monarchy should become honorable, the citizen of the republic virtuous, and the citizen of a despotic government fearful.

The different principles of government, however, with their idiosyncratic practices of education, not only differ by content and pedagogy and therefore their concept of citizenship but also by their investment in education. To Montesquieu, there is no doubt that the aim of education in the republic—virtue—requires the utmost efforts: "It is in a republican government that the whole power of education is required. The fear of despotic governments naturally arises of itself amidst threats and punishments; the honor of monarchies is favored by the passions, and favors them in its turn; but virtue is a self-renunciation, which is ever arduous and painful" (book 4, Chapter 5). The citizen of the republic obviously requires the biggest efforts to render him as what he is supposed to be: virtuous.

This virtue is directed to the common good and entails essentially the love of fatherland and the subordination of private interests: "This virtue may be defined as the love of the laws and of our country. As such love requires a constant preference of public to private interest, it is the source of all private virtues; for they are nothing more than this very preference itself" (book 4, Chapter 5). It goes without saying that in a democratic form of a republic, all the people need to be educated toward virtue, and that in an aristocratic form of a republic first and foremost those with the right to be in power need to be made virtuous. Back in 1748, when Montesquieu was writing his *The Spirit of Laws*, most countries were monarchies (France being in the eyes of Montesquieu a despotism), some were aristocratic republics (city states with subjected land according to the Greek model) such as the Swiss Cantons of Zurich or Berne, and only a very few cantons in the Swiss alps were considered to be democratic republics (although virtually dominated by "important" families).

Republicanism, Education, and Global Interpretations of World History

Obviously, Montesquieu could know only a few contemporary republics (aristocratic and democratic), and he identified in particular the confederations of the Netherlands and Switzerland plus a few German cities such as Lübeck and Bremen. However, by the end of the 18th century, two new republics emerged[6] that would prove to be of global importance, the United States and France, and today most of the powerful countries in the world are in some way or another republics. Within the "group of eight," for instance, six countries are considered to be republics (United States, Germany, Canada, Italy, France, and the semi-member Russia), and only two are (constitutional) monarchies (Japan, United Kingdom).[7] The republic—despite all the differences and the critical questions as to whether or not a republic is indeed a republic—is a successful model that seems to be highly attractive to a variety of political cultures.[8]

Consider that (a) republics (at least in the mind of Montesquieu) needed state systems of education to persist, (b) republics grew in numbers and importance throughout the world in the 19th and 20th centuries, and (c) mass schooling expanded rapidly in the 19th and 20th centuries throughout the world. In summary, this suggests that the combination of republicanism and education has been an extraordinary success on the world stage. The complementarity of the republic and education becomes even more necessary if the educational shift in the second half of the 18th century is considered, when social problems became more and more educationalized, as education increasingly seemed the answer to every social ailment. This shift first appeared in contexts that were not only republics but those that were dominated by reformed Protestantism[9] (Tröhler, 2008). Montesquieu had already identified the close relation between republics and Protestantism: In the 14th book of *The Spirit of Laws*, he claimed "[t]hat the Catholic Religion is most agreeable to a Monarchy, and the Protestant to a Republic" (book 14, Chapter 5). Montesquieu ascribed the fact that the republics and Protestantism were situated in the north of Europe (German city states, the Netherlands, and Switzerland) not to greater intelligence or rationality but to the climate: "The reason is plain: the people of the north have, and will for ever have, a spirit of liberty and independence, which the people of the south have not; and therefore a religion which has no visible head is more agreeable to the independence of the climate than that which has one" (book 14, Chapter 5).

However the emergence and local attractiveness of Protestantism is explained, a success story of the three "ingredients" seems to be all too obvious: The political form of the republic, (reformed) Protestantism, and education appear to be the globally successful amalgam, the engine of global development.[10]

Republics and Republicanisms

Despite the attractiveness of universal theories of progress, history proves to be much more complicated. Such theories suggest a linear and harmonizing vision of globalization, which neglects or at least marginalizes competing models, rather than analyzing the complexity of the historical processes (Tröhler, 2009). It will do to recall that the French Revolution not only referred to the republic Montesquieu had in mind, the republic of antiquity with its virtuous citizen, but also defined a completely new language of republicanism. These two very different languages or ideologies of republicanism have been challenging each other for the last 250 years and are often confused or blended with each other. And there is a third model of the republic (often forgotten), namely the Dutch, which merged pragmatically the idea of an aristocratic republic in the sense of Montesquieu with the capitalist idea of the citizen and exerted much more influence in the political debates than research has recognized (Mijnhardt, 2005). The two ideal types, however, have continued to be the classical republic and the modern republic. Or in light of the linguistic turn—which encourages us to look at republicanism rather than at the republic—we can call these two different republican languages, competing with each other up to the present day.

Today, the historically older strand, the so-called classical one (the one Montesquieu was thinking of in 1748) is still labeled as (classical) republicanism, whereas the other strand, the newer one, emerging in the late 18th century, is now mostly called liberalism (in the European sense). Attempts to distinguish them have been undertaken by intellectuals such as the Benjamin Constant in his famous 1816 talk *The Liberty of Ancients Compared with that of Moderns*[11] or by Isaiah Berlin in his inaugural lecture before the University of Oxford 1958, *Two Concepts of Liberty* (Berlin, 1958). Both authors defend the modern liberal version of republicanism with its concept of "negative liberty," whereas in another inaugural lecture in Great Britain in 1998, *Liberty before Liberalism*, the historian Quentin Skinner articulates more appreciation for the classical republicanism with its concept of "positive liberty" (Skinner, 1998). "Negative liberty" assumes an independent rational subject as a point of origin for any social or political thinking. In other words, in contrast to the classical republicanism, this modern form of republicanism starts from a non-historical and abstract point of view. It refers to freedom as freedom from interference by the government or other people, as we would find it in the writings of Condorcet.

Accordingly, education is focused on modern, rationally legitimated knowledge by which the young will be able—and free—to pursue their own interests and their own social position. The philosophical basis for this position is modern natural law, according to which every man is "free" by birth and has inalienable rights. Social cohesion is made by a social contract, and this contract, if it is an expression of justice, takes care of the equality among human beings. People live together in a political community not as friends or brothers—which was the vision of Aristotle and classical republicanism—but as contract partners, and they try to find laws that give every inhabitant a certain space of liberty, so that citizens can enjoy their lives as much as they want and in the way that they want. The ideal citizen is self-interested *and* enlightened by education in modern science. The ideal of this modern republicanism based almost exclusively on knowledge (and not on emotions such as the love of fatherland) was defended during the French Revolution by Condorcet (see Chapter 10, this volume).[12]

Whereas modern republicanism can be easily identified with the revolutionary French period after 1789, classical republicanism is undoubtedly the dominant language in Switzerland through the concept of "positive liberty."[13] This concept assumes less an independent rational subject as a point of origin than the political community as we would find it in Aristotle's practical philosophy. To be free refers to an idea of freedom as opportunity and an ability to act to fulfill one's own potential, especially as a political actor. To be free to create laws makes it necessary to obey them, which in turn requires some specific virtues, namely, the love of laws or, a bit more broadly, the love of fatherland as a place where the citizen finds fulfillment as a human being making and following these laws. Education, therefore, focuses at least as much (if not more) on virtue as on knowledge, as one might find in Rousseau's *Considerations on the government of Poland* (1772) or in his famous *Letter to d'Alembert* (1758).

The relevance of the distinction between the two concepts of ordering of social conduct, the ideal of the citizen or the "nature" of society, can be detected in the heated debate about the roots of the United States, a debate that has a great deal to do with the self-perception of Americans. It is the question of whether the ideals of republicanism were classical or liberal. An expression of this debate was the so-called communitarianism-liberalism quarrel in the 1980s, in which critiques of the present social and economic situation in the United States identified this situation as the result of a liberal political ideology (which they usually saw legitimated in John Rawls' *Theory of Justice*, 1972) and evoked ideals of community that had been shared by the people in the founding time of the United States (Bellah et al., 1985; Sandel, 1982). In the background of this communitarian vision (Etzioni, 1993) is the language of classical republicanism, as it was introduced by the New Zealander John G. A. Pocock, who sought to explain "that the United States was barely modern at all, but should—from the point of view of dominant languages—rather be traced back to Machiavelli's times" (Rodgers, 1992, p. 19; see also Pocock, 1975; Sandel, 1996).

The contribution of this volume is to explore how the different political concepts to order conduct are assembled, connected, and disconnected historically and to what extent they can be understood through the implicit ideal types of classical and modern republicanism. The notion of the long 19th century, for example, directs attention to the republicanism as a cultural language that intersects with salvation themes drawn from religious narratives, elements of the various enlightenments, pedagogical narratives about the technologies to make the good and virtuous citizen, and scientific narratives about the logic and rationality of thought and action. The schooling, however, is not merely the sum of the different narratives or an expression of particular ideal types. The intellectual, cultural, and institutional "outcome" of the school is a (re)visioning and (re)configuration of these different historical practices into particular patterns of thought and action about what constitutes schooling, the child, and the future citizen.

Republic, Republicanism, Democracy, and Enlightenment

Republicanism and democracy are not identical terms. Great Britain, for example, is both a parliamentary democracy and constitutional monarchy, but it is not a republic; the same is true for Sweden. Democracy can be the governmental system in both republics and monarchies. The meaning of the notion "republic" has now been more and more leveled to the meaning of "non-monarchy," which suggests that we should focus less on the form of government (monarchy and republic) and more on the languages of republicanism (classical or modern). The modern language of republicanism ("negative liberty") that arose in the French Revolution is unthinkable without democracy, but the classical language of republicanism ("positive liberty") is much more reserved in this respect. Most of the fervent defenders of the classical republicanism in Switzerland in the 18th century rejected full democracy and favored a "mixed system," the democracy of an elite minority (based on merits rather than on ancestry, of course), or (in Montesquieu's words) an aristocratic republic.

The rebirth of classical republicanism in the mid-18th century and the birth of modern republicanism at the end of the same century suggest a close relationship between republicanism and what is called the Enlightenment. The label "Enlightenment" serves in many accounts as an umbrella term for almost any intellectual movement in the 18th century. Because general historiographical narratives tells us that the American and French revolutions were political expressions of Enlightenment and at the same time the birth of modernity, we all seem to be heirs and successors of the Enlightenment.

This perspective, however, is closely related to what Walter Benjamin called the *emptying of time*. Some 12 years ago, it was the cultural historian Robert Darnton who challenged this generalization of the notion of Enlightenment as a case of de-historization. Darnton discussed the problem that in the general view, the late 20th century is more or less the direct descendant of the *Enlightenment* and, even more, of *the* Enlightenment. Darnton (1997) criticized the inflated use of the term "enlightenment" for almost all non-reactionary phenomena of the 18th century because, blown up to such a size, it loses its meaning: "The Enlightenment is beginning to be everything, and therefore nothing" (p. 34). Darnton was aiming for two things. First, he wanted to "reduce the Enlightenment to manageable proportions" (p. 35, p. 34f.). In the 18th century, he said, there was no homogenous intellectual tradition that could be called the Enlightenment. He therefore proposed limiting the notion to the place where the idea was "born" and to its exponents—to Paris and the circle of people who called themselves *"philosophes,"* and that represented a very different concept of modern thinking than, let's say, David Hume, Adam Smith, Edmund Burke, Johann Joachim Winckelmann, Immanuel Kant, or Johann Wolfgang von Goethe. In other words, the Enlightenment is, according to Darnton, a historically and locally specific way of thinking. And the second problem Darnton identified was that the inflated use of "Enlightenment" leads to a facile identification of the ideas of the 18th century with all modernity, as synonymous with much of what is subsumed under the name of Western civilization. Thus, it can be easily made "responsible for almost everything that causes discontent, especially in the camps of postmodernists and anti-Westernizers" (p. 35).

One does not have to agree with this rigid limitation of the notion of "enlightenment," but there are certainly good reasons to limit it to the way of philosophical and political thinking that is based primarily on modern sciences and the modern natural law. Modern republicanism, as continually expressed through the chapters of this volume, is undoubtedly emerged in the intersection of elements of the enlightenment, points where different forms of republicanism were placed in an intersection with some enlightenment motives but at other historical spaces in the forming of the nation and schooling considered part of a distinct intellectual, mostly anti-capitalist movement that is not identifiable with the enlightenment.[14]

PROMISED LANDS: MODERN NATIONS, SALVATION THEMES, AND SCHOOLING

Montesquieu was certainly right when in 1748 he pointed out the interdependency among form of government and educational practices, the educational potential of republicanism, and the close relationship between Protestantism and republicanism. However, he could not foresee the emergence of a second language of republicanism at the end of the 18th century, nor the fact that Catholic as well as Protestant countries in the long 19th century would initiate systems of schooling in order to educate the people and create national identity. But even if the attractiveness of education to all of the countries in this period can rather easily be established, the question still remains whether non-Protestant countries copied Protestant ideas and systems and what happened in the translation of these ideas and systems into local religious and cultural idioms.

To decipher the amalgam of factors shaping education—culture, history, and schooling—is the core aim of a modern, comparative cultural history of education that pays respect to the molding effects of the historically grown, inherited, and transformed contexts in which people grow up. Whereas similar words are used in school reform across nations about the child, the citizen, civic education, and citizenship, these words are given expression within particular historical contexts that are not identical, and they often unconsciously inscribe the national, ideological, and religious traditions on educational policy and educational research. The excavation of the different historical traces and the ideological, political, and religious backgrounds to schooling provide a way to consider distinctions and differences in the shaping of contemporary narratives of civic education and civic virtue.

These chapters, initially presented at a conference held in Zurich in 2007, aim to help provide an outline for a comprehensive comparative study of dominant cultural patterns of thought and self-conception—about the ideal form of government, the ideal citizen, and the ideal vision of social progress—that are embodied in schooling. The conference started out with a core idea: to examine how and to what degree countries sharing a specific political mode of thinking about the ordering of social conduct tried to reinforce and stabilize this specific mode of thinking and behavior by means of education, most of all by the organization of education into schools. From a different angle, we wanted to examine whether or not in these countries the establishment of modern schooling in the long 19th century could be understood as specific, effective, and efficient efforts to realize or improve the continuing idea of citizenship by education. The countries we examined most closely in a comparative way were the four republics at the end of the 18th century—The Netherlands, Switzerland, the United States, and France—comparing them not only to each other but to non-republican nations as well.

In this book, we examine five intersecting themes about the formation of schooling, which we briefly summarize in this section of the introduction:

- The modern school joined republican visions of the citizen with narratives about the liberty and freedom of the individual.
- Schooling embodied visions of salvation about the promised secular land of republican life.
- The democratic impulse to include also embodied processes of exclusion.
- The new social and educational sciences calculated and planned the reform of society.
- The different languages and institutional forms given to modern schooling existed in a global field.

The Modern School Joined Republican Visions of the Citizen with Narratives About the Liberty and Freedom of the Individual

Republicanism in the advent of the modern school embodied two registers that are often thought to be in opposition, as expressed in the separate notions of negative and positive liberty; that is, the social administration of freedom. Whether the discourses of schooling stressed negative or positive liberty, the practices of education in general and of schooling in particular encased in the term "modern" assumed that (a) the citizen was not born but made, and (b) the pedagogical projects of education and schooling would provide the principles and processes of social administration that would order the conduct necessary for the practices of liberty and freedom. As Cruikshank (1999) argues, "participation was not clear cut or naturally occurring; it was something that had to be solicited, encouraged, guided, and directed. Hence, the new sciences of politics needed to develop technologies of citizenship and participation" (p. 97).

Schooling brought together the registers of social and institutional governing with that of individual freedom and liberty. In the Preamble of the U.S. Constitution, adopted in 1787, the two registers are evident in its justification of government:

> We the People of the United States, in Order to form a more perfect Union, establish Justice, insure domestic Tranquility, provide for the common defense, promote the general Welfare, and secure the Blessings of Liberty to ourselves and our Posterity, do ordain and establish this Constitution for the United States of America.

The "We" consecrates government as responsible for the collective well-being of the commonwealth through securing "a more perfect Union." Institutional sovereignty of government, however, coexisted with the register of individual liberty and freedom. The latter brought to bear American Enlightenment principles of the citizen whose individual freedom and liberty were also to give expression to patriotism that was essential to the functioning of non-monarchic government. A similar relation can be found in the humanism of the Scottish Enlightenment influential in the formation of the American and British schools (Hamilton[15]; Hamilton, 1989). Education was institutionalized through a blueprint (a timetable of lessons and course of study) and sometimes administered and locally controlled by the citizens themselves (Labaree, Tröhler). That blueprint, Hamilton argues, is to produce liberty through the capabilities of the child who has communicative fluency, erudition, political and legal expertise, discretion, integrity, nobility of spirit, and humility coupled with assurance.

The school was to make the citizen needed for the republic. Education was central to ensure the moral development and growth of the child through education and the childrearing patterns of the family. From France, The Netherlands, Switzerland, and across the Atlantic, narratives of the school and family were about making virtuous citizens. The family was visualized as the cradle of civilization where a child learns to be civilized and a part of civilization embodied in the nation. Osterwalder argues, for example, that the familial morality and national virtue aimed at the same goal of good citizenship. Educational discourses were about the citizens who loved their country and embodied heroism and self-sacrifice in the name of the nation. Dutch 17th-century school reforms placed emphasis on the family morals such as the importance in upbringing for all mothers to breast-feed (Dekker). The Puritans in the United States called the family the "little commonwealth" (Popkewitz, 2008). Their notions of the family as the fundamental source of community and continuity—the place where most work was done, and the primary institution for teaching the young, disciplining the wayward, and caring for the poor—was re-inscribed in the school of the new republic.

The inscription of the enlightenments' cosmopolitan beliefs and political cultures created different sets of principles for organizing the pedagogy of the school. Osterwalder argues, for example, that in France in the late 18th century, the school entered the struggle over pluralist interests and republican morality by becoming a site for enabling freedom, liberty, and the participatory demands of the republic. Instruction was moral and civic. The state school was to guarantee that youth did not accept an anarchy of opinions that would lead to authoritarian manners. The collective values of "human," civil, and political rights became part of the conceptual principles safeguarding individual freedom and a prerequisite for the liberal tradition within French republicanism. Portuguese political and cultural circles, in contrast, argued for republican forms of educational governing that articulated enlightenment ideas about individuals capable of self-guided rational action

(Ó). Instruction, however, combined the subject of "reason" with that of learning the mysteries of the faith. Dutch national unification and reconciliation in the Batavian government entailed the adoption of an inclusive ideal of civil or moral citizenship in 1795 that stressed martial virtue connected with willingness to protect one's native town or country (Los). Textbooks point to republican ideas of citizenship that embodied a patriotic sense and restoration of society by industriousness and good morals like thrift, honesty, philanthropy, and impartiality, virtues propagated by republican authors.

Republicanism merged with notions of democracy to reshape the relation of the public and private, society and the individual, and individuality and collective. Democracy was a political practice that enabled personal interest and will be brought into a relation to public interest articulated as civic culture (collective obligations and responsibilities). In the late 19th century, Labaree argues in the United States, the balance between the *res publica* in school and individual interests, for example, shifted toward the latter. Individual liberty replaced civic virtue as the centerpiece of the educational enterprise. By the 20th century, notions of the republic disappear and are replaced with a homo economicus related to the social efficiency reforms for the American high school. Civic virtue was linked to the issues of access, opportunity, and the pursuit of happiness tied to existing social structures.

Schooling Embodied Visions of Salvation About the Promised Secular Land of Republican Life

To talk about schooling as salvation seems, at first glance, misplaced in the context of the secularization assumed as part of modernity.[16] Anti-clericalism was indeed part of the French Enlightenment, but this is only part of the story. American and early European state formation, for example, emerged through processes of faith and social discipline unleashed by the Reformation but that overlapped with the developments of capitalism and military competition (Gorski, 1999). Close readings of the cultural histories of the American and French Revolutions show a merger of discourses of religion with a state that is often given "divine sanction" (Becker, 1932/2003; Bell, 2001; Ferguson, 1997; Marx, 2003). When we closely examine discourses of modern schooling, themes of salvation, redemption, and fear of a fall from grace were embodied in the phenomena of modernity and secularization. It is thus, as Tröhler argues, no coincidence that the modern school of the liberal republic of Zurich was organized analog to the organization of the Zwinglian church, extending the Zwinglian perception of local democracy to a "universal" principle of school affairs.

The formation of the school involved different relations between citizens and religion. As Osterwalder argues, the secular required religious discourses for the production of morality itself. School was to develop the principles of the common good and individual liberty. This theme continues in Ó's chapter. Pedagogy was the project of learning sensibilities, emotions, and rationalities to order moral conduct in the inner life—a soul in concept if not in religious cosmology. The common morality in the French school was based on emotion in the form of Gallic religion of conscience and introspection, and political religion related to Rousseau's social contract (Osterwalder). In the United States, pedagogy entailed Puritan notions of salvation and individualization that inscribed to nation as "the chosen people" (Popkewitz).

If we take central notions of modern pedagogy to foster the child's abilities of reason, that reason was never merely cognitive and rational. Older religious forms of pedagogy leached into the instruction to produce the republican citizen. The sentiments, morality, emotion, and science overlapped in the cultural ascriptions of pedagogy. Ó argues that Portuguese republican discourses of education in the 19th century were intended to overcome what was seen as the failed models of the Catholic Church. But in fact that reform returned to Jesuit teaching practices. School was to produce a new man, an agent of progress, a citizen with clarified intelligence, sensitivity, and a robust body. Dekker, as well, identifies a new pedagogical discourse that emerged from adherents of the Dutch enlightenment in the Dutch Society of Public Welfare. The school reforms were to provide universal education in order to contribute to unification and modernization at the end of the 18th century. That education was to create a patriotic citizen through combining Dutch cultural norms of republicanism with Christian values (Los, Dekker).

Prior models related to teaching of religion that crossed Protestant and Catholic contexts were (re)visioned in the school. The heritage of the Scottish school, Hamilton argues, had roots in the awareness of two sources of social change in the middle ages—Providence (God's direction) and Fortuna (Lady Luck)—which joined with the notion of progress that was given expression through the ideas of conscious actions of human beings and human agency (i.e., their humanism). Education fostered the acquisition of wisdom, and, in turn, the public exercise of this wisdom was the basis for self-government (among wise male citizens). Scottish attention to *virtuous* education and godly upbringing in 1560 was parallel with Lutheran and Swiss Protestant notions of upbringing that were formalized outside the home in what can be thought of as modern schooling.

The different languages of republicanism in schooling were located, in part, in the Calvinist distinction between elect and reprobates and the Lutheran discussion of justification by faith not by works (Hamilton). One borrowed form was the catechism of churches to teach patriotism. In Spain thinkers of the counter-enlightenment at the end of 18th century did not differentiate republicanism from Church and monarchy (Viñao). For them, schooling entailed a mixture of religion, morality, and citizenship intended to produce industrious citizens whose happiness and prosperity for the republic included awareness of civic duties and love of their country. In the liberal periods in Spain (early 19th century), the constitution did not speak of the rights of man and citizen but of the Spanish nation and obligations to patriotism and obedience to laws. The educational law of 1823 required that alongside of the religious catechism would be a "constitutional catechism." In Sweden, the catechism of Martin Luther's Table of Duties represented the moral curriculum after 1686 to interpret the prevailing moral philosophy based on natural law. By the 1800s, this pedagogy of unconditional obedience was replaced by a pedagogy that emphasized a reciprocal relationship of care and respect. The *Patriotic Catechism* in Argentinean school reforms took the pedagogical format of questions and answers transmitting religious faith (Dussel). The Catechism relied strongly on memory and repetition and originally was thought of as an oral device. The new pedagogical sciences that were focusing on instructing large numbers of children broke down content to be taught into several small pieces, which were intended to cover the whole array of questions to be raised about a subject.

The salvation narratives embodied in the discourses and technologies of pedagogy of the modern school gave focus to the city. The city was the space where the enlightenment hopes of progress could be enacted, and it was the space of the dangers and dangerous populations to the envisioned notion of civilization. The city occupied a dual space in social and educational reforms throughout North America and Europe. The French, for example, associated the morality of the city with the right to education (Osterwalder). But this relation of the city to republicanism is not as straightforward as it might seem. In an interesting comparative study, De Vincenti and Grube compare the aristocratic republic of Zurich with the rural schools within the territory of the republic. Rural areas exhibited the participation norms of communes, which defended the rights to elect the schoolmaster and resist outside interference (De Vincenti and Grube). The schools were linked to being good Christians and to securing children's salvation within the canon of values of the communes themselves. When the high school of Zurich was examined 100 years later, the very notions of community and collective responsibility of the rural areas had been inscribed into the notion of civic virtue that circulated in the school. The making of the child as the future citizen did not ask for school republics, as Tröhler demonstrates for Zurich, but embodied patriotic catechisms, as Dussel calls the pedagogy of citizenship. American Progressive Education and the more general Progressive political and social reforms, Popkewitz argues, embodied the concern with urbanization. Called the Social Question, Protestant reforms focused on alleviating the contradictions produced by the dislocations and threats of moral disorder produced by industrialization and urbanization.

The Democratic Impulse to Include Also Embodied Processes of Exclusion

Republicanism as a political culture, we argued earlier, embodied two registers that related institutional forms of governing with conceptions of the capacities and actions of individuals that were necessary for government.

The very inscription of notions of civic virtue and the common good embodied a style of thought that enabled comparisons of people along a continuum of value. This comparative style of thought had two different but overlapping historical trajectories.

One was institutional and related to given identities, such as the way many earlier republican governments excluded women, religious minorities, non-citizens, and other races. The groups that would be citizens and vote, for example, changed over time as republicanism and representation were increasingly tied to notions of democracy, as illustrated in the chapters on Dutch school reforms and the Argentinean movement for universal male suffrage. The liberal elites of Argentina saw natives, blacks, and mestizos as barbarians in comparison to the civilized manners of the white population. While republican education was to provide the cement to overcome social and ethnic divisions, there were the policies of the boundaries of the civilized through the norms of what was "proper Spanish."

The other trajectory is the inscription of difference that relocated the Heavenly City into the City of Human Intentions and Purposes. The latter gave expression in the enlightenments to the idea of nations that could trace their histories through progressive developments of "civilizations" whose origins, for example, started in Ancient Greece or Rome and arrived at the present. The comparative style of thought often posed the pastoral image of community drawn from religious notions of salvation into the re-visioned city and its norms of civility from which difference was inscribed. In Australia, Green and Cormack argue, nation formation became embedded in English as a distinctive school subject, linked to Anglo-Celtic traditions and the particular geography of Australia. Within this, and at the primary level, the school subject Reading was able to register various rural imaginaries, link to racial, cultural, and economic conceptions of Empire and Nation, and provide space for the promotion of a subject-citizen for a newly formed democratic federation of post-colonial States. In the United States, pastoral images of community were brought into the new sociologies and psychologies of education in the Protestant reformism of Progressivism (Popkewitz). The concerns were with the moral disorder of the newly industrialized city and the need to redefine the patterns of communication in the families and schools.

The New Social and Educational Sciences Calculated and Planned the Reform of Society

The quest for moral improvement that joined the enlightenments with republicanism left no branch of the sciences or arts unexplored. The pursuit of science to discover God's given unity shifted by the 19th century to science as finding the processes and principles that gave physical and social harmony. Science that previously was a practice to master and technologically control nature traveled into social realms. The human sciences were remade into the service of republicanism rather than God. It was often called moral science and enlisted as to serve in remaking society by making the moral responsibilities and obligations of its citizen. Reason, it was believed, aided by observation and experience, was efficacious in leading people toward perfection. The search for rationally discovering laws of nature in society embodied the hopes of the enlightenments and fears of the dangers and dangerous populations to that future. Fears were expressed about, for example, the need to harness the passions and self-interest that prevented the promotion of the common good.

The methods of science began to distinguish with greater details about the characteristics and capabilities of the worthy from the unworthy. The modernizing of Portuguese liberalism in the 19th century used the language of scientific progress among governors to combat ignorance, a consequence of illiteracy (Ó). In the United States, it promoted the need to create useful schools that would educate skillful men in jobs and make them experts capable of multiplying the resources of the treasure of the entire nation, as seen in the shift toward education for social efficiency in the 20th century (Labaree). Schools were to create an equal society through which all have access to rational knowledge and science, as well as to promote a rationally negotiated moral unity and common ground among different classes and regions regardless of gender (Osterwalder). School was to be compulsory, non-denominational secular, and free, and in some places publically controlled (Tröhler). American progressive educators deployed the perspective of educational psychology to promote self-regulation and pedagogical control as prerequisites for an autonomous soul (Popkewitz, Labaree).

The planning in the name of liberalism and social progress, however, was not without limits. As Popkewitz explores in American Progressivism, a particular comparative style of thought was inscribed in the social and educational sciences. Progressivism, he argues, was social movements responding, in part, to the Social Question that directed Protestant reformism and civic movements to the moral disorder of urban life and its modes of life. That comparative style of thought, he argues, entails the particular assembly of American enlightenment notions that generated double gestures of hope and fears about who was not the citizen and populations abjected. The system of reason through which difference was inscribed, he argues, provides a way to consider issues of social inclusion and exclusion, expressed through categories of gender, ethnicity, and race in contemporary social and educational practices.

The Different Languages and Institutional Forms Given to Modern Schooling Existed in a Global Field

As this volume clearly illustrates, schooling acquired national identities within an international field. But the emergence of the modern school was not merely variations of a single theme. The theories and principles of the "educated" citizen and child entailed multiple trajectories and different assumptions about the relation of individuality, science, reason, and progress in the pedagogical organization of the school. In this instance, it is more appropriate to treat modernity and "the modern" schooling as having non-uniform differences and contextual distinctions rather than an epochal concept of uniformity in social experience (see Eisenstadt, 2000; Wittrock, 2000; in education, Popkewitz, 2005; Tröhler, 2010). The movement and assembly of ideas, institutions, and narratives across national boundaries, then, is not simply replication but acts of differential creation through which particular hopes, desires, and fears were expressed.

The complex relation between the pedagogical practices of "educating" the child and the political culture of the citizen is particularly evident in the historical studies in this volume. Whereas we associate republicanism with Europe and North America, the word circulated in Latin America and seemingly counter-reformation regions. Further, the different historical sites show different seemingly logical practices that overlap in the making of schooling. Argentina, for example, continually deployed republican language as a common trait across disparate projects of the nation, including defense of anti-monarchic systems and modernist traditions (Dussel).

If we think of the formation of the modern school as an expression of globalization before the concept was used, the chapters by Hamilton (Scotland), Lindmark (Sweden), Viñao (Spain), Dussel (Argentina), and De Vincente and Grube (Switzerland) direct our attention to the different historical paths that came together to make the school possible. Hamilton, for example, argues that the *institutional* forms taken in Scotland in 18th-century enlightenment need to be seen historically in relation to the Renaissance and Reformation—particularly Calvin, Knox, and Ignatius of Loyola, who were humanists involved in the demographic, political, and social circumstances of Scotland prior to the mid-19th century. Out of this hybrid emerged the school, Hamilton continues, combining medieval assumptions about text-based learning with 15th-century humanist assumptions about education. The values and norms of republicanism were mobilized in Spain, for example, in the battles of emancipation from the crown and the organization of independence in the mid-19t[h] century (Viñao). Where the liberal elite gave emphasis to a literate citizenship, republican education was an integrative ideal designed to overcome particularism in order to cement the common good. In Argentina, officials censored Rousseau's chapter on religious beliefs, arguing that he must have had a temporary dementia when he wrote his anti-Catholic diatribe (Dussel). Followers positioned in close alliance with the Catholic Church used Rousseau's social contract as a civic catechism to link literacy with citizenship, teaching children to serve the fatherland. For Switzerland, De Vincente and Grube compare rural school political cultures in the 18th-century province of Zurich and the 19th-century city of Zurich, arguing that the earlier participation norms of communes made possible what a century later became an urbanized political culture in schools. The school had multiple functions. It was to teach children to be good Christians and secure children's salvation within the cannon of values of the communes themselves and to educate to become useful members of the political commune.

CONCLUSION

The central focus of this book has been to explore the social, cultural, and political complexities of the formation of the modern school in multiple national settings, starting with the question of how the educational impetus in the idea of classical republicanism affected the emergence and organization of (modern) schooling even as schooling developed in non-republican countries. The pathway that formed the modern schooling was not merely a single, homogenous event with variations in different contexts. What became the modern school revolved around the interplay of existing languages and cultural ascriptions about individuality and the child, the taken-for-granted assumptions that linked individuality to the social, and new conditions that made visible problems of upbringing and pedagogy. The technologies of teaching and curriculum, for example, were not born from one model or ideal of the citizen. They arose from different historical practices that included, among others, competing visions about the social order that emerged in the new political philosophies about the relation of the individual to collective norms and values, and technologies often borrowed from previous religious pedagogical structures. In this mixture was also the emergence of the social and education sciences, particularly in the latter part of the 19th century, that enabled new forms of administration to carry the dispositional as well as knowledge requirements associated with the citizen.

We began with republicanism to engage the history of schooling in the broad question about nation and citizen. We argue that the modern school, an enterprise that begins to take shape in the 18th century and emerges at the end of the 20th century as a globalized institution, entailed certain similar but different conditions that made that institution possible and necessary. Republicanism oriented that discussion to explore the different cultural and institutional principles in pedagogical projects for governing how children (and families) were to think and act as future citizens. As important to this formation of the school was the formation of new forms of expertise that gave attention to science in planning for the reform of society through the pedagogical practices of the school. As we argued, the citizen was not born but made. Mass schooling became a major site for processes of "modernization" of the self whose self-responsibility and motivation are necessary for the adequate functioning of modern government.

The substantive discussions about the constitution of modern schooling is also a methodological approach for thinking about and potentially (re)visioning the historiography of schooling. At one layer and in relation to the particular phrase of contemporary U.S. schools, instruction is an instrumental problem "to reach desired goals" or to increase children's achievement. We can also point to the current emphasis on testing children's knowledge of school subjects that emerges in the U.S. No Child Left Behind (and Race to the Top) reforms and the OECD PISA assessments of children's practical knowledge of school subjects. The studies of this volume bring to the fore the inadequacy of such formulations in the reforms of schooling. The very acts of curriculum and teaching are not merely to improve or make more efficient what is taught to children. What became possible as modern schooling entailed the assembly, connections, and disconnections of different historical phenomena that are never neutral, but about who the child is and should be.

The pedagogy of the school embodied and brought together a variety of social and political changes as it was reconstituted at the level of transforming the self and organizing the problems of personal life. This transformation in seemingly secular projects of making the citizen, as multiple chapters in this book illustrate, was not merely shedding the past for the new but realigning and (re)visioning prior technologies of pedagogy, such as found in Jesuit and Lutheran modes of instruction. Without engaging a presentism that uses the past as merely a descriptive device to explain the present, historicizing how the commonsense of contemporary schooling was formed and its mutations in the present is an important strategy to denaturalize its ways of doing and thinking, and thus open up possibilities for other ways of acting and thinking.

The chapters of this book are organized in three parts. Part I, *Christian Souls, Enlightenment Ideals, and Pedagogical Forms*, includes five chapters that discuss educational concepts as religious traditions, and enlightened ideals were brought into the organization of the pedagogy of schooling. This part includes discussion of Sweden (Daniel Linkmark), The Netherlands (Jeroen J.H. Dekker), Portugal (Jorge Ramos do Ó), Spain (Antonio Viñao), and Scotland (David Hamilton). The four chapters of Part II, *Organizing Schooling as Rationalizing Moral Codes*, explore the rationalizing and organizing of the moral visions of the particular republican ideals. These chapters focus on Argentina (Inès Dussel), Switzerland (Daniel Tröhler), the United States (David F. Labaree), and France (Fritz Osterwalder). In Part III, *Curriculum, Science, and the Fabrication of the Virtuous Citizen,* the four chapters engage in examining the way the ideal citizen was to be educated in the United States (Thomas S. Popkewitz), Australia (Bill Green and Phillip Cormack), The Netherlands (Willeke Los), and Zurich, Switzerland (Andrea De Vincenti and Norbert Grube).

While we have organized the chapters through these three parts, it is important to recognize that the themes of the parts also have overlapping foci and emphases. For example, although Part I focuses on the significance of religious themes that are brought into secular concerns related to the formal of the modern schools, it also considers issues of the rationalization of moral visions of political cultures associated with republican ideals.

NOTES

1. The "political culture" arguments in this literature harken back to work in the post-World War II years in U.S. political science and education that stresses the importance of a global civic culture and the vision of "One World" under the leadership of the United States. This idea soon became educationalized after the Sputnik shock in 1957, and in Western Europe—via human capital theory—it grew into the main ideology of the OECD and its instrument PISA (Tröhler, 2010). There was a similar reaction within the educational establishment of the former Soviet Union and the call for reforms but with different political intent and ideological restrictions (see e.g., Popkewitz, 1984, particularly Chapter 3). The earlier comparative studies of national civic culture were intended to buttress the norms and values of participation that embodied liberal democratic notions of the common good and civic virtue in order to stand as a bulwark against the authoritarianism and totalitarianism associated with Nazi Germany and the Soviet Union. This geopolitics was carried into school studies through behavioral political science projects in education about the socialization processes of childhood (e.g., Easton & Hess, 1962; Merelman, 1971) that continue today as character education, adjustment psychologies, and citizenship education.
2. These two terms appeared as related concepts during this time in Europe. "Society," for example, was previously a word concerned with associations of people and not with some abstract conception about the general organization of a public, secular world.
3. Aristotle: "But of all the things which I have mentioned that which most contributes to the permanence of constitutions is the adaptation of education to the form of government, and yet in our own day this principle is universally neglected" (*Politics*, book 5, part 9).
4. The main work of sensationism was published in 1754 by Étienne Bonnot de Condillac (*Traité des sensations*); it was translated into English only in 1930 (*Condillac's treatise on the sensations*). However, already in his *Essai sur l'origine des connaissances humaines* in 1746, Condillac had developed John Locke's empiricism to sensationsism (translated into English 10 years later: *An Essay on the Origin of Human Knowledge, Being a Supplement to Mr. Locke's Essay on the Human Understanding*, London 1756).
5. Compare Aristotle's *Politics*: "For, inasmuch as every family is a part of a state, and these relationships are the parts of a family, and the virtue of the part must have regard to the virtue of the whole, women and children must be trained by education with an eye to the constitution, if the virtues of either of them are supposed to make any difference in the virtues of the state" (book 1, part 13).
6. There were some more, however short-lived, French client republics erected by Napoleon Bonaparte: The Cisalpine Republic (*Repubblica Cisalpina*) lasted from 1797 to 1802 and was then followed by the Italian Republic (*Repubblica Italiana*) from 1802 to 1805. The Ligurian Republic (*Repubblica Ligure*) was formed in 1797 too and consisted of the territory of the old Republic of Genoa, which covered most of the Ligurian region of Northwest

Italy. In 1805, the whole area was annexed by France. The French also converted the existing republics into new republics according to the centralistic French model: The Netherlands became the Batavian Republic (*Bataafse Republiek*) and Switzerland the Helvetic Republic (*Helvetische Republik*). After the defeat of Napoleon Bonaparte, the Netherlands turned into a monarchy in 1815, and the Swiss returned to a confederation of republics.

7. Some examples may serve here for today's situation: Federal presidential republics: Argentina, Brazil, Mexico; Federal parliamentary republic: Germany, Austria, Australia*, Canada*; Federal parliamentary republic with direct democracy: Switzerland; Federal constitutional republic: United States; Federal republic with parliamentary democracy: India; Parliamentary republics: Turkey, Italy, Portugal, Poland; People's republics: China, Cuba, Libya; Semi-presidential republics: Taiwan (= Republic of China), Finland, France, Algeria; Federal semi-presidential republic: Russia. Norway, Sweden, Denmark, Belgium, The Netherlands, United Kingdom, Luxembourg, Spain, and Thailand are parliamentary democracies under constitutional monarchies. Japan is a parliamentary constitutional monarchy.
8. Iran, for instance, calls itself an Islamic Republic, North Korea's name is officially Democratic People's Republic of Korea, and the Syrian Arabic Republic is a Presidential single party republic.
9. "Reformed-protestant" indicates the Calvinist and Zwinglian reformation in contrast to the Lutheran reformation.
10. This thesis, by the way, could easily be backed up by Max Weber's thesis on Protestantism. As a matter of fact, Weber's thesis on Protestantism inspired today's dominant global thesis on education, such as the neo-institutional concept of a world culture (e.g., Meyer, Boli, Thomas, & Ramirez, 1997; see also Tröhler, 2009).
11. See http://www.uark.edu/depts/comminfo/cambridge/ancients.html. Retrieved March 3, 2008.
12. Whether or not the American Revolution in 1776 was based on ancient or modern republicanism is disputed (see in favor for the ancient Gordon Wood, 1969, and in favor for the modern Michael P. Zuckert, 1996).
13. At that time, the opposition of classical republicanism was not the liberal republicanism of France (because it had not developed to a dominant langue for a long time), but the so-called commercial republicanism that merged widely with the modern-liberal version during the 19th century. The model for a commercial republic was The Netherlands and thus the counterpoint of classical republicanism in Switzerland (see Tröhler, 2005).
14. It is interesting that in the beginning of the 20th century, the Soviet Union defined itself as a republic and took French enlightenment notions in defining its state as the precursor stage of its eventual development of communism.
15. When an author appears without a date, it refers to a chapter in this volume.
16. Secularization was, ironically, a word used initially by Catholic priests prior to the Reformation who left the monasteries to minister to people in the local communities.

REFERENCES

Almond, G. A., & Verba, S. (1963). *The civic culture: Political attitudes and democracy in five nations*. Princeton, NJ: Princeton University Press.

Aristotle (1996). *The Politics and the Constitution of Athens*. Cambridge, UK: Cambridge University Press.

Bakhtin, M. (1981). *The dialogic imagination: Four essays* (C. Emerson & M. Holquist, Trans.). Austin, TX: University of Texas Press.

Becker, C. L. (2003). *The heavenly city of the eighteenth-century philosophers* (1st ed., 1932). New Haven, CT: Yale University Press.

Bell, D. (1962). *The end of ideology: On the exhaustion of political ideas in the fifties*. New York: Free Press; London: Collier-Macmillan.

Bell, D. A. (2001). *The cult of the nation in France: Inventing nationalism, 1680-1800*. Cambridge, MA: Harvard University Press.

Bellah, R. N., Madsen, R., Sullivan, W. M., Swidler, A., & Tipton, S. M. (1985). *Habits of the heart: Individualism and commitment in American life*. Berkeley, CA: University of California Press.

Benjamin, W. (1955/1985). Theses on the philosophy of history (H. Zohn, Trans.). In H. Arendt (Ed.), *Illuminations: Essays and reflections* (pp. 253–264). New York: Schocken Books.

Berlin, I. (1958). *Two concepts of liberty*. Oxford: Clarendon Press.

Condillac, É. B. de (1746). *Essai sur l'origine des connaissances humaines, ouvrage où l'on réduit à un seul principe tout ce qui concerne l'entendement humain*. Amsterdam: P. Mortier.

Condillac, É. B. de (1754). *Traité des Sensations, a Madame la Comtesse de Vassé*. London and Paris: Chez de Bure l'ainé.

Condillac, É. B. de (1756). *An Essay on the Origin of Human Knowledge, Being a Supplement to Mr. Locke's Essay on the Human Understanding*. Translated from the French of the Abbé de Condillac by Mister Nugent. London: J. Nourse (French original 1746).

Condillac, É. B. de (1930). *Condillac's treatise on the sensations*. Translated by Geraldine Carr, with a preface by H. Wildon Carr. London: The Favil Press (French original 1754).

Cruikshank, B. (1999). *The will to empower: Democratic citizens and the other subjects*. Ithaca, NY: Cornell University.

Darnton, R. (1997). George Washington's False Teeth (pp. 34-38). *New York Review of Books*, March, 27, 44(5), 34–38.

Easton, D., & Hess, R. (1962, August). The child's political world. *Midwest Journal of Political Science*, 6(9), 229–246.

Eisenberg, C. (1999). *"English sports" und deutsche bürger. Eine gesellschaftsgeschichte, 1800–1939*. Paderborn: Schöningh.

Eisenstadt, S. N. (Ed.) (2000). *Multiple modernities*. Daebalus: Winter 2000; 29. Cambridge, MA: American Academy of Arts and Sciences.

Etzioni, A. (1993). *The spirit of community. The reinvention of American society*. New York: Simon & Schuster.

Ferguson, R. A. (1997). *The American enlightenment, 1750-1820*. Cambridge: Harvard University Press.

Freedman, K., & Popkewitz, T. S. (1988). Art education and social interests in the development of schooling: Ideological origins of curriculum theory. *Journal of Curriculum Studies*, 20(5), 387–405.

Fukuyama, F. (1989). The end of history? *The National Interest*. Retrieved 10 December 2010, from http://www.wesjones.com/eoh.htm

Gorski, P. (1999). Calvinism and state-formation in early modern Europe. In G. Steinmetz (Ed.), *State/Culture: State formation after the cultural turn* (pp. 147-181). Ithaca, NY: Cornell Press.

Gustafson, R. (2009). *Race and curriculum: Music in childhood education*. New York: Palgrave Macmillan.

Hahn, C. L. (1998). *Becoming political: Comparative perspectives on citizenship education*. Albany, NY: SUNY Press.

Hahn, C. L. (1999). Citizenship education: An empirical study of policy, practices, and outcomes. *Oxford Review of Education, 25*(1&2), 231–250.

Hamilton, D. (1989). *Towards a theory of schooling.* London, England: Falmer Press.

Hüfner, K., Meyer, J. W., & Naumann, J. (1987). Comparative education policy research: A world society perspective. In H. Meinolf, N. Weiler, & A. B. Antal (Eds.), *Comparative policy research. Learning from experience* (pp. 188–243). New York: St. Martin's Press.

Hunter, I. (1988). *Culture and government: The emergence of literary education.* Hampshire, England: Macmillan.

Laslett, P. (1960). Introduction. In P. Laslet (Ed.), *John Locke: Two treatises of government* (pp. 3–122). Cambridge: Cambridge University Press.

Lawn, M. (Ed.). (2009). *Modelling the future. Exhibitions and the materiality of education.* Oxford: Symposium Books.

Lutz, D. S. (1984). The relative influence of European writers on late eighteenth-century American political thought. *The American Political Science Review, 78(1),* 189–197.

Macpherson, C. B. (1962). *The political theory of possessive individualism: From Hobbes to Locke.* Oxford: Oxford University Press.

Mellor, S. (1998). *What's the point? Political attitudes of Victorian year 11 students.* Melbourne: Australian Centre for Educational Research.

Merelman, R. M. (1971). *Political socialization and educational climates: A study of two school districts.* New York: Holt, Rinehart and Winston.

Meyer, J. W., Boli, J., Thomas, G. M., & Ramirez, F. (1997). World society and the nation-state. *American Journal of Sociology, 103*(1), 144–181.

Meyer, J. W., & Ramirez, F. O. (2000). The world institutionalization of education. In J. Schriewer (Hrsg.), *Discourse formation in comparative education* (pp. 111–132). Frankfurt am Main: Lang.

Meyer, J. W., & Rowan, B. (1977). Institutionalized organizations: Formal structure as myth and ceremony. *The American Journal of Sociology, 83,* 340–363.

Mijnhardt, W. W. (2005). The limits of present-day historiography of republicanism. *De Achttiende Eeuw, 37*(1), 75–89.

Montesquieu (1752). *The spirit of laws. Translated from the French of M. De Secondat,* Baron de Montesquieu, by Mr. Nugent. London: J. Nourse and P. Vaillant (French original 1748).

National Commission on Excellence in Education (1983). *A Nation at Risk: The Imperative for Educational Reform.* Washington, D.C.: Superintendent of Documents, U.S. Gov. Print. Off.

Nesbit, M. (2000). *Their common sense.* London: Black Dog Publishing.

Osler, A. & Starkey, H. (2001). Citizenship Education and National Identities in France and England: Inclusive or Exclusive? *Oxford Review of Education,* 27(2), pp. 287-305.

Overesch, A. (2007). *Wie die Schulpolitik ihre Probleme (nicht) löst. Deutschland und Finnland im Vergleich.* Münster: Waxmann.

Pocock, J. G. A. (1975). *The Machiavellian moment. Florentine political thought and the Atlantic republican tradition.* Princeton: Princeton University Press.

Popkewitz, T. (1984). *Paradigm and ideology in educational research: Social functions of the intellectual.* London & New York: Falmer Press.

Popkewitz, T. (Ed.). (2005). *Inventing the modern self and John Dewey: Modernities and the traveling of pragmatism in education.* New York: Palgrave Macmillan.

Popkewitz, T. S. (2008). *Cosmopolitanism and the age of school reform: Science, education, and making society by making the child.* New York: Routledge.

Rawls, J. (1972). *A theory of justice.* Oxford, UK: Clarendon Press.

Rodgers, D. T. (1992). *Republicanism: The career of a concept*. The Journal of American History, 29(1), 11-38.
Rousseau, J.-J. (1758). *J.J. Rousseau, citoyen de Genève, a Mr. d'Alembert, sur son article Genève*, dans le VIIme Volume de 'Encyclopédie. Amsterdam: Marc Michel Rey.
Rousseau, J.-J. (1783). *Considerations sur le gouvernement de la Pologine et sur la réformatoin projetée*. La Hate: P.F. Gosse et Lausanne: François Grasset & Comp. (Original: 1772).
Sandel, M. (1982). *Liberalism and the limits of justice*. Cambridge: Cambridge University Press.
Sandel, M. (1996). *Democracy's discontent: America in search of a public philosophy*. Cambridge, MA: Harvard University Press.
Schelbert, T. (1983). Mundart und Hochsprache: Segen oder Fluch? *Schweizer Schule, 13*, 598–604.
Skinner, Q. (1988). Meaning and understanding in the history of ideas. In J. Tully (Ed.), *Meaning and context: Quentin Skinner and his critics* (pp. 29–67). Princeton: Princeton University Press.
Skinner, Q. (1998): *Liberty before liberalism*. Cambridge: Cambridge University Press.
Smeyers, P., & Depaepe, M. (Eds.). (2006). *Educational research: Why "what works" doesn't work*. Dordrecht: Springer.
Stourzh, G. (1970/1989). William Blackstone: Teacher of revolution. In G. Stourzh (Ed.), *Wege zur Grundrechtsdemokratie. Studien zur Begriffs- und Institutionengeschichte des liberalen Verfassungsstaates* (pp. 137–153). Wien: Böhlau.
Torney-Purta, J., Lehmann, R., Oswald, H., & Schulz, W. (2001). *Citizenship and education in twenty-eight countries. Civic knowledge and engagement at age fourteen*. Amsterdam: IEA.
Tröhler, D. (2005). *Langue* as homeland: The Genevan of reception of pragmatism. In T. S. Popkewitz (Ed.), *Inventing the modern self and John Dewey: Modernities and the travelling of pragmatism in education* (pp. 61–84). New York: St. Martin's Press and Palgrave Macmillan.
Tröhler, D. (2008). The educationalization of the modern world: Progress, passion, and the Protestant promise of education. In P. Smeyers & M. Depaepe (Eds.), *Educational research: The educationalization of social problems* (pp. 31–46). Dordrecht: Springer.
Tröhler, D. (2009). Globalizing globalization: The neo-institutional concept of a world culture. In T. S. Popkewitz & F. Rizvi (Eds.), *NSSE yearbook. Education and globalism* (pp. 29–48). New York: Teachers College Press.
Tröhler, D. (2010). Harmonizing the educational globe. World polity, cultural features, and the challenges to educational research. *Studies in Philosophy and Education, 29*, 7–29.
Tröhler, D. (2011). *Languages of education. Protestant legacies in educationalization of the world, national identities, and global aspirations*. New York: Routledge.
UNESCO (2002). *Education for all: is the world on track?* Paris: Unesco.
US Congress (2001). *No Child left Behind Act*. Washington. D.C.: Department of Education.
Wittrock, B. (2000). Modernity: One, none, or many? European origins and modernity as a global condition. *Daedalus, 29*(1), 31-60.
Wood, G. (1969). *The creation of the American republic, 1776–1787*. Chapel Hill: University of North Carolina Press.
Zuckert, M. P. (1996). *The natural rights republic. Studies in the foundation of the American political tradition*. Notre Dame, IN: University of Notre Dame Press.

Part I
Christian Souls, Enlightenment Ideals, and Pedagogical Forms

2 New Wine into Old Bottles

Luther's Table of Duties as a Vehicle of Changing Civic Virtues in 18th- and 19th-Century Sweden

Daniel Lindmark

RELIGIOUS ROOTS OF MODERN SOCIETY—AN INTRODUCTION

In previous research, scholars have tried to identify the foundation blocks of the Nordic community, some pointing at cultural and religious unity (Østergaard, 1994), others at the similar social structure with a significant middle class (Rerup, 1994). While the "Nordist" activists of the 20th century would refer to historical, primordial criteria such as linguistic and political unity, scholars increasingly tend to view *Norden* as a constructed community based on the idea of Nordic coherence rooted in 19th-century Scandinavianism (Janfelt, 2005). The connection between "Nordism" and nationalism has been emphasized, including the prevalence of the nation-state idea (L. Hansen, 1994; S. Hansen, 1997; Hovbakke Sørensen, 1996; Sørensen & Stråth, 1997).

As an introduction to the present chapter, I would like to address perspectives on the historical roots of the Nordic model of society presented by Danish political scientist Tim Knudsen. By referring to actual historical phenomena, Knudsen's perspectives represent a primordial view of certain features of the Nordic model. Knudsen identifies *universalism* as a fundamental idea of the Nordic welfare systems, the ideological roots of which can be found in the Lutheran state church system (Knudsen, 2000, 2002). Whereas the social insurance system instituted by Otto von Bismarck in Germany was restricted to the labor force, the Nordic model embraced all citizens. According to Knudsen, this universalist approach was founded on the organization and ideology of the Lutheran state churches. In their function as state officials, Lutheran ministers were employed to organize poor relief and other social benefits. The parishes' responsibility for this is still recognizable in the persisting tradition of strong local government in the Nordic countries.

Knudsen also points at certain ideological correspondences between the Nordic welfare state and Lutheranism. Full employment and universal social security correspond to the Lutheran doctrines on daily labor as a divine calling and the universal priesthood, respectively. Furthermore, the mutual trust between authorities and citizens, and the high degree of national solidarity that characterizes the Nordic countries, can be traced back to the homogeneity created by the Lutheran state churches. The efficiency of the nation-building process of the Nordic countries is clearly demonstrated by the Swedification of the former Danish provinces of present-day Southern Sweden. In this process, the Church of Sweden played a role of vital importance.

The perspective of universalism is clearly applicable to the Swedish history of popular education. Ideologically, the roots of universalism can be found in Lutheran ambitions to bring the divine word to all and sundry. This makes the educational field an evident parallel to the social insurance system of the Nordic welfare states. Educational universalism was not only manifested in the early parish school system of Denmark-Norway, but also in the alphabetization campaign conducted through household instruction in Sweden-Finland. Regardless of which organizational model was preferred, all citizens of the Nordic countries were taught reading and religion in the 18th century (Apelseth, 2004; Johansson, 1977; Lindmark, 2004). Furthermore, there is reason to underline the long-term effects of Lutheranism in the field of popular education. With regard to organization, the state church continued to be responsible for popular education after the enactment of elementary school reforms of the 19th century (Denmark 1814, Norway 1827, Sweden 1842, Finland 1866). Local parishes were obliged to establish and maintain schools, and the connection between school instruction and confirmation prevailed into the 20th century. However, the most long-lived consequences of Lutheranism are not to be found in matters concerning organization and curriculum, but in the general philosophy of education. Whereas universalism in the early modern period was founded on the Lutheran conception of every man's access to the Word, universalism in the modern secularized Nordic states is motivated by democratic principles as to every individual's free and equal access to education. This is true for primary, secondary, and higher education, which are provided free of charge to all citizens regardless of sex, age, religion, ethnicity, socioeconomic status, and even place of residence.

Before modifying this one-dimensional picture of universalism as the dominant feature of the history of Nordic education, I would like to emphasize another pattern motivating the use of images and interpretations of the Nordic community. Knudsen traces the roots of specific traits of modern society back to early modern religious culture with its Lutheran ideology and ecclesiastical organization. From a general point of view, this chapter will apply a similar perspective by discussing the religious background to civic norms and values proffered by the secular, state-supported educational system of the 20th century. But instead of providing historical explanations of certain features of contemporary society, I will concentrate on a relatively short transitional period in the Swedish history of education, when Martin Luther's Table of Duties served as a bridge between religious and civic education or rather between Lutheran social ethics and civic values founded on natural law.

CIVIC EDUCATION BEFORE THE ERA OF COMPULSORY SCHOOLING—AIM OF THE STUDY

Of course, universalism was never the only idea guiding Nordic and Swedish education. Patterns of particularism are also easily recognizable in the history of Swedish education. From the 17th century, the social stratification of education becomes increasingly visible. Primary and secondary education were organized in two separate systems. The state-supported Latin school system prepared students from higher social strata for future careers in the church and civil service by providing classical education, whereas popular education was restricted to basic reading and religious instruction conducted at home and examined by the Lutheran ministers. Even though the classical curriculum was supplemented with a modern curriculum at the beginning of the 19th century, the social barrier between elite and mass education was upheld well into the 20th century. This general division of Swedish education reflects the widening cleavage between elite and popular culture characterizing the period after 1650. The social and economic segregation between the upper and lower strata of society was accompanied by educational separation between rural and urban areas and between men and women. Reading ability and catechetical knowledge were the only common denominators in education, where even the book market was divided into two distinct spheres, characterized by different genres and even print types. Not until the implementation of the elementary school system in the mid-19th century were conditions created for a broader reading culture based on national rather than religious symbols. Still, these parallel school systems prevailed for another century before being replaced by the integrated comprehensive school.

In an influential introduction to curriculum theory, Ulf P. Lundgren presented an analysis of the development of curriculum codes in the history of Swedish education in 1979. In his view, secondary education was dominated by a classical curriculum increasingly challenged by a modern curriculum, whereas popular education developed from a moral code to a rational curriculum code from the beginning of the 20th century, the rational curriculum bridging the cleavage between primary and secondary education (Englund, 1980, 1986a, 1986b; Lundgren, 1979). What kind of norms and values were promoted by the moral code of Swedish popular education? According to Lundgren, the elementary school system established in the mid-19th century was founded on "God and the Fatherland, its subjects being basic knowledge, its objective moral training in the Lutheran faith and ethics, in combination with knowledge of the Fatherland" (Lundgren, 1979, p. 65). Modifying Lundgren's interpretations of the 20th century, Tomas Englund (1980, 1986a) identified a civic curriculum code that replaced the moral code of primary education in its first two decades. This civic curriculum code was characterized by the notion of mutual interdependence between individual members of society—social integration and coherence being goals of vital importance. Methodologically, the civic curriculum code rested on students' self-activity and co-operation; in terms of organization, priority was given to an integrated "unitary school" for all citizens; and regarding contents, focus was placed on secular civic education, especially in social sciences.

In this chapter, I will discuss one of the most important texts for promoting social norms in the days before the compulsory elementary school system (i.e., Martin Luther's Table of Duties). I will address the following questions:

1. What position did the Table of Duties hold in primary education in the 18th and early 19th centuries?
2. How was the Table of Duties interpreted and how did interpretations change over time?
3. How does the Table of Duties refer to moral and civic curriculum codes?

The chapter will conclude with a preliminary discussion of the alleged universalism of the Nordic model of society and its possible linkage to civic values rather than religious ideology.

THE TABLE OF DUTIES IN SWEDISH EDUCATIONAL HISTORY

In the history of Swedish education, Martin Luther's Table of Duties (Germ. *Haustafel*, Sw. *Hustavla*) has played a huge role. This brief collection of Biblical quotations was linked to the Small Catechism, and because the Small Catechism of 1529 was included in the Book of Concord of 1580, the Table of Duties obtained symbolic status as well. However, the Small Catechism did not become the major textbook of popular education in Sweden until the 18th century. In the 17th century, religious instruction was still restricted to memorization of elementary texts, such as the Lord's Prayer, the Creed, Morning and Evening Prayers, and Table Blessings. These texts were found in the common ABC-book, which subsequently served as a bridge between oral and literate education.

By the end of the 17th century, an educational campaign was launched in Sweden. Confessionalism dominated state philosophy, according to which confessional coherence was seen as the fundament of a stable society. Consequently, each and every inhabitant of the Swedish Realm was requested to develop a thorough knowledge of the Lutheran faith. In the Church Law of 1686, the clergy was ordered to carry out annual examinations of their parishioners' catechetical knowledge by visiting them in their homes. The results of these examinations were recorded in special registers, which today provide the historian with unique individual data on reading skills and catechetical knowledge. This educational offensive was also an alphabetization campaign because the expansion of the requested knowledge required more sophisticated educational technology. The heads of the households were made responsible for the instruction of the members of their households, the Table of Duties legitimating this paternalistic structure (see below).

In Swedish historical research, the Table of Duties has attracted serious attention. An influential essay written by Church historian Hilding Pleijel appeared in the books *Från hustavlans tid* and *Hustavlans värld* of 1951 and 1970, respectively. For many years, Pleijel's interpretation of the significance of the Table of Duties went unchallenged. Pleijel argued that Luther's Table of Duties was so well known by the entire Swedish population that it served as a self-evident and, often enough, tacit precondition for all thinking and acting. This assessment of the significance of the Table of Duties was founded on normative statements about the teaching and learning of the text in question. "The learning of the Table of Duties created a certain general knowledge that enabled the congregation to follow the minister's explications of related issues, be it in sermons or various examinations," Pelijel (1970, pp. 37–38) stated. The assumed learning not only increased knowledge of the doctrine of the three estates but also made an impression on popular thinking: "Since the Table of Duties was continuously impressed on the congregants through catechetical reading and sermons, it is self-evident that it was imprinted on their world of ideas" (Pleijel, 1970, p. 43). This argument is founded on two presuppositions that have not been discussed by Pleijel or the scholars who have given their support to his view: (a) the Table of Duties held a prominent position in popular education during the period in question, and (b) learning of the Table of Duties meant that its norms and values were internalized. In this chapter, I will conduct a critical discussion of the first of these presuppositions by confronting it with empirical evidence.

The significance of the Table of Duties as the vehicle of an ideology of society can be discussed at several levels. On the highest level, the state ideology level or the intended curriculum level, the official opinion of the Table of Duties was created and expressed in the political, theological, philosophical, and pedagogical discussions. Previous research has primarily been focused on this level. The second level, the implemented curriculum level, concerns the educational practice (i.e., the clergy's efforts to disseminate the contents of the Table of Duties to the population). This level includes sermons, textbooks, and popular education. On this level, previous research has been restricted to the presence of the Table of Duties or the doctrine of the three estates in sermons, catechisms, and hymnals. How the common man received and internalized the norms and values of the Table of Duties is the focus of the third level, the attained curriculum level. To find evidence of this internalization, the scholar will be obliged to resort to such sources as judicial documents and minutes from parish meetings that reflect the observance of the norms and values of the Table of Duties.

When discussing what position the Table of Duties held in popular education, I will restrict myself to presenting data on the median level, the implemented curriculum level. When Pleijel drew his conclusions concerning the use of the Table of Duties, he referred to sermons, Diet minutes, and other sources reflecting the ideology of the educated layers of society. In this study, I will use the parish examination registers from various periods of time and geographical areas of Sweden.[1] I will both discuss the existence of a special column for the Table of Duties in the registers and present individual data from selected parishes. I will begin by discussing data from the four deaneries of Ångermanland, Härnösand Diocese, in northern Sweden (Table 2.1).

The information provided in Table 2.1 can be interpreted in different ways. If the parishes with extant registers dating from the period before 1810 are taken into account, the Table of Duties has recurred in the registers for an average of 47 years, varying from 9 years in Resele to 102 in

Table 2.1 The Table of Duties in the Parish Examination Registers of the Four Deaneries of Ångermanland, Härnösand Diocese

Parishes	Registers with Table of Duty	Time Periods	Number of Years	Remarks
Härnösand	AI:1–3	1732–1811	79	
Säbrå	AI:1–4	1727–1812	85	
Stigsjö	AI:1	1776–1814	38	
Häggdånger	AI:1	1750–1790	40	AI:2 1805–1814
Nordingrå	AI:1–4	1741–1803	62	
Nora	AI:1–3	1701–1803	102	
Gudmundrå			–	AI:1 1820–1829
Torsåker	AI:2	1778–1803	25	
Sollefteå	AI:1–2	1762–1802	40	
Boteå	AI:1	1782–1801	19	AI:2 1811–1820
Resele	AI:1	1769–1778	9	AI:2 1800–1815
Ramsele	AI:1–2	1767–1801	34	AI:3 1804–1817
Nätra			–	AI:1 1810–1817
Anundsjö	AI:1–4	1726–1806	42	Not AI:2-31743–1781
Sidensjö	AI:1–3	1727–1807	80	

(continued)

Table 2.1 (continued)

Parishes	Registers with Table of Duty	Time Periods	Number of Years	Remarks
Själevad	AI:1	1791–1815	24	
Arnäs	AI:2–4	1767–1815	48	AI:1 1749–1766
Grundsunda	AI:1	1786–1808	22	
Nordmaling	AI:1–6	1704–1805	101	
Åsele	AI:2	1778–1812	34	AI:1 1772–1780
Fredrika	AI:1	1800–1820	20	
Dorotea	AI:1	1798–1826	28	

Sources: The Research Archives, Umeå University, Microfiche Collection. Note: Each pastorate is represented by the mother parish only.

Nora. However, these figures tell more about the creation of new parishes and the preservation of archival sources than the use of the Table of Duties in popular education. In 17 of 20 cases, the Table of Duties can be found in the oldest extant register, and in these parishes no registers from the 17th century have survived. The two oldest registers date from 1701 and 1704, respectively, the early starting date explaining the long history of the Table of Duties in these parishes.

If the starting points vary considerably between the parishes, the endpoints of the Table of Duties display reasonable simultaneousness. In 16 of 20 parishes, the last register containing a column for the Table of Duties ends in the period 1800–1815. The reason for this is mainly the introduction of a new form of register developed by Dean Johan Erik Dillner. Recommended by the Härnösand Consistory in 1802, the new form soon replaced the old one created by Dean Pehr Högström. Whereas the Högström register reflected the contents of popular education with columns for all the texts of the catechism, including the Table of Duties, the Dillner register emphasized skills by reducing the columns to "Reading," "Catechism," and "Comprehension." Of course, this development represents an ideological shift in educational philosophy. The tradition of rote learning was attacked for promoting mechanical knowledge without true understanding, and reformers instead advocated improved reading skills as a basis for understanding and applying religious teaching.

Obviously, the examination registers of Härnösand Diocese cannot answer the question of when the Table of Duties was introduced in popular education. Therefore, we have to turn to other regions. From Västerås Diocese, many examination registers are extant from the 17th century. Egil Johansson has processed the notations of catechetical knowledge in the register of Mora, Dalecarlia, 1667–1685, and found that no more than 4% of the parishioners had recorded knowledge of the Table of Duties (Johansson, 1992). From Lund Diocese in southern Sweden, deans' reports from 1683 offer an opportunity to cover a larger area.[2] However, only one sixth of the reports provide information about the Table of Duties, and only from Vemmenhög Deanery is this information placed in a specific column. Whereas 2,168 youngsters in Vemmenhög master the main parts of the Small Catechism and 1,040 the explication, only 647 young people have recorded knowledge of the Table of Duties (30%).

As far as the ordinary parish examination registers from Lund Diocese are concerned, not many of the early ones contain information about the Table of Duties. Only in the 1730s are such registers found more than occasionally. In a sample of 16 parishes from Skytt Deanery, 1740, where the Table of Duties was included in the registers, the text in question was mastered by 24% of the parishioners, whereas 78% had recorded knowledge of the catechism and 47 of the explication.[3] However, there are considerable differences between the parishes. Gyllie and Kyrkköpinge are found at the 60% level, Trelleborg and Maglarp below 1%.

In order to study in more detail the introduction of the Table of Duties in popular education in Lund Diocese, I have processed data from 10 parishes in Skytt Deanery in 1731. When distributed on age cohorts, the recorded knowledge of the Table of Duties displays the following pattern. The text in question was mastered by 24% of the parishioners, the age cohort 30–49 representing the highest rate with 36%. This probably means that the population born between 1682 and 1701 was subjected to more intense religious instruction in its childhood and early youth than both previous and following generations. There is reason to assume that the Church Law of 1686, making instruction in the Table of Duties mandatory, can be identified as a factor behind this educational offensive around the turn of the 17th century.

The presented data show that the Table of Duties was introduced in popular education in the latter part of the 17th century, the ministers intensifying their efforts after the enactment of the Church Law. Still, the picture is very blurry, so further research is needed. However, more detailed information is available about the regression process, although only selected regions and parishes have been studied. Table 2.2 presents results from 130 parishes in Karlstad Diocese in central western Sweden.

Table 2.2 indicates that the Table of Duties was abandoned in popular education even earlier in Karlstad Diocese than in Härnösand Diocese. Whereas the decline starts after the turn of the century in Härnösand Diocese (Table 2.1), the percentage of registers with columns for the Table of Duties in Karlstad begins decreasing substantially as early as the 1780s.

In order to cover a larger geographical area, I have used a sample of registers from the first parish of every deanery in all the Swedish dioceses.[4] In the dioceses of Växjö, Lund, and Västerås, registers with a column for the Table of Duties can be found up to the 1860s, when Swedish Statistics (*Statistiska Centralbyrån*) standardized the form of parish registers. In the dioceses of Härnösand, Linköping, and Visby, the consistories launched new forms early in the 19th century where the Table of Duties had no place. In the dioceses where the regression seems to have been more spontaneous,

Table 2.2 The Table of Duties in Examination Registers from Karlstad Diocese, 1770–1829

Decades (Starting Point of Registers)	Number of Registers	Registers with the Table of Duties (%)
1770–1779	90	86
1780–1789	103	57
1790–1799	103	23
1800–1809	120	28
1810–1819	127	7
1820–1829	127	1

Sources: Examination Registers on microfiche. Swedish Archival Information, National Archives, Ramsele, Sweden.

the process started earliest in Karlstad and Skara, where not many registers from the 19th century include a column for the Table of Duties, whereas the decline accelerated from the 1810s in the rest of the Swedish dioceses.

However, forms and columns do not tell the whole story. Are there really any notations on knowledge of the Table of Duties in the registers in question? From the parish of Skellefteå in Härnösand Diocese in northern Sweden, the register of 1771 reveals a high degree of catechetical knowledge. Whereas 88% of the 4,676 parishioners mastered the explication of the Small Catechism, 70% were recorded for knowledge of the Table of Duties, this rate representing a major increase since 1724, when only 30% of the parishioners garnered similar notations.[5] In order to cover more than single parishes, I have studied a sample of youngsters, 16 to 20 years of age, from the mother parishes of all pastorates of Växjö Diocese in southeastern Sweden in the 1810s. The results show that among the newly confirmed youth, the Table of Duties was known by 39% (as compared with 83 for the Small Catechism and 76 for the explication).[6]

With due reservations for scattered evidence and regional variations, a rough picture of the Table of Duties' position in popular education can still be drawn. Introduced in the latter part of the 17th century, the text was more systematically promoted in popular education after the enactment of the Church Law of 1686. The Table of Duties seems to have had its peak in the last decades of the 18th century, already declining considerably at the beginning of the 19th century in many regions. In reference to Pleijel's view of the prominent position of the Table of Duties, the presented results indicate that such a position was not reached until the latter part of the 18th century and was held for no more than a short period of time. The Table of Duties was never prioritized at the expense of the more fundamental texts such as the Small Catechism and its explication. Its rise in popular education appears to have coincided with increasing reading ability, and its fall was at least partly connected to a pedagogically motivated renouncement of memorization.

THE IDEOLOGICAL CONTENTS AND CONTEMPORARY INTERPRETATIONS OF THE TABLE OF DUTIES

The Table of Duties consisted of a number of biblical excerpts mainly quoted from St. Paul's epistles. The Bible verses were organized under certain headings, indicating what social position or estate they referred to. In the Swedish catechetical tradition, special headings were inserted at the beginning of the 17th century, emphasizing the three main estates of society: the "ecclesiastical estate," the "political estate," and the "economical estate." In each of these main categories, there were biblical quotations referring to the superiors and inferiors of the estate in question. Consequently, the Table of Duties presented the social order in the following way:

ECCLESIASTICAL ESTATE
For Bishops, Pastors, and Preachers
What the Hearers Owe to Their Pastors

POLITICAL ESTATE
Concerning Civil Government
What Subjects Owe to the Magistrates

ECONOMICAL ESTATE
For Husbands
For Wives
For Children
For Male and Female Servants, Hired Men, and Laborers
For Masters and Mistresses
For Young Persons in General
For Widows
For All in Common

In the following, I will concentrate on two main components of Martin Luther's Table of Duties, the idea of the three estates and patriarchalism, respectively. With ideological roots in medieval theology, the idea of the three estates was founded on Luther's doctrine of the two kingdoms or "regimes," the church representing God's right-hand kingdom and the state his left-hand kingdom. These two kingdoms are easily recognizable in the ecclesiastical and political estates of the Table of Duties. The economical or "household" estate, as it was frequently referred to in Sweden, represented a society-in-miniature, a combination of the ecclesiastical and political estates at the domestic level, where the master was supposed to uphold religious as well as civil authority. According to Swedish legislation, the household should serve as a religious community, where the master was responsible for conducting morning and evening prayers and making sure that all the members of his household were literate and had mastered the catechism. In his capacity as "local" political government, the master was authorized to execute the corporal punishment of his family and servants whenever needed.

Although the relationships within each estate were organized hierarchically, the three estates were not placed in hierarchical order themselves. Instead, each estate embraced all individuals from the specific aspect the estate represented. This was the dominant interpretation of the doctrine of the three estates among theologians in early modern Sweden (Normann, 1948, pp. 56ff.). However, there were competing interpretations, and the view of the three estates developed over time. Often enough, the three estates of the Table of Duties were linked to the four estates of the Swedish Diet, the first two estates easily identified with the clergy and nobility of the Diet, and the economical estate representing the "third estate," or the "nourishing classes" with the peasantry and burgesses. Even more frequently, the first two estates of the Table of Duties were identified with the church and state, respectively. In the official catechism of 1810, the alteration of the order between the first estates of the Table of Duties not only serves as an expression of state sovereignty over the church but also indicates a new interpretation of the Table of Duties.

A truly new interpretation emerged in the latter part of the 18th century, when the exhortations and admonitions of the Table of Duties were increasingly redefined as natural law expressed in biblical quotations for different social relationships or "communities." This tendency of explicating the Table of Duties from the perspective of moral philosophy can be found in many contemporary textbooks. Heavily influenced by the Scottish school, Swedish moral philosophers tended to present the common duties of man in a certain order (the fourth category only occasionally appearing in Swedish textbooks):

1. Duties towards God
2. Duties towards Yourself
3. Duties towards Your Neighbour
4. Duties towards Animals

In a textbook authored by Samuel Wigelius (1803), *Kristelig Läro-Bok för Barn* ("Christian Textbook for Children"), we find a conspicuous wish to combine the traditional Christian teachings of the catechism with the new moral philosophy founded on natural law. When Wigelius opens the second part of his book, "Moral Philosophy or God's Law," by presenting the "Duties towards God," he resorts to the first three commandments of the Decalogue. The second section, "Care for Our Selves," had no counterpart in the prevailing catechetical tradition, and Wigelius therefore had to construct paragraphs and find suitable biblical sentences on his own. In the third section, "Duties towards Your Neighbour," Wigelius continues his explication of the Ten Commandments, whereas a brief three-paragraph section explaining the basics of "Duties towards Animals" also lacks correspondence with the prevalent catechetical teachings.

After having presented the common duties of man, Wigelius turns to the duties of the "particular communities." The fifth section of his textbook is dedicated to "specific duties relating to our different positions in the world." The paragraphs of this section follow the Table of Duties, although the order between the estates has been changed. The reader will find advice on relationships between members of the family, between masters and servants, governors and subjects, and teachers and hearers, followed by some advice for rich and poor, and young and old. In support of his teachings, Wigelius repeatedly refers to the biblical excerpts of the Table of Duties. Obviously, the fundamental idea of the Table of Duties to Wigelius was not the three estates, not even as an organizing principle, but the advice to people of different social status. In fact, in his presentation of the "particular duties," Wigelius uses common organizing principles popular among moral philosophers of his time. He starts with the "simple communities" (i.e., the communities of married couples, parents and children, and masters and servants) and then turns to "compound communities" composed of many simple communities.[7]

The Table of Duties was founded on a patriarchal ideology. According to Martin Luther, the relationship between God and mankind was basically a father—child relationship, in which the weak and sinful child needed education and guidance. In his catechisms, Luther expressed his idea that all civil and religious authority emanated from paternal power (Nordbäck, 2004). From a general perspective, the Table of Duties is a clear exponent of patriarchalism by organizing the members of each estate into superiors and inferiors. This hierarchical order appears to be an essential component of patriarchalism. Without discussing previous definitions of patriarchalism and paternalism, I would like to distinguish between hierarchical order and reciprocity as two different aspects of the patriarchalism of the Table of Duties. Furthermore, a distinction should be made between two types of mutual relationships. In the ecclesiastical and political estates, the relationships between superiors and inferiors are based on absolute authority and unconditional obedience. I will refer to this type of reciprocity as the "cold" power-and-obedience relationship. The presentations of relationships within the economical estate display more of the second type of reciprocity (i.e., fatherly care and guidance from above and respectful obedience from below). In the following, I will refer to this reciprocity as the "warm" care-and-respect relationship.

The patriarchalism of the Table of Duties becomes evident in the frequent links made between the Table of Duties and the fourth commandment. This connection was not restricted to Lutheran Orthodoxy but became increasingly prevalent in the course of the 18th century. Actually, in the official catechism of 1810, the relationships of the Table of Duties were all presented under the explication of the fourth commandment. First the catechism asks who are to be understood by the commandment's reference to "father and mother," and the answer is "our parents, parents-in-law, foster parents, governors, teachers, masters, and all others who fatherly care about us." The following paragraphs then deal with the relationships of the three estates:

[ECONOMICAL ESTATE]
53. What does it mean to love one's father and mother?
54. What does it mean to keep them before one's sight?
55. Are the children obliged to obey their parents in everything?
56. What does God promise them who honour their father and mother?
57. What does it mean to live long?
58. What are the duties of Christian parents towards their children?

[POLITICAL ESTATE]
59. What are the duties of a Christian subject?

[ECCLESIASTICAL ESTATE]
60. What are the duties of a Christian teacher?
61. What are the duties of a Christian hearer towards his teachers?

[ECONOMICAL ESTATE]
62. What are the duties of a Christian Master?
63. What are the duties of a Christian Servant?

In comparison with the previous Orthodox version of the catechism of 1689, the 1810 explication of the fourth commandment has incorporated major parts of the Table of Duties, paragraphs 58–63 representing complete novelties. An interesting fact per se, this connection between the Table of Duties and the fourth commandment emphasizes patriarchalism as an essential ideological component of the Table of Duties. Another example of this linkage is provided by Magnus Hjortsberg, who gives the following advice in his textbook of 1799: "The civic virtues can be presented under the explication of the Fourth Commandment and the Holy Table of Duties" (p. 53).

This quote not only reveals the patriarchal connection between the Table of Duties and the fourth commandment but also demonstrates the common conception of the Table of Duties as a collection of civic virtues designed for different strata of society. When Mor Kasim Pothmann's (1801) *Sittenbuch für den christlichen Landmann*, a textbook of moral philosophy, appeared in Swedish translation, it was given the title *Den*

Christliga Hustaflan ("The Christian Table of Duties"), even though it was not even organized according to Luther's Table of Duties. Although mostly a curiosity, it still provides an example of the common identification between the Table of Duties and civic virtues in Sweden. This identification also had an impact on the definition of relationships clearly discernible in textbooks issued by the turn of the 18th century. In general, there was a development from "cold" power-and-obedience relationships to "warm" care-and-respect relationships. This development within the patriarchal paradigm was also accompanied by a more detailed description of specific duties.

The "warm" accent of patriarchal reciprocity can easily be identified in the catechism of 1810. In the explication of the "incorporated" Table of Duties, the catechism explains parents' duties towards their children in the following way:

> To look after them and give them a Christian upbringing: early make them accustomed to diligence and good manners: give them good examples and advice: look not away from their faults, and in their prayers deliver them to God. (§ 58)

The paragraph is dominated by parental concern and education. Similar observations can be made in the paragraph dealing with the master's duties towards his servants, where patriarchalism is explicitly expressed:

> To take fatherly care of his servants' godliness, manners and order: to attend to their health and subsistence: to be reasonable in his demands: give them good examples: have concern for their future, and not prevent them from having their rightful salary. (§ 62)

This "warm" type of patriarchalism was not restricted to textbooks of religion and moral philosophy. Previous research has demonstrated that this type of "warm" patriarchalism challenged the "cold" patriarchalism in the debate on servants' rights and duties. The Servant Statute of 1739 was criticized for harshly restricting servants' rights. This restrictive policy reached its peak in the 1750s when a proposition promoting outright serfdom was discussed by the Diet. The proposition failed, and restrictive policy lost support in the following decades. Advocates of restriction managed to stop a more liberal statute in the 1770s, after which their influence diminished. By the turn of the century, the master's responsibility for his servants' moral education was widely recognized. Anders Chydenius was one of the most influential debaters. In his book on the natural rights of masters and servants of 1778, he argued in favor of the master's total responsibility for his servants' well-being. He maintained that servants usually received their fair share of material things, but "in daily supervision, in sensible guiding, in tender and loving punishment and in necessary encouragement," masters had failed to fulfill their duty towards their servants (quoted in Harnesk, 1990). In 1805, a more liberal Servant Statute was enacted that delineated the duties of masters in line with Chydenius' ideas.

The changing accent of patriarchalism in servant statutes and explications of the Table of Duties emerged in a time when the "social question" was frequently discussed. Population growth and the pauperization of the non-proprietary classes created grave concerns. By stressing the masters' responsibilities and intensifying moral teaching, the leading classes of society tried to solve the alleged problems of the "decay of religion and corruption of morality." The strengthened position that the Table of Duties gained in popular education should be interpreted against this background. The Table of Duties offered a set of rules for different positions in society, not least in the "household estate," and because it was readily available in all catechisms and hymnbooks, it was a handy vehicle for promoting civic virtues. Obviously, the interest shown in the Table of Duties was not motivated by its promotion of three-estate society but rather by the opportunities it offered to teach moral philosophy.

A VEHICLE OF CHANGING CIVIC VIRTUES—CONCLUDING DISCUSSION

When used as a vehicle of changing civic virtues, the Table of Duties had certain limitations that had to be compensated for. First, it did not express much of the "warm" care-and-respect type of patriarchalism that was being promoted by the turn of the 18th century. Second, it was not elaborate enough in its description of society and social status. Third, it did not specifically address all those duties, responsibilities, and virtues that were essential in the moral philosophy of the time. Fourth, except for the idea of the three estates and the hierarchical and patriarchal order of relationships, the Table of Duties neither expressed any general, coherent philosophy of society nor the moral qualities of social relationships. These limitations may explain why the Table of Duties appears to have experienced quite a short reign in the history of Swedish education.

More interesting than its parenthetical appearance is the indisputable fact that the Table of Duties was widely used in the latter part of the 18th century and the beginning of the 19th century. To render the obsolete text viable in a new era and a different social situation, certain compensatory techniques were employed. In certain cases, the Table of Duties could be supplemented with additional biblical excerpts. By the end of the 18th century, the authentic and symbolic status of the text was disputed, which opened for revisions of the contents. Not only was the order of the first two estates changed in the catechism of 1810, but also the biblical quotations. Quotations referring to teachers were reduced, and new citations were added to the sections for parents and children. Quotations from the

New Testament were supplemented with verses from the Old Testament emphasizing the significance of religious education.[8]

The Table of Duties could also turn up in new settings with slightly different contents. In the course of the 18th century, some new catechetical editions represented confessional alternatives to the Orthodox catechism of 1689. The many catechisms of Pietist and Neologist hue in particular paid more attention to the ethical aspects of the Christian faith by including more detailed paragraphs on the Christian way of living. Sometimes the categories of the Table of Duties can be found in the explications. For instance, in a Pietistic catechism of 1771, the categories of the Table of Duties are easily identified (Alnander, 1771). As demonstrated above, the catechism of 1810 introduced the "warm" care-and-respect type of patriarchalism in the interpretation of the categories of the Table of Duties under the explication of the fourth commandment, and in Samuel Wigelius' moral philosophy textbook, the same categories were explained as "different positions in the world," to which particular duties were linked. This re-interpretation of the contents of the Table of Duties represents an intermediate step in the direction towards a new set of civic virtues and occurred in a transitional period when the Table of Duties still held a strong position in popular education.

Another strategy for supplementing the Table of Duties was simply to develop new textbooks of moral philosophy and civic education, representing the next step in the evolution of a secular ideology of civic virtues. Some of the textbooks of moral philosophy have been mentioned above, but there were many more, of both Swedish and foreign origin. In the curricula of parish schools that reformers of popular education produced by the turn of the 18th century, social studies and civic education attained prominent positions. Consequently, new textbooks were issued to cover the need. Furthermore, the teaching of civic virtues could also find other channels than textbooks. Collections of quotations used in writing lessons frequently articulated advice for a moral life founded on natural law (Lindmark, 2009).

Unfortunately, not much is known about the contents of the textbooks that gradually replaced the Table of Duties in the teaching of civic duties and virtues. Even more hidden in darkness are the oral explications of the Table of Duties performed by teachers and ministers in their instruction of children and youth. Therefore, it is difficult to draw even preliminary conclusions about how far-reaching the re-interpretation of the Table of Duties was. More research is needed on the teaching of civic virtues in the period prior to the compulsory elementary school system of 1842.

At the outset of this chapter, I presented interpretations of 20th-century Swedish society in which mutual understanding comprised a major characteristic. Educationalist Tomas Englund identified mutual interdependence between individual members of society as a leading principle of the civic curriculum code of primary education in the early 20th century. When defining the unique traits of the Nordic states, political scientist Tim Knudsen emphasized the mutual trust between authorities and citizens that he considered to be rooted in the homogeneity created by the Lutheran state churches. I will conclude this chapter by briefly addressing the question of how to place the Table of Duties in the development of curriculum codes. How did the Table of Duties relate to the civic curriculum code and the previous moral curriculum code?

In itself, the Table of Duties represented an absolutist order of society, where civil and ecclesiastical government rested upon God-given authority. One of the reasons for the abandonment of the Table of Duties in Swedish popular education was probably its hierarchical order of society, including the subject-perspective that was applied to the political estate. A liberal perspective of free and independent citizens organizing society through contracts drawn up by mutual consent could not easily find its way into the Table of Duties. Nevertheless, through re-interpretations the Table of Duties could serve as a vehicle of new civic virtues during a transitional period.

In this chapter, I have identified reciprocity as a leading principle of the Table of Duties. The text rested on the fundamental idea of mutual relationships between individuals of different social status. However, the biblical quotations aimed at the superiors of the ecclesiastical and political estates did not reflect much of their relationship with their inferiors, the reciprocity at best represented by "cold" power-and-obedience relationships. The biblical quotations for the economical estate expressed more reciprocity, the mutual relationships being more characterized by a "warm" care-and-respect type of patriarchalism. Regardless of which type of patriarchalism the Table of Duties expressed, it established the idea that society could be divided into different social positions to which certain duties were linked, including responsibilities with regard to other people. This aspect of the Table of Duties was developed when the text and its categories were integrated into a moral philosophy based on natural law by the end of the 18th century. Consequently, this reciprocity offered the opportunity for the Table of Duties to serve as a vehicle of new civic virtues, thereby taking significant steps from a moral code to a civic curriculum code.

Only when more is known about interpretations of the Table of Duties and the contents of civic education in the 19th century will it be possible to address the question of the historical roots of Swedish and Nordic universalism. Until then, I do not challenge Tim Knudsen's thesis about the Lutheran state church ideology and organization as significant contributions to the Nordic model of society. However, this chapter has shown that that ideology underwent significant changes within the stable framework of the Lutheran Church of Sweden, the moral philosophy of natural law pouring new wine into the old bottles of the Table of Duties.

NOTES

1. For a more detailed presentation and discussion of the data used in this article, see Lindmark (1995).

2. Lund Consistory Archives, Regional State Archives, Lund (through photocopies in the Research Archives, Umeå University, Sweden).
3. Examination registers from respective parish archive, Regional State Archives, Lund (through photocopies in the Research Archives, Umeå University, Sweden).
4. Examination registers on microfiche, Swedish Archival Information, National Archives, Ramsele, Sweden.
5. Demographic Data Base, Umeå University, Sweden.
6. Examination registers on microfiche, Swedish Archival Information, National Archives, Ramsele, Sweden. The total number of individuals included in the sample is 1,813.
7. A similar presentation of the duties can be found in Wåhlin, 1802; cf. also Boëthius, 1807.
8. Proverbs 1, 8; Isaiah 38, 19. The tendency to use Old Testament wisdom literature in popular education can be found in Denmark as well, where the apocryphal book of Jesus Syrach achieved prominence (Markussen, 1988). Markussen concludes that intensified social teaching was needed in a time when the peasantry obtained greater freedom.

REFERENCES

Alnander, S. J. (1771). *Sammandrag Af den Christna Salighets-Läran*. Stockholm: Grefingska tryckeriet.
Apelseth, A. (2004). *Den låge danninga: Skriftmeistring, diskursintegrering og tekstlege deltakingsformer 1760–1840* (Diss.). Bergen: University of Bergen.
Boëthius, D. (1807). *Anvisning till sedeläran såsom vettenskap*. Uppsala: Uppsala University, Joh. Fr. Edman.
Englund, T. (1980). *Medborgerlig läroplanskod för folkskola, fortsättningsskola och grundskola 1918/19–?* Stockholm: Lärarhögskolan.
Englund, T. (1986a). *Samhällsorientering och medborgarfostran i svensk skola under 1900-talet*. Uppsala: Uppsala University.
Englund, T. (1986b). *Curriculum as a political problem: Changing educational conceptions, with special reference to citizenship education*. Lund: Studentlitteratur.
Hansen, L.-E. (1997). Den nordiska tanken—speglad i Norden-föreningarnas arkiv. In *Grannar emellan* (pp. 172–182). Stockholm: Riksarkivet.
Hansen, S. O. (1994). *Drømmen om Norden: Den norske foreningen Norden og det nordiske samarbeidet 1919–1994*. Oslo: Ad Notam Gyldendal.
Harnesk, B. (1990). *Legofolk: Drängar, pigor och bönder i 1700- och 1800-talens Sverige*. Umeå: Umeå University.
Hjortsberg, M. (1799). *Anvisning, huru Föräldrar av Allmogen Rätt böra Upfostra sina Barn* (2nd ed.). Strengnäs: Albrecht Julius Segerstedt.
Hovbakke Sørensen, L. (1996). Norden som idé och praksis: Den danske foreningen Nordens rolle som politisk-ideologisk pressionsgruppe 1940–1960. *Historie*, 22(1), 84–113.
Janfelt, M. (2005). *Att leva i den bästa av världar: Föreningarna Nordens syn på Norden 1919–1933*. Stockholm: Carlsson.
Johansson, E. (1977). *The history of literacy in Sweden and some other countries*. Umeå: Umeå University.
Johansson, E. (1992). "Kan själva orden"—ett grundtema för kyrkans undervisning. *Dalfolk*, 5(1), 4–6.

Knudsen, T. (Ed.). (2000). *Den nordiske protestantisme og velfærdsstaten*. Aarhus: Aarhus universitetsforlag.

Knudsen, T. (2002). Den nordiske velfærdsstat og de sækulariserede lutheranere. In *Velfærd og folkeoplysning* (pp. 11–28). Odense: Odense universitetsforlag.

Lindmark, D. (1995). *Uppfostran, undervisning, upplysning: Linjer i svensk folkundervisning före folkskolan*. Umeå: Umeå University.

Lindmark, D. (2004). *Reading, writing, and schooling: Swedish practices of education and literacy, 1650–1880*. Umeå: Umeå University.

Lindmark, D. (2009). Learning to write the right learning: The ideological function of copies in writing instruction in 19th-century Sweden. *History of Education and Children's Literature*, 4(1), 19–30.

Lundgren, U. P. (1979). *Att organisera omvärlden: En introduktion till läroplansteori*. Stockholm: LiberFörlag.

Markussen, I. (1988). *Visdommens lænker: Studier i enevældens skolereformer fra Reventlow til skolelov*. Odense: Landbohistorisk Selskab.

Nordbäck, C. (2004). *Samvetets röst: Om mötet mellan luthersk ortodoxi och konservativ pietism i 1720-talets Sverige*, Umeå: Umeå University.

Normann, C.-E. (1948). *Prästerskapet och det karolinska enväldet: Studier över det svenska prästerskapets statsuppfattning under stormaktstidens slutskede*. Stockholm: Svenska kyrkans diakonistyrelses bokförlag.

Østergaard, U. (1994). Norden–europæisk eller nordisk? *Den jyske historiker*, 69–70, 7–37.

Pleijel, H. (1951). *Från hustavlans tid: Kyrkohistoriska folklivsstudier*. Stockholm: Svenska kyrkans diakonistyrelses bokförlag.

Pleijel, H. (1970). *Hustavlans värld: Kyrkligt folkliv i äldre tiders Sverige*. Stockholm: Verbum.

Pothmann, M. K. (1801). *Den christliga hustaflan*. Linköping.

Rerup, L. (1994). Nationalisme og skandinavisme indtil Første Verdenskrigs udbrud. *Den jyske historiker*, 69–70, 79–87.

Sørensen, Ø., & Stråth, B. (Eds.). (1997). *The cultural construction of Norden*. Oslo: Scandinavian University Press.

Wåhlin, C. (1802). *Lärobok För Swerges Ungdom*. Lund: Johann Lundblad.

Wigelius, S. (1803). *Kristelig Läro-Bok för Barn, att nyttjas jämte Doktor Luthers lilla Katekes*. Karlskrona: Kungliga amiralitetstryckeriet.

3 From Imaginations to Realities
The Transformation of Enlightenment Pedagogical Illusions of the Dutch Republic into Late 19th-Century Realities of the Dutch Monarchy

Jeroen J. H. Dekker

INTRODUCTION

In the second half of the 18th century, in the Dutch Republic a new pedagogical and political discourse developed among adherents of the Dutch Enlightenment. Longing for unification and modernization of their decentralized country, in other words becoming modern republicans out of classical ones, they realized that only through education for all could an inclusive membership of the nation for all citizens be possible. They considered education as a necessity for their modern republicanism mission (see Introduction of the present volume). However, after some years of political euphoria that started in 1795, enthusiasm and belief in their political and educational imaginations slid down.

In this chapter, based on documents about education and schooling, on literature, in particular pedagogical poems for children, and on pieces of art, namely, paintings on parenting and education (Dekker, 2006), first the key elements of that new pedagogical discourse together with the concrete educational blueprints resulting from it are studied. Then attention is given to the growing awareness that the implementation of these blueprints for all citizens might turn into a mission impossible. It took a century before that awareness resulted into a historic deal on education between the adherents of Enlightenment and modern republican ideas and the main Christian groups.

Modern Republican Imaginations on Education and Childrearing: Education and Citizenship for All

A growing minority of mainly Protestant dissenters, adherents of the 18th-century Dutch Enlightenment, longed to be a nation and a new state instead of the decentralized and economically stagnating Dutch Republic, politically modelled on a 16th-century idea of local and regional autonomy, and, in the Golden Age in the 17th century, the most urbanized country of the world. In that new nation, built on modern republicanism, citizenship for all was crucial. This citizenship should be inclusive instead of the exclusive citizenship of the ancient regime Republic. Because education was, according to them, necessary in reaching patriotism and citizenship for all, these adherents of the new Dutch Enlightenment republicanism, in great majority moderate Protestants, developed a new pedagogical discourse. In 1778, Hieronijmus van Alphen (1746–1803), in one of his three volumes of poems for children, wrote a poem entitled "Patriotism" [De Liefde voor het Vaderland]. In that poem, he expressed the new patriotism effectively. On the drawing next to this poem, a Dutch boy stands before a pillar with the Dutch Lion, showing his patriotism, and promising that with the support of the national education, he will be useful for his country (Van Alphen, 1778/1998b; Van Sas, 1992, 1999, 2004). In this same patriotic spirit, Jan Hendrik Swildens (1745–1809), main ideologist of the most influential Dutch philanthropic society, *The Society for the General Good* [Maatschappij tot Nut van 't Algemeen, abridged as *Nut*], stated in 1781 in his *Patriotic A-B Book for the Dutch Youth* [Vaderlandsch A-B boek voor de Nederlandsche jeugd] that every Dutch child should love his country more than any other (Van Sas, 2004; cf. Hake, 2004).

In these years, Dutch society was disrupted by the struggle between patriots who were inspired by the Dutch Enlightenment and longing to one nation in one centralized and democratically governed modern republic, and the adherents of the prince of Orange. A civil war was far from imaginary. The famous patriot Joan Derk van der Capellen tot den Pol (1741–1784) blamed, in his 1781 anonymously published pamphlet *To the People of the Netherlands* [Aan het Volk van Nederland], the prince of Orange and his adherents for the suppression of the Dutch freedom. He even incited the population to make revolution with the help of their own militias, which was no less than an act of uprising (Israel, 1995; Van Sas, 2004). Without real fighting, the patriots fled to France after their defeat in 1787 against the prince, who got help from the Prussian troops of the Duke of Brunswick. In 1795, they returned to their country, and backed by the French troops they triumphed with their republicanism new style, or, modern republicanism, without any bloodshed. Now the prince fled and went to England. In the meanwhile, the patriots founded the modern republic they had dreamed of for years: the centralized Batavian Republic. This republic became the first centralized state in the history of the Northern Netherlands. After some preparatory years, in 1798, the new constitution came into force; as a result, the unified state became reality and the regional autonomy of the ancient regime and classic Republic over and done. According to Van Sas, this was a metamorphosis of the country.[1]

The new pedagogical culture that developed during that metamorphosis was part of the Dutch Enlightenment and was inspired by foreign examples from England (Locke), France (Rousseau), and in particular from the German tradition (Basedow, Campe, Salzmann) (Gobbers, 1963). Many books of these philosophers and pedagogues were translated in Dutch. This process started with the translation of John Locke's (1632–1704) *Some Thoughts Concerning Education* from 1693 by Pieter Adriaen Verwer in 1753. Next to the concept of *tabula rasa*, Locke's emphasis on child play was very influential on the Dutch pedagogical discourse (Cunningham, 1995/2005; Los, 1999). Jean-Jacques Rousseau's (1712–1778) radical pedagogical ideas, laid down in his *Émile, ou de l'Éducation* from 1762, were no doubt of influence in the Netherlands, but chiefly indirectly, through the didactic adaptation of his ideas by the German Philanthropists, the men behind the Dessau Philanthropium, founded in 1774 (Buijnsters & Buijnsters-Smets, 2001; Buijnsters, 1992; Dekker, 2001; Grandière, 1998; Lüth, 1997; Py, 1997; Rosenberg, 1990; Van Crombrugge, 1995, 2001). The reason why is that the Dutch pedagogical culture, with the exception of the Rousseau adherent Johannes Kneppelhout (1814–1885), was not so much interested in the romantic pedagogical movement as in practical ways of how to educate children into good citizens according to enlightened ideas (Dane, 2002; Kneppelhout, 1980). According to the Dutch, the Philanthropists supplied those practical ways. They had transformed part of Rousseau's ideas in practical and do-able programs, realized at their Philantropium in Dessau, and thus, according to their Dutch adherents, they proved that Rousseau's ideas could work, when transformed in a didactic direction. Although the writings of the founding father of the Dessau Philantropinum of 1774, Johann Bernhard Basedow (1724–1790), did not have much influence in the Netherlands, much of the work of Joachim Heinrich Campe (1746–1818), Basedow's successor in Dessau, and of Christian Gotthilf Salzmann (1744–1811) was translated in Dutch.[2] Salzmann, whose main moral books were reprinted several times in its Dutch translation, was of the opinion that children could be educated most efficiently to the virtues by letting them read books on virtuous men and women (Buijnsters & Buijnsters-Smets, 2001; Salzmann, 1780/1961). The already mentioned Swildens, ideologist of the philanthropic society the *Nut*, was a real adherent of the Philanthropists, as was made clear by his Patriotic A-B Book for the Dutch youth, published in 1781, a book full of social virtues, focused explicitly on citizenship and patriotism. In 1813, he also published his *Virtues booklet* [Deugden-boekje], inspired by Campe (Ter Linden et al., 1995; Van Sas, 2004).

Inspired by these foreign influences, the adherents of the new educational culture in the context of modern republicanism were of the opinion that the education of all Dutch boys and girls into good citizens should be realized in two different contexts: in the family and on the national primary school.

A Family for All: The Role of the Family in the New Pedagogical Culture

The family was by far the most important educational institution according to almost all modern republican patriots. In that respect, they built on a long tradition of the Dutch family education discourse, made popular by a series of best and long sellers of the 17th-century moralist and writer of emblematic books, Jacob Cats (Dekker, 2008, 2009a; Cats, 1655). At the same time, however, they changed the ultimate goal of that family education discourse, in now considering family education no longer as the preparation of religious education, but as the far most important educational power for the formation of future citizens. They even looked at the nation itself as a moral family, guided by the virtues of citizenship. Indeed, according to these adherents of the educational Dutch Enlightenment, nation virtues and family virtues aimed at the same goal, namely, good citizenship. From 1795, with the foundation of the centralized Batavian Republic and the 1798 liberal constitution, clear examples of modern republicanism according to the way used in this book, the new political elite inspired by the Enlightenment was in power. They developed a series of educational blue prints, and, apart from the radical anti-family ideas by the radical patriot and rector of the Gouda Latin School, Gerrit C.C. Vatebender (1759–1822), the vast majority of this enlightened elite focused on the family as the main pedagogical instrument. In addition, they developed legislation for primary schools resulting in the first national school acts of 1801 and 1806. The family became the key element of the new ideology. The *Domestic Book for Dutch Families* [Huisboek voor vaderlandsche huisgezinnen] from 1793, written by the moderate Protestant Reverend Johannes Martinet (1729–1795), became, in the words of Kloek and Mijnhardt (2001), the "icon of the domesticity ideology" (p. 200; see also Buijnsters & Buijnsters-Smets, 2001; Huussen, 1975; Mathijsen, 2002; Van Tilburg, 1998).

This new educational discourse was the Dutch variant of the European educational Enlightenment (Los, 2005). Specific for this variant was its didactic and explicit emphasis on family virtues and on citizenship as main goals of education (Van Tilburg, 1998). The *Little Poems for Children* [Kleine Gedigten voor Kinderen] by Hieronijmus van Alphen (1746–1803) were representative for this new culture. Van Alphen put into words this new pedagogical culture in a very effective way in these child-oriented poems, intended for both children and their parents. Van Alphen, pietistic patriot from Utrecht, obtained his doctorate in 1768 at the University of Utrecht and afterward worked as a lawyer (Buijnsters, 1973; Van Stipriaan, 2002). In 1775, after the death of his wife, he was left with his three young sons of 3, 2, and 1 year old. For these children, he wrote in 1778 anonymously his first volume of children's poems under the influence of Christian Felix Weisse (1726–1804) and Gottlob Wilhelm Burmann (1737–1805) (Buijnsters, 1973, 1998; Buijnsters & Buijnsters-Smets, 2001). In the second volume, also published in 1778, he put his name on the title page, as was in the third volume from 1782 (Van Alphen, 1778/1998a, 1778/1998b). These children's poems became very popular through their combination of text and didactic illustration, made by Jacobus Buijs (1724–1801). Their popularity continued for more than half a century, until ca. 1850. Then, they were criticized so strongly by the Reverend Petrus de Génestet (1829–1861) that their popularity went down. From then, they were considered as mainly moralistic and old fashioned, and they never recovered (Buijnsters, 1998).

Around 1800, however, on the peak of the Dutch Enlightenment pedagogical culture, they were very popular and read to children by their parents, as can be seen in the autobiography by Willem van den Hull (1778–1858) (Dane, 1998). It was not the content of those poems that was special, but the language, directed to the children themselves (Buijnsters, 1998). Indeed, these are *Vom Kinde Aus* poems *avant-la-lettre*. One of the reasons that Van Alphen succeeded in writing them in such a way must be the affective and intense relationship between him and his little sons. In writing for children, he was an exception in Dutch pedagogical Enlightenment whose texts on childhood and education (e.g., those by Wolff and Deken) were intended for parents and other adults and not for children. Van Alphen, however, tried to place himself in the position of the child, making a map of the mind of the child. In addition, his use of rhythm and his choice of words, which made them memorable, contributed to the attractiveness of his poems. In that respect, they were innovative. Whereas Wolff and Deken were part of the ancient tradition of child rearing advice, Van Alphen belongs to the newly emerging tradition of describing the child's world or making a map of the child's mind. Of course, he could only do that from the point of view of the culture in which he lived: His ideal child was the well-behaved, good child who wanted to become a good citizen. That explains both the popularity of his poems for more than 50 years, and, when this image of the ideal child changed in the second half of the 19th century, the decrease of that same popularity.

Van Alphen was a true representative of the Dutch Enlightenment: a moderate Christian, a patriot, and a pedagogic innovator. It is true that the Dutch Enlightenment started with emphasis on rationality with Justus van Effen and his *Hollandsche Spectator* (1731–1735). Van Alphen, however, also got inspiration from the second phase of that Enlightenment, during which emotions and feelings became more important (Israel, 1995; Sturkenboom, 1999). Therefore, his poems, in particular those that treat the relationships between parents and children, are a combination of childish rationality and sensibility. Examples are the poem in which Claartje is weeping at the portrait of her dead mother or the poem in which Willem is weeping on his dead little sister.

The central role of the mother in the pedagogical discourse and the genre painting on education of 17th-century Holland was again emphasized in the late 18th-century context of domesticity (Dekker, 1998a, 2006, 2008, 2009a, 2009b; Dekker & Groenendijk & Verberckmoes, 2000; Groenendijk, 2002). The innovation was the emphasis on the preparation of that role through education. Van Effen, pleading in his 17th *Spectatorial Writings* from 1731 in favor of good education for girls, was not doing that with the intention of preparing them for a position in the society, but with the idea of preparing them for their future role as a mother and a wife (Kloek & Mijnhardt, 2001). This argument for good education of girls for their future mother role was frequently used in other Spectatorial texts and shared by famous female authors such as Betje Wolff, Aagje Deken, and Petronella Moens. According to Betje Wolff in her popular *A Proof on Education* [Proeve over de opvoeding] from 1779, it was only by way of family education and through the effort of well-educated mothers that children could become decent citizens (Kloek & Mijnhardt, 2001; Sturkenboom, 1999). The 18th-century message on motherhood not only differed from the 17th-century message in its emphasis on good education for girls, but also through its didactic and explicit moralistic style. For the reader of these late 18th-century texts, it was clear that there was no alternative to this future for girls and mothers, everybody who did not accept that argument not yet being enlightened.

As was the case in the 17th century, also around 1800 genre-painters made use of the discourse on motherhood, although not in such great numbers and without the Golden Age quality. In addition to writers and politicians, artists became enthusiastic about the new ideals on citizenship and education, as, for example, the Frisian painter Willem Bartel van der Kooi (1768–1836). Van der Kooi, a moderate Protestant, a modern republican, and an adherent of the Dutch Enlightenment, was an autodidact, inspired by the portraits by Van Dijck and other famous portrait painters, which he studied during his travels, in 1804–1805, to Düsseldorf. He was an active participant in the 1795 Dutch revolution, becoming a substitute member of the Provincial Executive of Friesland. At the famous National Assembly, he voted for the unified modern republic. In 1798, he became a lector in drawing at the University of the Frisian city of Franeker and was both a successful portrait and genre painter. His large genre paintings breathe the didactic and educational spirit of the Dutch Enlightenment. They contain explicit and didactic messages that differ from the complex and often implicit messages of 17th-century Dutch genre painting on education and childhood. Whereas during his life his reputation as an artist was high, around 1900 it went down, and it took more than half a century before some appreciation came into being again. Nowadays, some of his paintings are even hanging prominently in the Amsterdam Rijks Museum.

Van der Kooi's painting from 1826, entitled *Breast-feeding Mother*, an oil canvas from the Leeuwarden Fries Museum, shows a Frisian mother from the country who breast-feeds her baby (Boschma, 1976, 1978; Van Tilborgh & Jansen, 1986). This painting, a secular caritas image, functioned as propaganda for breast-feeding for the upper bourgeois mothers. That is why his model was a Frisian woman from the country in traditional clothes. The painting contains the message that all mothers, not only those living on the countryside, but also elite women from the cities, could only become good mothers when they made the choice for breast-feeding their children. That message was popular in the Enlightenment and formulated explicitly by Rousseau. For the rest, in the Northern Netherlands, breast-feeding was already common use among the majority of mothers, in contrast with countries like France. The 17th-century moralist Jacob Cats also emphasized the relationship between good motherhood and breast-feeding. Due to the high infant mortality rate around 1800, however, it was according to Van der Kooi meaningful to renew this propaganda (Brandt Corstius & Hallema, 1981; Boschma, 1978; De Mooij & Kruijsen, 1997; Fildes, 1986, 1988; Groenendijk, 1976).

A School for All: The Mission of the Dutch Educational Enlightenment

Family education, notwithstanding its enormous importance according to Dutch Enlightenment adherents such as Van Effen, Van Alphen, and Van Kooi, was not the whole story. School was the other part. A private philanthropic society took the initiative for school reform. It was the modern republican, moderate Protestant, and Enlightenment-inspired *Society for the General Good*, founded in 1784 in the city of Edam near Amsterdam by the Anabaptist Reverend Jan Nieuwenhuijzen (1759–1793). Dutch-moderated Protestant minorities such as Anabaptists, Remonstrants, and Lutherans dominated this society. This *civil church* according to Simon Schama, governed by clergymen such as its founder Nieuwenhuijzen, J. F. Martinet and Bernardus Bosch (1747–1803), developed the ambition and then got the illusion of representing the nation as a whole. In reality, however, Catholics, Jews, orthodox Protestants, and moderate Protestant women, in other words the great majority of society, took no part in this society. The mission of the *Nut* was to transform by means of education all members of the nation into good Dutch citizens (Buijnsters & Buijnsters-Smets, 2001; Dekker, 1994, 1998b, 2001; Kloek & Mijnhardt, 2001; Kruithof, 1990; Mijnhardt, 1988; Mijnhardt & Wichers, 1984; Schama, 1977). This was an ambitious democratic mission of these modern republicans, as outlined in the first chapter of this book, for eventually this mission also focused on the uncivilized majority of the people, as formulated by IJsbrand van Hamelsveld in his *De zedelijke toestand der Nederlandsche Natie, op het einde der achttiende eeuw* [The moral situation of the Dutch Nation at the end of the 18th century] from 1791 (Kloek & Mijnhardt, 2002). The *Nut*, although inspired by the Enlightenment, was not against faith or religion, as was often the case among adherents of the French Enlightenment. On the contrary, their members were moderate Protestants. They, being themselves members of minorities with only limited civil rights during the Dutch Republic before 1795, strived for the abolishment of the privileged position of the Dutch Calvinistic Church and its members, and for making all Christian religions equal before the law (Boekholt, 1998).

In their opinion, reaching the Enlightenment and the civilization of all citizens, a goal explicitly mentioned in article 60 of the modern republican constitution of 1798, was only possible by giving the central state a monopoly on primary education (Boekholt, 1998). In order to realize that, the *Nut* developed, next to blue prints on health policy, detailed plans on educational policy. Indeed, education was the central issue for this modern republican philanthropic society. According to the *Nut*, learning was both a right and a duty, and the state-governed school should become the place to practice that. In emphasizing their argument for a national school, they purposefully exaggerated the negative aspects of the current school system, notwithstanding the fact that it had been improved substantially in the 18th century (Boekholt, 1998; Kloek & Mijnhardt, 2001). The school system around 1790 consisted of various schools, such as German schools, elementary schools, French schools, and of course the famous Latin School, all being Calvinistic (Frijhoff, 1983, 2004). In the 18th century, next to these Calvinistic schools, special schools developed for Catholics, Jews, and Protestant minorities. In addition, for the education of upper class children at least as important were private schoolmasters (Kloek & Mijnhardt, 2001).

The ancient school system, not focused on inclusion of all citizens, was no longer acceptable for the members of the *Nut* who saw the task of the school as the making of good citizens out of all boys and girls. In the words of the radical Enlightenment adherent and rector of the Gouda Latin School, G. C. C. Vatebender, every child—he gives the example of a future carpenter—should become "A human being and not only a Carpenter." In other words, the new national school should not only aim at traditional literacy by teaching children the three Rs, or at vocational training, but also at social literacy by teaching children how to become good citizens. An additional advantage of social literacy could be the diminution of poverty, for well-educated citizens should no longer be dependent on poor relief (Boekholt & de Booy, 1987). Main foreign sources of inspiration for such ideas were Locke with his emphasis on the relationship between knowledge and virtue and his concept of *tabula rasa*, and the German *Philantropinum* in the German city of Dessau, visited by the prominent Dutch school reformer Swildens in 1777 (Buijnsters & Buijnsters-Smets, 2001). Although the reformers of the *Nut* failed in introducing legal compulsory primary education that was realized not earlier than 1901, they succeeded in getting compulsory primary education generally accepted as an ambition to be realized soon. Everybody had to go to school in order to become a good citizen: That soon became the norm in the Netherlands. Getting virtues without getting knowledge was no longer possible, and getting that knowledge became possible through attending the national school.

Although being a private organization, the *Nut* dominated the school reformation in the Batavian Republic. The main document on school policy in these years, and the basis of the school acts of 1801, 1803, and 1806, was the report developed by the *Nut* in 1796 and published in 1798, the same year of the first Dutch constitution, and entitled *General*

Ideas on National Education [Algemeene denkbeelden over het nationaal onderwijs]. The *Nut* did ask the brand-new government to develop such a report, and that was an offer that could not be refused. Indeed, the new government was in favor of the introduction of a new national school system. The report's starting point was revolutionary. It stated that education and schooling should be "a state's affair and not a church affair." This caused a real blow in a country in which for centuries schooling was the affair of the church, or more precisely of the only privileged one, namely, the Calvinist Dutch Reformed Church (Boekholt & De Booy, 1987). For the *Nut* and for the new government alike, that starting point was necessary in order to reach the main goal of their political and societal plans, namely, making every member of society a good citizen and therefore teaching on school the elementary knowledge for all boys and girls. It was clear that a state with such an ambition also had the duty to supply the means for realizing it or to offer everybody, the rich and the poor, and men and women alike, state elementary education (Kloek & Mijnhardt, 2001). According to this overtly modern republican report, "The general happiness is the main law for everybody." That means that, on the one hand, society could ask its members to cooperate with each other in order to reach that goal of general happiness. On the other hand, the state had to prepare all citizens to this task by supplying sufficient schooling and education. The report offered a detailed proposal for school policy. It went further than only describing the main responsibilities of the state and of its citizens and the role function of elementary education in making possible these responsibilities. It also sketched the conditions the future schoolmasters should fulfill, and it asked for the introduction of teaching on class level instead of individual teaching in all schools. In this innovative new national school, children should be divided in groups according to their age and should form a homogenous class instead of the heterogeneous classroom of the ancient regime (Boekholt et al., 2002; Dodde, 1971, 2001; Van Essen & Imelman, 1999; Van Essen, 2006).

As said before, the reformers did not work in a national vacuum but got inspiration from foreign examples and ideas. Specific for the Dutch variant is the focus on primary education, whereas in countries such as France the innovation of secondary education got more emphasis (Amsing, 2002; Boekholt, 1998; Boekholt & De Booy, 1980, 1987; Frijhoff, 1983, 1985; Kloek & Mijnhardt, 2001; Savoie et al., 2004). For the Dutch educational Enlightenment, the new national primary school was the main vehicle in reaching their general goals, namely, the knowledge of national feelings, and of national and Christian virtues, and the making of good citizens out of all members of society. Indeed, the reformers were concerned both about national and Christian virtues. With Christian virtues, however, they meant general Christian virtues, not specific Calvinist, Lutheran, or even Catholic dogmas. The new national school was, according to them, Christian and enlightened at the same time, meaning rational and anti-dogmatic, a school that should make all boys and girls, Calvinists and Catholics alike, into good Christians and into useful citizens.

From Imaginations to Realities: The Failure of National Education for All

After some years, however, the patriotic and modern republican atmosphere of enthusiasm and of belief in the new political and educational imaginations slid down. The intended national curriculum on the national primary school, to be financed by the central modern republic, remained an ambition instead of becoming a reality. In the short term, this was the result of political change: The independent Batavian Republic (1795–1806) went down and was subsequently succeeded by the Monarchy of Holland under Napoleon's brother, Louis Napoleon (1806–1810), a department of France (1810–1813), finally, after the Vienna Congress, the independent Monarchy of the Netherlands. In addition, major financial problems of the young state made it almost impossible to implement major educational innovations.

These reasons, however, were not the main causes of the failure of the national education for all. In the long term, the main reason for the failure of implementing the most important blue print of the Batavian Republic, namely, the educational one, seems to be the growing opposition of the Roman Catholics and the orthodox Calvinists, groups that did not share the modern language of republicanism, as outlined in Chapter 1 of this book. The self-awareness and the political power of these groups grew enormously in the 19th century. On the one hand, the Roman Catholics, who were third-class citizens in the classical ancient regime Dutch Republic, eventually got equal rights through the 1798 constitution of the modern Batavian Republic. This became the start of their struggle for cultural and political emancipation, with as a first major result the restoration of the Episcopal hierarchy in 1853. The orthodox Calvinists, on the other hand, being first-class citizens in the Dutch Republic, were now in danger of becoming marginalized by their liberal Protestant counterparts. Of course, the orthodox Calvinists were principally opposed to all revolutionary and modern republican ideas of the moderate Protestants, and they considered the modernizing developments in the Dutch Calvinist Church a frontal attack against what they saw as the only true Faith. Although the Catholics and the orthodox Calvinists were far from natural allies, their growing self-awareness and political power eventually, after 1860, brought them together in the opposition against the attempt to implement the Enlightenment pedagogical ideas for all citizens, including orthodox Calvinists and Catholics.

Thus, paradoxically these very reformers prepared the conditions for the growing opposition in the 19th century against their reformatory plans in making in 1798 a constitution that ended the privileged position of the Calvinist church and made all religions, including the Roman Catholic Church, equal before the law (Israel, 1995; Kloek & Mijnhardt, 2001). It is true that the reformers, in majority Protestant dissenters, together with one of their main future ideological opponents, namely, the Roman Catholics, considered by them mainly as believers into superstition (Kloek & Mijnhardt, 2001, 192), took full advantage of this 1798 constitution. The orthodox Protestants, however, immediately were aware that their privileged position now was over and done. This growing opposition against the reformatory plans was the Dutch manifestation of a European-wide development of a new *Wendung zur Religion*, the expression with which the German historian Thomas Nipperdey refers to the phenomenon that after 1800 in Europe the meaning of religion grew again (Dekker, 2001; McLeod, 1997; Nipperdey, 1983). Consequently, the ambition of the *Nut* to become a national *civil church* failed, as was the case with their educational blue prints.

The first national school acts from 1801, 1803, and 1806, realized in the modern Batavian Republic, were prepared by Van der Palm and Van den Ende. Johannes Hendrik van der Palm (1763–1840), professor of oriental languages at the University of Leiden and a confirmed patriot and modern republican, became Secretary of Education [Agent van Nationale Opvoeding] from 1799 (Boekholt, 1998). Adriaan van den Ende (1769–1846), first assistant of Van der Palm, became Inspector for Elementary Education from 1806 to 1833 (Boekholt & de Booy, 1987). The dream of these two men was to build a national school system, governed from and financed by the central government, responsible for the quality of both the curriculum and the schoolmasters (Kloek & Mijnhardt, 2001). With, however, most dreams and blue prints of the Batavian Republic failing in their implementation, Van der Palm showed himself a pragmatic and opportunistic administrator (Kloek & Mijnhardt, 2001). When it became clear to him that the ambitious blue prints and dreams could not be realized, he modified them into do-able measures. For example, he cancelled the national school free for the poor, introduced by himself, for financial reasons; as a result, school attendance immediately diminished.

Yet, what remained of the blue prints in the 1806 national school act still is innovative. This act, mentioned after Van den Ende, characterized by Boekholt as a bookkeeper, survived until 1857. It increased the influence and responsibility of the central government on the quality of the primary school by the introduction of a central system of school inspection, but no state monopoly, the ambition of the Batavian reformers, was realized. Next to the public schools, private schools were recognized, and these schools, in fact Christian schools, flourished. So, the imaginations of the radical Batavian national school, managed and financed by the central state and based on general Christian and modern republican ideas, were transformed in the reality of a system in which various schools, based on various religions that were opposing the Enlightenment, existed together with the state school based on general Christian and Enlightenment ideas. A free primary school for all remained a dream. Perhaps the most important innovation through this act was the introduction of school inspection. Also, the introduction of special school buildings, separate classrooms with rows of school desks, and class-level teaching instead of individual teaching were innovative (Boekholt, 1978, 1982, 1998; Boekholt & De Booy, 1987; Kloek & Mijnhardt, 2001; Lenders, 1988;Smeding, 1987; Verhoeven, 1994; Visser, 1995).

In the first decade that followed this 1806 school act, the successors of the Batavian reformers exercised some compulsion to realize part of their original imaginations anyway. For that goal, the *Nut* adherents made a list of schoolbooks and children's books in their *General List of Books for the Primary Schools in Holland* [Algemeene boekenlijst ten dienste der lagere scholen in Holland]. This list only contained those books that did fit Enlightenment ideas. Genres such as life stories of children who died when being young, a popular genre among Calvinists, and popular literature intended for children were not present on this list (Buijnsters & Buijnsters-Smets, 2001). The policy of the makers of this list of books was to stimulate the use of only these books that contained "societal and Christian virtues," the acquiring of those virtues being the very goal of the primary school education according to the Batavian reformers (Boekholt & de Booy, 1987; Buijnsters & Buijnsters-Smets, 2001). The General List of Books was published in 1810 for the first time and was compiled by inspector Adriaan van den Ende with the help of the director of the Teacher College of Haarlem, P. J. Prinsen. It was the first Dutch national prescribed booklist. The first version of 1815 was 125 pages long and only contained books that fit the enlightened philanthropic ideas of the *Nut*. Many books were translations of German ones. Fairy tales, like the Dutch version of the European classic *Mother Goose* and the medieval *Reinaert the Fox* and *The Four Heems-children*, were not present on the list. These books were, according to the *Nut*, not good for the education of children. Children should never be brought in contact with a world outside reality, as is the main character of fairy tales. Catholic and Orthodox Protestant books were banned from the list too because both the magic and religious worlds of the child were unimportant according to this list. Entering this world could even be harmful for children, according to the moral paternalism of the *Nut*. For the rest, the list never got the status it pursued. Religious literature, fairy tales, and popular literature remained important (Buijnsters & Buijnsters-Smets, 2001; Parlevliet, 2009).

The history of the list is an example of the way the blue print of the national school for all eventually failed. That blue print and its manifestation in the school acts and in the list of books raised opposition from two sides. The Catholics were against it because the national school was eventually a Protestant school and not a neutral one. School inspection and the personnel were, with the exception of the southern provinces, in the hands of moderate, enlightenment Protestants. That was not the Catholic dream about the education of their children (Boekholt & De

Booy, 1987; De Haan, 1998; Dekker, 2006; Kruithof, 1998; Kuiper, 1998; Rietveld-van Wingerden, 2001; Schutte, 1998; Van Zuthem, 1998). The orthodox Protestants were also against the national school that was, according to them, more liberal than Protestant. They wanted schools based on the *Heidelberg Catechism* and the Bible. Their representatives like Isaac da Costa with his *Objections against the Spirit of the Century* [Bezwaren tegen de geest der eeuw] from 1823 and Guillaume Groen van Prinsterer with his *Unbelief and Revolution* [Ongeloof en revolutie] from 1847 on the equalization of revolution and unbelief organized the opposition. They considered themselves as the real representatives of the Dutch nation.

In the constitution of 1848, J. R. Thorbecke (1798–1872), liberal and founder of the constitutional Dutch Monarchy, guaranteed freedom of education. On this principle, the protestant politician and member of the cabinet J. J. L. van der Brugghen (1804–1863) founded his School Act of 1857. While Groen van Prinsterer pleaded for an orthodox Calvinistic national school, the Calvinist Van der Brugghen pleaded for the separation between state and church. He was of the opinion that both the state school and the religious schools should be guaranteed by the constitution, with the state school being a neutral one and no longer Protestant. His basic idea of freedom of education was similar with Thorbecke's, although the intentions of Thorbecke were different. The liberal Thorbecke wanted to entrust the responsibility of education to the citizens as far as possible. In order to realize that, freedom of education was necessary. Therefore, the School Act of 1857 served at least three different interests: of the liberals who wanted the freedom of education; of the orthodox Protestants who, at least in majority, realized that Groen van Prinster's ambition of an orthodox Protestant national school had to fail; and of the Roman Catholics, who now saw new opportunities for their own schools. The School Act of 1857 confirmed the defeat of two orthodox groups: those adherents of the Nut who wanted a national moderate Protestant school for all, and the orthodox Protestants who wanted a national orthodox Protestant school for all.

The spirit of the School Act of 1806, itself already being a poor substitute for the ambitious plans of the Batavian Reformers, was over and done now. The freedom to establish schools was guaranteed, and the national school became neutral. The first phase of the battle on the Dutch primary school was finished, and soon the second started. Now, the financing of the private or denominational school was at stake. This battle dominated Dutch political culture for more than 50 years. It was finished by a compromise that would determine the shape of Dutch society for many decades, namely, a society consisting of so-called pillars, in which Protestants, Catholics, and Socialists lived as separate from each other as possible in their own social, cultural, and political pillars, with their own schools, political parties, philanthropic societies, newspapers, mass media, and of course their own ideology and religion (Boekholt, 2003; Boekholt & De Booy, 1987; De Bruin, 1985; Langedijk, 1953; Van Essen & Imelman, 1999).

A Compromise Around 1900: Unifying the Nation by Accepting its Ideological Division

In the first phase of this educational battle, the liberals remained in favor of a strong national school and refused to finance the denominational schools. No state money to non-state schools, that was their position, and they could hold that position because of their political domination. That domination, however, ended when, in the last decades of the 19th century, the political and social power of the denominational parties accelerated. These parties got more influence in the Parliament, a result of the enlarging of the poll tax wanted by these very liberals who so, like their predecessors in 1798, again supported their opponents. Moreover, the orthodox Protestants and the Catholics built up an impressive system of schools and of re-educational residential institutions. Because of this changing balance between the main opponents, a deal became inevitable. With this deal, the illusion of that modern Batavian republicanism, full of educational imaginations of one homogenous pedagogical culture for all citizens of the nation, ended. After a struggle of more than 100 years, the new balance of power in the ideologically and religiously divided Dutch Monarchy resulted, in 1901 and 1905, in a series of political deals on Compulsory Education Acts and on Child Protection Acts. Eventually, in 1917, the liberals and the religious parties made a deal on the 100% financing of all primary education, state and denominational alike. Paradoxically, these deals unified the nation by dividing it ideologically (Boekholt, 1998; Boekholt & de Booy, 1987).

CONCLUSION

The imaginations of the late 18th-century modern republican Dutch Enlightenment were focused on an enlightened citizenship for all. Their dreams were expressed by politicians such as Van der Palm, authors such as Van Effen, Wolff, Deken, and Van Alphen, and artists such as Van der Kooi. To realize that dream, two things had to be done. First, the decentralized Dutch Republic, which was, according to them, an old-fashioned 16th-century model of local autonomy, had to become a modern republic that should end that local and regional autonomy. Second, they wanted to change the educational system in such a way that it fit with their dream of enlightened citizenship for all. They based their educational blue prints, developed when in power in the Batavian Republic they had dreamed of for so many years, on a new pedagogical discourse, inspired by the Enlightenment that glorified family virtues while emphasizing the meaning of the school. The school they dreamed of was a national primary school for all, being the consequence of their ambition for a citizenship for all or an inclusive membership of the nation of the republic for all citizens. Both, family education and the school, were according to them necessary means for the realization of citizenship for all.

These imaginations remained a dream. After some years of political euphoria, enthusiasm and belief in these political and educational imaginations slid down. The 19th-century Dutch Monarchy created new realities, and the intended national curriculum on the national primary school, financed by the central state, became a mission impossible. Apart from major changes in the structure of the Dutch state, from the Batavian Republic to the Monarchy of Holland, and from a department of France to the Monarchy of the Netherlands, as well as financial problems, the main reason for the impossibility of their mission was the growing opposition of the Roman Catholics and the orthodox Calvinists. They were strongly against a national school and wanted schools of their own. Their opposition was the Dutch manifestation of a European-wide development of the new *Wendung zur Religion*, the phenomenon that after 1800 in Europe the meaning of religion again grew.

Eventually, a deal became inevitable through the changing balance of power in the Dutch constitutional Monarchy in the last decades of the 19th century, with the power of the denominational parties increasing and that of the liberals decreasing. With this deal, the educational imaginations of the modern Batavian Republic of one homogenous and Enlightenment pedagogical culture for all citizens of the nation ended forever. The promised land the new children and future citizens had to live in became a divided land because the deal, finished off in 1917, unified the nation by dividing it ideologically.

NOTES

1. Van Sas' *De metamorfose* and Kloek and Mijnhardt's *1800* are examples of the modern approach of this period of Dutch history that started with Schama's *Patriots*. Cf. Israel, *The Dutch Republic*, 1098–1112; Kossmann, De Lage Landen; Beliën, Van der Horst, and Van Setten, *Nederlanders van het eerste uur*. For the local developments, see Prak, *Republikeinse veelheid*; Streng, *Stemme in staat*; and Van Wissing, *Stokebrand Janus 1787*. For the international context of the Batavian Revolution, see Frijhoff et al., "Revolutie en contrarevolutie."
2. Campe, the first professional German author of children books, in 1799–1780 published *Robinson der Jüngere*, a moralizing version of Defoe's Robinson Crusoe, the only book Rousseau let Émile read. On the history of the transformation of Dutch versions for the youth of Robinson Crusoe, and other classics, for the period 1850–1950, see Sanne Parlevliet's PhD thesis *Meesterwerken met ezelsoren* from 2009.

REFERENCES

Alphen, H. van. (1778/1998a). Proeve van kleine gedigten voor kinderen. In H. V. Alphen (Ed.), *Kleine gedigten voor kinderen* (pp. 9–61). Amsterdam: Athenaeum.

Alphen, H. van. (1778/1998b). Tweede vervolg der kleine gedigten voor kinderen, van mr. Hieronijmus van Alphen. In H. V. Alphen (Ed.), *Kleine gedigten voor kinderen* (pp. 115–163). Amsterdam: Athenaeum.
Alphen, H. van. (1998 or 1782). Vervolg der kleine gedigten voor kinderen, van mr. Hieronijmus van Alphen. In H. van Alphen (Ed.), *Kleine Gedigten voor kinderen* (pp. 63–113). Amsterdam: Athenaeum.
Amsing, H. T.A. (2002). *Bakens verzetten in het voortgezet onderwijs, 1863–1930. Gymnasium, h.b.s. en m.m.s. in onderwijssyteem, leerplan en geschiedenisonderwijs.* Delft: Eburon.
Beliën, H. M., van der Horst, D., & van Setten, G. J. (Eds.). (1996). *Nederlanders van het eerste uur. Het ontstaan van het moderne Nederland, 1780–1830.* Den Haag: Bakker.
Boekholt, P. Th. F. M. (1978). *Het lager onderwijs in Gelderland 1795–1858.* Zutphen: De Walberg Pers.
Boekholt, P. Th. F. M. (1982). *Het onderwijs in Drenthe in de eerste helft van de negentiende eeuw.* Assen: van Gorcum.
Boekholt, P. Th. F. M. (1986). *Een onderwijsrapport uit 1808. Verslag van een reis van onderwijsinspecteur Van den Ende via Noord- en Oost-Nederland naar Oost-Friesland.* Groningen: Groningen University Press.
Boekholt, P. Th. F. M. (1998). *Het ongeregelde verleden. Over eenheid en verscheidenheid van het Nederlandse onderwijs.* Assen: van Gorcurn.
Boekholt, P. Th. F. M., & de Booy, E. P. (1987). *Geschiedenis van de school in Nederland vanaf de middeleeuwen tot aan de huidige tijd.* Assen/Maastricht: van Gorcurn.
Boekholt, P. Th. F. M., Van Crombrugge, H., Dodde, N. L., & Tyssens, J. (Eds.). (2002). Tweehonderd jaar onderwijs en de zorg van de Staat. In *Jaarboek voor de geschiedenis van opvoeding en onderwijs* (pp. 1–366). Assen: van Gorcurn.
Booy, E. P. de (1977). *De weldaet der scholen. Het plattelandsonderwijs in de provincie Utrecht van 1580 tot het begin der negentiende eeuw.* Zutphen: de Walburg Pers.
Booy, E. P. de (1980). *Kweekhoven der wijsheid. Basis- en vervolgonderwijs in de steden van de provincie Utrecht van 1580 tot het begin der 19de eeuw.* Utrecht/Zutphen: de Walburg Pers.
Boschma, C. (1976). *Willem Bartel van der Kooi, Fries Museum-Leeuwarden.* Leeuwarden: Catalogue of the Exhibition.
Boschma, C. (1978). *Willem Bartel van der Kooi en het tekenonderwijs in Friesland.* Leeuwarden: De Tille.
Brandt-Corstius, L., & Hollema, C. (Eds.). (1981). *De kunst van het moederschap: Leven en werk van Nederlandse vrouwen in de 19de eeuw.* Haarlem: Frans Halsmuseum.
Bruin, A. A. de (1985). *Het ontstaan van de schoolstrijd. Onderzoek naar de wortels van de schoolstrijd in de Noordelijke Nederlanden gedurende de eerste helft van de 19e eeuw. Een cultuurhistorische studie.* Amsterdam: Bolland.
Buijnsters, P. J. (1973). *Hieronymus van Alphen (1746–1800).* Assen: van Gorcum.
Buijnsters, P. J. (1992). *Justus van Effen (1684–1735).* Leven en werk. Utrecht: HES.
Buijnsters, P. J. (1998). Nawoord. In H. van Alphen (Ed.), *Kleine gedigten voor kinderen* (pp. 173–196). Amsterdam: Athenaeum.
Buijnsters, P. J., & Buijnsters-Smets, L. (2001). *Lust en leering. Geschiedenis van het Nederlandse kinderboek in de negentiende eeuw.* Zwolle: Waanders.
Cats, J. (1655). *Alle de wercken.* Amsterdam: Schipper.
Crombrugge, H. van (1995). Rousseau on family and education. *Paedagogica Historica, 31,* 445–480.
Crombrugge, H. van (2001). Emile en Sophie wisselen boeken uit. Lectuur en meisjesopvoeding bij Rousseau. *Pedagogiek. Wetenschappelijk forum voor opvoeding, onderwijs en vorming, 21,* 68–87.

Cunningham, H. (1995/2005). *Children & childhood in Western society since 1500*. London/New York: Longman.
Dane, J. (1998). Zwarigheid voor het kinderverstand. *De Kleine Gedigten van Van Alphen*. NRC Handelsblad, Book Supplement, 7.
Dane, J. (2002). Meer en meer paedagoog geworden. Opvoeding rondom Johannes Kneppelhout. *De Negentiende Eeuw*, 26, 199–217.
Dekker, J. J. H. (1994). Philanthropie et rééducation, XVIIIe—XIXe siècles: Le modèle néerlandais. In C. Duprat, J. Petit, C. Bec, & J.-N. Luc (Eds.), *Philanthropies et politiques sociales en Europe* (XVIIIe-XXe siècles) (pp. 45–61). Paris: Anthropos.
Dekker, J. J. H. (1996). A republic of educators. Educational messages in seventeenth-century Dutch genre painting. *History of Education Quarterly*, 36, 163–190.
Dekker, J. J. H. (1998a). Message et réalité. L'iconographie de l'éducation des enfants et sa signification morale dans la peinture de genre hollandaise du XVIIe siècle'. In E. Becchi & D. Julia (Eds.), *Histoire de l'enfance en occident*. Volume 1, De l'antiquité au XVIIe siècle (pp. 374–401). Paris: Seuil.
Dekker, J. J. H. (1998b). Transforming the nation and the child: Philanthropy in the Netherlands, Belgium, France, and England, c.1780–c.1850. In H.Cunningham & J. Innes (Eds.), *Charity, philanthropy and reform. From the 1690s to 1850* (pp. 130–147). London/Basingstoke: Macmillan.
Dekker, J. J. H. (2001). *The will to change the child. Re-education homes for children at risk in nineteenth century Western Europe*. Frankfurt am Main/Berlin/Bern/NewYork/Paris/ Vienna: Lang.
Dekker, J. J. H. (2006). *Het verlangen naar opvoeden. Over de groei van de pedagogische ruimte in Nederland sinds de Gouden Eeuw tot omstreeks 1900*. Amsterdam: Bert Bakker.
Dekker, J. J. H. (2008). Moral literacy: The pleasure of learning how to become decent adults and good parents in the Dutch Republic in the seventeenth century. *Paedagogica Historica*, 44, 135–149.
Dekker, J. J. H. (2009a). Woord en beeld: Jacob Cats en de pedagogische cultuuroverdracht in de zeventiende eeuw. In J. W. Steutel, D. J. de Ruyter, & S. Miedema (Eds.), *De gereformeerden en hun vormingsoffensief door de eeuwen heen* (pp. 47–65). Zoetermeer: Meinema.
Dekker, J. J. H. (2009b). Beauty and simplicity. The power of fine art in moral teaching on education in 17th century Holland. *Journal of Family History. Studies in Family, Kinship, and Demography*, 34(2), 166–188.
Dekker, J. J. H., Groenendijk, L. F., & Verberckmoes, J. (2000). Proudly raising vulnerable youngsters. The scope for education in the Netherlands. In J. B. Bedaux & R. E. O. Ekkart (Eds.), *Pride and joy. Children's portraits in the Netherlands, 1500–1700* (pp. 43–60). Gent/Amsterdam/New York: Ludion.
Dodde, N. L. (1971). Een onderwijsrapport. *Een historisch-pedagogisch onderzoek naar de invloed van een onderwijsrapport over onderwijsverbetering en -vernieuwing op de onderwijswetgeving na 1801*. Hertogenbosch: Nalmberg.
Dodde, N. L. (2001). *Een speurtocht naar samenhang'. Het rijksschooltoezicht van 1801 tot 2001*. Den Haag: Inspectie van het Onderwijs.
Essen, M. van (2006). *Kweekeling tussen akte en ideaal. De opleiding tot onderwijzer(es) vanaf 1800*. Amsterdam: Boom.
Essen, M. van, & Imelman, J. D. (1999). *Historische pedagogiek. Verlichting, Romantiek en ontwikkelingen in Nederland na 1800*. Baarn: Intro.
Fildes, V. A. (1986). *Breasts, bottles, and babies. A history of infant feeding*. Edinburgh: Edinburgh University Press.
Fildes, V. A. (1988). *Wet nursing. A history from antiquity to the present*. Oxford: Basil Blackwell.

Frijhoff, W. (1983). Van onderwijs naar opvoedend onderwijs. Ontwikkelingen van opvoeding en onderwijs in Noord-Nederland in de achttiende eeuw. In *Onderwijs en opvoeding in de achttiende eeuw. Verslag van het symposium, Doesburg 1982* (pp. 3–39). Amsterdam: APA.
Frijhoff, W. (1985). Crisis of modernisering. Hypothesen over de ontwikkeling van het voortgezet en hoger onderwijs in Holland in de 18e eeuw. In *Holland. Regionaal-historisch tijdschrift, 17*, 37–56.
Frijhoff, W. (2004). La réforme de l'enseignement secondaire dans les départements hollandaise. In J.-O. Boudon (Ed.), *Napoléon et les lycées. Enseignement et société en Europe au début du XIXe siècle* (pp. 165–193). Paris: Fayard.
Gobbers, W. (1963). *Jean-Jacques Rousseau in Holland. Een onderzoek naar de invloed van de mens en het werk* (ca. 1760-ca. 1810). Gent: KVATL.
Grandière, M. (1998). *L'Idéal pédagogique en France au dix-huitième siècle.* Oxford: Vultaire Foundation.
Groenendijk, L. F. (1976). Piëtisten en borstvoeding. *Pedagogisch Tijdschrift/ Forum voor Opvoedkunde, 1*, 583–590.
Groenendijk, L. F. (2002). Piëtistische opvoedingsleer in Nederland. Balans van een kwarteeuw historisch-pedagogisch onderzoek. *Pedagogiek, 22*, 326–337.
Haan, I. de (1998). Het onderwijs in de Grondwet. Van staatszorg tot vrijheidsrecht. In N. C. F. van Sas & H. te Velde (Eds.), *De eeuw van de grondwet. Grondwet en politiek in Nederland 1789–1917* (pp. 182–217). Deventer: Kluwer.
Hake, B. J. (2004). Between patriotism and nationalism: Johan Hendrik Wildens and the "pedagogy of the patriotic virtues" in the United Dutch Provinces during the 1780s and 1790s. *History of Education, 33*, 11–38.
Huussen, Jr., A. H. (1975). *De codificatie van het Nederlands huwelijksrecht 1795–1838. Geschiedenis en analyse van de ontwikkeling van de huwelijkswetgeving en van de opvattingen omtrent huwelijk en gezin op het eind van de achttiende en het begin van de negentiende eeuw.* Amsterdam.
Israel, J. I. (1995). *The Dutch Republic. Its rise, greatness, and fall, 1477–1806.* Oxford.
Kloek, J., & Mijnhardt, W. (2001). *1800. Blauwdrukken voor een samenleving.* Den Haag.
Kloek, J., & Mijnhardt, W. (2002). De verlichte burger. In J. Kloek & K. Tilmans (Eds.), *Burger* (pp. 155–171). Amsterdam.
Kneppelhout, J. (1980). *Opvoeding door vriendschap* (Dutch translation of l'Éducation par l'amitié from 1835 by M. Mathijsen & F. Ligtvoet). Amsterdam: Querido.
Kossmann, E. H. (1986). *De Lage Landen. Twee eeuwen Nederland en België (1780–1980).* Amsterdam/Brussels.
Kruithof, B. (1990). *Zonde en deugd in domineesland. Nederlandse protestanten en problemen van opvoeding, zeventiende tot twintigste eeuw.* Groningen: Wolters-Noordhoff.
Kruithof, B. (1998). "Toegankelijk voor alle kinderen". De grondwet van 1848 en het lager onderwijs. In G. J. Schutte & J. Vree (Eds.), *Om de toekomst van het protestantse Nederland. De gevolgen van de grondwetsherziening van 1848 voor kerk, staat en maatschappij* (pp. 173–190). Zoetermeer: Meinema.
Kuiper, R. (1998). Antirevolutionaire partijvorming na de grondwetswijziging van 1848. In G. J. Schutte & J. Vree (Eds.), *Om de toekomst van het protestantse Nederland. De gevolgen van de grondwetsherziening van 1848 voor kerk, staat en maatschappij* (pp. 152–172). Zoetermeer: Meinema.
Langedijk, D. (1953). *De geschiedenis van het protestants-christelijk onderwijs.* Delft: Van Keulen.
Lenders, J. (1988). *De burger en de volksschool. Culturele en mentale achtergronden van een onderwijshervorming, Nederland 1780–1850.* Nijmegen: SUN.

Linden, J. ter, et al. (Eds.). (1995). *A is een Aapje. Opstellen over ABC-boeken van de vijftiende eeuw tot heden*. Amsterdam: Querido.

Los, W. (1999). Locke in Nederland: De receptie van zijn ideeën over individualiteit in opvoeding en onderwijs bij P.A. Verwer (1696-1757) en K. van der Palm (1730-1789). *De Achttiende Eeuw, 31*, 173-186.

Los, W. (2005). *Opvoeding tot mens en burger. Pedagogiek als Cultuurkritiek in Nederland in de 18e eeuw*. Hilversum: Verloren.

Lüth, Chr. (1997). Staatliche und private Erziehung bei Rousseau. In O. Hansmann (Ed.), *Seminar: Der pädagogische Rousseau. Deel 2, Kommentare, Interpretationen, Wirkungsgeschichte* (pp. 167-194). Weinheim: Beltz.

Matthijsen, M. (2002). *De gemaskerde eeuw*. Amsterdam: Querido.

McLeod, H. (1997). *Religion and the people of Western Europe, 1789-1989*. Oxford/New York: Oxford University Press.

Mijnhardt, W. W. (1988). *Tot Heil van 't Menschdom. Culturele genootschappen in Nederland, 1750-1815*. Amsterdam: Rodopi.

Mijnhardt, W. W., & Wichers, A. J. (Eds.). (1984). *Om het algemeen volksgeluk. Twee eeuwen particulier initiatief 1784-1984. Gedenkboek ter gelegenheid van het tweehonderdjarig bestaan van de Maatschappij tot Nut van 't Algemeen*. Edam.

Mooij, C., de, & Kruijsen, B. (Eds.). (1997). *Kinderen van alle tijden. Kindercultuur in de Nederlanden vanaf de middeleeuwen tot heden*. Zwolle: Waanders.

Nipperdey, T. (1983). *Deutsche Geschichte 1800-1866. Bürgerwelt und starker Staat*. München: Beck.

Parlevliet, S. (2009). *Meesterwerken met ezelsoren. Bewerkingen van literaire klassiekers voor kinderen 1850/1950*. Hilversum: Verloren.

Prak, M. (1999). *Republikeinse veelheid, democratisch enkelvoud. Sociale verandering in het Revolutietijdvak, 's-Hertogenbosch, 1770-1820*. Nijmegen: SUN.

Py, G. (1997). *Rousseau et les éducateurs. Etude sur la fortune des idées pédagogiques de Jean-Jacques Rousseau en France et en Europe au XVIIIe siècle*. Oxford: Voltaire Foundation.

Rietveld-van Wingerden, M. (2001). De Nederlandse wetgeving van 1806 en het joodse onderwijs. *De School Anno, 19*(3), 4-10.

Rosenberg, A. (1990). Rousseau's Emile: The nature and purpose of education. In J. Willinsky (Ed.), *The educational legacy of romanticism* (pp. 11-32). Calgary: Wilfrid Laurier University Press.

Salzmann, C. G. (1780/1961). *Krebstbüchlein oder Anweisung zu einer unvernünftigen Erziehung der Kinder*. Bad Heilbrun: Julius Klinkhardt.

Sas, N. C. F. van (1992). Nationaliteit in de schaduw van de Gouden Eeuw. Nationale cultuur en vaderlands verleden 1780-1914. In F. Grijzenhout & H. van Veen (Eds.), *De Gouden Eeuw in perspectief. Het beeld van de Nederlandse zeventiende-eeuwse schilders in later tijd* (pp. 83-106). Nijmegen: SUN.

Sas, N. C. F. van (1999). De vaderlandse imperatief. Begripsverandering en politieke conjunctuur, 1763-1813. In N. C. F. van Sas (Ed.), *Vaderland. Een geschiedenis van de vijftiende eeuw tot 1940* (pp. 275-308). Amsterdam: Amsterdam University Press.

Sas, N. C. F. van. (2004). *De metamorfose van Nederland. Van oude orde naar moderniteit, 1750-1900*. Amsterdam: Amsterdam University Press.

Savoie, Ph., Bruter, A., & Frijhoff, W. (Eds.). (2004). Secondary education: Institutional, cultural, and social history. *Paedagogica Historica, 40*, 6-227.

Schama, S. (1977). *Patriots and liberators, revolution in the Netherlands, 1780-1813*. London/New York: Knopf.

Schutte, G. J. (1998). Nederland in 1848. In G. J. Schutte & J. Vree (Eds.), *Om de toekomst van het protestantse Nederland. De gevolgen van de grondwetsher-*

ziening van 1848 voor kerk, staat en maatschappij (pp. 8–21). Zoetermeer: Meinema.
Smeding, T. U. (1987). *School in de steigers. De wording van de Friese lagere school in de periode 1800–1857.* Leeuwarden: Fryske Akademy.
Stipriaan, R. van. (2002). *Het volle leven. Nederlandse literatuur en cultuur ten tijde van de Republiek* (circa 1550–1800). Amsterdam.
Streng, J. C. (1998). *Stemme in staat. De bestuurlijke elite in de stadsrepubliek Zwolle, 1579–1795.* Hilversum: Verloren.
Sturkenboom, D. (1999). *Spectators van hartstocht. Sekse en emotionele cultuur in de achttiende eeuw.* Hilversum: Verloren.
Tilborgh, L. van. (Ed.). (1993). *The potato eaters by Vincent van Gogh.* Zwolle: Waanders.
Tilborgh, L., van, & Jansen, G. (1986). *Op zoek naar de Gouden Eeuw. Nederlandse schilderkunst 1800–1850.* Zwolle: Waanders.
Tilburg, M. van (1998). *Hoe hoorde het? Seksualiteit en partnerkeuze in de Nederlandse adviesliteratuur, 1780–1890.* Amsterdam: Het Spinhus.
Verhoeven, Th. H. T. (1994). *Ter vorming van verstand en hart. Lager onderwijs in oostelijk Noord-Brabant, ca. 1770–1920.* Hilversum: Verloren.
Visser, C. (1995). *Vernieuwing van het lager onderwijs in Zeeland in de eerste helft van de negentiende eeuw.* Utrecht: Universiteit Utrecht.
Wissing, P. van (2004). *Stokebrand Janus 1787. Opkomst en ondergang van een achttiende-eeuws satyrisch politiek-literair weekblad.* Nijmegen: SUN.
Zuthem, J. van (1998). Tegen de teloorgang van de protestantse natie. Enkele opmerkingen over de relatie tussen Groen van Prinsterer en de antipapistische stromingen en netwerken rond het midden van de negentiende eeuw. In G. J. Schutte & J. Vree (Eds.), *Om de toekomst van het protestantse Nederland. De gevolgen van de grondwetsherziening van 1848 voor kerk, staat en maatschappij* (pp. 128–151). Zoetermeer: Meinema.

4 Republican Deliveries for the Modernization of Secondary Education in Portugal in the 19th Century
From Alexandre Herculano, Ramalho Ortigão, and Bernardino Machado to Jaime Moniz

Jorge Ramos do Ó

INTRODUCTION[1]

This chapter stems from the clear fact that secondary schooling was encumbered with *fabricating citizens* in order to consolidate the nation-state. It also sets out to show how the pedagogical and organizational modernization of this educational level in Portugal was mainly articulated within the circles of republican liberalism. In doing so, it addresses a few of the core subject matters discussed throughout the book while ascertaining the Portuguese example as an act of "differential creation" within a global field. The general modern republican project of creating an "agent of progress" by means of education is analyzed through the historical singularity of the Portuguese Liceu. Its specific focus on the class regime and its concern with pupils' self-regulated rational action are directed toward the accomplishment of what had gradually become a self-evident truth for Western thought: that progress depended on improved citizenship, and that schooling was to provide the fundamental tools of civic education and virtue to fulfill it. The solutions that were put into practice in order to produce liberty, citizenship, and participation (the "social administration of freedom") became convergent regardless of political antagonisms. Indeed, the reformers' diagnoses and solutions at the end of the 19th century were included in discussions on political progress and civic and citizenship education previously undertaken by the republican opposition. It was this convergence of opinions that ultimately made it possible for liberalism to accomplish the aims of social integration and civic participation advocated by traditional republicanism. However, this would not be achieved by directly teaching virtue and values in view of creating a "political community" of ideal citizens, but by focusing on conduct and the pupils' exercise of self-discipline as the basic unit for the obtention of population homogeneity.

Republican Deliveries for the Modernization of Secondary Education 71

This chapter focuses on the discourse of a number of intellectual influencers who were dominated by the Enlightenment and effectively constructed an entire strategy around the theme of secondary school decadence in Portugal from the late 1830s onward. The aim of this was to explore the central epistemological values connecting the modern individual to collective belonging and citizenship that went on to acquire a decisive role in making the mechanics of later educational reforms more intelligible. The pedagogical rationality expressed in the political intervention texts, written by republicans such as Alexandre Herculano (1810–1877), Ramalho Ortigão (1836–1915), and Bernardino Machado (1851–1944) had, indeed, the greatest impact on the modernization of secondary studies in Portugal in the late 19th century and continued throughout the following century. In fact, they contain a vision of the child with a moldable soul who would learn to act as a self-motivated, self-responsible individual in the name of public interest.

In Portugal, during the transition from the 19th to the 20th century, the educational reformers' discourse was already very convergent with that of the republicans. I believe that it was precisely this convergence that gave rise to the modernization of secondary education. One may even say that from that moment on, and throughout most of the last century, secondary studies were accompanied by an important "differentiating and framing process of a particular class *based on age*," with a view to constructing the future citizen or youth. Republican ideas on social order, progress conditions, as well as concerns regarding civic virtues coincided with the diagnosis of the first education scientists who regarded the secondary education cycle as being determinant in the consolidation of a new age period, namely, adolescence. It was this convergence that formed the basis of the essentially psychological scientific discourse as well as the technologies of teaching and curriculum that went on to dominate educational theory. The association of both gave rise to taxonomies regarding the divisions and differences of the personality of youths as well as relational practices that legitimized civic and personal identities in the name of civilization and progress. Throughout the 20th century, the Portuguese State asserted itself as an *Educating State* mainly due to the spread of responsabilization technologies and the internalization of authority that had been systematized in earlier decades by the republican stance (Nóvoa, Barroso, & Ó, 2003).

With regard to the republican intellectuals and educational reformers of the last century, their main objective was to construct State power—equipping it with a body of employees capable of modernizing the rather incipient central government and Portuguese public services—and to give a practical expression to the concepts of civic virtue, citizenship, and, finally, democratic participation. In order to accomplish the aim of governing each and every citizen, they imagined a type of school organization within which a multiplicity of strategic games and relational situations were supposed to invite each member of the school population to constitute himself as an autonomous and rational individual. After leaving school, he would be capable of contributing toward the integration of the entire social fabric. It was accepted that secondary education should be structured to work around the "I," thus universalizing the idea that all its aims were to culminate in the educational preparation of authentic and true subjects, both in terms of their relationship with others as well as with themselves. In the 19th century, state secondary school, which focused on norms and values, started to be planned as a *political subjectivation* organization. In other words, it was capable of mobilizing its entire technical and practical resources to format the pupil's aspirations, needs, and desires in accordance with collectively shared great convictions. *Conduct* would be its greatest pedagogical problem, *culture of oneself* the pupil's most important occupation, and socioeconomic *integration* its ultimate aim.

HISTORICAL PERIODS OF THE PORTUGUESE LICEU

Although focusing on liberal and republican critical thought during a relatively short period of time, the exclusive historical backdrop to this chapter is based on the institutional reality of the *Liceu* (the name given to each establishment integrating the first state secondary school network, which, collectively, formed the so-called *Liceus*), created in 1836 and only terminated in the 1970s. In terms of curriculum and organization, the Portuguese *Liceu* was derived from the French Lycée, founded 34 years earlier; however, its claims had already been circulating among liberal intellectuals since the end of the 17th century. Within current historiography, it is consensual to affirm that there are three main stages in the life of Portuguese *Liceus*.

The first period, characterized by blurred definitions, advances, and withdrawals and always accompanied by intense critical debate, lasted from the time of its establishment up to 1894–1895, a period when a true rebirth and implantation of a more modern secondary education emerged. Indeed, this year marked the most important reform ever undergone by the *Liceus* in their entire history—the so-called Jaime Moniz Reform (1837–1917) (Ó, 2006; Proença, 1997). One of the main measures taken by the Lisbon government of the time was to create a curriculum plan that articulated pupils' progress throughout the course. Up to that point, the old practice of isolated lessons, handed down from the so-called *Minor Studies*, had been used, originally organized by the despot Marquis of Pombal in 1759, the year when he also banished the Jesuits from Portugal. However, the themes of these lessons were not coordinated nor were there clear rules regarding pupil distribution and governing. Until then, secondary education had been little more than a straight route to university. In other words, it had no importance in itself. As it will be shown at the end of this chapter, the Jaime Moniz Reform imposed a *common, consecutive, parallel distribution, by means of a gradual juxtaposition of subjects, placing particular importance on moral conduct.* Now, the main assumptions on which this modern, pedagogical program was based had been duly justified and systematized some centuries earlier by several important figures on the Portuguese cultural and political front—Alexandre Herculano, Ramalho Ortigão, and Bernardino Machado. The second stage corresponds to the consolidation of the so-called "Royal School," which lasted the duration of three different political regimes: the final years of the Constitutional Monarchy (overthrown by the Republican Revolution on October 5, 1910), the I Republic (1910–1926), and the Military Dictatorship (1926–1933). The final period lasted between the 1930s and the 1970s (when the *Liceu* was officially extinguished), a period marked by a population boom and expansion under the authoritarian regime that governed Portugal between 1933 and 1974 (Nóvoa, 1994; Ó, 2003).

In the case of Portugal, from the year of the *Liceus*' foundation up to the end of the 19th century, as was the case in many other European countries, the pedagogical debate began to cement a consensus around the purpose of secondary education. Over the years, two main ideas were consolidated: on the one hand, the general education of the citizen and his preparation for active life; on the other hand, the continuation of studies in higher education. Nonetheless, the intermediary school cycle gradually acquired its autonomy on the basis of the more general aim of the leading classes' constitution. By the beginning of the 20th century, the need for the formation of elites was already a general consensus and, among a number of advances and withdrawals, identified the secondary education of the *Liceu*. With respect to this, I will focus on the statements of two well-known academics, Marnoco e Sousa (1869–1916) and Adolfo Coelho (1847–1919), whose scientific and pedagogical works highlighted particular concern regarding the specificity of this branch of education:

> The middle classes should belong to the running of modern society as the people, themselves, and aristocracy have proven to be incompetent in this respect. As higher education seems to be geared towards the culture of a nation's intellectual elite and primary education towards the general education of all citizens, secondary education should play the social role of preparing these classes for the performance of such a high mission, thus, educating them on the basis of dedication to public interest and making them capable of guiding national interest, for example. Organizing the scope of general knowledge that secondary education should teach in order to prepare entry into higher education courses and active life is one of the most difficult tasks a legislator may be faced with. The required knowledge for the performance of all activities should be taught through secondary education and pupils trained on the basis of education and individual social awareness. (Sousa, 1903, pp. 4–5)

The organization of the *Liceu* puts an end to the false distinction between education and teaching, between theoretical and practical teaching methods, moving towards the construction of the full man, while taking the seeds of individuality into account in his work, thus, making further secondary differentiations possible between the two main course divisions. Hence, a special classification system will be proposed in lieu of the former routine. (Coelho, 1913)

The historical operation that spread the idea of the *Liceu* in Portugal, as António Nóvoa (1994) points out, is the result of an effort for the State to gradually replace the family and the Church through the consolidation of devices for providing a frame of reference for pupils' *comprehensive education* and social production of *social awareness*. It is crucial to understand that this organization was conceived by educators and psychological specialists, and its institutionalization depended on two factors. On the one hand, it corresponded to the assertion of a sociopolitical republican model that went on to regard citizenship as a central aspect of progress meant to link State and individual governing. On the other hand, it institutionalized self-governing practices, guiding the mechanisms of discipline toward the inner self, to the soul of the pupil. What mattered was that each future citizen internalized *Authority* and made it equivalent to *Liberty*.

THE MODERNIZING ILLUSION OF PORTUGUESE LIBERALISM IN THE 19TH CENTURY

Immediately after the Revolution of 1820, marking the triumph of liberalism in Portugal, there was a general feeling that it was necessary to recover what the new governors considered to be a lack of development in Portugal's state education. A new political context also imposed a different educational model. The language of scientific progress acquired increasing expression among the circles of governors to such an extent that the minister of the Kingdom, in 1822, requested not only the urgent combat of ignorance, a consequence of illiteracy, but also the need to promote the creation of *useful schools,* which would educate skillful men in their jobs, making them experts capable of multiplying the resources of the treasury and the entire nation. The theologians and jurists had to make way for the experts in production activities. The governor believed, at the time, that the buildings, previously belonging to the religious orders that were now extinct, could be rapidly occupied by the State, with a view to establishing "political and rural economy schools" there. The dissolution of the Courts the following year held back, so it seems, this developmental aim; nevertheless, it never ceased to leave its mark on the liberal and republican ideals. When, in 1836, a decree signed by Passos Manuel created the Secondary School in Portugal (the *Liceus*), we immediately realize that the legislator was overcome by such great intentions. The diploma, itself, has the importance of being the first official Portuguese document that systematized secondary studies, integrating curriculum, pedagogical, and administrative aspects. In his chapters, he presented a complete and articulate vision of the secondary school's aims and objectives.

The option for a technical, scientific orientation structured the entire Decree, which, in fact, opened with a criticism of the speculative type of education, presenting it as being void of any social, objective purpose: "Secondary education is, out of all the areas of State education, that which most requires a reform, since the current system consists primarily of sterile branches of learnedness, which is practically useless for the cultivation of sciences, possessing nothing that might produce the perfecting of the Arts and the progress of the country's material civilization." As far as religious education was concerned, only the existence of a "private" class for "ecclesiastical studies" was determined in the last article of the Decree and was composed of two subjects whose programs were to be "written by the Faculty of Theology." The State had very little to say on this. The new teaching method would be essentially practical, and, in compliance with the liberal democratic promise, it would have to be structured so as to accommodate the needs of the population as a whole. The foreword of the Decree was as follows: "There can be no general or useful illustration if the great masses of Citizens, who do not aspire to higher education, are not in possession of the fundamental scientific and technical elements required for life in current societies" (Decree of Passos Manuel, 17/11/1836).

Nevertheless, the list of subjects in the 1836 plan demonstrates the high value liberalism attributed to state education and how it equally defined the principle, which had innumerous future consequences, that *only one general and generalist education could shape the mind of the pupil with long-lasting benefits*. In order to establish a universalist vision of nature and humankind, the principles of *unity* and the *complementariness* of knowledge marked the secondary school curriculum, in the aim to distinguish it from the specialized, lacunal science that characterized higher education. Therefore, right from the start, the secondary school course would "form a *compact whole* for the development of the pupils' minds" (Nobre, 1936, p. 41).

The Portuguese legislator was concerned with creating material conditions for the development of the so-called *inductive methodologies*. On this basis, he obliged the secondary schools to set themselves up in "well located and healthy" buildings, which could be appropriately prepared for the "good order and economy of classes," and also established that interior and exterior spaces should be made available for the practice of live and *experimental* education. It was in this organization of space that the Passos Manuel Reform focused on "the good order and economy of classes" and moved away from the dogmatic, anachronic, and useless teaching that was characteristic of the Portuguese educational tradition. It seemed to promise that learning would cease to be synonymous of learning by rote; from then on the pupil would observe in order to be capable of understanding phenomena (Decree of Passos Manuel, 17/11/1836).

It seems that Passos Manuel started procedures during the course of 1836, to put the measures recommended in his legal diploma into action, namely, by looking for buildings that could be adapted to the complex establishment program proposed in the decree. However, the story that follows tells of the complete failure of the 1836 reform. Research carried out by Áurea Adão (1982) has led me to conclude that "by the year 1840–1841 secondary education was no longer corresponding to the originally defined aims" and that "the scientific and industrial subjects did not function while the law of Passos Manuel was in force" (p. 133). The secondary school did not manage to overcome the pragmatic intention and also remained throughout the 19th century tied to the function of serving the university. A simple, isolated observation of all Portuguese secondary schools during this initial phase allows one to verify that up to the end of the 19th century, all the breaks and recoveries had been irrelevant in relation to the full-scale failure of the liberal policies to transform the secondary school into a potentially useful school for the kingdom's future active population. It did not even come close to reaching the 4,000 pupils in more than half a century of secondary school education. The average per year was little more than 3,000 (Adão, 1982; Valente, 1983).

It is worth mentioning that awareness of this reality concerning secondary education may also be considered a historical detail in relation to Portugal during that period and was constantly referred to by many agents, both directly and indirectly, throughout the second half of the 19th century. Indeed, the anarchic adjective is what best describes the image of the texts produced by the headmasters, teachers, and governmental inspectors of the *Liceus*. This discourse was produced within an environment marked by severe criticism, which was always associated with the feeling of decadence in this branch of education. The extent to which this criticism spread is easy to establish. For some, the collapse occurred after the publication of the 1860 Regulation, which proposed to initiate a second stage of the Portuguese *Liceus*' establishment and organization. As far as others were concerned, the beginning of the failure dated back to 1870, when the Portuguese Statists became concerned "with the intrinsic value of the *Liceu* course" and aimed to "make it easier and quicker by simplifying the final exams, reducing the programs and doing away with subjects for entry to all types of higher education" (Veloso, 1927, p. 97). In spite of all this, it became clear through the 1880 Reform that there was an attempt to put the system in order because its study plan was already based on "the pedagogical distribution of subjects, gradually split into years in accordance with the pupil's psychological development, but always with emphasis on the value of each subject" (Deusdado, 1894, p. 536). However, this measure was no more than an intention. The most remarkable aspect of the years to follow was the "spiral towards absolute chaos: the reforms multiplied,

Table 4.1 Number of Pupils Enrolled in State Education between 1836 and 1893–1894

Years	No. of Pupils
1836–1837	1,361
1837–1838	1,083
1838–1839	1,872
1840–1841	2,038
1841–1842	2,039
1842–1843	3,446
1848–1849	1,998
1849–1850	2,036
1850–1851	2,073
1851–1852	2,396
1855–1856	3,256
1856–1857	3,649
1857–1858	3,613
1867–1868	3,121
1875–1876	2,558
1887–1888	2,372
1892–1893	3,617
1893–1894	3,630

(Adão, 1982; Valente, 1983)

intermingling in their different and simultaneous transitory regimes." There was not the slightest order or plan. The *Liceu* was transformed into an "administrative factory for the production of diplomas" (Nóvoa, Barroso, & Ó, 2003, p. 31).

The 19th-Century Portuguese Republican Flag: Decadence, Regeneration, and Progress. Alexandre Herculano, Ramalho Ortigão, and Bernardino Machado in the Combat Against the Moral Degeneration of Secondary Education

As expected, critical opinions of secondary school began to circulate among the political opposition and became increasingly identified with republicanism. In the mid-19th century, the issue regarding the theme of *the chaotic state of education* and the economic underdevelopment—the scandal of Portugal being behind Morrocco or of being the "Turkey of Europe"— was very obvious in historical and sociological explanations. Melancholy and servantship were then seen as characteristics that better defined the

Portuguese, whose minds were "warped" by a disconnected, mnemonic, and useless type of education. The metaphors for the spiraling decadence of the homeland, which found the permanent cause of all present and past woes in the educational system, legitimized a utopia based on regeneration and redemption with relative ease. This went on to dominate the agenda of the republican propaganda from the 1860s and 1870s onward; however, it was back in the 1830s that the first texts attacking the authorities, namely, the Absolute and Constitutional Monarchy on issues regarding secondary education, emerged (Pintassilgo, 1998).

Before looking at the arguments presented by each one of the three critical figures, it is important to note that several consensual points emerged among these texts. The agreement was constructed around a set of principles making up a considerable part of "the basic grammar of schooling," to use the expression of Tyack and Tobin (1994): The pedagogical program was meant to follow an organic and systematic subject plan in accordance with the various aims of secondary education; the curriculum was meant to be designed around the subjects' educational impact on the mind of the pupil and the subject matter organized on the basis of increasingly complex levels and according to blocks related to mental and physical activity, which would also positively reinforce moral examples; the pupil would be submitted to very short assessment and exam cycles geared towards verifying knowledge but also to reinforcing the homogeneity of the people in each class; the optimization of the teaching-learning tasks would result from an individualized and active type of education, in other words, one that would take the different intellectual, physical, and emotional skills of each pupil into account (Ó, 2003).

At the top of the list of critics was Alexandre Herculano (1810–1867), a political fighter of the liberal revolution and a historian who had become famous as the writer of several historical novels. From 1838, Alexandre Herculano differed when it came to "governmental precautions," which, as far as state education was concerned, had been taken from the time of the Marquis of Pombal. This meant that he equally disagreed with the Passos Manuel Reform and, even more so, with the situation of the "introduction to higher education." Nothing in the Portuguese educational panorama was connected with true "popular education." The latter "aims to make a useful and illustrious citizen out of any man, whatever his profession, and not only of him but of his neighbors and the rest of Society." Now, being sure that secondary education, which was called *instrução preparatória* [preparatory instruction], should not only be intended for the elite—"the professional of any mechanical line of work, the artist, farmer, salesperson, soldier, men of letters and sciences, everyone, with no exception should receive it"—the state in which this level of education found itself could only hinder the awakening of the learners' vocations and gifts. Herculano wondered about the usefulness "of the Latin and Greek anthologies, of the tropes of Quintilian, the cachetic philosophy of Genovesi or

Heineck" to the majority of men. This was a direct criticism of the Jesuit education and went on to conclude that what the preparatory instruction offered pupils was no better than "fodder," "which would be remembered by nobody ten years later." Latin was "taught by rancid means," whereas Rhetoric and Poetics had a "Scholastic nature" and were surrounded by "such aridity" that no pupil profited at all (Herculano, 1975 [1838], pp. 30–35). The Constitutional regime, born from the Revolution of 1820, kept the social mark of absolute monarchy for itself: Education continued to be a privilege, and that which was still designated as culture was no more than a fragrant, but sterile intellectuality of theatre halls, galleries, pulpits, and forums. The gap between the world of ideas and economic and social interests became more accentuated in the present. The Portuguese school could not contribute to the progress of general civilization because it had no knowledge of modern science, which it referred to as the *science of the material world*. The diagnosis of Herculano, who became a member of parliament in 1840 but was excluded from the *Comissão Parlamentar de Instrução Pública* [Parliamentary Commission of State Education] in 1840–1841, was already made in 1838. It was an impressive portrait of the decadence of the school and ignorance of the pupil under the Constitutional Monarchy.

> The main vice of our preparatory education is, above all, the fact that it is exclusive: what can he, who wishes to receive an intellect without reaching university, really learn? Latin, Greek and Rhetoric, something called Philosophy and a look at Euclides' geometrical figures. There is nothing beyond this, because the other kinds of classes, established in Lisbon and Porto, are only places and can not really be counted as anything other than private institutes. The second flaw in our preparatory education (. . .) is the fact that there is no connection with the past or the future; there is no connection with anything in this world; it is expensive and not productive; it wastes a lot of time on nothing in particular; in fact, it does not teach the receiver anything other than what it doesn't mind him forgetting, but is shameful not to have learned. That is why so many rush to the big cities in search of employment; and that is why the University is full of boorish scholars who, often devoted to decadence, waste away essence of the Homeland. (Herculano, 1975[1838], pp. 36–37)

After these statements, Alexandre Herculano did not return to educational issues. However, his name always lived on as a kind of critical conscience, and his country house became transformed into a sort of "Mecca for Portuguese Liberalism, to which young and old flurried" (Saraiva, 1977, p. 26).

The most articulate "attack" on secondary education was resumed by Ramalho Ortigão (1836–1915), whose thought on the subject was "it is a paradigm of all the others" in the period, and should be subject to "close examination" (Valente, 1983, p. 380). Ramalho Ortigão, a writer and journalist, had a sarcastic style that later developed into irony associated with the positive, liberal, and modern spirit of Europe at the time. He became known as a member of the Cenacle, from which the famous Casino Conferences emerged in Lisbon (1871), in which a criticism was elaborated by a group of intellectuals, of the institutions and the "bourgeois order," and especially as the author of *Farpas* [*Barbs*], the title of his monthly chronicles "on politics, arts and customs," which he published between 1871 and 1882, revealing his strong critical personality. In a long letter to the Minister of the Kingdom, dated August 1875 and later reproduced in Volume ll of *Farpas*, Ramalho also began by going along with those who demanded another secondary education reform or else "this branch of state education" would die "within a few years." Indeed, statistics seemed to corroborate his words, displaying at this specific time a significant fall in the already scarce secondary school population. This proof was enough for him to affirm that if the direction things were taking was not inverted, with constant failures of the secondary school's transformational experiences, then very shortly "no one" in Portugal would want "to hand over the education of a child to the State." He interpreted the flee of the pupils as an "opposition against disdain," "a rebellion against contempt" (Ortigão, 1943[1881], p. 146). A year later, he returned to the issue of "secondary school reorganization" in another letter sent to the same governor (Ortigão, 1946 [1882]). I will go on to systematize the arguments presented in both.

Ramalho Ortigão began by presenting a precise definition of the aims and purposes of secondary school education. Its existence was broadly justified by a specific "aim," which was to "prepare men for all professions outside scientific and public careers" (Ortigão, 1943[1881], p. 148). Like the rest of the educated nations, Portugal would have to win the social and economic development battle through an effectively democratized school: "A well managed secondary education is what makes the intellectual level of a people"; "it is through strong secondary education, common to all citizens, whatever their status, profession or hierarchy, that a true democracy is acquired in civilization and progress." The first great novelty that was introduced by Herculano was related to the defense of a "perfect educational system" that would include the "culture of all the faculties of our nature." Ramalho Ortigão believed that man's various dimensions were supportive of each other, and therefore the school should also take care of both the intelligence and soul of its pupils, and even look after their bodies. For the *free thinkers*, only an integral and full education could serve the interests of the secular Nation. The writer went on to add: "It is through the perfect, harmonious balance of these three faculties, the physical, intellectual and moral, that the truly superior men, the great useful men and citizens, the only ones who are absolutely worthy of society's gratitude and the respect of their neighbors, may be born" (Ortigão, 1946[1882], p. 45–50).

Ramalho Ortigão described the Portuguese situation in an even darker manner. He spoke, thus, of the youths of his time: "We are a generation of good-for-nothings, incapable of work, perseverance, order, economy, incompetent in everything but public and literary careers." Owing to an entire set of "abstract and useless knowledge," "Portuguese education" did everything but "arouse man's mental activity." During his time as a student, inculcation skills, which were typical of the convents and academies of the two former centuries, were still dominant: "dogmatism, classicism, rhetoric, metaphysics, oratory, grammatical theory." And so the liberal State obstinately continued to remove pupils from "alphabetical ignorance" to immediately launch them into "an even more pernicious ignorance than the alphabetical one: ignorance deriving from false education and false science" (Ortigão, 1943[1881], pp. 154–156).

His reflections immediately pointed to a legitimization of a new type of moral and civic virtue. However, and once again, even though the theses of Ramalho seem to criticize those that the Church transported to the school, they should be viewed as approaches to the same issue. After claiming that "unfortunately, all intellectual education in Portugal has always been more literary than scientific" (Ortigão, 1946[1882], p. 55), he gave a detailed characterization of the teaching of the main subjects in the secondary education curriculum. He regretted that the basis for all education continued to be "Jesuitical," in other words, based on "grammar." The latter consisted of "the most abstract of things! The most useless of things for daily life!" The teaching of the Portuguese language, the subject in which "oratory" was most developed, seemed, in his opinion, still very tied to "rhetoric, pedantism and triviality"; in other words, it was sterile to "shed light on the roots of the national language, its tradition, history, developments from the critical perspective of modern philology." The live languages were also a "pure grammatical application," which explained why "in one hundred pupils, not even two can speak French or English." As for Geography, he referred to it as a mere "memory exercise," which intended that a set of "names and definitions" of the "continents, countries, rivers, mountains, seas, straits, capes, etc., be learned by rote." In his "collection of biographical anecdotes," it was History that took the "absurdity" of Geography to extremes: The compendiums referred "invariably to the dynastic successions and biography of the emperors, kings, consuls and governors of all kinds," or, rather, of the different "funambulists" who, from the period of Roman Antiquity up to the present, "were only capable of keeping their balance just for a few days on the tightrope of temporal power, and which represents the most insignificant episode in the passing of generations." Finally, the so-called subject of Philosophy: "a verbose fraud, camouflaging the theft of the pupil's intelligence by education, itself" (Ortigão,1943[1881], p. 152; 1946[1882], pp. 28–33). Consequently, Ramalho tried to record what, at the beginning of the third quarter of the 19th century, made up the knowledge and gaps of a "complete pupil," the "typical pupil" of around

15 years of age. The image he gives back to us is of the greatest decadence: The Portuguese pupil seemed to be literally hollow in terms of knowledge and physically debilitated.

The school institution should have understood that it had to find a way of producing a new man, an agent of progress, a citizen with clarified intelligence, poignant sensitivity, and a robust body. A sequence of themes and subjects presented by Ramalho Ortigão brings to us the plan that was later systematized and followed by the men of New Education. Its pedagogical thinking reveals the typical republican concerns with civic virtue, in view of the education of people who were capable of self-guided rational action for public interest.

Ramalho began by using the "method" recommended by Augusto Comte and resorting to the fundamental division between the "abstract part " and "concrete part" in the set of sciences because he believed that it was the basis of "the limits by which secondary education has to be *restricted*." A rational program should surely cover the abstract part of the fields of intelligence, with a view to discovering the laws that rule the different classes of phenomena. It would be the role of the secondary school to essentially consider the concrete combinations, banishing from within everything "abstract and useless" (Ortigão, 1946[1882], pp. 46–47).

It is within the context of this discussion on the determination of curriculum knowledge that I wish to make another observation, this time with a view to specifying the historical feelings associated with the word *disciplina* [subject] in the educational field. We know that it re-emerged in the second half of the 19th century, in a way that was very close to its Latin meaning, in the sense of *discipline*, as being the education that the pupil receives from the schoolmaster. However, Chervel (1998) adds that it should be understood as the German term *disziplin*, which was also in circulation in the pedagogical discourse of the time. Indeed, this second meaning helps us to understand the renovation of the aims of secondary education. *Disziplin* was associated with the verb *disciplinar*, which, at the end of the 19th century, referred to something like *intellectual agility*. Ramalho Ortigão's way of thinking also tended toward establishing a vast program for secondary school that would permanently exercise the intellect of the pupils. His strong defense of experimental education can only have the first meaning of *disciplina*. Furthermore, it was not by chance that he thought of the content of the traditional methodologies as being the main causes of the "vice" and "moral dissipation" he saw increase among the school population. In support of my argument, it is important that this association is clear. Whether through school text books, immediately classified as "absurd," or through the "dogmatic method," in Ortigão's eyes, the Portuguese school was doing everything in its power for the pupil to become "a pedant or imbecile." Education was converted into "a mechanism for learning definitions by rote" and made the pupil "lose mental habits for research, analysis and reflection"; it instilled in him "the tedium of work" and, more important,

Republican Deliveries for the Modernization of Secondary Education 83

"the lack of consideration for himself." Furthermore, "the companionship with his peers, who were just as perverted," contributed to the "rapid development of all the bad qualities" that the pupil presented at the time: He became "indolent, rude and lascivious" and, in the short term, "a citizen irremediably lost to dignity and duty" (Ortigão, 1946[1882], p. 35).

On the contrary, experimental education could only have advantages: It would accustom the pupil to the love of work, encourage individual initiative, and even contribute to character formation and self-esteem. Ramalho Ortigão's great promise was that pedagogical training would, in itself, generate self-regulation mechanisms. The duties that were to be developed by the new type of secondary education would, therefore, have an impact on *discipline*, which is taken here in its modern sense (i.e., as a synonym of *hygiene* and looking after oneself). He recommended, then, that "a stupefying type of study that depressed all physical strength and mental faculties" be replaced by "notions of cosmography, anatomy, mechanics, hygiene, political economy and home economics." The lessons should, as far as possible, become "experimental and practical"; the live languages would be learned on the basis of "understanding and speaking them," constant "field studies" would be carried out with "great manufacturers, arsenals, customs, galleries and State branches, in big cities, in provinces, in industrial establishments, regional farms, large and small farming areas" (Ortigão, 1943[1881], pp. 154–155). Intellectual education would be alive as well as encyclopedic. And that was not all. "Solfeggio, ornate design and, mainly, the study of perspective and the mechanical profession" were to be added, as an "indispensable complement" to the knowledge of positive science. These *manual* subjects were equally "essential" for transmitting the universal language of "feelings." Finally, "physical education" would be adopted, a disciplinary practice of the body that, like the "mechanical arts," had the double advantage of keeping one healthy and physically vigorous while powerfully correcting laziness, lack of action, moral despondency, the tendency for perverse temperaments prone to vice, and finally of channeling all the activity the body is capable of practicing" (Ortigão, 1946[1882], pp. 49–52). As one may see, the archeology of the 20th-century secondary school curriculum is, here, a sequence of subject areas with the clear intention of accomplishing a balance between the faculties of the soul and the vigor of the body.

For Ramalho Ortigão, the problem was not only one of intentions, of substituting the old diet for the new list of programs. One was led to believe that the battle would be won through the development of methodologies that interested and kept the pupil active for a long period of time, each day, both in and out of the classroom. In this case, the work could no longer proceed under passiveness. As with the word *disciplina*, it is now important to clarify the historical content of a fundamental expression that, in the meantime, has come to acquire a different meaning to that of the time: *dar a lição* [giving the lesson]. Up to the end of the 19th century, the word lesson meant that the theme of the lesson was learned by rote and recited in class by a pupil. In other words, giving the lesson would be the practical demonstration of the memorization and undertaken by the pupil and its results: Studying at home corresponded to repeating, as often as necessary, until they were learned by rote and were often based on themes that had not yet been dealt with by the class. The time spent in the classroom was, more often than not, dictated by this circular exchange between pupil and teacher: The former displayed his knowledge of the subjects in the previous session and the latter revised it and then demonstrated his knowledge of the theme by having it at the tip of his tongue for the next session.

If we focus our attention on Bernardino Machado (1851–1944)—member of parliament for the Regenerative Party in the 1880s, Master Mason the following decade, board member of the Republican Party from 1903 and President of the Republic twice—we immediately realize that, as far as secondary education is concerned, we are faced with a diagnosis that is identical to the one identified by Ramalho Ortigão (Machado, 1882a, 1882b, 1899). In spite of the fact that his contribution was in a political, parliamentary register, Bernardino Machado's discourse allows us to go even further in the organization of such crucial pedagogical aspects, such as those related to the different variables to be considered in the organization of secondary education or even to the type of influence the teacher could and should have on the pupil in order to accomplish perfect socialization. His entire intervention was motivated by the construction of an alternative model to that of the time, characterized by the provision of a type of education with a list of independent subjects and isolated exams, left to the consideration of the youths and their families. The system in force from the 1880s onward had, in his estimation, two "serious" and "irreparable" flaws. On the one hand, it offended the "grading of work" and jeopardized the "normal growth of the pupil" because it barged into "the lessons of the same subject"; on the other hand, "in order to tear the place away from each one," it "removed the lessons of the other subjects" with obvious damage "to the diversification of work, thus, putting the harmonious development of the pupil at risk" (Machado, 1899, p. 276).

It is obvious that the arguments defending the articulation of the curriculum subjects leads us to the *grading* concept; at this point, its main argument was based on the pupil's period of growth and corresponding level of knowledge, which were what legitimized the reform. The curriculum construction, which gave rise to the ordering of knowledge in academic years, was, first and foremost, accomplished according to age. What was unavoidable for Bernardino Machado was that the secondary school course unfolded "in a conjugated series, from term to term, with the development of the pupil: this is what grading was." Furthermore, of all the possible ways of distributing the work of the pupils, the "only good way would be to make it proportional to age." Given that "adolescence" was considered to be a period of "gradual growth of ability," the secondary school was meant to be capable of "waiting for it," to make the most of "all the skills of each moment zealously, but cautiously and appropriately" due to the fact that the faculties of observation, application, experience, and abstraction, of induction and deduction, could not be the same in a pupil of 12 as in one of 15 years of age. Once again, liberal educational reasoning is presented to us as being in perfect harmony with individual nature: The grading of the secondary course in academic years would consequently be an essential requirement of school work. However, it was precisely due to not wanting to know about the "natural orders" that the subject regime, which piled into 1 year what should have been spread over several, transformed secondary education into a huge failure (Machado, 1899).

Of course, it was not working with the technology later proposed by Binet, but, as predicted, Bernardino Machado finally came to the unavoidable class concept—in secondary school, the alternative regime to the subject is not called class by chance—through the same process of governing each and every one. Indeed, the notion of skill, even though it had less to do with idiosyncrasy and personality trait and more to do with the age and knowledge displayed by the pupil on entering the school, was the rational path of differentiation and homogenous grouping of the entire school population: During each year of the secondary school cycle, the pupil had to be in possession of a certain amount of global knowledge, and it was here that the principle that still exists today was established—that no school subject could be acquired independently of the others and that progression is achieved, from year to year, through levels of increasing complexity.

Seemingly, the main issue for Bernardino Machado was an effective management of the collective. It was necessary to find "a point" around which "all the pupils would oscillate" given that it is this intersection that determines and specifies "the intensity of collective education" and the "grading of the whole class." In these terms, the class is historically tied to a kind of social anchorage in which the variations between the pupils should be eliminated "little by little" with a view to "systematizing all of them into a common career" (Machado, 1899, pp. 268–269). The concept of class was more than a reference to reality; it was already seen as its constructor, operating through the *a priori* of the average standard model—age, skill—and hoping that in the end, in active life, equally standardized behavior might be registered, at least of a socially compatible type. A thorough and constant evaluation would have to be undertaken in the school, and difference would be handled through the inclusion of individuals in minimally varied groups. Bernardino Machado also seemed to wish to write "individual" as a synonym of "collective" when he directly related social *equilibrium* to particular *vocation*. I need to reproduce *ipsis verbis* his argumentation, which gives me an archetypical image of my theory. His aim was to show that $1+1=1$, in a context of clear optimization and profitability of the modalities of knowledge transmission and the effective socialization of the young pupils.

Here, the far more complex work of the teacher than giving a lesson should be recognized as a *social construction of unity,* and preferably act on the vocation of the pupil, in the framework of governing the collective class. This is where a separation could be established from the tradition of open disintegration that characterized secondary school education. The most important aspect consists of verifying that educational intervention in this context becomes conceived on the basis of surprising the "imbalance" in the pupil, with a view to pressing correct "guidance" on him. Thus, the old task of transmitting and managing curriculum contents became less of a priority. That which Bernardino Machado tended to call "the power of hygiene" on personality was also defined. Knowing and being started to coincide in educational discourse: Subjectivity could begin to define itself as the preferred method adopted by the new teacher. Machado outlined his intervention as "double, negative and positive": Acting correctively on the "temperament," "in the imbalance of more or less," he could never legitimately "curb the innate dispositions" of the pupil. There is no doubt that modern disciplinary logic was being insinuated here: A socializing practice that establishes "harmony as the *desideratum* of education," it claims to respect individual vocations—"saliences are not deformities"—but making them converge, as if to eliminate singular disproportions. Such a soul-saving task, based on actual individual material, demanded moderation and "immense tact, extremely fine tact, without a doubt" and was acknowledged by Bernardino Machado (189, pp. 267, 262). For the republicans in the last quarter of the 19th century, the biggest and final demand was that the secondary school should put entirely self-regulated discipline into action.

The implantation of this new juvenile socialization logic within the secondary school would require the universalization of the *exam,* according to Foucault (1975) (i.e., in the formalization of individuality codes and in the construction of the population's homogeneity). The exam would then be the formalization of a link that would simultaneously particularize the pupil and make the group, in which he would be included, homogenous. Further back, we saw how Bernardino Machado linked the exam to the register of the pupil's skills and abilities. It was based on the result, expressed through the objective strictness of the figures that the decision was made to safely include or exclude each one of the individuals in the class, and even defining for him an exact place in the tight hierarchy of the class group. It is still worth mentioning that at this historical time, and by means of this debate, the exam emerged as a promoting and encouraging instrument of action. Furthermore, he also went on to be seen, undoubtedly, as the constructor of results before being their actual expression. Hence, the proselytes of the modernization of education also defended its extension and multiplication throughout the secondary school cycle. The need to promote an exam at the end of each year to test knowledge emerged as a guarantee of separation and maintenance by different years of the study plan, with the respective grouping of classes, also on an annual basis. The final secondary school exams, the only ones that remained throughout this whole period and that granted a diploma, turned out to be insufficient. It was no longer an issue of certifying acquired knowledge, but rather of organizing a mechanism that would regularly pressure the pupil to achieve or maintain a social position. For this reason, it was referred to as a real *system of perfection* of pupils' knowledge. In a word, the evaluation ritual, which obliged constant comparison with each member of the population, of the class, began to be viewed as an important organizational element of the type of school he wished to construct.

The Jaime Moniz Reform (1894–1895): Re-establishment of the Portuguese Liceu

It is not an exaggeration to say that nobody within the pedagogical field dared to defend the *Liceu* model as it was in the late 19th century in Portugal. Such a situation was only of interest to families—for whom secondary education was still seen as a *"nuisance* needed for entry into university" and who were only interested in the final diploma—or to the owners of private schools, which offered short school cycles and, thus, absorbed most of the Portuguese pupils. From an organizational perspective, the *Liceu* limited itself to a set of isolated subjects: Teachers were not guided by any type of pedagogical coordination, and the pupils were grouped in an arbitrary manner. The Jaime Moniz Reform—and the fact that it was in force during the dictatorship should be noted—emerged as an attempt to contradict this situation and was characterized on the basis of its utilitarian, pragmatic, and mercantile nature, which marked the secondary education of the time.

The 1894–1895 reform, undersigned by someone who was mainly concerned that the pedagogical principles of education should develop pupils' minds both intellectually and morally, through the methodical and progressive acquisition of the knowledge related to each subject, marked the "beginning of a new evolutionary period in Portuguese secondary education" and represented "the most important fact in its history since the establishment of the Liceus in *1836* by Passos Manuel" (Valente, 1983, p. 441). It should be closely examined for two reasons: because both the diagnosis and the solutions spread the republican interpretation and also because the problems and solutions that were formalized by Jaime Moniz lasted throughout the 20th century.

As with the texts by Alexandre Herculano and Alexandre Ortigão on the decadence of education, the legislative writings of Jaime Moniz opened with a harsh sentence. "The pitiful state of secondary education in Portugal cannot continue" followed by several more that endeavored to show how "the ruin of an entire social function" had arrived. The aim was to broadly justify the creation of a "new order" geared toward "the intellectual and moral progress" of the country. Obviously, the most negative aspect identified by Jaime Moniz's team was the fact that the regime of the time completely ignored the pupil's mental age. It was here that the failure of this branch of education was rooted. Consequently, knowledge could not be converted into "a factor of individuality" or a "mould for personal qualities" (Decree of Passos Manuel, 22/12/1894).

The preface of the Reform went along completely with the complaints regarding the quantity and quality of knowledge the pupils displayed on leaving the *Liceu*. It shed light upon a type of pedagogical relationship whereby the youth received no strength from the ideas and representations supplied by the teachers, nor did he get involved in major aims or aspirations. He remained in a permanent state of lethargy and inaction. The legislator once again picked up on the discursive republican treasure, persisting with the images of an incapable and incompetent pupil: The learning of the subject content was more than deficient, and due to a lack of civic education, a connection to social action was also impossible. It was in this context that the need to work on the mind of the *Liceu* pupil was imposed from a completely different perspective, clearly on the basis of a kind of support that would bring together *power* and a desire for *knowledge*. This was the historical moment when the Portuguese state adhered to the language of the pupil's education:

> The majority of pupils enter further studies without having sufficiently developed their minds; they faint at the sight of the most elementary analytical task; they reason wrongly if they reason at all; they can not observe; they deduce badly and induce even worse; indeed, they drag themselves along the school benches, forced to have dealings with people who are incapable of monitoring their practices (...) There is no method or real acquisition of subjects, which equally lack an efficient correlation with the mentality of those learning them, nor can there be formation of the mind through the simple appropriation of multiform ignorance. We learn to gain power and knowledge. Therefore, in this field, it is as important as ever to assist with a possible remedy for such a sad, overall vision. (Decree of Passos Manuel, 22/12/1894)

The establishment of this new organization implied that a clear choice had been made, and the political risk of producing a reform without important social support among the frequenters of the *Liceu* had been run. This is what happened: In the words of the law, it was registered that "for most families" everything was being completely reduced to "the rapid ascension of their children in order to attain certificates for further education studies": Knowledge had no price, and the "best system" was the "toughest one." Nowadays, "it's quite the opposite": The Executive council is based on "not giving in" to pressure. So, the 1894–1895 reform was presented as an instrument capable of allowing all public power to stop being "a victim of complacency itself" and to give it back a new public side, characterized by independence, rigor, and organization (Decree of Passos Manuel, 22/12/1894).

The system's crucial and structuring measure was based on a regime of pupil admission and attendance. It was established that in the future there would only be "one class of pupils" in the *Liceu*, and the respective enrollment would be made per "year or class, and so on from the initial class of entry" (Decree of Passos Manuel, 14/8/1895). It would no longer be possible to have pupils of different ages in the same classroom. This alternative to the previous regime of isolated subjects created a framework for the distribution of knowledge, leveled into years or classes in which it was dissected, in terms of its own particularity as well as the contribution it effectively gave to the absolute value of secondary education. At the end of the 19th century, the reformer made *curriculum alchemy* one of his most important tasks, along the lines of one of the senses presented by Popkewitz (1998): as an operation that, on transforming the several subjects—mathematics, literature, science, etc.—into secondary education themes or programs, emphasized the transmission of information through small blocks. Such knowledge was meant to be nationalized, and the State took this task on board fully and wholeheartedly: (a) the subject programs were printed in the government's journal, thus making their use compulsory throughout the country; (b) teachers and pupils went on to use the same school manuals for each subject, and they were also approved centrally in Lisbon; (c) a new time flow technology was constructed through the organization of strict timetables; and (d) an evaluation system was constructed with six types of written and oral exams aimed at all secondary education pupils. The homogeneity that characterizes modern school began to emerge in a very clear and unequivocal manner.

In addition to this *gluttonous* curriculum format, another was created that was directly related to the pupil and based on a wide range of *diversity*. To state that effective learning of the program content would only have a long-lasting effect on the mind if it was carried out progressively was the same as defending the principle, according to which any grading of subject matter would have to be done on the basis of the pupil's physical and mental age. Uniformity and idiosyncrasy were the two instigators of this system. The latter was established in accordance with a conceptual framework connecting it to psychological science. The notions of law, the evolution of the mind, and individual ability began to influence the official discourse (Decree of Passos Manuel, 22/12/1894). The legislator of 1894–1895 seemed to adopt the modern pedagogical *habitus* maxim, according to which "to teach is to intern."

The reforming act ended with the reiteration that it was the purpose of secondary education to provide civic training. The issue regarding "character" dominated the law. It is worth noting that the Jaime Moniz Reform marked the beginning of the long institutionalization of lay moral through secondary education. Because his core concerns were in relation to curriculum organization, his legislative text defended, furthermore, that all subjects would have "an ethical value" and clear "moralizing properties." The organization of school work became geared toward personality, and each of the various curriculum subjects was expected to give its contribution to this central aim. In fact, this reform connected all the areas of knowledge contained in the *Liceu's* study plan through "main moral aims," which were to function precisely as points of contact to ensure the existence of an authentic "civic cultivation of character." In a simple way, Jaime Moniz's imagined that pupils would simultaneously work on "thought, will and feeling." The final aim of this educational unit was to align these structures of the conscience. In the different classes divided by age, regardless of the subject being taught, the teacher was obliged to adopt an "affectionate connection" with his pupils. He became the conductor of souls and promoter of autonomy and self-fulfillment. For instance, with regard to initial years, he had to be sensitive "to the vivacity and mobility," to the "impulsive" natures and to the "easily influenced and unsteady minds" of the pupils. However, for those in the middle of their secondary education, at the stage of transition from boyhood to adolescence, he had to ensure that "camaraderie acquired the utmost importance." Finally, in relation to those about to reach adulthood and in the final stages of their secondary education, he had to understand that they were equally in need of "guidance" and a "firm hand" even though fully aware of the fact that these pupils generally "kept themselves to themselves" and did not allow "their inner feelings to be easily influenced." However, although these differences in level had to be respected, invariably, the educational act was meant to cultivate "the feeling of self dignity." Said in a more direct manner, all the rules and precepts had more of a "stimulating" impact than an "oppressive" one. He had to take the greatest care to ensure that all the "demands" and "requirements" made to pupils also led "to the harmony of individual work and personal independence, in the interest of will formation and the healthy development of individuality" (Moniz, 1919, pp. 495–498). It was a pedagogy based on civic moral and emerged as a technology of the ego with the purpose of putting *liberty* and *authority* on a par.

There is no doubt that the 1894–1895 reform institutionalized rules and ways of functioning that brought about the modernization of the secondary school in Portugal. Years later, with a view to assessing the impact of the reform he had undersigned, Jaime Moniz stated that a "radical change" had taken place, and he had finally managed to put an end to the "old fashioned styles" that had been operating. The results were easy to systematize: "an incoherent and counter-productive form of distribution and the teaching of subjects had been replaced by another which was psychologically and pedagogically organized, attentive to individuals and to the country it was aimed for." He concluded that he had supplied the Portuguese secondary school with a "progressive nature," which was already "very much alive among the more advanced populations" of Europe (Moniz, 1919, p. 40).

CONCLUSION

It was the aim of this chapter to show that the arguments developed by the republican intellectuals are reasonably verifiable in view of the curriculum diagnosis and solution adopted by the Portuguese State in 1894–1895, which went on to identify secondary school throughout the 20th century. In their own way, these three figures based their pedagogical considerations on the line of discourse that characterized the decadence of the Portuguese cultural circles that had been against the governments of the constitutional monarchy, accusing them of dragging the country toward economic collapse and moral decay since the 1930s. The accounts of Alexandre Herculano, Ramalho Ortigão, and Bernardino Machado marked the beginning of a permanent layering of political rhetoric with the discourse on educational change. Since their intervention and up to the present moment, two things have continuously been repeated in the Portuguese educational arena: (a) the entire social reform of education assumes and is based on a vehement condemnation of the past that should be clarified by long, ill-speaking criticisms and eloquent metaphors alluding to its imminent collapse; and (b) only a school constructed under modern standards can trigger the reform of mentalities that the country needs to get on the path toward economic progress and political democracy. It is important to acknowledge that within this invariant, the scientific rationalization of curriculum issues is not historically an appanage of the specialists in Education Sciences because there are perfectly capable agents in the political field to systematize it.

Finally, it is worth mentioning that the defense of the so-called class regime—the model that imposed the division and grading of pupils' knowledge, with a view to methodically and progressively perfecting their mental abilities—emerged in the writings of Herculano, Ortigão, and Machado as an institutional ideal for the full development of civic virtues, citizenship, and, finally, democratic participation. All their considerations were geared toward issues on the moral and cultivation of character. Indeed, it was precisely in view of the crucial connection with the construction of a new social order that, in the opinion of these three men, science needed to become a field of practice that would then directly intervene in the notions of individuality and in the way the development of the young pupil was to be conceived: as a subject with a moldable soul who would learn to act as a self-motivated, self-responsible individual in the name of public interest. Therefore, it was essential that a curriculum technology be found that would act and intervene in attitudes, dispositions, and behavior. If the school institution was to primarily configure a huge social movement favoring the constitution of a kind of social agent mainly defined by the relationship it shared with the school itself, then for sure concerns for the rationalization and universalization of ways of governing men and things were at the root of its reforms. It was toward this point that all the republican concerns throughout the 19th century were directed.

NOTES

1. I would like to thank Tomás Vallera for his useful suggestions.

REFERENCES

Adão, Á. (1982). *A criação e instalação dos primeiros liceus portugueses: Organização administrativa e pedagógica (1836–1860)*. Lisboa: Fundação Calouste Gulbenkian.
Chervel, A. (1998). *La culture scolaire: Une approche historique*. Paris: Belin.
Coelho, F. A. (1913). Relatório da comissão encarregada da elaboração do projecto de reforma do ensino secundário (Primeira parte). Publicado no *Diário do Governo* n° 127, de 2 de Junho.
Deusdado, F. (1984). Observaçoes à proposta de lei sobre o ensino secundário. *Revista de Educação e Ensino 9*, 534-543.
Foucault, M. (1975). *Surveiller et punir: Naissance de la prison*. Paris: Gallimard. pp. 635–657). Paris: Gallimard.
Herculano, A. (1975) [1838 a 1ª edição]. Instrução Pública. In A. Ferreira (Org.), *Antologia de textos pedagógicos do século XIX português* (Vol. III, pp. 27–38). Lisboa: Fundação Calouste Gulbenkian.
Machado, B. (1882a). *O estado da instrução secundária entre nós: Ofício ao senhor António Augusto Soares de Sousa Cirne*. Coimbra: Imprensa da Universidade.
Machado, B. (1882b). Palavras pronunciadas a propósito do projecto de lei sobre exames de instrução secundária. In *Afirmações públicas (1882–1886)* (pp. 377–380). Coimbra: Imprensa da Universidade.
Machado, B. (1899). *O ensino primário e secundário*. Coimbra: Tipografia França Amado.
Moniz, J. (1919). *Estudos de ensino secundário*. Lisboa: Imprensa Nacional.
Nobre, J. B. (1936). I° Centenário da criação dos liceus em Portugal. *Labor, 75*(11), 31–47.
Nóvoa, A. (1994). *História da educação*. Lisboa: Faculdade de Psicologia e de Ciências da Educação
Nóvoa, A., Barroso, J., & Ó, J. R. do. (2003). O Todo Poderoso Império do Meio. In A. Nóvoa & A. T. Santa-Clara (Dir.). *Liceus de Portugal* (pp. 17–73). Porto: Asa.
Ó, J. R. do. (2003). *O governo de si mesmo: Modernidade pedagógica e encenações disciplinares do aluno liceal*. Lisboa: Educa.
Ó, J. R. do. (2006). A Reforma de Jaime Moniz (1894–95) e a construção do ensino liceal de características modernas em Portugal. *Estudos do Século, XX* (6), 77–93.
Ortigão, R. (1943–1946) [1870–1881 a 1ª edição]. *As farpas*. Vols. II e XV. Lisboa: Livraria Clássica Editora.
Pintassilgo, J. (1998). *República e formação de cidadãos: A educação cívica nas escolas primárias da I República portuguesa*. Lisboa: Colibri.
Popkewitz, T. S. (1998). *Struggling for the soul: The politics of schooling and the construction of the teacher*. New York: Teachers College Press.
Proença, M. C. (1997). *A Reforma de Jaime Moniz: Antecedentes e destino histórico*. Lisboa: Colibri.
Saraiva, A. J. (1977). *Herculano e o liberalismo em Portugal*. Lisboa: Livraria Bertrand.
Sousa, M. (1903). O regime de instrução secundária e os seus resultados. *Boletim da Direcção Geral de Instrução Pública, 1–4*(2), 1–50.

Tyack, D. & Tobin, W. (1994). The grammar of schooling: Why has it been so hard to change? *American Educational Research Journal*, 31(3), 453-479.

Valente, V. P. (1983). O estado liberal e o ensino: Os liceus portugueses (1834–1930). In *Tentar perceber* (pp. 363–571). Lisboa: Imprensa Nacional-Casa da Moeda.

Veloso, J.M. de Queiroz (1927). A tormação profissional dos professores liceais: Simples esboço da história do ensino secundário em Portugal, *Labor 6(2)*, 91-105.

5 Republicanism and Education from Enlightenment to Liberalism
Discourses and Realities in the Education of the Citizen in Spain

Antonio Viñao

What historians of political ideas refer to as "the republican tradition" or "republicanism" offers various historical models and concepts that often relate to notions of the citizen and citizenship. They approach this in this manner for the simple reason that republicanism is not one thing but made up of a series of discourses formulated in differing circumstances, contexts, and situations.

Various basic aspects of the republican tradition or ideology, however, have some overlapping themes such as the need for civic virtues, the readiness for social and political participation, the emphasis put on obligations and duties, and the pedagogic value of knowledge of the law, among others. These themes are directly related to the education of those who, as citizens, would be part of a republican community. This chapter aims to analyze these relationships embedded in the notion of republicanism in a specific case of Spain in the last third of the 18th century and the first third of the 19th century. This period entails the transition from the Enlightenment to liberalism with the revolution began in the "Cortes" of Cadiz[1]—and its political-legislative icon—the 1812 Constitution. This period shows the lapse between proposals and reality of the republican tradition as it gave rise to hybrid situations, accommodations, and adaptations to its circumstances that also conditioned elements from the model or theoretical ideology based upon it.

REPUBLICANISM AND ENLIGHTENMENT: BETWEEN THE CLASSICAL TRADITION AND THE NEW REVOLUTIONARY IDEAS

The presence and persistence in the academic world of the concepts and meanings of the no less academic republican discourse, a discourse referring above all to an idealized Roman Republic, are similarly present in many works of enlightened writers dealing with these matters in Spain. This is especially true because of the polysemy of the discourses—their power to be used in different contexts and with differing, even opposing, meanings. This is evident as when republicanism appears as a simple rhetorical resource or as a discourse strategy to refer in positive terms, in a hidden or indirect way, to the republic as a form of government in order to elude or outwit state censorship and the Inquisition. One way or another, in the Spanish Enlightenment, the ambiguous notion of the citizen is mixed up with the idea of a subject, a cultivated, industrious subject who knows his social duties, even those of his social estate, but does not participate in political life.

In the words of Fernández Sebastián (2002):

> The duties and obligations of the citizen are much talked of in the newspapers of the last third of the eighteenth century, in the writings of Campomanes and Jovellanos (. . .), or in the dissertations of economic societies[2]. There is much less on the corresponding rights. Deeply rooted in the classical tradition that has formed the basis of Western education over centuries, later revitalised by the works of Montesquieu and Rousseau, the notions of a citizen and civic virtue are widely used in the later years of the Enlightenment in Spain. While in principle these terms referred to the cities and Republics of Antiquity, during the final decade of the century the historical perspective gave way to a growing application in contemporary contexts.[3] (p. 139)

In effect, the idea was that education, particularly religious/moral and political/civil education, formed the basis for "happiness" or "prosperity" of the "republic." Virtually present in all the writings on education of the enlightened Spaniards was that only through a "good and solid" education, as Jovellanos (1963[1802], p. 232) was to say, would it be possible to form virtuous and enlightened citizens, aware of their civil duties and steeped in the "social virtues" and "love of one's country" or "patriotism."[4] This is true dealing both with the utopias of the early Enlightenment as that of *Sinapia* ("Having good citizens depends on education and upon this the preservation and the good of the republic" (Fernández, 1976, p. 116) and with texts from well-known authors such as Vallejo (1998) or Jovellanos (1963[1802]), among others. Even the Economic Societies of the Country's Friends, created in different parts of the country in 1774 at the initiative of Campomanes as "Fiscal" for the Council of Castille,[5] had the aim of advancing education, social welfare, industry, and agriculture that included members of the nobility, clergy, magistracy, bureaucracy, and the upper class. The programs, in some cases, were given the name of patriotic societies and their teaching establishments.

Nevertheless, this discourse rooted in republicanism was or had to be reconciled with the supremacy of the Catholic Church and absolute monarchy as a form of government. The result would be the so-called Catholic or Christian Enlightenment and, tightly linked, the defense of an absolute but enlightened monarchy that would govern under the well-known motto "all for the people, but without the people."

For the enlightened Spaniards, it was Catholicism that had to be the main aim of education as the key instrument to form habits, hold back wicked inclinations, and keep the social and political order, consequently prohibiting any other religion. A consequence of this religious supremacy would be the crucial role assigned to the clergy in the task of producing enlightened citizens. Another, as shall be seen, would be the confused mix of religious, moral, social, and civic aspects and virtues in the preparation of citizen, in spite of the distinction sometimes made between moral/religious and political/civil education.

Almost all of the enlightened Spaniards (Arroyal, Floridablanca, Campomanes, Jovellanos, Sarmiento, Olavide, Vallejo, and Traggia), with the unique exception, later referred to, of Cabarrús, gave a fundamental role in education to the Catholic Church, not excluding buildings and incomes. Not surprising, then, was their interest in training and counting on an enlightened clergy to exert state control. This control took the form of royal prerogative or galicanism), the training received in the clerical seminaries and the tendency, clearly visible in early Spanish liberalism, to establish a national church independent of Rome and regulated by National Councils.

All of the above took place within the framework of reform of the clergy and the Catholic Church. This was common among the most advanced, enlightened Spaniards and a significant section of the clergy from the perspective of philo-Jansenism. The philo-Jansenism was characterized as the return to the original Church, the preaching of reform, and the use of the pulpit as a search for greater simplicity. It also included the encouragement of the reading of the Bible in the common tongue; an interior spirituality in contrast to external manifestations of faith; and the criticism of the clergy of the religious orders, congregations, and mendicant orders, as well as superstitions and miracles. These reforms also served to strengthen the archbishops' power (episcopalism) and the revitalization of parish priests as ecclesiastic and state agents. Without this religious-political tendency or current, it would be impossible to understand the position of the Cortes of Cadiz, the Spanish constitutional liberalism of 1812.

Well aware of Montesquieu's assignment of the principles of honor, virtue, and servile fear to monarchical, republican, and despotic forms of government, respectively, the enlightened Spaniards carefully remarked that the principle of virtue and civil virtues could be encouraged and found as much in republican as in monarchic government. Thus, after proclaiming the "need for schools to teach all citizens their duty to love and serve their country, their common fatherland, thus following the example of the Greeks and Romans," Vallejo (1998) pointed out that in this there was no need to "draw any distinction between monarchies and republics" (p. 50). This circumstance and the need to harmonize civic virtues with the exclusive supremacy of the Catholic religion in social, political, and educational spheres meant that both the establishment of and the type of education required a combination of religious, moral, political, civil, and social aspects. Picornell, for example, set the aims of a "well-directed education" as "love of one's country," in "maxims of sound morality," "submission to the rightful Sovereign," and the "respect for the national laws and the supreme truths of Religion" (Gomila, 1786, p. V). With reference to the "ethic or science of customs," Jovellanos (1963[1802]) included, among the "civil virtues" or "science of the citizen," the "duty to be instructed" and the "respect for the constitution." The latter was understood as the existent form of political organization, "obedience of the laws and submission to the legitimate authorities and love of peace and order" as well as, in particular, "public spiritedness" that "makes all the necessary sacrifices of personal interest for the common good and ensures that the welfare and prosperity of everyone form part of the happiness of each and every citizen" (Jovellanos, 1963[1802], p. 256).

This mixture of religion, morality, and citizenship explains the juxtaposition of these aspects in selecting the texts that they believed children should read at school. It was generally recognized that such a book as they desired—one that would emphasize knowledge, encourage virtue, and present a diversity of proposals on the matter—did not exist and would have to be written. At the same time, the majority were in favor of adding to this book the virtues of urbanity, defined by Vallejo (1998) as "the external religion of civil dealings" (p. 52). But there were significant differences among them on the type of book and its contents. For Vallejo, it was a "religious, civil and natural catechism" that contained the teachings of religion and holy scriptures, urbanity, social obligations, and natural history (p. 52).

Jovellanos recommended "in the meantime" the *Compendio de historia de España* by Tomás de Iriarte and the *Tratado de las obligaciones del hombre* by Juan de Escoiquiz. The use of this book was imposed by the ruling on Elementary Schooling of 1797, along with a treatise on courtesy for the teaching of "morality and good habits." In order to teach children to read, Traggia (1998) suggested a book in four parts: History of the Christian religion, Christian morality, Politics ("an idea of the purpose of government for the general weal; domestic order, economy, some ideas about industry and personal and private comfort; notions of patriotism and the way to make villages flourish"), and some "lessons on agriculture" and the "cultivation of species and raw materials" that should "preferably be given priority in the villages" (p. 493). Finally, Vargas and Ponce, in their report to the Committee for Public Instruction of Joseph Bonaparte in the middle of the War of Independence (1808–1814), pointed out that one thing was the teaching of morality and another was that of "social duties." The latter was reduced to the teaching of politeness and the norms of common courtesy (Lorente, 1989).

The exception to this attempt to create a monarchic government that combined a Christian republic with the clericalism and religiosity of the

Catholic Enlightenment with classical republicanism was one that anticipated the principles and ideas of the constitutional liberalism of Cadiz—that of Francisco Cabarrús (1752–1810). In his *Cartas sobre los obstáculos que la naturaleza, la opinión y las leyes oponen a la felicidad pública*, written in 1792 and unpublished until 1808, Cabarrús expressed political ideas that were influenced by Locke, Montesquieu, and Rousseau.

The second of these letters dealt with "obstacles to opinion and the means of removing them with the spread of light," that is, freedom of the press and "a general education system." Here Cabarrús proposed compulsory education for children between the ages of 6 and 10 "common to all citizens." "Children of the same country should grow up together," said Cabarrús, without exception of any kind. "Do they not all go to church? Why should they not go to this temple to patriotism?" he asked. This temple had no place for the teaching of religion, and clergy were excluded.

On the other hand, the clergy was to be integrated into a national church. Cabarrús (1933) argued that the teaching of religion belonged to "the church, the clergy and, above all, the parents; national education, however, is completely secular and should be administered by laymen" (pp. 83–85). In contrast, alongside reading, writing, arithmetic, and "practical geometry," he promoted "a political catechism in which are made clear the elements of the society in which they live and the benefits derived from this" should also be taught. A catechism still to be drawn up in which the following would be taught:

> the state constitution, the rights and duties of the citizen, a definition of the laws, the benefits of their observance, the harm of their non-observance, taxes, coins, roads, commerce, industry (...). The abstract dogmas of theology are instilled into us in childhood, so why should we not be taught social principles, elements of legislation and be shown the common and individual interest that unites us? (Cabarrús, 1933, pp. 82–83)

The need to train good citizens was not to be reduced, from the point of view of the academic school curriculum, to the inclusion in elementary schools of a civic-political reading book or catechism, whether mixed or not with the teaching or religion, morals, courtesy, or similar matters. At the same time it demanded teaching at the level of higher education of what Jovellanos called the science or sciences of citizenship. These were disciplines that, from an academic-scientific viewpoint, dealt with (a) duties, rights, and freedoms of citizens; (b) the political organization of the state that would encourage and demand compliance with citizen's duties and would ensure the existence of their rights and freedoms; and (c) a new economic order in line with the duties, rights, freedoms, and political organization that emerged in the Industrial Revolution and liberal ideas and doctrines. This was the understanding of Vallejo (1998) when he argued in his *Discurso sobre la necesidad de una reforma general de los métodos de educación* of 1791 that the study of jurisprudence begins with "human and citizens' rights,", that is, "Public Law." Also included in his study plans were Natural Law, Law of Nations, and Civil Economy or Commerce, which he preferred to call Political Economy (Vallejo, 1998, pp. 84–85, 105, 108).

In fact, Natural Law and Law of Nations as well as Civil or Political Economy in late 18th-century Spain, in some instances indeed was a Trojan horse hiding ideas and proposals that would undermine the foundations of the Ancien Régime and absolute monarchy, enlightened or despotic. The introduction and spread of economic science in late 18th-century and early 19th-century Spain were linked to the Economic Societies of the Country's Friends, the Trade Boards existent in some cities such as Barcelona and Malaga, and the work of some enlightened and proto-liberals. Vicente Alcalá Galiano and Ramón Campos, for example, translated and promoted the works of Adam Smith. The writings and studies in this field of Ward, Jovellanos, and Campomanes, among others, with a few exceptions, brought these ideas into the universities or teaching centers.

This was not the case with Natural Law and Law of Nations. Mayans (1975) required their teaching in the studies of Civil Jurisprudence in his plan for the university reform of 1767,[6] and the government itself imposed their teaching in the Royal Studies of San Isidro set up in 1770 to replace, in Madrid, the Jesuit Imperial College, the Jesuits having been expelled from the country in 1767. In 1790, it was demanded that "notions" of the discipline feature in the *Plan de gobierno y estudios* established in the "seminaries for the education of nobility and gentry" alongside the teaching of "Lessons in Commerce, Arithmetic, Politics and Economics" (*Plan de gobierno y estudios*, 1790, p. 21). In some cases, Natural Law and Law of Nations would overcome the traditional conservatism of the universities and, with differing outcomes, would be included in the reforms of the study plans for Seville and Valencia in 1769 and 1786, respectively.

Although it is true that the texts chosen for their study (those by Heineccius, adapted and expurgated, and by Almici, among others) or those expressly written by the professors charged with their study, such as Joaquín Marín y Mendoza (1776), caused no problems to the Catholic orthodoxy and enlightened monarchy, it is also true that in other cases the content of studies influenced by Locke, Montesquieu, Rousseau, Condillac, or Adam Smith opened the doors to political and economic liberalism and were completely unacceptable even for enlightened Catholics. These unacceptable texts were found in those of Manuel Joaquín de Condado, professor since 1782 in the Noble Seminary of Madrid and from 1792 in the Royal Studies.

In 1789 the French Revolution would mark a division in the development of political and cultural life in Spain. The repressive measures and the quarantine imposed to isolate the country from the events in France meant a tightening of government censorship. Natural Law and Law of Nations that had been cultivated in Europe by authors on the

Inquisition's Index contained ideas and proposals that served as a threat as much to Catholic orthodoxy as to absolute monarchy. Finally, in 1794, the government suppressed all the professorships in and teaching of Natural and Public Law. Both subjects would have to wait for more suitable times and circumstances.

REPUBLICANISM AND EDUCATION IN THE FIRST LIBERAL PERIODS IN SPAIN (1810–1814 AND 1820–1823)

The deputies making up this Congress and who represent the Spanish nation, declare themselves legitimately constituted in general and extraordinary "Cortes" and that national sovereignty resides in them.

> The "Cortes" (...) recognise, proclaim and swear once more their only legitimate King to be Fernando VII of Borbon; furthermore they declare null and void the cession of the Crown to Napoleon, not only because of the violence that took place in these unjust and illegal acts, but principally for the absence of the Nation's consent.

These were the first words of the first Decree passed on September 24, 1810, by the "Cortes" gathered in Cadiz in representation of the "Spanish Nation." Two years later, on March 18, 1812, these same "Cortes" passed the "Political Constitution of the Spanish Monarchy." For Spain, in the eyes of the enlightened and liberal Europeans (Montesquieu and Hume among them), no revolutionary process was forthcoming. So quickly passing a constitution of clearly liberal intent made it immediately a revolutionary model for other countries, particularly given the passion of Spain's legislative body that, between 1810 and 1814, tried to destroy all the institutions and structure of the Ancien Régime. As Marx was to write in 1854,

> How are we to account for the curious phenomenon of the Constitution of 1812, afterward branded by the crowned heads of Europe, assembled at Verona, as the most incendiary invention of the Jacobinism, having sprung up from the head of the old monastic and absolutist Spain at the very epoch when she seemed totally absorbed in waging a holy war against the Revolution?

How can this sudden upsurge of the Nation as the subject for political sovereignty and the establishment of a close link between Nation and citizenship have come about in a country where, with very few exceptions, the concept of citizen was identified with subject and even, among the antienlightened, with that of vassal? From the viewpoint of the relationship between education and citizenship arises the question of how to interpret, in light of the above, a Constitution that:

1. Dedicated its first chapter I (articles 1–4) not to the establishment of the rights of man and the citizen, to which there was no explicit reference or listing. The reference was rather to the definition of the "Spanish Nation," declared "free and independent" and not belonging to the "patrimony or any family or individual" and to establish political sovereignty in the Nation, and the right to make and pass its "fundamental laws."
2. Determined in chapter II (articles 6–9) that among a Spaniard's obligations were "love of one's country," "to be just and charitable," faithfulness to the Constitution and obedience to its laws, contribution to state expenses "according to means" and "to bear arms in defence of the country".
3. Established the religion of this "Spanish Nation" to be Catholicism, with the practice of any other forbidden (article 12).
4. As from 1830, linked the exercise of citizens' rights—the right to vote or hold public office at municipal level, for example—to the ability to read and write (article 25).
5. Commanded that in elementary schools the catechism of the Catholic Church be taught with the inclusion of "a short outline of civil duties" (article 366) and that the Constitution be explained "in all the universities and teaching establishments where ecclesiastical and political sciences are taught" (article 368).
6. In his "Preliminary Discourse" on the presentation of the project of the Constitution to the "Cortes," Agustín Argüelles (1776–1843), one of the most noteworthy liberals, would claim that "The State" needed "citizens" who would illuminate "the Nation" and "promote its happiness with all manner of knowledge and discoveries." And as a result, one of the "first concerns" the "representatives" of the "people" should address was "public education." To this end, education should be "general and uniform" and "national in character" as well as be the responsibility, in centralized form, of the "Cortes" and the government and not entrusted "to mercenary hands, limited minds, imbued with false ideas or mistaken principles" (Argüelles, 1989, p. 125).

The events that made these facts possible are multiple. They include the country's occupation by the French army, the flight of the royal family to France under the supposed protection of Napoleon, the abdication of Charles IV in favor of his son Fernando VII and of the latter in favor of Napoleon, the declaration of Joseph Bonaparte as King, and the beginning of the so-called "War of Independence" (1808–1814). These events entailed as well the formation first of provincial assemblies to organize the struggle against the invader. The summoning of the "Cortes" was to fill the power vacuum left by the Royal family's absence. The meeting of "Cortes" in Cadiz was selected as a place, isolated from the war in the rest of the country where liberal ideas enjoyed a certain acceptance. As it tended to be claimed in liberal circles, these exceptional circumstances and the heroism associated with the Nation, with a capital N, had made possible the recovery of rights strangled by despotism. The Nation's declaration of sovereignty would be buffered by a political constitution.

On the other hand, how could the Catholic nature of the Spanish nation with its corresponding demand for protective treatment and the establishment of religious intolerance square with an undeniably liberal constitution? For strategic or pragmatic reasons but also because of the weight of the Catholic Enlightenment (source of the liberal Catholicism later to be suffocated within the Catholic Church itself), the "Cortes" was possible with the so-called philo-Jansenism. As it has already been mentioned, this was a partisan current of anti-Romanic Episcopalism and the creation of a national church (at the nation's service) whose supporters, along with the defenders of royal prerogatives, considered the reform of the Spanish Catholic Church both desirable and possible. That would imply, among other aspects, the suppression of the Inquisition (not of ecclesiastical censorship, which was in the hands of the bishops) and of a large part of the existing convents and monasteries, along with the reform of the clergy and a better training for and distribution of parish priests. All these aspects, in conjunction with the disentitlement of the properties of the abolished convents and monasteries, the suppression of the tithes and sinecures or ecclesiastical privileges, and press freedom, were bound to produce widespread rejection not only in the religious orders and congregations but also in a substantial sector of the clergy.

Last, to what extent, regarding the relationship between education and republicanism, could it be said that the "Cortes" took concepts and ideas already present in enlightened absolutism and simply put into a legal text what had already been proposed by some enlightened thinkers? Could their agreements really be seen as a qualitative leap from subject to citizen, typical of liberal democracies? Was education by and for the monarchy, where the monarchy was the state, the same as education by and for the nation? Are we faced with two different projects—the enlightened and the liberal—with the same objective: bringing the subject/citizen into a specific political project via education? Or, are we dealing with the same project? What role would the political catechism, the teaching of the Constitution, or those disciplines most closely linked to the idea of citizenship play in all this?

As in the 1813 Report of the Commission created to propose "a plan" for public instruction, the dramatist, poet, and politician, Manuel José Quintana, said that because of the recently established freedom of press and the circumstances described above, once the "obstacles" had been "destroyed" or "weakened," it would be possible to carry out the "complete and radical reform" of education that Spain needed. The country needed "a system of public instruction appropriate and worthy of a free people" (Quintana, 1979, pp. 374–376). It is evident that the 1813 Report, the Dictum on the project for the Decree for the "general plan for public teaching" of March 7,

1814, drawn up by the Commission for Public Instruction of the "Cortes," as well as the aforementioned project and the General Ruling on Public Instruction of June 29, 1821, passed during the second operational period of the Cadiz Constitution, between 1820 and 1823, established the legal bases of "a complete and radical reform" for the creation of a national education system. However, in connection with civic education or education for citizenship, the only measure taken was to pass what had already been proposed by some of the enlightened Spaniards. Quite another thing would be the practical consequences of the legalization of those proposals.

As for the legal, official, semi-official, or private proposals concerning the civil or political catechisms, a slightly heavier emphasis can be perceived (although not in all cases) on the rights of the citizen alongside the duties that included, in some cases, a separation of the political from the religious catechisms. In their essence, these proposals or legal texts could have well been written 10 or 20 years before. In the previously mentioned Report of 1813, they went no further than suggesting the teaching of "religious dogma," "first maxims of good morals and upbringing" and "the principal rights and duties" of the "citizen" via clear, short and simple catechisms" (Quintana, 1979, p. 382).

In article 10, the project of the Decree of 1814 distinguished between a religious and moral catechism and a political one. But in the Ruling finally passed in 1821, article 12 referenced a sole religious, moral, and political catechism. In the Report on the project for the new study plan put forward by Salamanca University in 1814, it was termed a "civil and moral catechism" or "Spanish catechism" (*Informe de la Universidad de Salamanca*, 1820, pp. IX & XI). For its part, the project for the general Ruling on Elementary Education of March 16, 1822, which was never passed because of the return of absolutism in 1823, insisted on the constitutional and legal requirement to teach in school a single religious and civic catechism, by rote, of course. But, until such a catechism could be produced, the law ordered that, alongside the religious catechism, the children would memorize a "constitutional catechism." At the same time, it stated, and there was novelty in this, that boys and girls "in all schools" of Madrid, except those who followed the Lancasterian system, read the Constitution and learned by heart "some of the constitutional catechisms and even the Constitution itself" (Dirección General de Estudios, 1822, pp. 60–61, 84).

Other proposals from individuals, typical of a period in which private plans and projects flourished, did not significantly differ from those of the Age of Enlightenment. Manuel de Valbuena, professor of Latin studies in the Royal Studies of Saint Isidro, in his manuscript *Memoria* of 1813 did no more than mention the need to know the two catechisms by heart, the religious and the civic, placing more emphasis in the latter on the citizens' duties rather than rights (Valbuena, 1813). Marcial López, lawyer and translator of Constant, in his *Plan de educación nacional* presented to the "Cortes" in 1813, did his utmost in the work's preamble to link the concepts of citizen, rights, and education. However, except for suggesting that the Constitution be the first book children read, supposedly when they read fluently, he defended the existence of a single "civil and religious catechism" whose "maxims" with respect to the "duties of the citizen" were "submission to the Authorities, respect for elders, word of honour, fraternal charity, tolerance of faults in others, friendship, mutual benefit and all those age-appropriate virtues that shaped the soul, binding it to society with sacred bonds" (López, 1813, pp. 9, 10, 22). In short, something that could have been written by an enlightened scholar with no more than moderate ideas; something that supposed the autonomy stemming from civic or public morality and a civic-political catechism with respect to Catholic religion, morality, and a catechism to whose principles, dogmas, and criteria this emergent civic and public morality should be subject. Nevertheless, the 1812 Constitution, largely thanks to freedom of the press, did offer greater novelty in the appearance and spread of political, civil, liberal, or constitutional catechisms.

These catechisms show the diversity and internal complexity of a textual and didactic genre with scarcely defined boundaries. Naturally, virtually all conform to the question–response model common to religious catechisms. However, some take a dialogue form. Almost all are called catechisms, of course, but some are also identified as "Cartilla" (Primer) and "Catón" (name of the second school book for learning to read), "Lecciones" (Lessons) or "Instrucción" (Instruction). They tend to be short (some even consisting of very few pages), given their popularizing and proselytizing purpose, but some are of considerable length.

The question is further complicated when their titles and contents are analyzed. The liberal-enlightened catechisms tended to include, in their titles, the adjectives "political" or "constitutional." But there were also Catholic-political, Christian-political, political-Spanish-constitutional, and civil catechisms. This latter term, civil, is the one used in some of the catechisms, occasional in nature, printed in the early years of the War of Independence with the aim of enhancing the figure of Fernando VII and demonizing Napoleon and the French, while encouraging a Holy War against the invader. However, title and contents do not always correspond. The style and title of catechism were also used to spread the absolutist, clerical, anti-revolutionary and anti-liberal cause and ideas, moral or civil norms, and subjects such as agriculture and economy. Among the strictly political/constitutional catechisms, written in the glow of the Constitution in the three periods when it was in force (March 1812 to May 1814, March 1820 to October 1823 and in provisional form from August 1836 to June 1837, when it would be substituted by the liberal-progressive Constitution of that year), it is even necessary to distinguish those that deal with subjects of a general nature (origins of civil society, forms of government, natural law, political law, etc.), from those that confine themselves to the simple laying out of the Constitution, and those that combine both aspects in their turn. Likewise, it is important to distinguish between publications with an exclusively general purpose with an informative and proselytizing tendency and those written primarily for educational use and shaping the new citizens that the nation needed.

Concerning the teaching of the Constitution and citizen sciences more directly linked with citizenship, its approval was often the source of communications to the "Cortes" by municipalities or educational institutions explaining that some cleric or graduate had offered to teach them for free and requesting the creation of "Constitution" as a specific teaching post. At the same time, following the constitutional mandate and without waiting for the passing of a new plan of studies for the Universities, Valencia University opened "to the general public" a Chair in Constitution held by Law Professor, Nicolás Mª Garelli. The position was set up, as an explicit symbol, in the previous buildings maintained by the Inquisition prior to 1814. On the other hand, the effect of the Decree passed in 1820—shortly after the re-establishment of the Constitution of Cadiz—saying that the teachers should explain the Constitution in the elementary schools and those of Latin studies or Humanities remains uncertain. What is known is the non-compliance and outright rejection of the requirement made by the "Cortes" to parish priests, under threat of heavy sanctions, that they explain the Constitution on holidays at the end of the Mass.

With regard to the proposals, the Report of 1813 suggested, as an innovation, that in secondary studies (a recently established level), "social sciences" should be included alongside sciences and humanities. "Social sciences" were understood as those "studies that enable us to know our rights and duties as individuals, as members of an association formed to attain and ensure the common happiness of those composing it, and as a society in relationship to another society." The "studies" specifically included the disciplines of ethics or moral philosophy, natural law, political law, and law of nations. Added to these "moral and political studies" would be "the study and analysis of the Spanish Constitution which is the outcome and application of those moral and political principles taught," as well as statistics and political economy (Quintana, 1979, pp. 391–393). In line with this proposal, the Dictum on the project of Decree of 1814 established, as it would later be included as article 26 of said project and article 24 of the above mentioned Ruling of 1821, that at the secondary level students would study a new third science called "political and moral sciences," made up of three disciplines: Morals and Natural Law, Public or Political Law and Constitution, and Political Economy and Statistics. The "knowledge" of these sciences, the Dictum said, was "beneficial for all nations and absolutely essential in those that enjoyed a just freedom, difficult to maintain [without] public and domestic virtues." It added that the aim of the subject of Morals and Natural Law was "knowledge of man's duties with respect to his Creator, himself and his fellows, the inference of these duties that directly derives from man's nature, the rights that lead from these same duties and the various relationships that bind man according to the differing estates he may have in society." The contents of Political Law and Constitution were "the general principles of this science" and the study of the "fundamental laws" of the country "in order to see their agreement with the principles underlying society and from personal conviction to love which must be respected out of duty."

In the matter of university education, the first treatise of Public and Constitutional Law would come out in 1821 from the Professor of Salamanca University and translator of Destutt de Tracy and Bentham, Ramón de Salas (Salas, 1821). This work, as the author writes in the prologue, is made up of two parts: the former dedicated to the "fundamental principles generally recognised as Constitutional Public Law" and the latter on the 1812 Constitution in the light of the "principles" established in the former (Salas, 1821, p. XLIV). Its publication was partly the result of the Decree of August 6, 1820, by which the "Cortes" temporarily re-established the University study plan of 1807 replacing, in the Faculties of Jurisprudence, the study of the *Novísima Recopilación* and the *Siete Partidas* of Alfonso X the Wise (the former a compilation of the legislation of the Ancien Régime, printed in 1805, and the latter a code drawn up in the 13th century with the aim of achieving a certain legal standardization in the Kingdom of Castille) with that of Natural Law and Law of the Nations and the Political Constitution of the Monarchy, respectively. The Chair in Constitution was once again to be suppressed in 1823 with the return to absolutism. It would not be reinstated until 1836, in full liberal revolution, although then with the title of Public or Political Law.

SYNTHESIS AND FINAL REFLECTIONS

The current of thought known as the "republican tradition" or "republicanism" offers a certain diversity of perspectives from a historical point of view, as well as a series of common themes. The emphasis attached in that tradition to the importance or need of civic virtues—to willingness to participate in social and political life, to the social and civil rights and duties, and to the educational worth of the law and adherence to it—put education of the republic's citizens at the heart of what is understood by republicanism and citizenship.

The republican tradition in its enlightened version had to come to terms with the exclusive supremacy of the Catholic Church. The Catholic Enlightenment, philo-Jansenist in orientation, had therefore to adapt and neutralize the revolutionary potential of the new republicanism of the French and North American Revolutions to the Spanish context, as well as the ideas, doctrines, and works of the philosophers, economists, and jurists who gave ideological support to both Revolutions. The presence of a national Church and the role assigned to the clergy, especially the parish priests as agents and collaborators of the government, in the programs and proposals for social, political, economic, and educational reforms, are two of the most characteristic aspects of this adaptation. The confusion or mingling of religion with religious morals and citizenship, public spiritedness, and patriotism and civility did not, however, undermine the predominance of the first all the others. The same confusion or mingling and predominance can be found in the contents assigned (excepting Cabarrús) to this school reading book or reading primer, in which the civic-religious virtues and duties unanimously acclaimed by enlightened scholars were to be taught. The events of the French Revolution and the need to establish a quarantine to prevent the propagation of a revolutionary epidemic throughout the country increased the suspicion and rejection of the new language and the republican concepts and interpretations as well as of the "citizen sciences." The 1794 suppression of the Chairs of Natural Law and Law of the Nations that had been created only a few years before such events was yet another sign of suspicion and rejection.

Only exceptional circumstances such as the people's war initiative against the French occupation and the sovereign power vacuum created can explain the summoning of the "Cortes," their establishment in 1810, and their self-assignation of national sovereignty. The Constitution of 1812 would go on to proclaim the Nation as the source and starting point of citizenship. A new concept of the Nation was emerging and, along with it, a new concept of citizen. Thus, it was in the days when the Cadiz Constitution was in force that Spaniards took to the concept of citizenship "with most enthusiasm," and "the speeches of the time overflowed with invocations" to the Constitution, "political virtue," and "public spiritedness" (Sebastián, 2002, p. 139).

It was not only that "royal" establishments had to change to be called "national," but additionally that the word "citizen" had ceased to be a synonym for inhabitant. Rather, although it continued to carry that meaning, it added two more: that of "Spanish national," that is, a citizen of Spanish nationality as specified in articles 18 and 26 of the Constitution and, in a more restricted sense, a Spanish national with the right to "accede to municipal employment" (article 23), be an elector on the parish electoral boards and be elected representative of the nation in the "Cortes" (articles 45 and 91). In this sense, the citizen would be a male inhabitant who could be an elector if he could read and write, a necessary condition as from 1830 (article 25) and deputy to the "Cortes" if he possessed "a proportionate annual income, derived from his own property" (article 92). The educational instrument to prepare these new citizens, at least in the sphere of formal or school education, would be the religious and civil catechism (article 366) and the teaching of the Constitution in all educational institutions of mid- and higher level (article 368).

Once again, all this had to be fitted into the Catholic faith of the Spanish nation and the special protection the nation granted it at the expense of all other faiths, as set out in article 12 of the Constitution. From the contemporary viewpoint, this article can only be justified as stemming from caution given the force among enlightened and liberal Spaniards of the idea of a national Church. On the first count, the liberal deputy Agustín Argüelles, in a book edited in London in 1835, recognized that in article 12 of the Constitution, "a serious and disastrous mistake, a source of great but inevitable damage" had been committed. In his opinion, this was motivated by political caution to avoid radical confrontation with "the intolerant spirit reigning over much of the ecclesiastical estate," whereby the liberals accepted this statement of "religious intolerance" believing that a gradual "shedding of the light" would correct the error "without fight or scandal" (Argüelles, 1970, pp. 262–263).

As to the second point, the new Catholic Church that liberals believed could be established in Spain was a *national* Church, subject to a whole series of articles that guaranteed the faithfulness of the clergy to state interests before those of Rome. This was a foolish error because a group of moderate liberals would recognize when including religious freedom among the "individual rights" in a Constitutional Act, destined to supplant the Cadiz Constitution, drawn up in 1819 in the wake of a conspiracy against the monarchy of Fernando VII. The clergy and Catholics who supported the concept of the national Church were a minority. They were as enlightened and educated as could be desired but were nevertheless a minority that naturally faced the opposition of Rome and that found itself distanced from the people, whom they considered on the whole to be superstitious and uneducated. The numerical weakness of those Catholic liberals and their limited power and influence within the Catholic Church was problematic. So was the overwhelming support among the existing ecclesiastical hierarchy, parish priests, and the religious orders and congregations for the return of absolute monarchy, in the figure of Fernando VII. The result was an unbridgeable gulf between liberalism and the Catholic Church.

The disentitlement of the properties of the religious orders and congregations, begun in 1837, would further widen the gulf separating the Church and the liberals. Later events (fear of the European revolutions of 1848, the rise to power in 1844 of moderate or doctrinaire liberals) and the interests of both parties would ensure the attainment of a political agreement in the form of the Concordat between the Vatican and the Spanish state in 1851. However, in 1855, the main author of the study plan of 1845, Gil de Zárate, a liberal leaning toward moderation, faced with the ecclesiastical opposition found himself obliged to affirm with raw sincerity:

> for once and for all, let us admit that the educational issue is a question of power: he who teaches, dominates; since education is the moulding of men and men shaped in the light of those who indoctrinate them. To leave the teaching to the clergy is to want men for the clergy and not for the State (...) it is, in brief, to grant sovereignty where it is not due (...).

The question, as I have said, is one of power. It is about who should dominate society: the government or the clergy (...). Civil society admits ecclesiastical society as a fellow companion, no longer as a dominator. (Zárate, 1855, pp. 117, 118, 146–147)

However, let us consider that it was no longer a matter of educating men for the nation, as in 1812, but for the state; it was not about creating a national education system but a state educational system. Sovereignty no longer lay in the nation but in the state and, within the state, more in the executive power, presided over by the monarch, than in the legislative power; it was a phenomenon, as it has been mentioned, in line with the "social power" of the property-owning and moneyed classes. By then, under the reigning ideology of moderation, the various liberal governments had given up the idea of including the civic and social virtues in elementary schools (they had more confidence in the teaching of Catholic religion and morality and the treatises on courtesy than in the political-constitutional catechisms) as well as the teaching of the Constitution and "citizen sciences" at the secondary level. Nevertheless, the struggle between the Church, on the one hand, and constitutional and republican liberalism, on the other hand, began a series of ups and downs and periods of greater or lesser conflict that continues even today.

NOTES

1. The "Cortes" of Cadiz was a national legislative body. "Cortes" was the traditional name, in Spain, for the Parliament.
2. Economic Societies of the Country's Friend: societies driven by the government and composed of members of the aristocracy, clergy, and the high civil service, as well as lawyers and some well-to-do people, in order to promote economy, social welfare, and education.
3. Campomanes (1723–1802) and Jovellanos (1744–1811) are two of the most outstanding representatives of the Spanish Enlightenment.
4. The distinction between "love of one's country" as a feeling of attachment to the birth country (a natural tendency) and "patriotism" as a constant willingness to work for the good of the country (a civic virtue) can already be found by 1789 in some texts of the Spanish Enlightenment.
5. "Fiscal": high civil servant in charge of defending the rights of the Monarch and promoting the common interest.
6. Mayans proposed the study of *Elementa Juris Naturae et Gentium (1737)* by Heineccius and *Prelectiones* by the same author on the books by Grocio and Puffendorf, suitably expurgated.

REFERENCES

Argüelles, A. de. (1970). *La reforma constitucional de Cádiz*. Madrid: Iter ediciones.
Argüelles, A. de. (1989). *Discurso preliminar a la Constitución de 1812*. Madrid: Centros de Estudios Constitucionales.

Cabarrús, C. de. (1933). *Cartas sobre los obstáculos que la naturaleza, la opinión y las leyes oponen a la felicidad pública*. Madrid: Espasa Calpe.

Dirección General de Estudios. (1822). *Esposición sobre el estado de la enseñanza pública hecha a las Cortes, por la Dirección General de Estudios*. Madrid: Imprenta de Alban y Cª.

Fernández, M. A. (1976). *Sinapia. Una utopía española del siglo de las luces*. Madrid: Editora Nacional.

Gomila, J. P. y. (1786). *Discurso teórico práctico sobre la educación de la infancia dirigido a los padres de familia*. Salamanca: Andrés García Rico.

Informe de la Universidad de Salamanca sobre plan de estudios, o sobre su Fundación, altura y decadencia: con cuyo motivo presenta un proyecto de ley de instrucción pública. (1820). Salamanca: Vicente Blanco.

Jovellanos, G. M. de. (1963) [1802]. Memoria sobre educación pública, o sea tratado teórico-práctico de enseñanza, con aplicación a las escuelas y colegios de niños. In *Obras de D. Gaspar Melchor de Jovellanos*, (pp. 230–267). Madrid: Biblioteca de Autores Españoles, Ediciones Atlas.

López, M. (1813). Plan de educación nacional. s. l., s. d., but ca. 1813.

Lorente, L. M. L. (1989). El Informe de José Vargas Ponce a la Junta de Instrucción Pública. *Historia de la Educación*, 8, 293–313.

Marx, K. (1854, November 25). Revolutionary Spain. VI. *New York Daily Tribune*, p. 4.425.

Mayans, G. (1975). Idea del nuevo método que se puede practicar en la enseñanza de las universidades de España. In Mariano Peset & José Luís Peset (Eds.), *Gregorio Mayans y la reforma universitaria* (pp. 179–351). Valencia: Ayuntamiento de Oliva.

Mendoza, J. M. y. (1776). *Historia del Derecho Natural y de Gentes*. Madrid: Manuel Martín.

Plan de gobierno y estudios, formado de Orden del Consejo, para los seminarios de educación de la nobleza y gentes acomodadas que se establezcan en las capitales de provincia. (1790). Madrid: Imprenta de la Viuda de Marín.

Quintana, M. J. (1979). Informe de la Junta creada por la Regencia para proponer los medios de proceder al arreglo de los diversos ramos de Instrucción Pública. In *Historia de la Educación en España. Texto y documentos. Tomo I. Del despotismo ilustrado a las Cortes de Cádiz* (pp. 373–414). Madrid: Ministerio de Educación y Ciencia.

Salas, R. de. (1821). *Lecciones de Derecho público constitucional, para las escuelas de España*. 2 volumes. Madrid: Imprenta de D. Fermín Villalpando.

Sebastián, J. F. (2002). Ciudadanía. In Javier Fernández Sebastián & Juan Francisco Fuentes (Dirs.), *Diccionario político y social del siglo XIX español* (pp. 139–143). Madrid: Alianza.

Traggia, J. (1998). Idea de una feliz revolución literaria en la nación española, 1791. In Alejandro Mayordomo Pérez & Luís Miguel Lázaro Lorente (Eds.), *Escritos pedagógicos de la Ilustración, t. II*. Madrid: Ministerio de Educación y Ciencia.

Valbuena, M. de. (1813, March 1). *Memoria sobre la educación, e instrucción pública*. Sevilla. (author's archive).

Vallejo, P. (1998). Discurso sobre la necesidad de una reforma general de los métodos de educación de las Escuelas, Universidades y Colegios de la Nación e idea general de esta reforma (1791). In Carmen Labrador, Herráiz, & Pascual Vallejo (Eds.), *ilustrado y reformador de los estudios* (pp. 27–129). Madrid: Ministerio de Educación y Ciencia.

Zárate, A. G. de. (1855). *De la instrucción pública en España, t. I*. Madrid: Imprenta del Colegio de Sordo-Mudos.

6 Republicanism, National Identity, and the Scottish Enlightenment

David Hamilton

> When the sole end in view is the communication of knowledge, the natural connection of the subjects to be explained will, in all probability, dictate to the teacher the order which ought to be pursued, and, at the same time, deprive him of any alternative as to the succession of the different topics. But in the case under consideration, as the subjects are chosen with a reference to the improvement of the student in the use of his intellectual faculties, rather than with the view of putting him in possession of any class of facts, the method of instruction will be calculated to meet the natural growth of the understanding and to follow the order in which the several powers of the mind are found to develop themselves.
>
> (George Jardine, *Outlines of Philosophical Education Illustrated by the Method of Teaching the Logic Class in the University of Glasgow*, 1825, p. 257)

The above epigraph, written by a professor at Glasgow University, is evidence of a transformative moment in the development of republican schooling. It looks back to the 17th century when the body of knowledge relevant to schooling was believed to be divine in origin and fixed in content; and it looks forward to an age—the long 19th century—when the body of knowledge relevant to schooling was gradually accepted as rational in origin and evolving in content and form. Earlier attention to divine right and an associated belief in hierarchical authority was replaced by belief in human understanding and authority by consent. This chapter examines the role of education and schooling in such a transformation and the particular form it took in a small corner of northwest Europe.

I choose, however, not to start with republicanism but, rather, with the blurred binary of education and schooling. The boundary between these categories is blurred whenever English-language texts that claim to be histories of education are revealed as merely narratives about the successive institutional forms taken by schooling. Fortunately, other modern languages, like Italian, Spanish, French, and German, retain a more sophisticated appreciation of the distinction between education and schooling; as when they refer to notions of formation, destiny, scholarization, and, not least, the psycho-pedagogical idea of Bildung.

Cutting across this education/schooling binary is another problematic notion, also strongly rooted in English-language and, particularly, North American discussions of education and schooling. Education is identified as a transitive process—something that one person does to another while both are sitting, in the archetypical instance, on opposite ends of a log. Such bucolic imagery, however, denies the historical primacy of self-education or, as it is sometimes known in English, autodidacticism.

My chapter, then, uses these binaries to focus on the institutional forms taken by education/schooling in Scotland around the time of the 18th-century Enlightenment. To resolve the problems described earlier, I concluded that to understand what happened in the long 19th century, it was equally important to embrace what had happened previously.

Yet, this stance brought me to a second problem. I became acutely aware that earlier narratives of republicanism, together with discussion of the Scottish Enlightenment, already constitute a "historiographical juggernaut." Their combined weight has already given earlier research a "formidable momentum" (Allan, 1993, p. 1), one that has been repeatedly energized by waves of "reassessment" (cf. Wood, 2000). This scholarly apparatus has arisen from work conducted in fields of inquiry as diverse as philosophy, law, politics, sociology, cultural geography, gender relations, and military studies. To pay their own homage to this juggernaut, educational historians must, therefore, insert themselves into a bulky yet ill-defined and fluid field. Like me, they must find their way through the debris left in the wake of the juggernaut's path. At best, then, this chapter is merely a prelude, an earnest ground-clearing exercise.

The net result is an account of Scottish Education between the 16th and 19th centuries. I start with the Renaissance and Reformation, remembering that Jean Calvin, John Knox (Calvin's Scottish counterpart), and, indeed, Ignatius of Loyola (founder of the Jesuits) were all reformers as well as humanists. In the process, I identify arguments about the relationship of humanism and republicanism. The main part of my chapter, however, is taken up with the interaction of ideas about republicanism and the economic, demographic, political, and social circumstances of Scotland prior to the mid-19th century.

THE FLUID HUMANIST INHERITANCE

Scottish schooling in the 16th and 17th centuries was dominated by two pressures felt elsewhere in Europe. On the one hand, there was pressure to come to terms with the humanism that spread from Italy over the Alps into Northern Europe, and, on the other hand, there was internal pressure to reform Church organization. The former pressure constituted

Republicanism, National Identity, and the Scottish Enlightenment 113

the Renaissance, the latter fostered the Reformation. Together, however, these pressures created a "shared European heritage" of "republicanism" (Gelderen & Skinner, 2004).

What was this republican heritage? Its roots were an awareness that the two main sources of social change in the Middle Ages—Providence (God's direction) and Fortuna (Lady Luck)—had been joined by a new force—the conscious actions of human beings (i.e., their humanism). Humanists believed, in effect, that members of the human species could make their own contribution to history. In other words, they could improve themselves. To clarify this project, humanists returned to ideas excavated or recovered from classical, non-Christian sources. Gradually, they arrived at the assumption that education fosters the acquisition of wisdom, and that, in turn, the public exercise of this wisdom offers a basis for self-government among wise, male citizens.

At the same time, the promotion and acquisition of civic wisdom was to be fostered by the refurbishment of existing educational practices. Insofar as these practices were translated into texts, their traces remain as surrogates in the educational record. The eloquence, spoken and written, embodied in these texts is evidence that their authors possessed wisdom. Indeed, as a demonstration of wisdom, eloquence was the crowning humanist virtue—the mark of the "true" Renaissance man (Skinner, 1978, p. 87).

The humanist identification of wisdom and eloquence was achieved through the revision of earlier assumptions about rhetoric—one of the arts associated with medieval trivium (viz. grammar, logic, rhetoric). Previously, grammar involved stringing words together in a meaningful way, logic involved stringing propositions together as plausible arguments, and rhetoric involved stringing words and propositions together such that the initial argument also became persuasive. Humanists reworked this triad. Principally, they blurred the boundaries between logic and rhetoric. In the process, they created the humanist field of *dialectic*—the formulation of arguments that were both plausible and persuasive. Indeed, if an argument was both plausible *and* persuasive (i.e., eloquent), it could be regarded as "true" (see e.g., Hamilton, 2002, 2003; Ong, 1958).

The truth-creating potential of dialectic underwrote the humanists' endeavor. It enabled them to "struggle against the tide of fortune [viz. lady luck], to channel and subdue its power, and in this way to become, at least to some extent, the master of their own fate" (Skinner, 1978, pp. 96–97). Through the acquisition of virtue, humans would recover something that had been taken from them in the Garden of Eden. In the words of the Old Testament, they would know the difference between good and evil; they would be able to eat from the tree of knowledge; and they would, in the process, live forever.

But, as noted earlier, their progress beyond the Garden of Eden was interrupted by other forces—those associated with church reform. These pressures were, in part, transposed into a new social development: the idea that the new power of wise humans also extended to the upbringing (or disciplining) of other adults and other parents' children. In Scotland, this attention to "vertuous (sic) education and Godly upbringing" was identified in the *First Book of Discipline* prepared by Scottish reformers in 1560, following similar initiatives by Lutheran and Swiss Protestants. Not only was everyone to be "compelled to bring up their children in learning and virtue," these activities were also assumed to be of "great instruction to the aged" (see Cameron, 1972, pp. 130, 132).

Ceasing to be predominantly a feature of domestic life, upbringing could be formalized into an outside-the-home instrument of social engineering, which, for the sake of argument, I describe as "modern schooling." This formalization was also associated with the emergence of new ideas about syllabus, class, curriculum, catechesis, and didactics between about 1500 and 1650. It was seen as a mechanism for disciplining other people's children and, in the process, enhancing their prospects of salvation on earth and/or in heaven. As Hotson (2005) has commented, the reformed pedagogical tradition had the aim of "restoring perfection to human nature" (p, 2; see also Hotson, 2000). Indeed, it was the power immanent in this reconstitution of education that drew the attention of Protestant and Catholic reformers. Could humanity be rescued from the biblical Fall by education as well as by the hand of God?

One of the most persuasive English-language accounts of this reconstitution is Anthony Grafton and Lisa Jardine's (1986) *From Humanism to the Humanities: Education and the liberal arts in fifteenth- and sixteenth-century Europe*. Their analysis of the transition from humanism to the humanities echoes my own distinction between education and schooling. They claim, in a thesis reiterated by Hotson (2007), that humanist ideas about *learning and studying* generated in the 15th century, became corrupted (or replaced) by regimes of *instruction* consolidated in the 16th century. Moreover, these regimes sought to direct learning to particular ends, themselves related to emergent conceptions of piety, public service, and civic humanism.

Put another way, these regimes were intended to steer learners. They were not merely regimes of learning and studying; they were also regimes of power. Indeed, such *power over learning* rendered them as regimes of *instruction*. The Jesuit *Ratio studiorum* (1599) constitute one such regime; likewise, Johan Comenius' 17th-century *Didactica Magna* (see e.g., Blekastad, 1969). Moreover, such developments straddled the confessional boundaries that existed in Europe—a time when, as Grafton and Jardine (1986) report, a member of the "European academic elite," Justus Lipsius (1547–1606), played the "Lutheran at Jena, the Calvinist fellow-traveller in Leiden, and the ultra-orthodox Catholic in Louvain" (p. 197). Although this fluidity may have been reduced in later confessional divisions, it assisted the pan-European spread of modern schooling in the 17th century (e.g., at the hands of the Jesuits and sponsors and followers of Comenius).

STEERING LEARNING

Although it may be helpful to contrast *learning and studying*, on the one hand, with *instruction*, on the other, this distinction should be treated with caution. Like any dualism, it has appeal as a teaching or preaching device ("on the one hand . . . on the other hand . . ."). Yet, in practice, the one-sided association of power with instruction does not survive closer scrutiny? Can learning and studying, for instance, take place in the absence of power? Do institutional settings exist—inside or outside the family—where learning takes place in a power-free bubble? Adoption of such a perspective is to underwrite comparisons of education and schooling that are utopian, romantic, ahistorical, and, ultimately, illegitimate. It is preferable, I suggest, to regard schooling and education as processes that combine self-fashioning and other-fashioning. They are better seen, therefore, as a continuum than as discontinuous entities.

This last view of education and schooling stems, in my case, from the assumption that intellectual development is an intra- as well as an interpersonal process. Learning may not come directly from teachers but, rather, may be sponsored by their absent or invisible presence. Teachers may be present in person; they may be absent yet simultaneously present in the form of learning devices (e.g., textbooks); or teachers may exist merely as the inner voices, inherited from the language of others, that steer the desires, self-regulation, and self-direction of learners.

Whether a teacher is physically or virtually present, educational practices remain intrinsically goal-directed. Human beings are socialized, acculturated, formed, led-out, or self-directed into new realms of knowledge and new ways of knowing. Indeed, such purposive—or reflexive—*drawing out* is a defining feature of *educational* practice. The historical question, then, is how is this drawing out achieved? And by whom? Is it the responsibility of an external agent (a parent, home tutor, or schoolteacher)? Is it the result of an internal agent (e.g., a student's own motivation or desire)? Or is education fostered by disembodied agents—the invisible hands, for instance, that shape the layout of textbooks, schoolrooms, and websites?

As this suggests, the steering of learning is multicausal. Projections are always interrupted by mediating minds and hands. Sixteenth-century educational ideas, for instance, were selectively crystallized in the writings of Erasmus, Castiglione, Vives (etc.), who, in doing so, drew upon classical sources such as Cicero and Quintilian. The subsequent representation of these ideas was influenced by the 15th-century advent of moveable-type printing, which meant that *mise en page*—or layout—considerations became part of the conscious or unconscious corruption of sources used by copyists and printers. And these representations underwent further "modernization" as they were circulated by preachers and teachers working through the medium of modern European languages rather than Latin, Greek, or Hebrew (a historical issue discussed extensively in Hotson, 2007).

Collectively, these practices served as systems and relations of production. Authors, copyists, type-setters, bookbinders, publishers, booksellers, librarians, teachers, and preachers overlapped in their contributions (see e.g., Hotson, 2007). Separate agents in the process acquired new knowledge as they interacted with other aspects of the system (e.g., as editor-printers, author-booksellers). All of them used this hybridized knowledge in their engagement with the production process. And all, in a non-trivial sense, were educational practitioners engaged in steering the course of human history. Learners are made, just like textbooks (cf. Johns, 1998).

A notable instance of this interaction of ideas and practices is provided by the title of the Jesuit school program. It became known as the *Ratio studiorum*—a label that, paradoxically, is more reasonably translated as "scheme of studies" than as "scheme of instruction." Yet, as the Jesuit historian, John W. Padberg, has noted, the version of the *Ratio studiorum* approved by the Pope in 1599 had a "two-fold ancestry." It comprised "plans of studies" as well as a "series of rules." The final stages of its "production" centered on the formulation of rules to be followed by Jesuit colleges, yet, in practice, these revisions retained the label favored in earlier discussions, around 1560, which had related to the plans of study developed in the diversity of Jesuit colleges that, after about 1550, had spread inside and outside Europe (Padberg, 2000, p. 81).

By the end of the 16th century, then, schooling was a hybrid institution. It was an amalgam of at least three earlier sets of assumptions and practices. It was woven together from:

(1) medieval assumptions about text-based learning and studying that originated in monasteries and cathedrals (cf. Illich, 1993; Jaeger, 1994; Olson, 1995);
(2) 15th-century humanist assumptions about education as the "training" of "ideal, cultivated" citizens (Grafton & Jardine, 1986, p. xiv); and, finally,
(3) 16th-century assumptions about teaching as an efficient and methodological process of inculcation (cf. Green, 1996; Ong, 1958).

Yet, in this broader process, the promotion of humanist eloquence became problematic. Grafton and Jardine's (1986) "dilemma of late humanism" intervened. The intention of the humanist curriculum—the fact that while the promotion of humanism—"fluency, erudition, political and legal expertise, discretion, integrity, nobility of spirit, humility coupled with assurance"—had to compete with the humanities curriculum—an "educational blueprint: a timetable of lessons and a course of study" (Grafton & Jardine, 1986, pp. 200, 212).

At this point, I return to the Scottish case.

HUMANISM AND REFORMATION IN SCOTLAND

The Scottish Reformation, like similar European initiatives, was fuelled by generic humanist sentiments. These not only introduced a sense of human self-identity into politics but also, as a by-product, a sense of historical identity. The question "who am I?" necessarily led to the questions "where am I from?" and "where am I going?" The prevailing theological narrative was that humanity had fallen from grace (i.e., out of God's reach) in the Garden of Eden. Nevertheless, humanity had subsequently cleansed itself, reaching a state of recovery which allowed true believers to advance towards worldly and heavenly salvation. Despite reliance on Biblical authority, however, the way forward was never clear. Different pathways were proposed and different practices (e.g., regarding baptism) were chosen to accomplish deliverance. The Calvinist distinction between "elect" and "reprobates" and the Lutheran discussion of justification by "faith" not "works" are two examples of confessional distinctions that divided Europeans over social and educational practices.

In Scotland (and, I assume, elsewhere), questions about citizenship and political identity spilled over into questions of national identity. The humanist basis of these political discussions was a general republican concern for liberty and self-determination. One agent who made "creative use of the scanty evidence for deliberative government and elective monarchy" was George Buchanan (1506–1582), a Scottish-born humanist who taught in the universities of Paris, Bordeaux, Coimbra, and St Andrew's (Allan, 1993, p. 36).

Buchanan was not alone in this respect. Such attention to "history" by "all kinds of Scottish historians" was, as Allan (1993) suggests, "especially provocative in an age when the established medieval orthodoxies, habitually defended as divine, immutable, and unchallengeable, were under sustained attack" (pp. 37–38). Nevertheless, as Allan adds, such narratives were as creative as they were historical. Rhetoric was used, for instance, to mask "their more seditious political implications" (p. 38).

The composition of such "histories" was, therefore, not merely the production of an attractive narrative; it also represented participation in political debates. Moreover, such debates were broadcast through many channels. Narratives were not only published in printed versions, they also fuelled sermons preached by church officials, lessons taught by schoolteachers, and, presumably, the moral tales, fables, poems, and songs that circulated anonymously across the oral as well as the literary landscape of Scotland.

Allan's (1993) perspective on Scottish history appears in *Virtue, Learning and the Scottish Enlightenment: Ideas of scholarship in Early Modern History*. His study is pertinent to this chapter because it focuses on learning and scholarship not schooling or even education. It is about Scottish authors and their contribution to the circulation of ideas. Accordingly, it devotes little attention to the artifacts, practices, or audiences that sustained this circulation. Nevertheless, Allan offers occasional glimpses of the reading practices that accompanied the circulation of these works. For example, he includes the comment of Dundee-born Hector Boece (1465–1536), a friend of Erasmus, that "frequent" reading of histories was, itself, a profitable "exercise" (p. 56); and he reports that the author of *History of the World* (1652), Alexander Ross (1590–1654), believed that such a work would be of especial value among two agents of popular dissemination—"orators" and "schoolmasters" (Allan, 1993, p. 81).

Allan's (1993) failure to attend to the readers rather than the writers of texts is defensible. His general assumption is that the republican discourse of Scotland was limited to an elite—"men of letters" who practiced "enlightened scholarship" (p. 160) through the eloquence of their "authorial rhetoric" (p. 55).

THE MANAGEMENT OF REPUBLICANISM

As suggested, Allan's historical attention was not directed toward literacy practices. Instead, his work presents claims about continuity and change in a humanist/republican paradigm that emerged in the Scottish Reformation and that survived at least until the end of the 18th century.

The narrow focus of his argument, however, raises a parallel set of questions about the social distribution of republican ideas. Were they restricted to a literate, reading, composing, and corresponding elite? And what boundaries were imagined to limit or channel the circulation of such ideas? Such historical questions are legitimate. They relate to literacy, power, social topography, and gender relations, all of which remain contested areas of Scottish historiography. In this chapter, I can only address them in a foreshortened form—by reference to an influential account of the subsequent history of national or republican identity in Scotland—George Davie's (1961) *The Democratic Intellect*.

Davie's (1961) claim was that Scotland's national identity has been marked by a "democratic intellect" of "polymathic values" (p. 336) whose foundation was affirmed in the 18th-century Scottish Enlightenment, and whose traces could still be discerned, in the 1950s, when Davie worked as a "lecturer in Logic and metaphysics" at Edinburgh University. The word *democratic* in his title implies, moreover, that Davie believed republican sentiments existed throughout Scottish society and were not, that is, restricted to an elite.

Whatever the merits of Davie's original argument, *The Democratic Intellect* has remained important to educationists. It is not only a comment on Scottish identity, it is also a curriculum and pedagogic history—one that, in the words of its subtitle, embraces *Scotland and her universities in the nineteenth century*. Davie argued that the Scottish universities underwent a transformation in the 18th century. Influential professors, like Adam Smith, abandoned lecturing in Latin, followed a broad curriculum that united classics, science, and philosophy and encouraged their students to write essays and engage in class discussions. Davie believed that, by the 19th century, such reforms not only projected a "humanist flavour" (p. 13) but also acted as a bulwark against the encroachment of elitist (i.e., nondemocratic) educational ideas from England (via the universities of Oxford and Cambridge).

The historical foundation of Davie's republican argument is that, despite the amalgamation of the crowns and parliaments of Scotland and England in 1603 and 1707, respectively, Scotland retained the right to follow prior national usage in religion, law, and education—a devolved privilege that is still protected. Since 1707, then, policy debates in the areas of religion, law, and education have always been animated by parallel considerations of national identity.

Davie (1961) claimed that as the 19th century unfolded, the "chief point at issue" was the relationship between "school and university" (p. 7). Supporters of the English education system felt that Scottish schools and universities should follow more specialized pre-university curricula, whereas a (not *the*) Scottish position, itself debated in a succession of government inquiries, was that university institutions should not only remain open to students able to meet the fees, but they should also retain a general humanist curriculum that fostered wisdom and eloquence. According to Davie's argument, these Scottish protagonists repeatedly harked back to the role of universities in national life—emphasizing their "genuinely democratic character" and their association with the "traditional Scottish machinery of schooling," which, in the first place, had been "designed to neutralize the inequalities of scholastic and family backgrounds" (p. xvii).

THE SCOTTISH MACHINERY OF SCHOOLING

What, then, was this traditional machinery of democratic schooling? The role of schoolmen and grammar schools in the cultural life of Scotland between 1650 and 1800 is not easily described. As demonstrated, for instance, in a pioneering article (Withrington, 1965), records of post-Reformation teaching must be interpreted carefully. In particular, care should be taken over the interpretation of the *First Book of Discipline* (1560) and a law of 1696, both of which stipulated that a school should be erected (i.e., set up) in every parish. In the event, the residual historiographic problem is that a gap remained between stipulation and deed.

Likewise, terms used in the 17th century, for instance, should not be judged against later assumptions and definitions. For example, the reported existence of a Latin "master" does not necessarily mean the existence of a grammar *school*. It merely denoted the existence of someone who had attended university classes and could offer Latin tuition. Further, schools were usually one-teacher institutions. Tutoring could be offered in any suitable setting, including the learner or teacher's home. Even if these setting came to be known as "schools," the designation *grammar* school was not the same as *English, Scots,* or *parish* school. Teachers linked to English or Scots schools offered reading (from the Bible), less often writing, and even less frequently arithmetic. *Parish school,* however, was also an ambiguous designation. The teacher, who received part of his income from parish sources, covered the same ground as *English* or *Scots* schools but might also offer Latin to those pupils who could pay extra fees.

Equally, teaching need not be a full-time occupation: It was regularly combined with other church responsibilities such as assisting the minister on Sundays and acting as a clerk on weekdays. Equally, teaching Latin need not be a life-long career. It might be a transient occupation for young men while they gathered funds and/or waited for an opening in the church—in Scotland or overseas. In this respect, too, young men could also work as teachers outside the formal structure of the established Church—typically as family tutors. Indeed, such tutors may have been the main source of formalized (book-based) tuition in eloquence (i.e., humanity). Finally, school attendance was not compulsory, nor was it necessarily a continuous activity. Students attended according to their circumstances. They might attend only in summer (if access was difficult in winter) or only in winter (if they were required as field laborers in the growing season). And it was not unknown for siblings to attend on alternate days—for one set of fees. Irregular patterns of attendance were also shown by teachers. Their service in the parish school could be interrupted by their infirmity, death, or absence due to other parish or personal business.

My feeling is that until the end of the 18th century, the Scottish parish school was a site of both instruction and tutoring. The existence of instruction is symbolized in the creation, in 1648, of Scotland's longest-surviving textbook—the *Shorter Catechism* (see Carruthers, 1957). The evidence for tutoring, however, is more circumstantial. It is based on two inferences that can be made about the "traditional machinery" of Scottish schooling. First, there was a more lucrative mode of teaching for university teachers and their successful students—tutoring in families. Second, the small size of schools, the diverse ages and backgrounds of the pupils, and their irregular admission and attendance meant that some of the teaching was individualized. It was conducted *seriatim,* a practice where pupils had their lessons "heard," in turn, by the teacher. What, in fact, occurred during these interactions remains, of course, a matter of conjecture. But there is no reason to rule out the promotion of learning and studying.

This structure predominated in the central lowlands of Scotland. In the highlands, however, the existence of parish schools could not be assumed because their establishment was subject to hindrances of geographical scale, the vagaries of a subsistence economy, the survival of Gaelic as a home language, and the reluctance of local "patrons" to meet the costs of maintaining a school. Young people, particularly those living in rural areas, acquired their learning, like their literacy, in many ways and from many sources. To an unknown degree, some were educated; some were schooled; and some used their learning/schooling to make the journey from home education, through school education, to further and higher learning in urban areas.

By such means, ideas about humanism and republicanism were exchanged. In turn, they were nourished by the changing circumstances of Scottish life, notably the attention given to question of self-determination. Schooling was implicated in this process, contributing to the transmission and transformation of such sentiments. This machinery survived until at least the end of the 18th century, when it began to be undermined by the spread of wage labor and the modernization of agricultural practice—both of which led to further migration from rural to urban centers.

Whether this 18th-century, pre-industrial machinery generated the "democratic" circumstances imagined by Davie is unclear. What, in fact, happened in the 18th century? Was it a period of democratic continuity or change? Although many Scottish historians highlight the impact of social change without using comparative data, it may be useful to draw attention to the interpretation offered by Fania Oz-Salzberger (1995), an Israeli who wrote her doctorate in Oxford and published it as *Translating the Enlightenment: Scottish civic discourse in eighteenth-century Germany*. Oz-Salzberger's doctoral interest was the translation process as it operated across Europe as an engine of both "inter-cultural affinity" and "cultural peculiarism." She suggests that, during the 18th century, there was a:

> transformation from a "republic of letters" dominated by erudite bilinguists or multilinguists, to a budding "democracy of letters" encompassing masses of monolingual readers. (Oz-Salzberger, 2006, p. 385)

It was a period of history when Latin was displaced as the "universal language" in favor of "Europe's vernaculars." Indeed, her conclusion is that "the Enlightenment lent itself to translation" through its "highly translatable" ideas about "progress, dispersal of knowledge, freedom of thought, universal humanity and critical reasoning" (Oz-Salzberger, 2006, p. 389).

From this perspective, it is reasonable to be cautious about Davie's (1961) claim that the democratic intellect was an expression of the "Presbyterian [Protestant] inheritance" in Scotland, which, in turn, nourished an "an evolving pedagogic tradition" during the 18th century (pp. 3, 19). Had it originated in the 17th-century aspiration of a school for every parish? Or was it, instead, a product of the "variegated diffusion" (Oz-Salzberger, 2006, p. 389) of republican and other moral sentiments around the north Atlantic during the 18th century?

My own feeling is to suspend judgment on the democratic intellect while giving attention to the ideas and practices of the Enlightenment, notably the

18th-century idea of establishing a natural order in society. Moreover, these ideas took shape in different ways in different local and national contexts. In Carla Hesse's (2006) apt characterization, the history of the Enlightenment should be understood as an "ongoing dialectic between aspirational ideals and local incarnations"—a story "laden with contingencies and heterodoxies" (p. 507).

SCIENTIFIC REPUBLICANISM

Insofar as their work was subject to translation and international dissemination, all Enlightenment authors can be described as eloquent. They served as a republic of letters whose ideas could be read, adapted, and applied to local circumstances. Yet, as Oz-Salzberger suggests, these thinkers also contributed to the establishment of a "budding" democracy of letters. Many of these thinkers were both authors and teachers. As authors, they revised their thinking; and as teachers, they also revised their pedagogic practices.

In this last respect, Davie's (1961) *The Democratic Intellect* remains a seminal text. It highlights the curricular and pedagogic changes that occurred in the Scottish universities toward the end of the 18th century. In particular, the Scottish Enlightenment extended the secularization of moral philosophy. A new version of rationalism substituted natural for supernatural explanations. Such scientific republicanism supplanted the humanist or civic republicanism of earlier centuries. During the 18th century, that is, rationalism was a sustained attempt to apply Newtonian assumptions about law-like behavior to other realms of human experience such as society (sociology), commerce (economics), the natural world (biology and geology), natural phenomena (statistics), the mind (psychology), and even religion. Such initiatives led to the break-up of philosophy (viz. the work of *philosophes*) into different disciplines.

A Scottish example of such rationalist thinking can be found in the works of Adam Smith (1723–1790). In 1751, Smith was recruited to the chair of Logic and Rhetoric at Glasgow University, but, because the existing professor of Moral Philosophy (Thomas Craigie) was ill at the time, he also shared in teaching the moral philosophy class. Professor and students met at 7:30 a.m. for lectures on ethics, politics, jurisprudence, and natural theology and then reconvened for an "examination" hour at 11 a.m., where the same ground was covered in a more conversational manner. Finally, students who had taken the public course in the previous year were also admitted to the professor's "private," class which met at 12:00 p.m., 3 days a week. According to the 20th-century editor of these lectures, J. C. Bryce, Smith (1983) devoted these lectures to "the first subject he had ever taught, Rhetoric and Belles Lettres" (p. 9).

These lectures were not published in the 18th century and may have been included in the material that was burned, at Smith's request, by his literary executors. Students' notes from these lectures eventually came to light in the 1950s (see Howell, 1975; Smith, 1983). They follow the 16th-century humanist idea that rhetoric is integral to the composition of arguments. Accordingly, Smith gave 10 lectures on style (*elocutio*) and 19 on the arrangement of an argument (*dispositio*). Into this second group of lectures, however, Smith introduced a new, rationalist category, which he called the *didactic* style. Indeed, Bryce suggests that this category had a "central place" in Smith's "whole conception of discourse" (p. 14). "Descartes," Smith suggested to his students, "was in reality the first who attempted this method," closely followed by Isaac Newton. This "Newtonian method," he duly claimed:

> is undoubtedly the most philosophical and, in every science whether of morals or natural philosophy etc, is vastly more ingenious and for that reason more engaging. (Smith, 1983, p. 146; lecture 24, punctuation and spelling modernized; see also Miller, 1995)

In highlighting the relevance of the didactic style to the conduct of Enlightenment arguments, Bryce maintains that Smith was showing his dissatisfaction with the "ancient division," which had prevailed between logic and rhetoric. Didactic, that is, was not a branch of humanist rhetoric but "a procedure of thought: the scientific. . . . [It is] concerned with the exposition of a system, [and] the clarification of a multitude of phenomena by one known or proved principle" (p. 14). In other words, Smith rejected the 16th-century idealization of dialectic. In the light of debates about a science of society, he began to regard rhetoric merely as a device for decorating or masking an incomplete argument, not as a means of strengthening or validating its propositions. In Smith's words, that is, rhetoric had degenerated more into "reverence for antiquity" than into a regard for the "beauty or usefulness of the thing itself" (Smith, 1983, p. 149, lecture 12). He was clear, that is, in his rationalist preference for *didactic* over *rhetoric*.

> Persuasion, which is the primary design in the rhetorical, is but the secondary design in the didactic. It endeavors to persuade us only so far as the strength of the arguments is convincing: Instruction is the main end. In the other, persuasion is the main design, and instruction is considered only so far as it is subservient to persuasion and no farther (Smith 1983, p. 149; spelling and punctuation modernized).

This retreat from 16th-century dialectic was matched, if not caused, by the gradual disappearance of Latin as a medium of instruction in universities and the consequent marginalization of Latin in school curricula. Indeed, Adam Smith subsequently used *The Wealth of Nations* to argue for a reorientation of the Scottish parish school, which embraced a rejection of Latin instruction:

> If in those little schools the books by which children are taught to read were a little more instructive than they commonly are, and if, instead of a little smattering of Latin which the children of the common people are sometimes taught there, and which can scarce ever be of any use to them, they were instructed in the elementary parts of geometry and mechanics, the literary education of this rank of people would perhaps be as complete as it can be. (Book 5, chapter 1; see also Withrington, 1970)

EVOLVING PEDAGOGIES

Eighteenth-century rationalism focused on seeking truth in the order of nature and, in turn, the application of these truths to, among other things, the question of national identity, the abolition of slavery, and the rights of women (discussed in more detail in Gelderen & Skinner, 2004; Skinner & Stråth, 2003). Natural logic was substituted for formal logic such that, in the process, new attention was given to mental philosophy and faculty psychology.

Access to this transformation is offered in the writings of George Jardine (Professor of Logic at Glasgow University between 1774 and 1827). Although not known for his philosophical writings, Jardine is remembered in the history of Scottish education for the commentary on higher education that he offered in his *Synopsis of the Lectures on Logic and Belles Lettres Read in the University of Glasgow* (1797) and in his *Outlines of Philosophical Education* (1825). To set the scene for the replacement of formal by natural logic, Jardine expressed the following (Scottish) view on the teaching of Latin:

> We do not, in this part of the Kingdom attach to classical learning that high and almost exclusive degree of importance which is ascribed to it elsewhere; thinking it of greater consequence to the students, to receive instructions in the elements of science, both mental and physical, than to acquire even the most accurate knowledge of the ancient tongues. (Jardine, 1825, p. 418)

As a professor of logic, the study of mind was the *"mother science"* for Jardine (1825), a source "from which all others derive at once their origin and nourishment" (p. 45). By introducing students to the workings of various mental powers or faculties (e.g., perception and attention), Jardine's intention was to give them access to the "tools and engines" that were "to be used in every activity and disquisitions [written or verbal presentations]" (Jardine, 1797, p. 7). He also recognized that if a student's faculties were to operate at full power, they also needed regular exercise. Thus, Jardine envisaged the existence of a system of extempore questioning within or alongside lectures. By such means, lectures should cease to be construed as "the dictating of notes"—also known as "dictates" (Wood, 1993, p. 1). Rather, they were to be regarded as a vernacular discourse—an "easy dialogue" (Jardine, 1825, pp. 17, 464).

Like Adam Smith, Jardine was also making a break with 16th-century dialectic, albeit one that seems to differ from Smith's adoption of didactic. To this end, Jardine explicitly referred to Francis Bacon's critique of "magistral teaching" (see Spedding, Ellis, & Heath, 1860, pp. 448ff.), a mode of teaching where, Jardine felt, the "pompous teacher" sought to impress upon the mind of the pupil that his, the teacher's, own "sense and reflection were the only true guide to knowledge" (Jardine, 1925, pp. 12–13).

Instead Jardine's work echoed Bacon's view of "initiative" teaching. He sought to create an "active discipline" in the university Logic class, one that placed "constant demands" upon the "attention" of all students (Jardine, 1825, p. 284). Moreover, such ideas about the replacement of seriatim with *class* teaching rapidly spread to other sections of society. The mechanism, form, and extent of this diffusion deserves further inquiry, but one explanation is that the rationalist or republican appeal of so-called "natural," "scientific," or "positive" forms of social organization spread, during the 19th century, from the universities and colleges of the Enlightenment throughout the organs of the nation-state and the institutions of civil society. In the years that followed, such ideas were addressed, contested, and revised by a wide variety of educational innovators, in early education, school education, adult education, and college education.

CONCLUSION

This chapter has focused on a pivotal episode in the history of republicanism in education: the replacement of humanist republicanism by scientific republicanism. To round off my argument, I would like to return to a sentiment raised at the outset: the fact that Enlightenment *philosophes*, like George Jardine and Adam Smith, were as aware of their humanist past as much as they reached for a sense of their republican and scientific future. But they were not alone in this respect. Another European figure who discussed public education in his lectures and writings was Immanuel Kant (1724–1804). At the time of Kant's death, these lectures were edited into '*Über Pedagogik*, and, in 1899, they first appeared in an English translation (based on different German versions) that acquired the title *Education* (1960).

In these writings, Kant (1960) looks forward because he shares Jardine's assumption that all humans have a mind of their own and, above all, can think for themselves. Kant celebrated this sense of mind and the power of reason that accompanied it. "Man needs a reason of his own," he wrote, and "all the natural endowments of mankind must be developed little by little out of man himself, through his own effort" (pp. 2–3). Only through education according to "human nature" (p. 2) could man "become man" (p. 6).

At the same time, however, Kant (1960) felt that, "on the whole, public education is the best" (pp. 26–27). Yet, in this last claim, Kant was looking back to humanist practice. His writings did not refer to "public" education in the sense that dominated the long 19th century. Instead public education was to be designed merely for the "children of rich people" (Kant, 1960, p. 24). It was to be a preparation for senior positions in the public sphere. Thus, Kant disparaged the use of *home* education "carried on either by the parents themselves" or "by others who are paid to assist them." He felt that it might not be an adequate "preparation for the [public] duties of a citizen" (p. 25).

But Kant's usage was not peculiar to German thought. Pre-Enlightenment usage also remained in England. Indeed, it still remains in the 21st century—in the generic label (*Public* school) given to a small corpus of schools whose male alumni still exert a disproportionate influence in the public spheres of English life.

Overall, then, this chapter has focused on the distinction between public education and republican schooling as the former emerged in the 16th century and as the latter came to cast a long shadow over education debates that energized 18th-century educational practice. While accepting that these debates had a variegated diffusion in the 19th century, it also recognizes that their local incarnation in Scotland became tied up with parallel discussions of how national identity should be expressed in the organization of schools, colleges, and universities. Internal debates about Scottish schooling during the 19th century—which extended from Thomas Dick's (1836) *On the Mental Illumination and Moral Improvement of Mankind*, through Alexander Bain's (1879) *Education as a Science*, to Henry Craik's (1896) *The State and Its Relation to Education*—embraced an amalgam of the ideas and practices of civic humanism and republicanism, which, themselves, were revisited in George Davie's (1961) *The Democratic Intellect: Scotland and her universities in the nineteenth century* and continue to exercise the intellectual faculties of men and women seeking to understand Scotland's position in the late- or post-Enlightenment world of the 21st century.

REFERENCES

Allan, D. (1993). Virtue, learning and the Scottish Enlightenment: Ideas of scholarship in early modern history. Edinburgh: Edinburgh University Press.

Bain, A. (1879). *Education as a Science*. London: Kegan Paul.

Blekastad, M. (1969). *Comenius: Versuch eines Umrisses von Leben, Werk und Schicksal des Janos Amos Komensky*. Oslo: University of Oslo Press.

Cameron, J. K. (Ed.). (1972). *The first book of discipline*. Edinburgh: The Saint Andrew Press.

Carruthers, S. W. (1957) *Three centuries of the Westminster Shorter Catechism*. Fredericton, New Brunswick: University of New Brunswick Press.

Craik, H. (1896). *The state and its relation to education* (2nd ed.). London: Macmillan.

Davie, G. E. (1961). *The Democratic intellect: Scotland and her universities in the nineteenth century*. Edinburgh: Edinburgh University Press.

Dick, T. (1836). *On the mental illumination and moral improvement of mankind*. Glasgow: Collins.

Gelderen, M. von, & Skinner, Q. (2004). *Republicanism: A shared European heritage* (2 vols.). Cambridge: Cambridge University Press.

Grafton, A., & Jardine, L. (1986). *From humanism to the humanities: Education and the liberal arts in fifteenth and sixteen-century Europe*. London: Duckworth.

Green, I. (1996). *The Christian's ABC: Catechisms and catechizing in England c1530–1740*. Oxford: Clarendon Press.

Hamilton, D. (2002). From dialectic to didactic (with curriculum and textbooks in mind). *Paradigm (Journal of the Textbook Colloquium)*, 2(5), 15–24.

Hamilton, D. (2003, April 21–25). *Instruction in the making: Peter Ramus and the beginnings of modern schooling*. Paper presented at the annual convention of the American Educational Research Association, Chicago. Available at http://brs.leeds.ac.uk/~beiwww/beid.html.

Hesse, C. (2006). Towards a new topography of Enlightenment. *European Review of History*, 13 (3), 499–508.

Hotson, H. (2000). *Johann Heinrich Alsted 1588–1638: Between Renaissance, Reformation and universal reform*. Oxford: Clarendon Press.

Hotson, H. (2005). The instauration of the image of God in man: Humanist anthropology, encyclopaedic pedagogy, Baconianism and universal reform. In M. Pelling & S. Mandelbrote (Eds.) *The practice of reform in health, medicine and science,1500–2000* (pp. 1–21). Aldershot: Ashgate.

Hotson, H. (2007). *Commonplace learning: Ramism and its German ramifications 1543–1630*. Oxford: Oxford University Press.

Howell, W. S. (1975). Adam Smith's lectures on rhetoric: An historical assessment. In A. S. Skinner & T. Wilson (Eds.), *Essays on Adam Smith* (pp. 11–43). Oxford: Clarendon Press.

Illich, I. (1993). *In the vineyard of the text: A commentary to Hugh's Didascalicon*. Chicago: Chicago University Press.

Jaeger, C. S. (1994). *The envy of angels: Cathedral schools and social ideals in Medieval Europe, 950–1200*. Philadelphia: University of Pennsylvania Press.

Jardine, G. (1797). *Synopsis of lectures on logic and Belles Lettres read in the University of Glasgow*. Glasgow: At the University Press.

Jardine, G. (1825). *Outlines of philosophical education illustrated by the method of teaching the logic class in the University of Glasgow* (2nd. Ed.). Glasgow: Oliver & Boyd.

Johns, A. (1998). *The nature of the book: Print and knowledge in the making*. Chicago: University of Chicago Press.

Kant, I. (1960). *Education*. Ann Arbor: University of Michigan Press.

Miller, T. P. (1995). Frances Hutcheson and the civic humanist traditions. In A. Hook & R. B. Sher (Eds.), *The Glasgow Enlightenment* (pp. 40–55). East Linton, Scotland: Tuckwell Press.

Olson, P. A. (1995). *The Journey to Wisdom: Self-education in patristic and medieval literature*. Lincoln: University of Nebraska Press.

Ong, W. J. (1958). *Ramus, method and the decay of dialogue: From the art of discourse to the art of reason*. London: Harvard University Press.

Oz-Salzberger, F. (1995). *Translating the Enlightenment: Scottish civic discourse in eighteenth-century Germany*. Oxford: Clarendon Press.

Oz-Salzberger, F. (2006). The Enlightenment in translation: Regional and European Aspects. *European Review of History*, 13 (3), 385–409.

Padberg, J.W. (2000). Development of the Ratio Studiorum. In Vincent. J. Duminuco (Ed.), *The Jesuit Ratio Studiorum: 400th Anniversary Perspectives* (pp. 80-100). New York: Fordham University Press.

Skinner, Q. (1978). *Foundations of modern political thought* (vol. 1). Cambridge: Cambridge University Press.

Skinner, Q., & Stråth, B. (Eds.). (2003). *States, citizens: History, theory, prospects,* Cambridge: Cambridge University Press.

Smith, A. (1983). *Lectures on rhetoric and Belles Lettres* (J. C. Bryce, Ed.). Oxford: Clarendon Press.

Spedding, J., Ellis, R. L., & Heath, D. D. (Eds.). (1860). *The works of Francis Bacon.* London: Longman.

Withrington, D. (1965). Lists of Schoolmasters teaching Latin, 1690. *Miscellany of the Scottish History Society, 10,* 121–142.

Withrington, D. (1970). Education and society in the eighteenth century. In N. Philipson & R. Mitchison (Eds.), *Scotland in the Age of Improvement* (pp. 169–199). Edinburgh: Edinburgh University Press.

Wood, P. B. (1993). *The Aberdeen Enlightenment: The arts curriculum in the eighteenth century.* Aberdeen: Aberdeen University Press.

Wood, P. B. (2000). *The Scottish Enlightenment: Essays in reassessment.* Rochester, NY: Rochester University Press.

Part II
Organizing Schooling as Rationalizing Moral Codes

7 Republicanism "Out-of-Place"
Readings on the Circulation of Republicanism in Education in 19th-Century Argentina

Inés Dussel

INTRODUCTION: ON THE HISTORY OF LATIN AMERICAN IDEAS AND THE NOTION OF A "RIGHT PLACE" FOR REPUBLICANISM

This chapter deals with a question that is central to this book: How are we to understand the history of modern schooling and its relation to the language of republicanism in a way that makes room for a global perspective as well as for its local configurations? In their introduction, Tröhler, Popkewitz, and Labaree stress that the answer sides with a comparative history that understands that schooling and the political discourses and cultures that it mobilizes are not single or homogenous events but rather complex scaffoldings of technologies, ideas, and rationalities that are played out differently in different contexts and time frames.

The Latin American experience can provide a case in point to excavate the multifarious ways in which republicanism has been intertwined with the configuration of modern educational systems. And it also gives a good example to discuss the historiographic approach to the multiple ways in which the global articulates with the local. It is important to note that for most of the 19th and 20th centuries, that is, since its independent history, Latin American ideas have been read as an application—even if as a distorted or deviated one—of their European "original" counterparts. They have been considered as a derivative stance that has taken place when political modernism—coming from overseas—was juxtaposed into the social and economic backwardness and archaisms that prevailed on this side of the Atlantic Ocean (Palti, 2007). The model of "ideal types" and "applications or derivations" constituted a powerful frame for understanding the circulation and adoption of modern institutions and ideas.

Although in the 19th century this was not seen as particularly problematic, given that the "import" of European ideas was regarded as a sign of a civilizing attitude, by the turn of that century the affirmation of nationalistic narratives began to denounce and oppose "foreign ideologies" such as liberalism or positivism. Revisionist historiographies claimed that the "nation" resided in what was left when foreign and exotic ideas were substracted (a "substractive nationalism," as Schwarz [1997] has called it). The nation was the folkloric, pastoral life prior to the industrial and urbanization transformation; for most, it did exclude the pre-Hispanic aboriginal peoples, still considered as a menace or a backward influence, and included the Spanish heritage, sufficiently distant to be regarded as a civilizational impulse.

In 1977, the Brazilian cultural historian and literary critic Roberto Schwarz wrote an essay that challenged this view, which prevailed even in the leftist dependency theories of the 1960s and 1970s. Studying Latin American liberalism, he claimed that "liberal ideas could not be practiced but were at the same time completely impossible to reject" (Schwarz, 1977 p. 22). This was one of the constitutive paradoxes of Latin American societies; his favorite example was the Brazilian liberal constitution of 1822 that subscribed to republican ideals and the Declaration of the Rights of Man at the same time that it endorsed slavery. He advanced that the combination of the two was possible because liberal concepts functioned as legitimating ideals, but politicians and intellectuals assumed that liberalism, when introduced into the Brazilian society, was an "out-of-place idea" that had to be twisted and transformed in order to fit in the local society.

The consideration of liberalism and republicanism as "out-of-place" ideas has given way to sophisticated and ground-breaking analysis on the history and the sociology of culture in the region (García Canclini's *Hybrid Cultures (1996)* or Sarlo's *Una modernidad periférica (1988)* among them). In its effort to understand Latin American particularisms, this literature has looked at the peculiar ways in which modern institutions have been constructed in contexts in which politics and subjectivities were not organized in classical liberal terms.[1] Yet, as a growing critical literature has pointed, there is a risk in this kind of analysis. It may end up reproducing the "ideal-types and deformations" model, as the "out-of-placeness" assumes that there is a right place for ideas (see Palti, 2007, for a detailed discussion).

The study of the history of republican ideas in the education field across the globe runs a similar risk, which by now can be overtly termed as *Eurocentrism*. There is a Eurocentric vision that believes that *true* Republics can only emerge in European contexts—moreover, in European cities.[2] In order to avoid it, the historian has to give up the idea that there is a *true* republicanism or *false* deviations and instead look at the particular settings in which republican statements have been deployed, and how they have constituted a particular political language. But also, she has to perform a theoretical move so that different questions can emerge. If the project is not to find the true meaning of republican concepts (its semantic meaning) but its effects when spoken and set in motion in particular contexts (its pragmatic significance), then the focus should be put on understanding the range of alternatives that were available at a particular time and the contexts of debate in which they became possible.[3] As an Argentinean scholar has put it, one should look for "not how the pieces were moved, but how the playing field was itself transformed" (Palti, 2005, p. 475).

This chapter analyzes how the republican ideas were put into play in Argentinean education during the 19th century, trying to avoid the ideal-types model and incorporating the questions and methods of the new intellectual history (especially as understood in Palti, 2005, 2007). It will do so considering how these ideas were deployed in different moments, that of emancipation, that of the organization of the national state, and that of the turn of the century and the consolidation of nationalism.[4] It will follow the meanderings of the republican ideals through a turbulent century, with the project of debating against essentialist and purist notions of republicanism and of illuminating its accommodation to different political strategies. It will conclude discussing whether there is a right place for particular ideas or if ideas are always "out of place" in some respects.

There is a short story written by Jorge Luis Borges that is particularly enlightening for understanding how republicanism circulated, or became articulated into, pedagogical ideas in Argentina at the end of the 19th century. In Borges' fable, Pierre Ménard tried to re-write the book of Cervantes, "Don Quixote," exactly in the same way it had been written in the 17th century. Even in the act of literally transcribing it, Borges remarked, Pierre Ménard was already producing a different book. The same terms and phrases written by Cervantes meant completely different things in the context of the end of the 19th century in which supposedly Ménard worked. Pierre Ménard failed to write the Quixote again and felt utterly disappointed.

Disappointment was the feeling that several Argentinean republicans at the end of the 19th century expressed openly about the fate of their ideals. Domingo F. Sarmiento (1811–1888) and Juan Bautista Alberdi (1810–1884), two of the main thinkers and politicians in the mid-19th century who had strong intervention in the design of constitutional models, institutions, and policies for the new Argentinean republic, had that feeling by the end of their lives, which (some say unfortunately) were long enough to reach the end of the century and see what their ideal designs had brought into life (Botana, 1991). However, if one wants to avoid anachronistic readings, as well as the kind of empiricism that takes the words and dichotomies of the contemporaries in a literal and univocal way, one needs to put that sentiment aside. No disappointment, then, or ideal-type look that only sees disadjustments, infidelities, or degradations of the true version.

To end this introduction, I will use another quote, this time from the French historian Lucien Jaume. In reading the history of political ideas, he asks himself, "The right question is not 'Did Rousseau had any influence on the Jacobins?' because that question is undecidable, and also compares things that are not comparable; the question might be, 'Why certain Jacobins quoted Rousseau?' It is necessary to consider in which context, in which game. What makes room for another fertile question: 'Why did they stop quoting him in reference to the revolutionary government in Year II and during the Terror time?'" (Jaume, 2004, p. 118). It is to this articulation between discourse and action, what he calls the ideopraxis, that this chapter will intend to look at when considering the circulation of republican ideas in Argentina's education during the 19th century.

REPUBLICANISM AND EDUCATION AT THE MOMENT OF EMANCIPATION

The reader might be familiar with the magical realism that became Latin America's trademark in the 1960s. From García Márquez *One hundred years of solitude* (1972) onward, much of the region's history and present has been narrated in terms of a contradiction between historical and social inequalities and backwardness, and political and aesthetic inventiveness and creativity.[5] It is probably due to the effects of the "magical realist" narrative that many analysts consider Latin America as a non-republican context. Its baroque "logic of excess" seems at odds with the sensibilities and institutions of republicanism.

However, in fact, this perception should be surprising because this region was one of the first in the globe to fully endorse republicanism as a way of government (Halperin Donghi, 1987; Sábato, 2006) and to do it on a large scale. As early as the first half of the 19th century, most Latin American nations (themselves in the middle of defining territories, boundaries, identities) subscribed to the "republican adventure", which was essayed in different forms. Republic pre-dated the nation form or, to be more precise, "the adoption and put into practice of republican forms of government was previous to the consolidation of nations and constituted a main feature of their histories" (Sábato, 2006, p. 22). In Hilda Sábato's account, republican ideas were strong and powerful, and they nurtured both political projects and collective imaginaries. The nation was built upon republican grounds. "However conflictive it was, the adoption of a modern form of the nation, as an abstract entity of unique and undivided sovereignty and composed of free and equal individuals, was done by the half of the 19th century. And the nation was constructed with a modern way of representation, with popular representatives emerging out of citizens' choice"(Sábato, 2006, p. 24).

In the case of Argentina, as early as 1810, with the emancipation of the Spanish crown, republican ideas and projects played a significant role in the organization of the nation. At the time of the independence (1816), it became clear that monarchic proponents were a small minority and that the majority of the independence leaders adhered to republicanism. As Carmen McEvoy (1999) has shown, they did not appeal to the *Ancien Régime* mechanisms to solve the problems of social and political organization of the new spaces; rather, they creatively rewrote republican ideals, as in the case of Bernardo de Monteagudo, an Argentinean lawyer who fought in Argentina, Chile, and Peru and became a sort of prime minister of the latter.

Following Sábato, in Latin America there were three initiatives that locked together the nation and the republic: elections, militias, and the institutions of public opinion. In Argentina, universal masculine suffrage was proclaimed as early as 1821 (although the reality of elections was far from democratic) (Sábato, 1997). The formation of popular militias had actually begun before the emancipation, with the attempt of an English fleet to invade Buenos Aires in 1806–1807. The experience of the "people in arms" was, according to some historians, one of the main catalysts in the process of independence, as the local elites and the city neighbors had had the experience of popular organization and successful military action against the British invaders (González Bernaldo, 1999).

But it is to the institutions of public opinions to which we should address our attention because education was ranked first among them, together with the press. In 1810, one of the first measures of the newly constituted First Council of Government (Primera Junta de Gobierno) was to translate Rousseau's *Social Contract* in order to be used as a civic catechism.[6] Schools for "the first letters" (primeras letras) were created on the charge of the *Cabildos* or City Councils because citizenship was intrinsically linked to literacy. Liberal conceptualizations of childhood were central to most of the revolutionary leadership. This can be traced through the debates on corporal punishment, which was abolished several times, as many times as it was re-instituted, during the first decades of the 19th century. Even the national congress that was meeting to write a national constitution revoked it in 1817, giving the affair a national prominence. In 1819 the government produced a new decree that turned it into anathema:

> [The government] cannot ignore the transcendental aspects of this abuse [corporal punishment], nor the influence it has in degrading the youth who ought to be educated for the service of the Fatherland with decency and with honor. The objections raised by the schools' principals against the just measures of the Government in this regard are so worthless as not to merit a response. (quoted in Szuchman, 1988, p. 112)

Historian Mark Szuchman has provided an account of educational practices at that time that shows the ambivalence or contradictions that republican ideas on education faced when set into practice. In many respects these contradictions can be seen as products of the emerging tensions between classical republicanism and modern republicanism, with its praise of individual freedom and autonomy. Yet, the idea of a republic that is based on a strict system of hierarchies and authorities is the prevalent one at the beginning of the 19th century.

This can be seen in teaching of *urbanidad* or manners, which was one of the aspects that education emphasized for the formation of a literate citizenship. Interestingly, it had little to do with autonomy or self-government and much more to do with the respect of authority and on the learning of "decent" habits. An exercise on handwriting done by a student at the barrio of San Telmo in 1817 makes these prescriptions evident:

> A person must be very conscious of himself at the dinner table, since it is there that he must observe an infinite number of rules in order to avoid all forms of rudeness and ill-breeding. Parting from the notion that cleanliness is never more necessary than at the table, the Child will wash his hands after all other persons superior to him have done so, taking care not to wash them at the same time as these others, unless he is expressly not forbidden to do so, in which case the man-servant should be nearby to provide a towel. (quoted in Szuchman, 1988, p. 158)

What is striking in this example is the explicit and repeated enforcement of authority over the notion of cleanliness or hygiene, which would become prevalent by the end of the century. For children, it is more important not to break the hierarchy than to have their hands cleaned (an act backed by the authority of science, but which apparently was not as powerful as traditional authority). Also, there is a loose reference to a code of elegance, a certain notion of performance of the whole operation that enacts social and cultural values: The man-servant being nearby to provide a towel is an important aside, a secondary intervention in the play, reinforcing at its turn that the little man, the child, is also a privileged character.[7]

The learning of obedience implied also an education of the body that circumscribed and restricted the movements that the young child could make. Again, historian Mark Szuchman provides a wonderful example in another handwriting assignment that was left incomplete by the student Mariano Rivero:

> A hurried walking cadence is seen poorly, as is the heavy step, while the artificial and effeminate form of walking suggests arrogance or shallowness. Shaking the body, or walking in a slanted fashion, or too straight, is. . . . (quoted in Szuchman, 1988, p. 159)

The parallels with the teachings of the Lasallean Brothers are remarkable, and in fact the textbooks on manners used by children at that time were most likely updated versions of the same manuals themselves. According to different sources, in early 19th-century Argentina, young women were still educated through Juan Luis Vives' "The Education of the Christian Woman" (1524) (Braccio, 1999), and young men read the "Catón Cristiano"and Patriotic Catechisms (Cucuzza, 1997). The "Catón," whose first version was written in 1494, was a small book that included short sentences and morals and was used as a reading practicum, a third step in the teaching of literacy after the primers and writing books (Demerson, 1985). It persisted across centuries and shows how the genre of manuals on manners has its own dynamic (for an example on the U.S. case, see Arditi, 1999).

The "Patriotic Catechism" is also an interesting text to consider in terms of the relationships to authority and to knowledge that it assumed, and it shows to what extent there were much more complex processes at stake than a simple adoption of republican ideas. The catechisms, as it is well known, are books for transmitting religious faith organized under the format of questions and answers. The catechisms laid strongly on memory and repetition and were originally thought of as an oral device.[8] But during the Enlightenment, they received new impulses from the emerging pedagogical sciences, and they served the purposes of instructing numerous children (see Dussel & Caruso, 2000). The catechism broke down the content to be taught into several small pieces and intended to cover the whole array of questions to be raised about a subject. Thus, it contributed to defining a universe of "thinkables and unthinkables," and in a way it ensured a more pervasive disciplining of the thoughts of children than simply telling a fable or morale.[9]

During the independence wars, the new authorities wrote a "Patriotic Catechism" that was supposed to replace the Spanish version of the catechism, written by Father Astete. This new catechism was called "Public Catechism for the Instruction of the Neophytes or Recently Converted to the Guild of the Patriotic Society" and was published between 1810 and 1811 (Cucuzza, 1997). One of its lectures read:

> *Question:* Tell me, sons, is there somebody who has to rule us?
> *Answer:* Yes, Father, there is He who has to rule us.
> *Q:* How many have to rule us?
> *A:* Just one.
> *Q:* Where is He who has to rule us?
> *A:* In Spain, in Chile, and any place.
> *Q:* Who is He who has to rule us?
> *A:* The People and its Representatives, and the City government, which are three and the same thing (...)
> *Q:* According to what you are saying, those who are set to discredit the Juntas, picturing them as a monster destroying the Americas, are in fact their enemies, and are trying to ruin them.
> *A:* It is human faith.
> *Q:* You do believe so.
> *A:* I do believe so. (quoted in Cucuzza, 1997, pp. 7–8)

What becomes visible in these examples is that the children were thought of as calculable, manageable bodies, but not as calculating, self-administered selves. As Nikolas Rose (1999) has said in relation to colonial government, disciplinary technologies were deployed "in the service of order and docility rather than self-regulated liberty" (p. 109). The "order and docility" has to be related in this case to previous experience and to the reshaping of political, racial, and social hierarchies in the post-colonial world (Dávilo, 1998).

In 1821, under the lead of a liberal politician, Bernardino Rivadavia,[10] elementary schools started to depend on the University of Buenos Aires, following the Napoleonic model of an educational system topped and run by the university. It was, among others, due to Rivadavia's impulse that the 1826 Constitution endorsed the republican form of government. Although it had a short life (in 1827 there was a secession from several provinces and the idea of a republican nation declined), it nonetheless marked a point to which antagonic groups would refer in the next three decades.

REPUBLICANISM AND EDUCATION IN THE MID-19TH CENTURY: UTOPIAN DESIGNS, "DISAPPOINTING" REALITIES

But it was in the 1850s that a vigorous effort to expand primary schooling took place. After several years of civil wars led by provincial leaders (*caudillos*), in 1853 a new Constitution was passed that proclaimed the republic. Bartolomé Mitre, one of the first presidents of the new republic, thought that they were just developing what had already been there since the emancipation: "The South American revolution was essentially republican, and the frustration of monarchic tendencies in the long course of its development shows that historically it was refractory to monarchy" (quoted in Botana & Gallo, 1997, p. 25). In his view, as well as in his contemporaries, the republicanization of the whole world was an unstoppable force since the 18th-century revolutions.

For this generation, strong believers of liberalism, education was to civilize the plebe that had been mobilized during the independence and civil wars, forming a citizenship that would stop backing the provincial leaders and embrace the liberal ideals. Pacifying and disarming the people in arms, bringing civilization to rural areas, and transforming the backwardness and ignorance into republican virtues were the aims of the new national endeavor. The republican order and the national union imagined by the liberal *elite* would rest on this "literate citizenship" (Sábato, 1992) educated by the schools.

Among this generation, Domingo Faustino Sarmiento (1811–1888) stands as a canonical figure in the development of education—some kind of *founding father* of schools.[11] An intellectual and thinker formed by the exile during the civil wars, Sarmiento is a representative of the republicanism that was deemed *feasible* in this part of the world. He was part of the "lettered elite" that admired Europe and that tried to adapt the utopian ideas to the social realities of South America. In an essay written in 1845, "Facundo: Civilization or Barbarism," Sarmiento sought to understand the "origin of the Argentine tragedy—as he called the civilian wars that followed the independence from Spain. He found a cultural explanation: "Barbarism" was the obstacle for unifying the nation. It could be healed through a series of actions that ranged from extermination ("The Pampas have to be watered with the gauchos' blood," he claimed unapologetically) (cf. Puiggrós, 1990) to immigration and education. The immigration that he had in mind was the Northern European, Protestant family, which he pictured as hardworking and austere.

The "civilization vs. barbarism" opposition was a powerful one, and it structured the analytical and political frames not only of the Argentine elite but also of many other Latin American countries (see Rojas de Ferro, 1995). Practicing what has been called "internal colonialism" (Mignolo, 2000, 281),[12] these intellectuals adopted the European model as the one to be imitated and considered that indigenous practices were "vices to be eradicated" (Rojas de Ferro, 1995). Civilization implied a process of whitening (as seen in the whitening of Rivadavia and other patriotic heros), in which the non-white identities (Natives, Blacks, Mestizos) were to be suppressed either through the transplanting of a new, white population into the Pampas or through acculturation ("education"). This frame defined the nation in cosmopolitan terms: As the Constitution of the unified state in 1853 said, the Argentine Republic would welcome "all those who would like to inhabit Argentine soil."

In 1845–1848, Sarmiento traveled extensively to Europe and North America in the charge of the Chilean government (where he spent most of his exile years in the 1840s due to internal civil wars) in order to produce reports on their educational systems. Interestingly, he was caught by the U.S. experience, which he found much more advanced and progressive than the European one, and he exchanged correspondence with Horace and Mary Mann, of whom he became a follower. Upon his return to Argentina, he was appointed as the head of the Education Department of the province of Buenos Aires (1856–1862), the largest of the country. From 1868 to 1874, he was president of the Argentine Republic; when he retired, he came back to the Department of Education of the province of Buenos Aires (1880–1884). He died in Paraguay in 1888, in another sort of exile, this time from his political enemies.

Sarmiento's ideas are interesting to analyze the paths of republicanism in Argentina's education. A self-proclaimed republican, he believed that education was to be the ground for the formation of solid institutions. In the first part of his seminal work, titled *Popular Education*, written in 1845 in Chile, he wrote:

> Up to now two centuries there was education for the ruling classes, for the priesthood and for the aristocracy; but the people, the *plebe*, did not conform, strictly speaking, active part of the nations (...) Public Instruction has as an objective to prepare the new generations (...) and the nations in mass for the use of rights that today belong

to some or other class. (Sarmiento, 2001, p. 7; quoted in Oria, 2006, p. 3, her translation)

Republican education was to provide the "cement" to overcome social and ethnic divisions. At that time, he was a strong supporter of social initiatives and thought that the public system of education should have a mixed tax funding and a participatory way of government through local councils and boards. In relation to taxing, he said that:

> The most perfect system of tax and public administration has political advantages which can't be neglected. Leaving the funding and management of the education to the people is vital in order to make them grow in the practice of self-government. This is not at all an innocent element of public action. In contrast, those expenditures that come all the way from the top, and all those interventions of the state in affairs that affect the people who are left without any influence, only extends their generalised indifference. (Sarmiento, 2001, p. 354; quoted in Oria, 2006, p. 7, her translation)

For Sarmiento, elementary education was a pivotal center of the society that he was designing. Thus, he believed that popular participation should be combined with a strong commitment by the state, which would ensure that all got what they needed:

> Primary education constitutes a branch of the public administration. The State is in charge of education, it controls it and inspects it. Towns, divided in school districts, determine taxes, enforce their payment and decide on investments (...) *The State does not finance education*. Self-interest and the fatherly love in each town will provide the school's with an income, via contributions that will benefit their own children, as well as the children of the poor families in their communities. (Sarmiento, 2001, p. 63)

He devoted several pages of his work on popular education, and also many articles in newspapers, to grammar and orthographic issues. As Angel Rama has said, this generation of republicans believed that writing was the epitome of knowledge and civilization. There was a particular "reverence towards writing," a confidence on the letter (an insistence on the letter, as Bill Green [1989] has said) that might be at the basis of popular culture's revolt against it (and the appeal of ironic characters such as Cantinflas in Mexico or Catita in Argentina in the 1940s, when this reverence started to decline). It is remarkable that one of the "founding fathers" of Latin American pedagogy, Simón Rodríguez, tutor to Simón Bolivar (and today's hero in Chávez' Venezuelan educational reform), proposed that "words be drawn with signs that represent the mouth," so that citizens would master the most needed art: "the art of drawing Republics"(quoted in Rama, 1996, p. 45).

But Sarmiento belonged to the party of the letter, the grammar, the orthography. At the time he advanced his ideas on popular education, he also wrote the *Facundo*, in which, as has been said before, he posited the opposition between civilization and barbarism, and where he judged that "indigenous forces" were to be fought and exterminated by the school or by the army. He had an ambivalent opinion of the social forces that were supposed to ensure the success of his utopian design: On the one hand, he considered them indispensable in the control and funding of the educational system, but on the other hand, he thought they were potentially dangerous, apathic, ignorant, and immoral. That ambivalence and contradiction can be seen in the following statement:

> I hope the government finds cooperation from the people, as small as it may be, and that the generalised state of apathy that characterises our populace doesn't get the government stuck along with all the resources it is now putting into such noble end. We shall not get tired of repeating it: every government action tending to the improvement of society is slow in its results, and not always achieves the desired results. The government can only help impulses emerging from the heart of society. (Sarmiento, 2001, p. 263; quoted in Oria, p. 9, her translation)

As he got into action, first as Head of Education for the province of Buenos Aires and later as President of the Republic, his design became less and less confident on society´s impulse. His equivalence between "public instruction" and "popular education" soon implied that the public was conflated with the state's intervention. He designed an increasingly centralized educational system of public instruction, with national control over teacher training and secondary schooling (directly organized and funded by the national government), and a National Council of Education that had to oversee curriculum and expenditure for the whole country.

Sarmiento thought of the republic not only as an institutional design but also as a moral cement for the country. "Those who know how to read usually dress tidier and have greater order and method in all their actions, as well as a constant aspiration to improve their condition" (Sarmiento, 2001, p. 35). Schools should serve as the "internal police of the people" and would also reduce crime and delinquency: "The instruction moralises the population, for there are more accused among the illiterate than among the ones that have received some instruction" (Sarmiento, 2001, p. 31). Republicanism became a moral discourse in an association that would prove fertile for education and pedagogy during the 20th century.

During his years as an administrator, this tension between confidence and disavowal of civil society and participation became more and more important in Sarmiento. That can be seen in his own efforts to organize local Boards of Education following the U.S. example, which were frustrated when the social participation he cherished did not have the results he intended but instead produced the occupation of civic spaces by political *cliques*. Sarmiento ended up supporting their suppression or marginalization (Caruso & Dussel, 1996).

This tendency to centralization became more evident in the 1880s, when the laws establishing compulsory and free education were passed, and the school councils were effaced from legislation. Angela Oría (2006) refers to this process as follows: "In a Report to Congress in 1884, Minister Eduardo Wilde wrote: 'It seems like modern societies have already consecrated as a doctrine inherent to civilization this tripod which serves as the grounds of legislation on "*popular* education": compulsory instruction; *free* instruction; non-religious instruction.'" She goes on to ask herself: "Popular education is deployed in an opposite way and the components of this fundamental 'tripod' are characterized as 'inherent' or essential to civilization. A 'reversal of a relationship of forces, an usurpation of power, an appropriation of a vocabulary turned against those who had once used it'? (Foucault, 1971, p. 21)" (Oria, 2006, p. 14). Sarmiento's essays of a republicanism that combined top-down reforms with social participation ended up in a clear failure; however, as noted earlier, this did not prevent him from becoming an educational hero, whose memory is still revered in Argentinean schools.

REPUBLICANISM AT THE TURN OF THE 19TH CENTURY: THE NATION AS INTEGRATIVE IDEAL

If Sarmiento's republican design was in the line of a cosmopolitan self, which nonetheless acknowledged the realities of what he thought were local failures or weaknesses, the generation that followed him slowly changed the balance between the republic and the nation. What was needed, in order to overcome the continuous civil conflicts, was a strong republic, a kind of conservative reformism that should centralize power and set a sustainable order. In the 1880s, another political party took over not only the government but also the intellectual field. The "unicato" system (a one-party system) was established under two main principles: peace and administration.

During this period, which extended itself until 1912 (with several revolutionary attempts in the middle), the nation became the integrative ideal. If Sarmiento's generation still doubted between confidence and disavowal of social action, the 1880s generation chose disavowal and opted for a top-down definition of citizenship that claimed to be equally republican. The nation was to be the superior self to which particularisms and localisms should be subsumed. Education, as has been said before, was to play another major role in the development of a national self.

Republicanism "Out-of-Place" 143

There are many studies on the contribution of schooling to the building of nation-states in the 19th century. These studies have generally assumed that one can derive from an account of prevailing ideologies "evidence about the organization of the mundane everyday practices and presuppositions that shape the conduct of human beings in particular sites and practices" (Rose, 1997, p. 128). Again, one can see here a derivative stance that, although much criticized in recent critical theory (Dean, 1994), has been nonetheless productive. Scholars have looked at history and geography textbooks, civic lessons, military and gymnastic disciplines, among other traces, to see how particular narratives of nationhood have been constructed. In these works, "school history" appears as much more patriotic and state-oriented than the university discipline, and it seems to have operated through the selection of historical characters and events so as to produce coherent and teleological narratives on the nation. Characteristically, Ernest Lavisse, one of the most prolific writers of history textbooks at the turn of the century in France, said that, "The history of France is, in many aspects, no more than a set of examples for a civics textbook" (quoted in Gagliano, 1991, p. 290).[13]

Another line of investigation has been the domain of rituals. Civic festivities, patriotic feasts, and the use of national symbols like the flag, the national anthem, and national heroes have also been part of the cement of this new solidarity.

Rituals were particularly important in Argentinean schools, closely tied to military and religious practices (Amuchástegui, 1995). It has been said that what was at stake was a certain "order of the signs," a particular grammar that intended to construct an order in what was perceived as a disordered social life (Rama, 1996). This grammar, transformed in the morality of the state, deployed itself not only in textbooks or in the glotopolitics (politics of language, privileging the standard Spanish against localisms, "barbarisms," "alienisms," etc.), but also in a monumental politics, a monumentalization of memory that renders invisible the plurality of bodies, gestures, sexualities, rhythms, and tones. Through the construction of monuments and buildings ("the most significant markers" according to the European image of "culture") (cf. Shapiro, 1997, p. 23), "the monumental space renders invisible the conflict of memories" (Barbero, 2006, p. 238). Statues epitomized which events and characters were to be included in the national pantheon of heroes and which ones would be excluded, and they were especially powerful due to their spread distribution across the city. One of the leading intellectuals of the nationalistic movement in the first decades of the century said that:

> History is not only taught in class lessons: the historical sense, without which lessons are sterile, is formed in the spectacle of daily life, in the traditional names of places, in the sites that are associated to heroic memories, in the remains and pieces preserved at museums, and even in the commemorative monuments, whose influence on the imagination I

have called *the pedagogy of statues*. (Ricardo Rojas, Nationalist Restoration, 1909, quoted in Gorelik, 1998, p. 206)

For example, in the capital city, Buenos Aires, during the first decade of the 20th century, there were hard debates around the statue erected in honor of the Italian leader Garibaldi in 1907, and an older one to pay homage to Mazzini in a central square near the city's port, erected in 1878 (Gorelik, 1998). Both were the object of severe scrutiny and complain due to their association to Italy. Whereas decades before, the statues symbolized cosmopolitan values (liberalism, republicanism) that were thought to be central to the newly constituted Argentine republic, by the turn of the century the nationalism that became prevalent was too exclusivist and chauvinist to tolerate the integration of foreign heroes in the national pantheon. One can clearly see the shift from a republican nationalism to a nationalism that marginalizes its republican heroes.[14]

These debates were also expressed in the urban plans for the modernization of cities. Buenos Aires was perceived by part of the elite as an enemy, a cosmopolitan monster. Its central avenue, Avenida de Mayo (in honor of the month of the Revolution), was seen as a mask ball that represented the new civic barbarism, the new rich immigrants. The historian Ricardo Rojas updated Sarmiento's opposition between civilization and barbarism in terms of urban decay and degeneration: "[Barbarism's] theatre is the city, and no longer the country; the barbarians do not ride horses but tramways" (quoted in Gorelik, 1998, p. 214). The monuments and statues had to stand in opposition to the city, producing a new sense of the past as a collection of patriotic icons (Gorelik, 1998, p. 216). This conviction led Rojas to build his Buenos Aires house imitating the façade of the building in which independence from Spain was declared in the northern province of Tucumán. This house, already demolished, was for him the symbol of the "true," authentic nation, against the urban Babel that mixed all styles and confused all symbols. He declared in his will that his house should be transformed into a museum after his death. The "invention of tradition" of which Eric Hobsbawm and Terence Ranger have talked is clearly at work: The creation of a historical house in the 1920s was to be transformed into a landmark of Argentina's memory of the early 19th century.

The school system participated actively in this campaign (which was called the "Patriotic Crusade" in 1908–1912), policing the boundaries of "proper Spanish," "proper memories," and "proper rules."[15] One school officer, Juan P. Ramos, wrote in a seminal report on the state of schools in 1910:

> We have not known yet how to make schools contribute to affirm the principle of nationality . . . We have lacked the aptitude to be a melting pot . . . Collective persuasion, produced by imitation, is unavoidable during the childhood years . . . We lacked the principle of a national school textbook, even of a national history itself from which we only

knew the chronicle and fragmented episodes. [From now on,] We have to establish a patriotic cult in schools, a cult for our Patriotic symbols and heroes, we have to retain the facts, the dates, and the names in our national history. (Juan P. Ramos, History of Public Instruction in Argentina, 1810–1910; quoted in Quatrocchi de Woisson, 1995, p. 41)

Patriotic rituals and "liturgy," as Gorelik calls them, became part of the daily life of schools. The honoring of the flag, the marching ceremonies of patriotic celebrations, and mural paintings and inscriptions proliferated across the country. This shift can be observed in the transformation of school rituals. Whereas in the last decades of the 19th century there was a day that commemorated "The Tree," celebrating nature and its positivistic laws, in the first decades of the 20th century it disappeared and gave way to a continuous schedule of patriotic feasts commemorating independence, revolution, the founding fathers, and the "discovery of America." Also, it should be noted that Andrés Rodríguez, the writer of one of the best-selling textbook of all times, "El Nene" ("The Kid," 1895, reprinted as late as the 1940s), started writing a series of books that were called "The Patriot," "The Family," and "The Soldier." The space of the "child" had to be filled with particular semantic associations attached to this militaristic nationalism.

The teaching of shooting was introduced for the upper grades of elementary schools (only for boys), and between 1911 and 1915 there were short experiences of "school battalions" that taught military drills to children.[16]

Classrooms were permeated with this patriotic impulse, which became quite chauvinistic. A report from a foreigner in 1915 recalled the following scene in a classroom:

> *Q:* How do you esteem yourself in relation to your compatriots?
> *A:* I consider myself bound to them as a sentiment unites us.
> *Q:* And what is that?
> *A:* The sentiment that the Argentine Republic is the finest country on earth.
> *Q:* What is the duty of a good citizen?
> *A:* First of all to love his country.
> *Q:* Even before his parents?
> *A:* Before all. (quoted in Spalding, 1972, pp. 44–45)

The nation or Fatherland was thus turned into the best representative of the collective body, which was to be placed above all other authorities. One can confront this dialogue with the Patriotic Catechism quoted in the first section of this chapter and see, on the one hand, the continuities in the format of instruction and, on the other hand, the replacement of the collective will or the republican ideals of the People by the Nation, following the trend of European nationalisms of the late 19th century (Hobsbawm, 1990).

This late 19th-century republicanism, then, is hardly recognizable as the heir of the early emancipation ideals and Sarmiento's utopian designs.

However, one should not forget that these practices were performed using the language of republicanism, and that among its effects stands the configuration of a lettered citizenship, to a degree that by 1930 Argentina had higher school enrolment rates than many Southern European countries (Puiggrós, 1990). How should we understand these combinations of republican ideas and different political projects? The last section will discuss some possible answers.

CONCLUDING REMARKS

Throughout the chapter, I have tried to show that the language of republicanism was central to the emergence of a modern educational system in Argentina and that it underwent significant shifts and transformations throughout the period considered. In the analysis of three different moments where republican ideas were significant in education, the emphasis has been put on the tensions and contradictions involved in the mobilization of the language of republicanism, on the different strategies to which it became associated, and on which challenges it intended to respond. Moreover, as said in the introduction, the focus was put on how the playing field itself got transformed. From a society that was highly mobile and was discussing how to organize itself, to a very centralized state that led patriotic crusades in order to produce a homogeneous citizenship, the contexts in which the pragmatics of the republican statements should be understood changed dramatically.

In the first moment, that of emancipation, Republican ideas were brought into play to support the fight against the Spanish rule and to promote the cause of liberty. The translation of Rousseau's *Social Contract* as a reading primer, the advancement of public instruction, and the abolishment of corporal punishment co-existed with the persistence of practices where traditional authority was enforced. Thus, it would not be easy to call it a "liberal republicanism," even though many of its supporters considered themselves as liberal thinkers. Citizens were supposed to be calculable, manageable bodies, but they were not educated as calculating, self-administered selves. To read this as a distortion or a deviation from republican ideals ignores that much of the same contradictions were visible in European countries in the tensions between classical and modern republicanism, and also that they speak of particular political fields and specific historicities (as in the case of Patriotic catechisms) and of the singular political coalitions within which the republican language was mobilized.

The second moment, in mid-19th century, is the time of the organization of the nation-state. To illustrate this generation of thinkers, the figure of Domingo Sarmiento, one of the most notorious republican *ideologues* and politicians and a main figure in the development of the educational system, was chosen. Sarmiento thought of the republic not only as an institutional design (e.g., when devising the tax system or the education participatory government) but also as a moral cement for the country, whose values would be disseminated by schools. Building an opposition between "civilization" (republic, schools, Western ideals, industries, and cities) and "barbarism" (gauchos, indigenous peoples, and rural lands), he constructed a powerful political rhetoric for the republic that would persist for decades. During his own life, he became disenchanted with the results of civic participation and supported the abandonment of local boards and civic participation in education.

The third moment was that of the consolidation of an exclusionary nationalism, which put the nation above the republic. Through a monumental pedagogy, patriotic rituals and liturgy, school textbooks and syllabi, the educational system turned into a fabulous assimilation machine for the thousands of immigrants who were coming to Argentina. Less worried with the political dimensions of participation and more concerned with a cultural and moral cement for the masses, the generation of conservative republicans who led the expansion of the educational system were very successful in the configuration of a lettered citizenship.

Throughout my analysis I have stressed discontinuities, but the appeal to the republican language remained a common trait across these disparate projects. The defense of anti-monarchic systems and of modernist traditions, as well as a definition of a common morality and a participatory self, are elements that are present in all three moments. However, one should avoid trying to "capture" specific traits of republican discourses because it is possible to find contradictions or ambivalences everywhere. As Elias Palti (2005) says, to define republican language is "precisely to determine everything that separates ourselves from it; that is, the network of assumptions on which they were built upon, that include scientific reasons, ideas about temporality, visions of nature, etc., completely alien or strange to us. To do the history of languages it is not enough to point at the crossroads or interactions between discourses, to underline the shifts in their problematics; it is also necessary to inquire into the thresholds that determine their historicity, that which gives them a principle of temporal irreversibility" (pp. 489–490). That those republicanisms might seem at odds with our own views on these issues should not prevent us from reading how republican ideas were articulated and within which projects they were mobilized.

Does this mean that anything goes, that no distinctions could be made between different readings and circulations of republican ideas? Of course not. Roberto Schwarz, whom I quoted at the beginning of this chapter, says that when studying the history of liberal or republican ideas in Latin America, it is useless to insist on their obvious falseness; on the contrary, "one should observe their dynamic, of which their falseness is a true component" (Schwarz, 1977, p. 26). "False" or "right," republicanism circulated widely among Latin American educators during the 19th century and was integrated into utopian designs and conservative daily practices. And in that respect, it was never out of place: paraphrasing Elias Palti's remarks for liberalism, one could say that if republican ideas were brought and mobilized for different purposes, that means that there were already conditions for this political language to be read and put into use. Argentina proved to be a good place for republicanism, at least as good as any other place.

NOTES

1. It has also pointed to the complexities of the liberal ideas themselves in their European contexts (cf. Guerra, 1993; Hale, 1991). I have dealt with this issue in Chapters 3 and 4 of my doctoral dissertation, discussing how pedagogical rationalities "imported" from Europe assumed a calculating subject that was far from the concrete social interactions and practices that prevailed in Argentinean society (Dussel, 2001).
2. McIntyre's *After Virtue (1981)* is an example of such a view. When I say "Eurocentric," I mean the kind of reading that has been done by postcolonial theory, which emphasizes the intertwining of locality and knowledge. As it has been said, "Europe" itself is a geopolitical category that needs to be rethought, questioned, rubbed against what it is deemed to represent, and how it is mobilized for or against particular causes at singular times. For such an analysis, see Bauman (2004).
3. Context is not to be understood as the "material structures" that explain "superstructure productions"—as in determinist Marxism—but as built into the texts, as the language game, the playing fields, the discursive constructions in which particular statements arise.
4. The analysis will be shorter than needed for the sake of the argument and for space reasons. Each of these moments has been analyzed in depth by several scholars, and I have studied them at length in my doctoral dissertation (Dussel, 2001). But I hope that showing these three moments together will help the argument of historicizing republicanism in a non-historicist way, that is, stop considering it as an ideal that was distorted or wrongly applied in different settings, but also not reducing it to particular contexts and understanding how it has its own historicity, how it constitutes a political language that recognizes links and traditions, and whose political weight is determined by that very fact.
5. That this rhetorical trope has many links with revisionist historiographies and has given way to neo-nationalistic narratives has not gone unexamined (see e.g., Schwarz, 1997).
6. It is interesting to note that Mariano Moreno, his translator and one of the more radical advocates of Rousseauianism at this time, censored the chapter on religious beliefs, arguing that Rousseau must have had a "temporal dementia" when he wrote his anti-Catholic diatribe (Weinberg, 1984). One can see how the politics of translation is a complex one: Rousseau's followers in Argentina chose to position themselves in close alliance to the Catholic Church, and this seems to have been productive, at least initially, if one looks at the numbers of priests enrolled in the patriotic army.
7. Szuchman provides yet another example of an assignment in which obedience is THE precept to be taught to children: "The fourth [sic] Commandment of the Decalogue indicates to us in the strongest fashion the reverence and respect that must be shown toward our parents. It is the first precept imposed on us by the second tablet of the Law of Grace, and which must be

obeyed in the strictest fashion after the first three precepts of the first tablet which refer to God. The Child will look with horror upon all deeds or words that may be interpreted as disobedience, contempt, mockery, or inattention toward his Parents. He will kiss their hands upon entering the house or wherever He encounters them" (quoted in Szuchman, 1988, p. 158).
8. According to Rubén Cucuzza (1997), "catechismus" in Medieval Latin meant "instruction in loud voice."
9. I thank Marcelo Caruso for pointing out this use of catechism to me.
10. Rivadavia remains an interesting character in Argentina's history. He was called "the Chocolate president" by his contemporaries presumably because of his African descent, which is obvious in the paintings and portraits of his time; but he was "whitened" by the official historiography that emerged in the 1880s, and the portraits made by the end of the 19th century depict him as a white man (see e.g., the lithographs at the National Historic Museum in Buenos Aires).
11. There is an Anthem for Sarmiento that is sung in Argentinean schools that ends up saying: "Father of the classroom, immortal Sarmiento" (Padre del aula, Sarmiento immortal). Generations of normal school teachers were educated in Sarmiento's ideas and considered themselves his heirs (the "sarmientinos/as").
12. Sarmiento wrote an early autobiography in which he claims that, while he was crossing the Andes Mountains from San Juan, his native province, to Chile, going into exile, he wrote on a stone: On ne tue pas les idées (ideas cannot be killed) in French!
13. One interesting example on this line of inquiry is provided by some French historians of education who have studied how textbooks written between 1870 and 1914 dealt with the defeat against the Prussians and their annexation of Alsace-Lorraine. The most popular primary school textbook at that time, *Le Tour de la France*, consisted of a narration by two siblings, a boy and a girl, born in Alsace and whose parents had perished in the Franco–Prussian war. The kids travel across France looking for their relatives and observe its geography and get to know about its history. Thus, they "learn" to love their country, and by the end of the tale, they express their readiness to become soldiers or teachers (Caspard, 1984). Coincidentally with Ernest Renan's remarks that forgetting the violence underlying the unity was crucial for the development of nations (Renan, 1882/1990), this story of reconciliation neglects the traces of the divisions in the country and of the exclusions that constituted the nation.
14. It is not a matter of European vs. non-European symbols. Gorelik notes that, paradoxically, the sculptors and aesthetic patterns used to produce the nationalistic statues were also of European origins, showing that the quest for an "authentic" national style was more of a winding road than a clear-cut pathway.
15. This campaign did not limit itself to schooling. Urban historian Adrián Gorelik shows in the following example the extent to which this ritualization penetrated daily life: "The patriotic liturgy invades different realms, and in this movement several institutions and discursive supports are added. [For example,] As an homage to the centenary of our country, the oil 'Bou' gives to Argentine children a copy of a plate belonging to General José de San Martín [a hero in the war against the Spaniards], as exhibited in the Historical Museum, adhering to the motto with which the English reproduced the dinner service of Admiral Nelson: 'to eat in the plate of a hero is to be inflamed with the fire of the highest patriotism'" ("Caras y Caretas", Buenos Aires, January 21, 1911, quoted in: Gorelik, 1998, p. 217).

16. As it has been said, the use of military metaphors and technologies had been in vogue before this chauvinistic movement. Shooting was introduced into the school curriculum in 1902. The "school battalions" imitated a French experience that was instituted after the defeat against Prussia in 1871.

REFERENCES

Amuchástegui, M. (1995). Los rituales patrióticos en la escuela pública. In A. Puiggrós (Ed.), *Discursos pedagógicos e imaginario social en el peronismo (1945–1955)* (pp. 13–41). Buenos Aires: Galerna.
Anderson, B. (1990). *Imagined communities*. London: Verso.
Arditi, J. (1999). Etiquette Books, Discourse, and the Deployment of the Order of Things. *Theory, Culture & Society*, 16 (4): 25-48.
Armus, D. (2000). El descubrimiento de la enfermedad como problema social. In M. Lobato (Ed.), *Nueva Historia Argentina. El progreso, la modernización y sus límites (1880–1916)* (pp. 507–551). Buenos Aires: Editorial Sudamericana.
Balibar, R., & Laporte, D. (1976). *Le Français National*. Paris: Hachette.
Barbero, J.M. (2006). La razón técnica desafía a la razón escolar. In M. Narodowski, H. Ospina and A. Martínez Boom (2006), *La razón técnica desafía a la razón escolar* (pp. 11-26). Buenos Aires: Noveduc.
Bauman, Z. (2004). *Europa: Una aventura inacabada*, Buenos Aires, Losada. In M. Lawn & A. Nóvoa (Eds.), *Fabricating Europe: The formation of an Education space*. New York: Kluwer Academic Press.
Bhabha, H. (Ed.). (1990). *Nation and narration*. New York & London: Routledge.
Botana, N. (1991). *La tradición republicana*. Buenos Aires: Sudamericana.
Botana, N., & Gallo, E. (1997). *De la República posible a la República verdadera*. Buenos Aires: Ariel Historia.
Braccio, G. (1999). Para mejor servir a Dios. El oficio de ser monja. In F. Devoto and M. Madero (Eds.), *Historia de la vida privada en la Argentina*. Tomo I: País Antiguo: De la colonia a 1870 (pp.225-250). Buenos Aires: Taurus.
Caruso, M., & I. Dussel (1996). *De Sarmiento a los Simpsons. Conceptos para pensar la escuela contemporánea*. Buenos Aires: Ed. Kapelusz.
Caspard, P. (1984). De l'horrible danger d'une analyse superficielle des manuels scolaires. *Histoire de l'éducation*, 21.
Colmenares, G. (1987). *Las convenciones contra la cultura*. Bogotá: Tercer Mundo Editores.
Cucuzza, H. R. (1997). *Ruptura hegemónica, ruptura pedagógica: catecismos o contrato social durante el predominio jacobino en la Primera Junta de Buenos Aires*. Paper presented at the Jornadas Nacionales de Historia de la Educación, Salta.
Dávilo, B. (1998). *Religión y política: Formas de sujeción en las sociedades de Antiguo Régimen*. Rosario: National University of Rosario, mimeo.
Dean, M. (1994). *Critical and Effective Histories. Foucault's Methods and Historical Sociology*. London & New York: Routledge.
De Certeau, M., Julia, D., et al. (1975). *Une politique de la langue. La révolution française et les patois: l'enquête de Grégoire*. Paris: Gallimard.
Demerson, P. (1985). Tres instrumentos pedagógicos del siglo XVIII: la Cartilla, el Arte de Escribir y el Catón. In: *L'enseignement primaire en Espagne et en Amérique Latine du XVIIIe siecle a nos jours. Politiques educatives et Realites scolaires* (pp. 31-40). Actes du Colloque de Tours, 29-30 novembre 1985.
Dussel, I. (2001). *School uniforms and the disciplining of appearances. Towards a comparative history of the regulation of bodies in early modern Europe, France,*

Argentina, and the United States. Ph.D. Dissertation, University of Wisconsin-Madison.
Dussel, I. & M. Caruso (2000). *La invención del aula. Una genealogía de las formas de enseñar.* Buenos Aires: Santillana.
Gagliano, R. (1991). Nacionalismo, inmigración y paranoia cultural. Polémicas educativas en torno al Centenario. In A. Puiggrós (Ed.), *Sociedad civil y Estado en los orígenes del sistema educativo argentino (1885–1916)* (pp. 281–307). Buenos Aires: Ed. Galerna.
García Canclini, N. (1996). *Hybrid Cultures.* Strategies for Entering and Leaving Modernity. Minneapolis: University of Minnesota Press.
García Márquez, G. (1972). *One Hundred Years of Solitude.* New York: Harper and Row.
González Bernaldo, P. (1999). *Civilité et Politique aux origines de la nation argentine. Les sociabilités à Buenos Aires, 1829–1862.* Paris: Publications de la Sorbonne.
Gorelik, A. (1998). *La grilla y el parque. Espacio urbano y cultura urbana en Buenos Aires, 1887–1936.* Buenos Aires: Editorial Universidad Nacional de Quilmes.
Green, B. (Ed.). (1993). *The insistence of the letter: Literacy studies and curriculum theorizing.* London: Falmer Press.
Guerra, F.-X. (1993). Modernidad e independencias. Ensayos sobre las revoluciones hispánicas. México D.F.: Fondo de Cultura Económica.
Hale, Ch. (1991). *La transformación del liberalismo en México a fines del siglo XIX.* México D.F.: Vuelta.
Halperin Donghi, T. (1987). *El espejo de la historia. Problemas argentinos y perspectivas latinoamericanas.* Buenos Aires: Sudamericana.
Hobsbawm, E. (1990). *Nations and nationalisms since 1789: Programme, myth, and reality.* Cambridge, England: Cambridge University Press.
Hobsbawm, E., & Ranger, T. (Eds.). (1983). *The invention of tradition.* Cambridge: Cambridge University Press.
Jaume, L. (2004). El pensamiento en acción: por otra historia de las ideas políticas. *Ayer*, 53, 1.
Julia, D. (1995). La culture scolaire como objet historique. In Nóvoa et al. *The colonial experience in education* (Suppl. Series 1). Gent: Pedagógica Historica.
McEvoy, C. (1999). *Forjando la nación: Ensayos de historia republicana.* Lima: PUC.
McIntyre, A. (1981). *After Virtue.* Notre Dame: University of Notre Dame Press.
Mignolo, W. (1995). *The darker side of the renaissance. Literacy, territoriality, & colonization.* Ann Arbor, MI: The University of Michigan Press.
Mignolo, W. (2000). *Local Histories/Global Designs. Coloniality, Subaltern Knowledges, and Border Thinking.* Princeton, NJ: Princeton University Press.
Mosse, G. L. (1975). *The nationalization of the masses. Political symbolism and mass movements in Germany from the Napoleonic Wars through the Third Reich.* Ithaca, NY, and London: Cornell University Press.
Oria, A. (2006). *The changing meanings of 'public education' in Argentina. A genealogy.* Unpublished doctoral dissertation, Institute of Education, University of London.
Palti, E. (2005). *La invención de una legitimidad. Razón y retórica en el pensamiento mexicano del siglo XIX (Un estudio sobre las formas del discurso político).* México D.F.: Fondo de Cultura Económica.
Palti, E. (2007). *El tiempo de la política. El siglo XIX reconsiderado.* Buenos Aires: Siglo XXI editores.
Puiggrós, A. (1990). *Sujetos, disciplina y curriculum en los orígenes del sistema educativo argentino (1885–1916).* Buenos Aires: Galerna.

Quattrocchi de Woisson, D. (1995). *Los males de la memoria. Historia y política en la Argentina.* Buenos Aires: Emecé.

Rama, A. (1996). *The Lettered City.* Durham, NC, & London: Duke University Press.

Renan, E. (1990). What is a nation? In H. Bhabha (Ed.), *Nation and narration.* London: Routledge.

Rojas de Ferro, C. (1995). Identity formation, violence, and the nation-state in nineteenth-century Colombia. *Alternatives, 20,* 195–224.

Rose, N. (1997). Identity, genealogy, history. In S. Hall & P. Du Gay (Eds.), *Questions of cultural identity* (pp. 128–150). London & Thousand Oaks, CA: Sage.

Rose, N. (1999). *Powers of Freedom. Refraiming Political Thought.* Cambridge: Cambridge University Press.

Sábato, H. (1992). Citizenship, political participation and the formation of the public sphere in Buenos Aires, 1850s–1880s. *Past and Present, 136.*

Sábato, H. (1997). *La política en las calles.* Buenos Aires: Sudamericana.

Sábato, H. (2006). República y nación en América Latina: notas breves sobre una historia turbulenta. In J. Nun & A. Grimson (Eds.), *Convivencia y buen gobierno. Nación, nacionalismo y democracia en América Latina* (pp. 21–31). Buenos Aires: Edhasa.

Salessi, J. (1995). *Médicos, maleantes y maricas. Higiene, criminología y homosexualidad en la construcción de la Nación Argentina (Buenos Aires, 1871–1914).* Rosario: Beatriz Viterbo Editora.

Sarlo, B. (1988). *Una modernidad periférica.* Buenos Aires 1920 y 1930. Buenos Aires: Nueva Visión.

Sarmiento, D. F. (1987). *Educación Común.* Buenos Aires: Ediciones Solar.

Sarmiento, D. F. (2001). *Obras Completas. Tomo 11.* Buenos Aires: Universidad Nacional de La Matanza.

Schwarz, R. (1977). *Ao vencedor as Batatas.* Sao Paulo: Duas Cidades.

Schwarz, R. (1997). *Que horas sao?* São Paulo: Companhia das Letras.

Shapiro, M. J. (1997). Winning the West, unwelcoming the immigrant: Alternative stories of "America." In S. Schram & P. Neisser (Eds.), *Tales of the state. Narrative in contemporary U.S. politics and public policy* (pp. 17–26). Lanham, MD, & Oxford, Rowan and Littlefield.

Spalding, Jr., H. A. (1972). Education in Argentina, 1890–1914: The limits of oligarchical reform. *The Journal of Interdisciplinary History, III*(1), 31–62.

Szuchman, M. (1988). *Order, family, and community in Buenos Aires, 1810–1860.* Stanford, CA: Stanford University Press.

Tyack, D., & Cuban, L. (1995). *Tinkering toward Utopia. A century of public school reform.* Cambridge, MA, & London: Harvard University Press.

Weinberg, G. (1984). *Modelos educativos en la historia de América-Latina.* Buenos Aires: Ed. Kapelusz.

8 Classical Republicanism, Local Democracy, and Education
The Emergence of the Public School of the Republic of Zurich, 1770–1870

Daniel Tröhler

In Zurich, Switzerland, the modern public school was developed over approximately 100 years between 1770 and 1870.[1] This development had to overcome different obstacles, especially the primordial close linkage of the school to the church and the traditional separation between the urban and rural school systems. Zurich had been an aristocratic republic[2] with different privileges of its inhabitants until in 1798 the Helvetic Revolution set a temporary end to the *Ancien Régime*. Its achievements, however, were diminished during the period of Restoration after the Vienna Congress and restated in the new constitution inaugurating representative democracy in 1831. In 1869 a new constitution introduced direct democracy to the people.[3] The major tasks of decoupling the school from the church and the establishment of one comprehensive school system for all inhabitants of the Canton of Zurich had required cultural and mental changes and adaptations that both followed and preceded the constitutional, legal, and institutional modifications. In 1870 the public school was so firmly anchored culturally and politically that subsequent changes or reforms later on were essentially extensions or elaborations of what had already come to exist. The school had become a *Volksschule* of the Republic of Zurich, a public school, itself shaped by the heritage of Reformed Protestantism and republicanism, and the persons responsible for the school were skeptical toward radical reforms but open to incremental adaptations.

Basically, this process leading toward this publicly borne *Volksschule* was possible because it occurred in the background of a common religious-political heritage, Zwinglianism,[4] foreseeing in its theoretical foundations much more than any other form of Protestantism, such as Calvinism or Lutheranism (and certainly much more than Catholicism, too), the classical republican idea of self-government: according to its ideology, the church is subordinate to the state; however, the clergy is responsible for the evaluation of the individual behavior of the people in general and the political rulers in particular. Whereas in the 16th and 17th centuries Zwingli and his followers had conceded the peasantry a comparatively large range of decision-making autonomy, the aristocratic element of the aristocratic republic had become more and more dominant during the following centuries. Therefore, the power of decision of the citizens of Zurich had grown, whereas in the peasantry it had decreased: toward the end of the *Ancien Régime*—that is, in the second half of the 18th century—the legal and institutional order had become rather alienated from the religious-political self-understanding of the Republic of Zurich. This tension triggered two different political movements that amalgamated in the course of a century. The two movements led to institutional secularization, a thorough democratization of the republic, and the erection of the public school. However, in the process of institutional secularization and democratization, the religious energy behind this process was not eclipsed but rather was (partly) translated into the sanctification of the democratic republic—or the Promised Land, in which public education was to play a crucial role.

One of the two different political movements triggered by the contradiction between legal and institutional order on one side and the cultural self-understanding on the other side was a Renaissance of classical republicanism discourse in the city of Zurich after 1750. This discourse aimed for more virtues on the part of its citizens, including the idea of a stronger common-good orientation with consideration of the fate and the rights of the peasantry, but it did not include the idea of equal rights. The aristocratic element of the aristocratic republic was not to be changed institutionally but rather to be legitimated by the virtuousness of the rulers. This classical republican discourse became fundamentally educational and partly radical, especially in younger citizens' circles. Using the language of classical republicanism, these circles publicly accused the rulers of corruption, and they organized their own republican education aiming toward a moral and political Renaissance of the republic of Zurich (Tröhler, 2008, 2009a). Whereas this movement was decidedly elitist, the second of the two political movements was more participative. Nurtured by news of the Declaration of Independence by the American Congress and the U.S. Constitution and the French Revolution, toward the end of the 18th century the rural elite claimed political and, most of all, the economic rights that they had lost over the centuries to the citizens of the city of Zurich. These claims drew upon old chartered rights and on the culture of the Zwinglian ideal of self-government (at least on a local level). The interaction of these two principles in the course of the 100 years between 1770 and 1870 led to the cultural and legal changes, modifications, and adaptations mentioned earlier, reinforcing the development of the school and, by that, eventually causing new adaptations. Whereas the constitution in 1831 guaranteed equal democratic rights to all its (male) citizens, even more political rights were given to citizens in 1869, and around 1870 the school became not an institution aimed at forming elitist virtuous leaders of the republic—as had been the case in the *Ancien Régime* in the circles of the angry young men upset by the alleged corruption of the rulers—but instead a modern public school in the context of a republic that was democratically authorized by the people, which prevented the school from being exposed to inopportune experiments.

In the following, I will support my thesis about the secularization, the democratization of elitist classical republicanism, and the emergence of the public school between 1770 and 1870 in six steps. First, I describe the school situation around 1770 in both the city and subject territory of Zurich. Second, I demonstrate how the development of the school had to deal with the delicate issue of the church and religion. Third, I look at Reformed Protestant origins of the idea of self-government of the school. Fourth, I analyze how republican *topoi* of anti-commercialism fostered the fundamental democratization of the constitution, putting a final end to the formal influence of church on the school. Fifth, I identify *topoi* of republicanism in school subjects and textbooks. Sixth, I show how stable this school was in its background, having emerged out of a secularization and democratization process of Reformed Protestantism, and how it was able to reject both explicit Republican and religious (Catholic and Evangelical) reform attempts, allowing only gradual development of the school in the decades thereafter.

THE ZURICH SCHOOLS AROUND 1770

The Republic of Zurich in the *Ancien Régime* is in a classical sense a republican city-state, or an aristocratic republic, in which the political rights entitled elected citizens[5] to make decisions not only for the political unit, the commune—that is, the city, but for the whole territory of Zurich. Furthermore, this aristocratic republic was Christian in the Zwinglian tradition. Zwingli had formulated his reformatory ideals in the language of the civic humanism that arose at the beginning of the 16th century and banded together political and religious leaders of the republic.[6] Citizens were male persons with civil liberty living in the city, which had a population of approximately 10,000. In contrast, the political rights of the rural population of about 200,000 were restricted to affairs of their communes. People in the communes around Zurich were not allowed to study at the Zurich Academy or to trade, and they were forbidden to enter into some specific tradesman occupations and military careers, which were reserved for citizens of the city. The Zurich countryside was a subject territory in which the individual communes possessed relatively great autonomy in local affairs that were based on old, vested (chartered) rights. Because these vested rights differed from commune to commune, there was great confusion about what the communes were authorized to do, which in turn made it impossible for the city of Zurich to administer the subject territory efficiently. The city was represented in the countryside by higher administrative officials, the district bailiffs (*Landvögte*), and the pastors. All other administrative offices were filled in the commune by members of the rural population and usually through democratic elections at the commune assemblies. In some communes, there was even an institutionalized *Weibergemeinde*, at which the women of the villages elected their midwife (Kunz, 1948).[7]

The rural school was controlled by the pastor, and, accordingly, religious contents predominated in the school subjects of reading and singing. Writing was not promoted as strongly, and arithmetic—if it were offered at all—was taught outside regular hours. Innovations in the school system met not infrequently with resistance on the part of the village residents. School was often held only in winter, and in the areas that were becoming industrialized there was a marked increase in school absences (Rosenmund, 2006). There was no official age for starting school, and there were no grades based on age. Pupils were to stay in school for as long as it took for them to satisfy minimal requirements. The period between school leaving and confirmation at the age of 16 was supposed to be filled by lessons once a week at the repetition schools.

In contrast, in the city, there was a subdivided school system for future citizens, the lowest level being the "Home School," where children of both sexes learned religion, reading, and writing in German at the teacher's home. The next level was the "German School," which was for the boys only,[8] where boys learned some arithmetic in addition to religion, reading, and writing in German. Then the boys moved on to the "Latin School" for 8 years (from ages 8 to 16). Here, in addition to religion, they studied Latin, Greek, and later also Hebrew and arithmetic—a classical humanistic education at a lower school level. Following Latin School, there was a 2-year *Collegium Humanitatis*, which served as a kind of preparatory school for the Academy. At the *Collegium* the young men read a lot of Latin and Greek and practiced grammar. At 18 years of age, the young men were permitted entry to the Academy, the *Collegium Carolinum*, where philosophy and theology dominated as the main topics. But the young men were also taught Swiss history and politics to inspire them with patriotism and political knowledge. Upon completion of their studies at the Academy, some of the young men went into government service. But most of them became pastors. All together, the city's school system provided the next generation for the political and administrative staff of the aristocratic republic in the tradition of Reformed Protestantism.[9]

Around 1770 there were initial decisive changes that turned out to be very different for the rural and city schools. In both cases the reforms were determined through the economic developments in agriculture and early home industry. In the countryside in the more industrialized areas, it was noted that school absenteeism was high, which caused concern about the carrying out of the religious and moral tasks of the school. As a result, we find what was probably one of the first comprehensive school surveys: the School Inquiry of 1771/1772 in the Canton of Zurich, which was conducted by one of the numerous moral societies in the city of Zurich.[10] Noticeable in the countryside is a revision of the school and teaching regulations in

Classical Republicanism, Local Democracy, and Education 157

1778, which did not so much strive after substantial reform as it sought to strengthen the old structures by means of organizational measures (Erneuerte Schul- und Lehr-Ordnung, 1778).

In the city there was a comparable phenomenon, insofar as both the Latin School and the *Collegium Humanitatis* experienced a striking decline in enrollment in the years 1750 and 1770. Parents sent their children to schools outside of the canton or even to schools abroad, where they received far better preparation for their commercial or artistic vocations (Tröhler, 2006a). The authorities in the city responded completely differently than in the countryside, however, and they implemented reforms in the years from 1770 to 1773. The entire foundation of the school system was modified: history, geography, writing, and arithmetic were given more room at the cost of Latin, which still predominated, and the *Collegium Humanitatis* added an art school, providing an alternative for young men who wished to pursue not the life of a pastor but of a tradesman or an artist. Even the highest level of schooling, the *Collegium Carolinum*, was moderately reformed. Starting in 1773 the academy was to produce not only theologians but also "Politici"—that is, future politicians and civil servants. Following upon this reform, a number of private schools were founded toward the end of the 18th century in the city: in 1774 a school for girls, in 1782 the medical/surgical institute, in 1786 a school for the poor, and in 1791 what was called a "country boys' institute," a school for children of families that worked for urban companies in the countryside and wanted to offer their children better education.

THE SCHOOL REFORM OF THE LIBERAL REPUBLIC AND THE DECLINING INFLUENCE OF THE CHURCH

The need for reform was ubiquitous and by no means limited to the schools. Many citizens had been concerned about the development of the Swiss republics and complained about luxury, alienation, capitalism, and corruption, and it is in this context that the language of radical classical republicanism re-emerged within the city of Zurich, borne by young theologians such as Johann Caspar Lavater, Johann Heinrich Füssly (later the painter John Henry Fusely), or Johann Heinrich Pestalozzi, and aiming for a virtuous non-commercial republic (Tröhler, 2009a). Thus, the invasion of Switzerland by the French revolutionary troops in spring 1798 was appreciated by many of the reformers, for most of them believed that the ideas of the French Republic were identical with the republican ideals of the Swiss and would help to reinforce them. However, neither the basic ideology of the French Revolution, the modern Natural Law,[11] nor Napoleon's interpretation of a republic turned out to be compatible with the classical republican dreams that many of the reformers had fostered.

In the short period of the Helvetic Republic (1798–1803), a fully new school law was written based on the model of Condorcet's reform plans in France, but it was never passed by the Helvetic legislature and therefore could never be implemented fully (Bütikofer, 2006). With the important exception of the state school board, which was to consist of publicly highly esteemed men who would serve office without payment,[12] Napoleon's Mediation Constitution of 1803 canceled many of these reforms. Against that background, the demand for a more adequate school system was not covered by the educational policy, so that the period of the new founding of private schools—starting in the 1770s—continued after 1803. In 1806 both a teacher training institute[13] and a political institute were established, and in 1812 a "country girls' institute" was set up in analogy to the institute for boys. Numerous schools came into being as private undertakings, and many rapidly disappeared from the scene (Tobler, 1944). Napoleon's downfall and the era of European Restoration after the Congress of Vienna 1814/1815 limited even more strongly the possibility for innovations in the public educational system.

The Restoration era did not solve the problems of the European nations in a sustainable way. Particularly the economic pressure caused by the British industry after the annulment of Napoleon's Continental System coerced the economic systems of the continent to modernize, a coercion that eventually joined liberal visions of political and educational reform proposals. The July Revolution in France in 1830 had signaling effects in different European countries. The most visible effects were in some of the Swiss cantons, first of all in Zurich, where in November 1830 at what is called the *Ustertag* more than 10,000 men of the Canton of Zurich asked for a new constitution, which was in fact passed in 1831.[14] The school was a core element within the idea of the new republic, and accordingly the constitution held: "Care for the perfection of youth instruction is duty of the people and its deputies. The state will cultivate and support the lower and higher school institutions to the best of its ability" (Staatsverfassung, 1831, § 20). The public body was represented by the state school board, which had already been inaugurated in the Helvetic Republic and was to supervise all of the schools of the canton. The members of the education council were elected by parliament (§ 70, paragraph 1). A year later in 1832, a new school law was passed by parliament; it was based on the liberal idea of social stratification, that is, the allocation of social positions according to the educational level of the individual (and not according to birth).

The events of 1830–1832 appear to be a radical break with the *Ancien Régime*, respectively, with its conservative reappearance in the era of Restoration, and in many respects it was a break indeed: (Representative) democracy and the principle of the public control had won supremacy over the old privileges, and the equality of rights of all the (male) inhabitants of the canton was guaranteed. In order to strengthen the principle of public rather than church control of the school, the education council mandated with revising the school law instituted lay school boards in the districts and in the communes of the state. The lay school boards had to be elected by the people (and are similar to the American school boards). However, the break was not as radical as it may seem (and as many historians believe). The law foresaw that in the communes, pastors would be the heads of these school boards (Gesetz betreffend die Organisation der Gemeinds-Schulpflegen, 1831, § 1) and that the other members of the school board would be elected by the members of the church parish (§ 2). And moreover, the teachers still had to take over the duties of cantor and sexton of the church in their commune, and only after violent battles and political initiatives by the teachers' organization (Synode, 1835, 1837) were the teachers relieved of the duties of church cantor in 1838 (Gubler, 1932, p. 144). Particularly at the lower school levels, a great part of the school culture remained church culture, or religious culture, for decades after 1831.[15]

The rather moderate break corresponded to the fact that the people of the canton by no means became irreligious by the events of 1830–1832 and certainly not in terms of education. Local self-government had been legitimized by the Zwinglian culture, and the privileged participation by church members did not interfere with the cultural self-understanding—at least not with that of the vast majority of the people. This "conservative" motive became evident a few years after the new constitution had been accepted: Together with other decisions by the liberal government that offended the Christian worldview of the people, the Catechism was banished from the school curriculum. In 1839 the conservative aristocrats of the city and the conservative people of the rural territory formed an alliance, marched into the city armed for a coup d'état, and then governed the canton for six years, reintroducing the Catechism to the school, extending the religion lessons to three hours per week, and guaranteeing the church council control authority over the teaching of religion (Gesetz betreffend einige Modificationen . . . , 1839; Gesetz betreffend einige Abänderungen . . . , 1840).

However, the conservative interregnum from 1839 to 1845 did not stop the development of an ongoing secularization, meaning the gradual reduction of a formal institutional influence of the church on the school. Accordingly, the local people step by step took over more responsibilities from the church and its personnel. A decisive moment was the new constitution of the Canton of Zurich in 1869, which unequivocally gave all people in the state the same rights (Verfassung des eidgenössischen Standes Zürich, 1869, § 2) and which, consistently, did not include any privileges of the pastor in the paragraphs on the schools (§ 62). In accordance with this tendency—and not by chance first at the level of higher schooling—pupils with conscious objections were excused from religious instruction classes in 1860. Starting in 1872 religious instruction was even declared optional (Hunziker, 1933). And 7 years later, religious instruction was declared "not obligatory" for the lower school levels (Kreisschreiben des Erziehungsrates, 1879, Folgerung 1).

REFORMED PROTESTANTISM AND SELF-GOVERNMENT OF THE SCHOOL

How closely handed-down and modern ideas were tied together in the representative democratic constitution of 1831 is expressed in two successive paragraphs of the constitution of 1831 (§69 and § 70). Paragraph 20 declares the school a public matter and charges the state to organize it—and thus emancipates the school from the church at the constitutional level. However, this separation of church and school was little radical, as shown by not only the legal determination of the privileged position of the local pastor on the commune school boards (see above) but also the organization of the school area: The organization of the church was laid down in Paragraph 69 of the constitution, the organization of the school in the following Paragraph 70. The succession is not by chance, nor is the order of the paragraphs: The perception of how the school could be organized autonomously from the church was strongly determined by how the church was organized, right down to the vocabulary. For the church, the same continued to apply as had always applied since Zwingli's Reformation—namely, extensive self-government of all belonging to the church, and their right to examine the policy of the lawmaking government authorities of Zurich. This self-government was democratic: Every pastor, whether important or not, had a vote in the church assembly, the synod. Church affairs were supervised by the church council (Staatsverfassung, 1831, § 69) that was elected by parliament (§ 44).

As stated in Paragraph 70, the school was to be organized analogously. As in the church area, a school synod was established comprising the people engaged in the school (mostly the teachers), and the whole education system was to be supervised by the state school board that had already been set up in 1798 in the Helvetic Republic (§ 70). As in the case of the church, the education council was to be elected by parliament (§ 44), and the law determined that the head of the school synod would be elected by the synod itself (Gesetz über die Einrichtung der Schulsynode, 1831, § 4). The school synod was to serve the continuing education of teachers and was to have a say in the education policy of the canton as a whole (§ 1). The education council, as the highest school authority, embodied the republican principle of the public next to the state. And the school synod was a kind of self-government of those acting in the school area, and it also had an obligation to the public through the publication of its acts of the annual meetings. Through their characteristics—representation of the public on the one hand, and self-government of the professional actors on the other—both institutions guaranteed a rather pragmatic development of the school that refrained from, or prevented, thoughtless reform ambitions.

The state school board acquired importance with the political upheavals of 1830 and the new constitution of 1831 insofar as the planned school reform was turned over to it. It first set up its own procedural rules and then organized the regional and local school authorities, the district school board, and the commune school board. The district school board was to be made up of seven members, whereby the church chapter (part of the church synod) elected two members, the teachers elected two, and the public elected the other three. The president of the district school board was selected by the education council from the elected members. The determination for the commune was more democratic, even though the local pastor was set as president; all of the other members of the commune school board were elected by the commune assembly (held each Sunday in the church following the church service) (Frey, 1953).

The delegation of school-political power to regionally and locally elected public institutions was a decisive step for the development of the school system. The most important point was not even that with this shift of power the rural population, which was often skeptical about changes, could be reassured, particularly as the education council—as the highest authority—was made up of predominantly urban, academically educated people exclusively. Much more important was the fact that the principle of local control of commune affairs accorded with a self-understanding of the people in the countryside that was hundreds of years old. Against this background the Helvetic Republic (1798–1803) had extended the political powers that the peasants had originally possessed and then lost, step by step, in the late 17th and 18th centuries: it had legalized the principle of local autonomy that was familiar to the peasantry. What at the level of the law appears as a modern republican principle based on the rational natural law following the French model[16] was in the context of the countryside's localism the legal institutionalization of the traditional cooperative understanding of freedom and—therefore successful (Muralt, 1941; Wyss, 1892).

In this context, the school synod demonstrates exceptionally well how the Zwinglian idea of (self-) government was sustainable and effective after the legal secularization with the new constitution in 1831. The perception that the members of the school (teachers, inspectors, etc.) had effectively the right of self-government was never challenged at all, not even when it became evident that this principle could be in contrast to the political authorities: What had been "right" for the (Zwinglian) church simply was equitable for the school. Against this background the school synod would prove to be successful: In addition to efforts in support of their profession for better pay[17] and clear separation from the church,[18] the synod worked toward improved social security for teachers and their families.[19]

But the teachers' central concern was the issue of textbooks. The new school law of 1832 had defined new school subjects and school grades by age, but there were hardly any textbooks available. The traditional church/religious textbooks (see Scherr, 1840b) were incompatible with the new guidelines, and the pressure on the teachers was accordingly strong.[20] Requests concerning the right of control over the new textbooks and about the question as to who should define the mandatory textbooks in all schools were the regular result of the assemblies of the synod.[21] Many of these requests were successful because they corresponded to a need that was conceived to be real. To be mentioned especially is, among other things, the synod's request in 1850 to organize the textbook production at the state level in order to reduce prices, which led to the establishing of an official, state-run textbook publishing house in 1851 that still exists today (Tröhler & Oelkers, 2001) or also the requests of the synod in 1874 and 1875 to make the textbooks accessible at one central location.[22] The result was the Permanent School Exhibition, established in 1875, along with the added Pestalozzi-Stübchen, which would later become the Pestalozzianum and then the Pestalozzianum Research Institute for the History of Education.[23]

TOPOI OF REPUBLICANISM AND THE DEVELOPMENT OF THE DEMOCRATIC PUBLIC SCHOOL

Although the Zwinglian idea of self-government had laid the groundwork for both the local autonomy and the synod, with its contribution to the development of the public school, the official rhetorical agenda was still in the language of classical republicanism through the political upheavals in 1798, 1803, 1815, and 1831. Expressions of that self-understanding are the emergence of gymnastics and shooting clubs, which contributed to both national unity and fitness for service in its militia army and whose festivals became impressive manifestations of Swiss republicanism in the 19th century. The festivals were occasions to celebrate the unity and freedom of the fatherland, especially at times when the perception of crisis dominated. A greater crisis began starting in 1840, when religious tensions in cantons with equal numbers of Protestants and Catholics increasingly challenged the national unity. In the face of the fermenting tension, the national competition (*Schützenfest*) held by the town guards in Chur in 1842 was dominated by slogans of national unity, which were not derived from natural law but were the result of shared historical experiences that had led to freedom:[24] The participants at the national *Schützenfest* were again and again reminded of the heroic history of their free Switzerland and of their fraternity and modesty. The motto of the festival was, accordingly, "*Gottesliebe, Vaterlandsliebe, Tyrannenhass*" [love of God, love of the fatherland, and hatred of tyranny] (Tröhler, 2001, pp. 17–27). On the national level, the traditional Christian aristocratic republics of the *Ancien Régime* had become the sanctified democratic republic.

Just how virulent the classical republican language was in the liberal era became evident around and after 1860. On both the federal and cantonal levels the representative democratic constitutions had permitted the rise of a rather capitalist economy that had more and more influence on politics; one of the most charismatic figures was Alfred Escher, founder of the *Schweizerische Kreditanstalt*, the mother organization of today's bank *Credit Suisse*,

Classical Republicanism, Local Democracy, and Education 163

banker, railroad pioneer, secretary of education in the Canton of Zurich, and member of the national parliament.[25] The constitution of 1831 had made such outstanding economical careers possible, but it had not fundamentally changed the classical republican language within which such monumental capitalist careers and wealth were interpreted as wrong and the political influence of those people as corruption of the idea of the republic. Especially when in 1865 an economic crisis—due, among other things, to the Civil War in the United States—affected mainly the rural population, the republican rhetoric became more radical and dominant. In pamphlets, politicians were called corrupt plutocrats that followed their own interests exclusively. And the "patriots and republicans" were publicly exhorted to erect "the democracy of honest people" against this system of power. The new democracy would be based strongly upon the local democratic communes (see Weinmann, 2002, p. 293ff.). The result of this upset was not, as it had been 100 years before within the city limits of Zurich, an elitist movement seeking more individual virtues for the citizens of the city but rather a broad democratic movement. It led to the total revision of the national constitution in 1874, which, following the example of some of the cantons (including the example of Zurich in 1869), massively extended the rights of the people in all of Switzerland.[26] In the analysis of a witness (Vogt, 1873, p. 358), this demand for the direct democratic revision of the constitution had grown out of a political "crisis of the representative system." Accordingly, against the new wealth demands were raised for estate taxes and luxury taxes as well as progressive taxation of income (Schaffner, 1982, p. 36f.). Motives of classical republicanism, in other words—skepticism toward economic liberalism and strengthening self-government—had fostered direct democracy with the instrument of the referendum and increased the public character of the public school by setting an end to the privileges of the pastors as *ex cathedra* members in the local and district school boards.

In the wake of the electoral success of classical republicanism by the democrats the educational character of classical republicanism became official. The republican rhetoric in the area of the public school had had a long tradition, but it had never been an important part of the official policy in the liberal era of the representative democracy.[27] In 1838, it had been the school synod that dealt with the issue of whether political government should be taught in the primary school or especially in the secondary school. A clear plea was made that the pupils should be taught not only the bodies and procedures of the state but that rather, going beyond that, the guiding principles were to be impressed on the pupils' minds and "according to republican concepts." One speaker at the synod had declared that the secondary school was called to implant patriotism traditionally so that future citizens would be oriented to the common good (Honegger, 1838). The publication of the synod report at the end of 1838 immediately set off public discussion. And the newspaper *Der Republikaner* (*The Republican*) wrote accordingly:

> If we want to educate republican citizens—and this is truly the duty of our secondary schools—if we want men of freedom, of virtue, of devotion, this best character of any patriot (may we be allowed to use this sometimes frowned upon expression), then we have to conduct politics in our schools in a certain sense. This politics consists in utilizing the school subjects, especially history, as a means towards the great purpose of the ennoblement of, the enthusiasm for, the people and fatherland. (...) History education is unfertile and useless, if the young person's heart does not glow with enthusiasm and love for the big ideas and the noble men that lived and died for them. (...) No teacher that is not a republican in action and thought should teach history in the republic. ("Darf Politik," 1839, pp. 21f.)

Thirty years later, against the background of the democratic constitution passed in 1869, it seemed that the time had come to realize this educational republicanism officially. The new constitution had indeed not only increased the rights of the people massively and relieved the pastors of their privileges in the commune school board but also added to the "general education of the people," explicitly the "republican citizen education" as a state matter (Verfassung des eidgenössischen Standes Zürich, 1869, § 62). However, the cultural commitment to classical republicanism and its educational preoccupation led to an educational rhetoric that, in answer to the question of *how* concretely a schooling of that kind should be organized, often remained rather monosyllabic. The legal codification of republicanism as the task of the public school in the constitution of 1869 changed this little.

CLASSICAL REPUBLICANISM, SCHOOL SUBJECTS, AND TEXTBOOKS

Essentially, inner-institutional effects of the republican language can be demonstrated only at the third level of compulsory schooling (Grades 7 to 8 or 9) and in Zurich's Upper High School. Specifically, three school subjects at the Upper High School could have shown an identifiable republican inheritance—namely, German language, physical education, and history. But the beginning of this was to prove difficult. Physical education had already been foreseen by the curriculum of 1833, but it could not be introduced until 1843, when the building of a gymnasium and a sports field was completed.[28] The school subject German was dominated by German emigrant teachers in the first decades of the 19th century, and in their teutophilic German Studies they often had little sensitivity for the republican tradition of Switzerland. Republican authors like Gottfried Keller came to be taught only toward the end of the 19th century, when Swiss teachers had already been teaching German for quite a long time (see here the contribution by De Vincenti & Grube, Chapter 14, this volume). And the school subject History suffered under the fact that at the beginning, "all of general history" as well as "the entire history of the Swiss" was to be taught, followed by the political and cultural history of Greek and Roman Antiquity and of the Swiss. This obviously excessive demand as to content led to neglect especially of the second part (Hunziker, 1933, p. 71).

With the completion of the gymnasium and the sports field, which occurred in the midst of general national enthusiasm for sports, the public sports festival mutated into an obligatory school festival in 1844. In 1850, the education council mandated that physical education be expanded. In addition to general physical exercises and sports, the school would have its own cadet school with infantry and artillery, making pre-military training possible. This was justified on the basis of Switzerland's republican militia army (see also Niggeler, 1875, p. IV). Connected with the school festivals, large maneuvers were conducted, which were described proudly in the Upper High School annual reports (see e.g., Programm der Zürcherischen Kantonsschule, 1856, Teil II, p. 38f.).[29]

The third level of compulsory schooling (Grades 7 to 8 or 9) was divided into two achievement levels: secondary school and (the intellectually lower) "Repeating School." The latter was paid little attention for many decades, it had just a few required school hours, and accordingly it was not provided with appropriate textbooks. The purpose of the school—mainly to repeat what had been taught previously—was not achieved and was questioned by the public, so that from time to time proposals were made to turn the school into a "civics school," which would teach the weaker pupils not so much knowledge but "national virtues" instead (Bericht des Erziehungsrates, 1848, p. 12). The demand to establish a school for citizen education had already been raised in 1842 (Scherr, 1842, p. 56f.), and from that time on it had occupied the school synod again and again but without success. This was due not least to the fact that the issue remained open as to whether it was appropriate for the public school and for pupils to conduct political education (Frey, 1867; Wettstein, 1867).

In the framework of compulsory schooling, political education could unfold at the intersection of German and history, and two textbooks in particular came to meet the need. Already in 1835 the textbook *Bildungsfreund* was published for the secondary level. The author explicitly called the textbook a republican textbook for secondary school classes (Scherr, 1835). That the reference to republicanism was not mere rhetoric is shown by the foreword to the second edition (1838). The author, Scherr, wrote of himself that when writing the reader he had taken "free Switzerland into particular consideration," based on the principle that readers for families of the middle class and the secondary schools in a republic should always "pursue promotion of republican rights and virtues" (Scherr, 1838, p. V).

Starting with this second edition, *Bildungsfreund* could be purchased in two separate parts: prose and poetry. The prose part contains seven chapters. The first chapter contains 73 tales as "Historical examples for developing and forming noble convictions" (p. VII). Already the first two historical examples refer to the Spartans to show the quintessence of republicanism, namely, law-abidance and patriotism:

> 1) Solon, a Greek law-maker, was asked how a state could best flourish. Solon answered, "When the citizens obey the authorities and the laws."
> 2) A Spartan woman whose son had gone off to fight for the fatherland received the news that he had been killed. "I bore him for the fatherland," she said, "and he was willing to sacrifice his life for it" (p. 1).[30]

A second textbook appeared alongside the reader in 1875, in the wake of the differentiation of the school subjects and in the endeavor to ensure republican citizen education as guaranteed by the constitution (1869). *Lehr- und Lesebuch für die Volksschule* [Textbook and reader for the public school] was a textbook for the higher public school grades (Grades 7 to 8 or 9). In the foreword, the authors (Vögelin & Müller, 1875, p. II) write:

> The goal is especially to make it possible for the young person to gain an understanding of the present and its objectives through a correct view of the past. [. . .] Teaching accords with a republic only if . . . it awakens and nourishes the spirit.

And in a section of the textbook on "The task and value of the teaching of history," the authors confirm: "First and foremost, citizens of a free land have to be enthused for freedom by knowledge of its history. This will make them love their fatherland above all and enable them to prove his ethos by action" (p. 5). When the textbook was to be declared obligatory, the newspapers that advocated free individualism and the free market, and thus opposed obligatory textbooks produced by the state-run textbook publishing house, responded sharply, using ever stronger progressive education argumentation—that is, religious glorification of the child's soul. The textbook, as the criticism in one journal stated, was ultimately the expression of the "political dogmatism of the ruling system of the present," and if it were definitely introduced into the schools, it would be "a public disaster, a sin against the child's nature," because the book represented not only "tactlessness" but "a despicable violation of all piety, a terrible sin against the child's unbiased nature, and educational scandal" ("Das Geschichtliche Lehrmittel," 1874, p. 1). Despite the criticism, the book was introduced into the curriculum, but it disappeared shortly thereafter, not only for ideological reasons but also because it was found too difficult to use as a teaching material.

THE DEMOCRATIC BRIDLE OF REPUBLICAN AND RELIGIOUS SCHOOL REFORMS

Never before had the opportunity to introduce a decisively republican curriculum to the public school been as great as right after the passing of the new constitution in 1869 with its commitment to "republican citizen education" as a state matter (Verfassung des eidgenössischen Standes Zürich, 1869, § 62). The new education secretary issued a public invitation to the "communes, authorities, associations and societies, teachers, professors, and every single citizen" to formulate wishes and suggestions for reorganizing the school. More than 170 reports were submitted, but experiences with other proposed laws had shown that the constitutional tool of the referendum had made it quite hard to govern. Therefore, the new law proposal was slim, focusing on a few fundamental issues only and leaving many issues to provisions that were—in contrast to the laws—not subjected to the referendum. One of the innovations in the school law drafted by the democratic government was the assignment of teacher's education to the university and another one—in accordance with the 1869 constitution—was an obligatory civics school for 18- to 19-year-olds. About 80% of the voters rejected the new law in 1872, which was a slap in the face for the democratic rulers who had not counted on the local and anti-elitist character of Zurich's democracy and self-government. The strong democracy that resulted, from anti-capitalist movements, in the new constitution in 1869 had evidently not opened the door for a school idea that aimed at creating republican citizens in the sense of classical republicanism or for the idea of a central academic expertise.[31]

Around 1870 the public school of Zurich had taken a shape that could differentiate further due to its stability, but it could no longer change in any decisive way. The reason for the stability lies essentially in the school being embedded in the cultural-political self-understanding of the Canton of Zurich as a Reformed Protestant democratic republic far from an elitist ideal of republicanism as had been dominant in the reform circles of the city in the 18th century. In the 100 years between 1770 and 1870 this city elitist republicanism had been combined with rural localism and had become decisively democratized. The educational polity of the people refrained from both central expertocracy (and academization of teacher education) and elitist republicanism. The latter was universal in the 19th century. Already in 1832 outstanding school reformers opposed Robert Owen's idea about forming a constitutional state out of the school because it seemed ridiculous to grant children "judgments, and constitutional rights opposite the teacher" (Scherr, 1835, p. 5). Also later attempts to organize the school as a republic met with no success (Hepp, 1910)—one experience with a school republic ended after only 2 years with the officially declared conclusion that the "English-American organization of the students is not transferable to our soil" (Programm der Kantonsschule, 1915, p. 76).[32]

The school had become a secular institution that was widely embedded in the Reformed Protestant culture of self-government, and this kept it safe not only against attempts to make the school more political but also against efforts to again bring it back closer to religion: The steadily decreasing influence of the church and the decreasing importance of religious instruction as a school subject, or the elimination of religious instruction as an obligatory subject, were not approved of everywhere. An expression of the school's stability is the founding of an Evangelical Teachers' Seminary by Pietist circles in 1869 and the first free Evangelical school in 1874. The first annual report of the Evangelical Teachers' Seminary begins as follows: "No matter how great the difficulties besetting Christian teacher education, greater still is the need for it. We need Christian teachers . . . that practice their profession for God's sake" (Erster Bericht, 1870, p. 3). The anti-republican rhetoric of the Evangelical school is shown clearly in the first annual report of the *Freie Schule Zürich*. As they described themselves in the report, they were not a sect, and they wanted to be no "*Winkelschule*" [private, second-rate school] but rather a public school. The school should be a Christian school. It was supported by a small group of fathers of families who loved the Lord Jesus and waited for His Coming. And although they accepted that they would be misjudged by the world, they formed a people that "serves its King freely in Holy ornament, and we live in the firm belief that this voluntary service will also uphold our school. It is a thing of the Kingdom of God and stands open to all" (Erster Jahresbericht, 1874, p. 3).

The majority of the people of Zurich did not opt for this Pietist Protestantism because they identified themselves with "their" public school. How sustainable this school in the Reformed Protestant Promised Land of the prosperous democratic republic of Zurich was to be, was proved very soon by the integration of the Catholic immigrants to Zurich toward the end of the century. Whereas in 1850 only 2,700 Catholics had lived in the canton of Zurich, there were 59,000 in 1910, mostly of lower social status and employed in the expanding industries of Zurich, and in 1930, almost 22% of the inhabitants were Catholic. In 1874 the first Catholic Church (St. Peter and Paul) was built in the outskirts of Zurich and in 1894 a second in the city of Zurich itself (*Liebfrauenkirche*), and soon the more radical Catholics began to criticize the public school. In the focus of the critique was the secular tendency of the school in general and more particularly the fact that according to the law, religion was taught by laymen—which at bottom was a Reformed Protestant idea (every man is a preacher). The refusal of radical Catholics to accept (any) Reformation led them to accuse the entire public school of Zurich of being un-Christian, meaning un-Catholic, and at the same time the stakeholders of the school defended the secular character of the public school that in fact had emerged out of Reformed Protestantism. The Catholics sought the reintroduction of the confessional school, interpreting the existing school as non-Christian, whereas the school was secular Reformed Protestantism (which to the radical Catholics was the same thing). In 1920 the Bishop of Chur[33] said, "The freedom of a Christian education will not be derived from the Church and the Christian people forever," and speaking toward Zurich, he stated: "No human institution will last forever in this world. Also the alleged modern, creedless state is, as everything else, an appearance, an abnormal appearance in the lives of the peoples," and therefore youth should be educated in a Christian and patriotic manner (Hardegger, 2008, p. 50).

However, the school was firmly under public control, with values rooted in Reformed Protestant ideals. On this basis, the school, in the years to come, would become continuously differentiated and its value in society as a whole would be strengthened, so that for instance private schools would never have an enrollment of more than 5 percent of school-age children.[34] It had grown into a system that was largely uniform across the canton; compulsory schooling had been extended to eight years; free-of-charge schooling was guaranteed by the constitution; the different levels of schooling followed one upon the other; the transitions were regulated by a standard certification system; coeducation was largely realized; the school subjects were defined; knowledge was divided into identical time units, and pupils were divided into grades by age; teacher education was established; the social security of teachers and their families was secured; and the importance of the school was guaranteed in public opinion. Accordingly, the state and communal funds dedicated to education increased, which also affected the teacher/student ratio, which had decreased enormously in the 100 years previously. What had proved to be a stop-and-go development in times of varying turbulence in the 100 years between 1770 and 1870 became after 1870 a comparatively continuous development for another 100 years until a new idea of school governance, raised in the midst of the Cold War (Tröhler, 2010), started to shatter the fundamentals of the continuous development.

NOTES

1. I would like to thank Anne Bosche, Ruth Villiger, and Michael Geiss for their help in finding the sources, and Tom Popkewitz for his very helpful comments.
2. For more details, see the Introduction of the present volume.
3. Direct democracy indicates the constitutional right of the people to call for a referendum on political issues. It is different from representative democracy in terms of the political rights of the people.
4. Huldrych Zwingli (1484–1531) was a leader of the Reformation in Switzerland. Zwingli was born during a time of emerging Swiss patriotism. He attended the Universities of Vienna and of Basel, a scholarly center of humanism, becoming influenced by the writings of Erasmus. In 1519, Zwingli became a pastor in Zurich, where he began to preach ideas on reforming the Catholic Church. In his works, written in the language of civic humanism or republicanism, he accused the ecclesiastical hierarchy of corruption. The ideal republic, in Zwingli's doctrine, should be republican *and* Christian: The Christian community was at the same time a political community,

integrating the people, the political authorities, and the clergy in one. This idea was promoted by Zwingli's successor, Heinrich Bullinger (1504–1575), who took in many Calvinist refugees from England. These refugees introduced Zwinglianism to England upon their return to their country after the death of Mary I of England in 1558. Zwinglianism became a decisive element of the political and religious philosophy of the Puritans and modified English Calvinism from theocracy to more democracy.

5. In order to be elected, one had to be a citizen of Zurich, which also meant being a member of a guild. The authority of the guilds had been established in 1336 against a ruling class of nobilities. In the 18th century most of the prominent guild members (and thus of the political authorities) were no longer the traditional artisans but wealthy commercial men.
6. Many of the decisive administrative committees provided equal representation of politicians and theologians.
7. There was an exception for teachers and communal bailiffs (*Dorfvögte*). They were also elected in the village, but a list of the candidates placing in the top three had to be sent for definitive selection to the city, where, however, almost without exception the candidate who had received the most votes was confirmed.
8. At this time the girls attended only the Home School; further education had to be private. However, with the reforms around 1770, a successful private girls' school was opened in 1774.
9. There were no studies of medicine or law. Knowledge and certificates in medicine and law had to be acquired at universities in foreign countries.
10. The questionnaire with its 81 questions and approximately 200 responses has been made available to the public (Tröhler & Schwab, 2006).
11. For the basic ideological background of the French Revolution and its evolution, see the Introduction.
12. I return to these education authorities, who were for the most part elected by parliament, further below.
13. This short-lived institution, although it was official, was supported by the initiative and experience of a private man. I thank Luca Godenzi for this specification.
14. Nobody seemed to have questioned that all the (male) inhabitants of the Canton of Zurich were allowed to vote on the new constitution, which assigned constitutional civil liberties to all inhabitants of the canton and brought the old system of privileges to an end. It is no wonder that the new constitution providing a representative democracy was accepted by 96% of the voters (40,503 vs. 1,721 votes).
15. The official celebrations, such as the founding of the Teachers' Seminary in 1832 or the annual teacher assemblies, were held in churches and opened with a prayer. The school morning also began with prayer, and the curriculum continued to look to the pupils' religious education. Even though the curriculum of 1832 had been clearly "modernized" and included arithmetic as well as geometry, geography, history, and civics, "religious education" was still listed. The passage of this new law in 1832 ignited the anger of church and conservative circles. The law did not provide for religious education as taught by a pastor but instead "only" for the "awakening and development of moral and religious feelings and concepts as a preparation for church lessons" (Gesetz über die Organisation . . . , 1832, § 4, Alinea 4).
16. For the difference between the classical and modern republic, see the Introduction.
17. In the years: 1835, 1838, 1839, 1841, 1843, 1844, 1847, 1860, 1864, 1867, 1872.

18. In the years: 1835, 1837, 1859, 1868.
19. In the years: 1856, 1857, 1858, 1863, 1868, 1872, 1873, 1874.
20. The battle for and against modern textbooks was impressive and was played hardball. Especially the newspapers became the battleground of educational policy, inventing their own history (success or decay, according to their own political ideology) (see Tröhler, 2009b).
21. In the years: 1835, 1836, 1841, 1843, 1847, 1849, 1850, 1855, 1857, 1858, 1859, 1860, 1861, 1862, 1863, 1864, 1866, 1867, 1869, 1872, 1873, 1874, 1875, 1885.
22. The synod underlined their requests using republican arguments, such as the demand in 1848 to end the privilege of the education council to submit three candidates to the commune for teacher elections and the demand to give the communes complete autonomy—the missing autonomy, it was argued, that "impedes the development of a republican life" (Bericht über die Verhandlungen der XIV und XV) (Schulsynode, 1848, p. 4; Strehler, 1848). The cantonal legislature agreed to this proposal on October 23, 1849, and retained for itself only the right to determine who has the right to be elected as teacher–that is, certification (Verfassungsgesetz betreffend Abänderung §§ 85, 86; der Verfassung, 1849, § 1).
23. This Research Institute was dissolved by Zurich University of Teacher Education in 2009.
24. Accordingly, a printed handkerchief was distributed on which were depicted, among others, Wilhelm Tell, Jean-Jacques Rousseau, and Johann Heinrich Pestalozzi—that is, the mythological founder of Switzerland, the probably most radical theoretician of republicanism, and the man who, in the field of tension between classical republicanism and modern commerce, had developed a specific pedagogy, respectively.
25. Alfred Escher's father, Heinrich Escher, had made a fortune during his two stays in the United States, 1795–1806 and 1812–1814.
26. These instruments aroused interest especially in the republican tradition of the United States, as shown, for example, by the 1894 article, "What Is the Referendum? Swiss Solutions of American Problems" (McCrackan, 1894). See here also the lengthy source list in Rappard (1912, p. 118 ff.).
27. A school plan of 1830, for instance, wanted to introduce more study of Greece and Rome at the Secondary School because the "moral and political convictions" of these republics were so "purely human and yet so sublime" that they could be of particularly proper use and avail to the free Swiss (Orelli, 1831, p. 31). Antiquity was said to strengthen the moral sense and true republican understanding (p. 32), so that also Books I to X of Livy's history of Rome were recommended for use as textbooks (p. 38). Also Ignaz Thomas Scherr, the most important school reformer after 1831, steered the seminary according to "republican principles" (Scherr, 1832, p. 7), praised the "freedom of the fatherland," the "rights of all citizens," and "true republicanism" (Scherr, 1840a, p. 61), and took his seminary students on field trips to a *Landsgemeinde* so that they could see true freedom with their own eyes (Scherr, 1840b, p. 16f.). The *Landsgemeinde* (German for "provincial assembly") is one of the oldest and simplest forms of direct democracy practiced in some cantons of Switzerland.
28. But many of the students attending the Upper High School participated in private gymnastics clubs and associations (Hunziker, 1933, p. 168f.).
29. The success of physical education at the high school level led the Swiss Military Society to conduct a contest with a prize for the best essay written on how military training could be "welded together" with education—that is, with compulsory schooling. The motto of one of the winning entries

was "A Republican School Should Also Be a Preparatory School for Military Occupations" (Niggeler, 1863, p. 4). The demands were not for the founding of a cadet system at the secondary school level but instead for appropriate education of the teachers and for targeted physical education (p. 22), for which textbooks were written (Niggeler, 1875). But the issue of physical education at the two lower levels of schooling (Grades 1 to 6) was remarkably different. Here, physical education became a part of the curriculum only with the law of 1859, but teachers were supposed to teach it for 30 minutes twice or three times per week outside of their regular teaching responsibilities, which was not motivating. In 1861 the executive issued a bylaw according to which a spacious field for physical education exercises was to be constructed in the proximity of every newly built schoolhouse, and it was also to have a covered (roofed) area if possible (Verordnung betreffend die Erbauung . . . 1861, §§ 4–5).

30. The second chapter contains "Detailed accounts of the lives of great and noble men," and it begins not by chance with Thebes' greatest military leader and politician, Epameinondas, and then focuses on heroes of the 18th and 19th centuries, among them George Washington and Pestalozzi. The third chapter offers "Principles for a noble and sociable life." The first sentence states: "Freedom makes everything more perfect." It contrasts freedom with the "passions of man," which destroy everything (p. 76). Unity, freedom, and patriotism are the pillars supporting the republican "noble and sociable life": "Our forebears sacrificed all for the idea of freedom. The old Swiss in the mountains forever remain the fathers of the Confederation. Without love of the fatherland the statesmanship of a free people means nothing" (p. 76). All in all, the textbook *Bildungsfreund* was extraordinarily successful. After the establishing of the Swiss Confederation with the Swiss Federal Constitution of 1848, the book called itself the *Schweizerische Bildungsfreund*, and in 1866 it was subtitled: *A republican reader*. A 10th and last edition appeared in 1882.

31. A certain change occurred only when the Federal Constitution of 1874 transferred military training from the hands of the cantons to the federal government, which led to the termination of weapons practice in the Upper High School in 1877 but also strengthened *Vaterlandskunde* (geography, history, and constitutional history of Switzerland) as a school subject. This school subject has to thank the Recruits Examinations that were conducted yearly starting in 1875. These were comprehensive national examinations of the military recruits, testing their achievement in reading, essay writing, arithmetic, and *Vaterlandskunde*. As the test results were made public, in a spirit of competition the cantons strove to improve the teaching of these subjects. As a consequence, to improve outcomes in *Vaterlandskunde*, the teaching of history was expanded, and pupils were encouraged to attend a voluntary civics (or citizens') school, which despite vehement demands was never made obligatory (Zürcher, 1907).

32. In the 1914 review of the year's events (1913), it is noted that one section of the Upper High School had experimentally introduced "student self-government" with a student council, student court, and student board. Despite no major problems within this experiment, the review stated that not all of the high expectations had been fulfilled, in particular when it came to education of the character. Namely, the jurisdiction suffered lengthiness, thoroughness, and independency, so that the experiment was to be shortened in 1914 by the student court (Programm der Kantonsschule, 1914, p. 78). The experiment was abandoned a year later because of lack of interest and authority of the student council (Programm der Kantonsschule, 1915, p. 76).

The interpretation of this failed experiment argued on the basis of cultural differences (see main text).
33. The Zurich Catholics were integrated into the *Dioecesis Curiensis* with the seat in Chur. The affiliation is only provisional (and has been since 1819!) because there was hope that a diocese of Zurich would be founded (*Dioecesis Turicienses*).
34. In 1920, for example, there were no private schools for Grades 1 to 6 and 7 to 8/9 (lower achievement level) at all. About 16.7% of secondary school children (Grades 7 to 8/9, higher achievement level) attended private schools. Altogether only 3% of all school-age children attended private schools. To compare: 47% of preschool children attended private schools (Archiv für das schweizerische Unterrichtswesen, 1920, pp. 102–115).

REFERENCES

Archiv für das schweizerische Unterrichtswesen. 6. Jahrgang 1920. Zürich.
Berichtes des Erziehungsrathes über den Zustand des Schulwesens im Kanton Zürich im Schuljahr 1846-1847 (1847). In: *Bericht über die Verhandlungen der 14. und 15. Schulsynode des Kantons Zürich in den Jahren 1847 und 1848* (pp. 40–82). Zürich.
Bericht über die Verhandlung der II. Schusynode des Kantons Zürich. (1835). Zürich.
Bericht über die Verhandlung der IV. Schulsynode des Kantons Zürich. (1837). Zürich.
Bericht über die Verhandlungen der XIV. und XV. Schulsynode des Kantons Zürich in den Jahren 1847 und 1848. (1848). Zürich.
Bütikofer, A. (2006). Staat und Wissen: *Ursprünge des modernen schweizerischen Bildungsystems im Diskurs der Helvetischen Republik* [State and knowledge: Origins of the modern education system in Switzerland in the discourse of the Helvetic Republic]. Bern: Haupt.
Darf Politik in der Volks-, zumal in der Sekundarschule gelehrt werden [May politics be taught in public, or more precisely, in secondary schools?] (1839, January 18). *Der Republikaner, Nr. 6*, pp. 21–22.
Das Geschichtliche Lehrmittel der Ergänzungsschule [The history textbook in the supplementary school] (1874, November 8). *Zürcher Presse, Nr. 263*, pp. 1–2.
De Vincenti, A., & Grube N. *The masters of Republicanism? Teachers and schools in rural and urban Zurich in the eighteenth and the long nineteenth Century.* (in this volume).
Erneuerte Schul- und Lehr-Ordnung für die Schulen der Landschaft Zürich. Aus Hoch Obrigkeitlichem Befehl zum Druck befördert. (1778). Zürich.
Erster Bericht über das Evangelische Lehrerseminar in Unterstrass bei Zürich. (1870). Zürich.
Erster Jahresbericht über die Freie Schule in Zürich. Schuljahr 1874–75. (1875). Zürich.
Frey. J.C. (1867). Die sozial-bürgerliche und politische Ausbildung unserer Jugend. In *Bericht über die Verhandlungen der Zürcherischen Schulsynode von 1867* (Beilage 3). Zürich.
Frey, P. (1953). *Die zürcherische Volksschulgesetzgebung 1831–1951*. Ein Beitrag zur zürcherischen Volksschule. Affoltern am Albis: Weiss.
Gesetz betreffend die Organisation der Gemeinds-Schulpflegen vom 29. November 1831. Zürich.

Gesetz betreffend einige Abänderungen in den bestehenden Gesetzen über das Unterrichtswesen vom 25. Juni 1840. Zürich.

Gesetz betreffend einige Modificationen in den bestehenden Gesetzen über das Unterrichtswesen vom 27. Juni 1839. Zürich.

Gesetz über die Einrichtung der Schulsynode vom 26. Nivember 1831. Zürich.

Gesetz über die Organisation des gesammten Unterrichtswesens im Canton Zürich. (1832). Zürich.

Gubler, H. (1933). Die zürcherische Volksschule von 1831–1845. In Erziehungsrat des Kantons Zürich (Ed.), *Volksschule und Lehrerbildung 1832–1932. Festschrift zur Hundertjahrfeier* (pp. 103-341). Zurich: Verlag der Erziehungsdirektion.

Hardegger, U. (2008). "Wer die Schule hat, der hat das Volk". Zum Verhältnis der Zürcher Volksschule zur Religion. In D. Tröhler & U. Hardegger (Eds.), *Zukunft bilden. Die Geschichte der modernen Zürcher Volksschule* [Building the future: History of the modern public school in Zurich] (pp. 41–53). Zurich: NZZ Libro.

Hepp, J. (1910). Die Selbstregierung der Schüler. In *Bericht über die Verhandlungen der Zürcherischen Schulsynode von 1910*. Pfäffikon. (Separatdruck, 65 pages)

Honegger. (1838). Abhandlungen über die zürcherische Sekundarschule, auf die Schulsynode 1838. In *Bericht über die Verhandlungen der fünften Schulsynode des Kantons Zürich im Jahr 1838* (pp. 33–50). Zürich.

Hunziker, F. (1933). *Die Mittelschulen in Zürich und Winterthur 1833–1933*. Zurich: Verlag der Erziehungsdirektion.

Kreisschreiben des Erziehungsrates an die Primar-, Sekundar- und Bezirksschulpflegen vom 15. Januar 1879. (1886). In *Die Gesetze und Verordnungen des Kantons Zürich betreffend das Unterrichtswesen* (pp. 77–79). Zurich: Verlag der Erziehungsdirektion.

Kunz, E.W. (1948). *Die lokale Selbstverwaltung in den zürcherischen Landgemeinden im 18. Jahrhundert* [Local self-government in the rural communes of Zurich in the eighteenth century]. Affoltern am Albis: Weiss.

McCrackan, W. D. (1894). What is the referendum? Swiss solutions of American problems. *New England Magazine*, 17(4), 448–459.

Muralt, L. v. (1941). *Alte und neue Freiheit in der helvetischen Revolution* [Old and new freedom in the Helvetic Revolution]. Zurich: Schulthess.

Niggeler, J. (1863). *Über die Vereinigung der militärischen Instruction mit der Volkserziehung*. Zurich: Zürcher und Furrer.

Niggeler, J. (1875). *Anleitung zum Turnen mit dem Eisenstab*. Zurich: F. Schulthess.

Orelli, J. K. (1831). *Pädagogische Ansichten über äussere Trennung und geistige Einheit der wissenschaftlichen und technischen Schulen, nebst einem Bruchstück aus dem Zürcherischen Schulplane von 1830 und einem Vorschlag für die neue Organisation des Unterrichtswesens im Kanton Zürich*. Zurich: Orell, Füssli.

Programm der Kantonsschule in Zürich (1914). Zürich.

Programm der Kantonsschule in Zürich (1915). Zürich.

Programm der Zürcherischen Kantonsschule zur Eröffnung des neuen mit Ostern beginnenden Schuljahres.(1856). Zürich.

Rappard, W. E. (1912). The initiative, referendum and recall in Switzerland. *Annals of the American Academy of Political and Social Science*, 43, 110–145.

Rosenmund, M. (2006). Volksbildung als Verzichtsleistung: Annäherung an die politische Ökonomie des Zürcher Landschulwesens im 18. Jahrhundert. In D. Tröhler & A. Schwab (Eds.), *Volksschule im 18. Jahrhundert. Die Schulumfrage auf der Zürcher Landschaft 1771/72: Quellen und Studien* [Basic primary

school in the eighteenth century: The School Inquiry of 1771/72 in rural Zurich: Sources and studies] (pp. 51–63). Bad Heilbrunn: Klinkhardt.
Schaffner, M. (1982). *Die demokratische Bewegung der 1860er Jahre. Beschreibung und Erklärung der Zürcher Volksbewegung von 1867* [The democratic movement of the 1860s: Description and explanation of the Zurich uprising of 1867]. Basel: Helbing und Lichtenhahn.
Scherr, I. T. (1832). *Rede, gehalten in der Kirche zu Küssnacht den 7. Mai 1832 bei Eröffnung der Lehrer-Bildungsanstalt für den Kanton Zürich*. Zurich: Orell, Füssli & Co.
Scherr, I. T. (1835). *Entwurf einer Verordnung über Ordnung und Zucht in den Zürcherischen Volksschulen*. Zurich: Orell, Füssli und Compagnie.
Scherr, I. T. (1838). *Der Bildungsfreund, ein Lesebuch für den häuslichen Kreis und für höhere Volksschulen. Prosaischer Theil*. Zurich: Orell, Füssli und Compagnie.
Scherr, I. T. (1840a). *Meine Beobachtungen, Bestrebungen und Schicksale währen meines Aufenthaltes im Kanton Zürich vom Jahr 1825 bis 1839*. Erstes Heft [First issue]. St. Gallen.
Scherr, I. T. (1840b). *Meine Beobachtungen, Bestrebungen und Schicksale währen meines Aufenthaltes im Kanton Zürich vom Jahr 1825 bis 1839*. Zweites Heft [Second issue]. St. Gallen.
Scherr, I. T. (1842). *Die Notwendigkeit einer vollständigen Organisation der allgemeinen Volksschule*. Zurich and Winterthur: Verl. d. literar. Comptoirs.
Staatsverfassung für den Eidgenössischen Stand Zürich. (1831). Zürich.
Strehler (1848): Abhandlung des Hrn. Sekundarlehrer Strehler in Schöfflisdorf. In *Bericht über die Verhandlungen der XIV. und XV. Schulsynode des Kantons Zürich in den Jahren 1847 und 1848* (pp. 22-28). Zurich.
Tobler, E. (1944). *Instituts-Erziehung. Ein Beitrag zur Geschichte der praktischen Erziehung in der deutschen Schweiz von der Zeit Pestalozzis bis zum Ende des 19. Jahrhunderts* [Education in institutions: A contribution towards the history of practical education in German-speaking Switzerland from Pestalozzi's time to the end of the nineteenth century]. Aarau: Sauerländer.
Tröhler, D. (2001). Politischer Liberalismus und staatlicher Lehrmittelverlag. In D. Tröhler & J. Oelkers (Eds.), *Über die Mittel des Lernens. Kontextuelle Studien zum staatlichen Lehrmittelwesen im Kanton Zürich des 19. Jahrhunderts* [On learning materials. Contextual studies on state textbooks in the Canton of Zurich in the nineteenth century] (pp. 10–48). Zurich: Pestalozzianum.
Tröhler, D., & Schwab, A. (Eds.). (2006). *Volksschule im 18. Jahrhundert. Die Schulumfrage auf der Zürcher Landschaft 1771/72: Quellen und Studien*. (Quellen und Dokumente zur Alltagsgeschichte der Erziehung, Band 1) [Basic primary school in the eighteenth century: The School Inquiry of 1771/72 in rural Zurich: Sources and studies (Sources and documents on everyday history of education, volume 10]. Bad Heilbrunn: Klinkhardt.
Tröhler, D. (2006a). *Republikanismus und Pädagogik. Pestalozzi im historischen Kontext* [Republicanism and education: Pestalozzi in historical context]. Bad Heilbrunn: Klinkhardt.
Tröhler, D. (2006b). Schulgeschichte und Historische Bildungsforschung. Methodologische Überlegungen zu einem vernachlässigten Genre pädagogischer Historiographie. In D. Tröhler & A. Schwab (Eds.), *Volksschule im 18. Jahrhundert. Die Schulumfrage auf der Zürcher Landschaft 1771/72: Quellen und Studien* [Basic primary school in the eighteenth century: The School Inquiry of 1771/72 in rural Zurich: Sources and studies] (pp. 65–93). Bad Heilbrunn: Klinkhardt.
Tröhler, D. (2008). The educationalization of the modern world: Progress, passion, and the Protestant promise of education. In P. Smeyers & M. Depaepe (Eds.), *Educational research: The educationalisation of social problems* (pp. 31–46). Dordrecht: Springer.

Tröhler, D. (2009a). Curriculum, languages, and mentalities. In B. Baker (Ed.), *New curriculum history* (pp. 97–115). Rotterdam: Sense Publishers.
Tröhler, D. (2009b). Schulgeschichte als Argument der politischen Presse. In M. Caruso & H. Kemnitz & J.-W. Link (Eds.), *Orte der Bildungsgeschichte* [Locations of history of education] (pp. 125–135). Bad Heilbrunn: Klinkhard.
Tröhler, D. (2010). Harmonizing the educational globe: World polity, cultural features, and the challenges to educational research. *Studies in Philosophy and Education*, 29, 7–29.
Verfassung des eidgenössischen Standes Zürich vom 31. März 1869. Zurich.
Verfassungsgesetz betreffend Abänderung §§ 85 und 86 der Verfassung vom 23 Oktober 1849. Zürich.
Verordnung betreffend die Erbauung der Schulhäuser vom 26. Juni 1861. Zürich.
Vögelin, S. & Müller, J. J. (1875) *Lehr und Lesebuch für die Volksschule. 7. bis 9. Schuljahr. Zweiter Theil. Allgemeine und vaterländische Geschichte*. Zurich: Verlag der Erziehungsdirektion.
Vogt, G. (1873). Referendum, Veto und Initiative in den neueren schweizerischen Kantonsverfassungen. *Zeitschrift für gesamte Staatswissenschaft*, 29, 350–380.
Weidenmann, B. (2002). *Eine andere Bürgergesellschaft. Klassischer Republikanismus und Kommunalismus im Kanton Zürich im späten 18. und 19. Jahrhundert* [A different civil society: Classical republicanism and communalism in the Canton of Zurich in the late eighteenth and nineteenth century]. Göttingen: Vandenhoeck und Ruprecht.
Wettstein, U. (1867). Die sozial-bürgerliche und politische Ausbildung unserer Jugend. In *Bericht über die Verhandlungen der Zürcherischen Schulsynode von 1867* (Beilage 2). Zurich.
Wyss, F. v. (1892). Die schweizerischen Landgemeinden in ihrer historischen Entwicklung. In F. von Wyss, *Abhandlungen zur Geschichte des schweizerischen öffentlichen Rechts* (pp. 3–160). Zurich: Orell, Füssli.
Zürcher E. (1907). Der staatsbürgerliche Unterricht. In *Bericht über die Verhandlungen der Schulsynode von 1907* (pp. 1–19). Affoltern am Albis.

9 Citizens and Consumers
Changing Visions of Virtue and Opportunity in U.S. Education, 1841–1954

David F. Labaree

This is a story about the evolving rhetoric of educational reform in the United States. It starts in the early 19th century with a republican vision of education for civic virtue and ends in the mid-20th century with a consumerist vision of education for equal opportunity. The story is about how we got from there to here, drawing on major reform texts that span this period.

I argue that this rhetorical transformation was characterized by two main shifts, each of which occurred at two levels. First, the overall balance in the purposes of schooling shifted from a political rationale (shoring up the new republic) to a market rationale (promoting social efficiency and social mobility). And the political rationale itself evolved from a substantive vision of education for civic virtue to a procedural vision of education for equal opportunity. Second, in a closely related change, the rhetorical emphasis shifted from viewing education as a public good to viewing it as a private good. And the understanding of education as a public good itself evolved from a politically grounded definition (education for republican community) to a market-grounded definition (education for human capital).

I explore these changes through an examination of a series of representative reform documents. These include: Horace Mann's *Fifth* and *Twelfth Annual Reports* as Secretary of the Massachusetts Board of Public Education (1841 and 1848); the *Report of the Committee of Ten on Secondary School Studies*, appointed by the National Education Association (1894); *The Cardinal Principles of Secondary Education*, report of the National Education Association's Commission on the Reorganization of Secondary Education (1918); and *Brown v. Board of Education of Topeka*, a decision of the U.S. Supreme Court (1954).

This American case study in the evolution of educational rhetoric fits within a larger cross-national pattern in the evolving republican discourse of schooling. As the other chapters in this volume show, republican ideas played a foundational role in the formation of public education in a number of countries during the long 19th century. Although this role varied from one context to another, the republican vision in general called for a system of education that would shape the kind of self-regulating and civic-minded citizen needed to sustain a viable republican community. That system was the modern public school. At the heart of its mission was the delicate and critical task of balancing two elements at the heart of republican thinking—the autonomous individual and the common good. The primary contribution of the school was its ability to instill a vision of the *res publica* within future citizens in a manner that promoted individual choice while inducing them to pursue the public interest of their own volition. This effort posed twin dangers: Too much emphasis on individual interests could turn republican community into a pluralist state that is constituted as a competition of private interests, but too much emphasis on community could turn the republic into an authoritarian state that sacrifices individual freedom to collective interests. A liberal republican state requires an educational system that can instill a commitment to both individual liberty and civic virtue.

In this chapter, I explore the evolution of the tension between liberty and community in American education through an analysis of key documents in the history of American educational reform. I argue that over time the rhetoric of education shifted from a political vision of the civic-minded citizen to a market vision of a self-interested consumer. But the idea of a republican community did not disappear from the educational mission. Instead the political goal of education shifted from the production of civic virtue in the service of the republic to the production of human capital and individual opportunity. The end result, however, was to reconstruct the republican vision of education sharply in the direction of private interests and individual opportunities.

A major factor in the transformation of American reform rhetoric was the market. While a number of reform efforts—the common school movement, the progressive movement, the civil rights movement—occupied center stage in the drama of school reform during this period, initially the market exerted its impact from a position off stage. Over time, however, the market gradually muscled its way into the center of American education, shaping both the structure of schooling (characterized by stratification and credentialism) and more recently the rhetoric of school reform (with its emphasis on producing human capital and promoting individual opportunity). In the current period (50 years past the end of this story), when the market vision is driving the educational agenda, the political vision of education's social role remains salient as an actor in the reform drama, frequently called upon by reformers of all stripes. But the definition of this political vision has become more abstract, its deployment more adaptable, and its impact more diffuse than in the early 19th century, when a well-defined set of republican ideals drove the creation of the American system of common schools.[1]

Below I explore these themes in the changing rhetoric of educational reform in the United States, focusing on major reform texts. In the interest of space, and to avoid turning this analysis of changing educational rhetoric into a history of American schooling, I spend minimal time locating these texts historically. These are familiar documents to scholars who have an acquaintance with the history of American school reform, so I operate under the assumption that the reader is reasonably familiar with them and focus my attention on the position they occupy within the larger story of evolving educational rhetoric.

THE COMMON SCHOOL MOVEMENT: SCHOOLS FOR THE REPUBLIC

As secretary of the Massachusetts Board of Public Education in the 1840s, Horace Mann became the most effective champion of the American common school movement, which established the American public school system in the years before the Civil War. Its primary accomplishment was not in increasing literacy, which was already widespread in the United States, but in drawing public support for a publicly funded and publicly controlled system of education that served all the members of the community. What was new was less the availability of education than its definition as an institution that both expressed and reinforced community.

Mann's *Twelfth Annual Report*, published in 1848, provides the most comprehensive summary of the argument for the common schools. And he makes clear that the primary rationale for this institution is political: to create citizens with the knowledge, skills, and public-spirited dispositions required to maintain a republic and to protect it from the sources of faction, class, and self-interest that pose the primary threat to its existence. After exploring the dangers posed by social class to the fabric of a republican community, he proclaims:

> Now, surely, nothing but Universal Education can counter-work this tendency to the domination of capital and the servility of labor. . . .
> Education, then, beyond all other devices of human origin, is the great equalizer of the conditions of men—the balance-wheel of the social machinery. I do not here mean that it so elevates the moral nature as to make men disdain and abhor the oppression of their fellowmen. This idea pertains to another of its attributes. But I mean that it gives each man the independence and the means, by which he can resist the selfishness of other men. It does better than to disarm the poor of their hostility towards the rich; it prevents being poor. . . . The spread of education, by enlarging the cultivated class or caste, will open a wider area over which the social feelings will expand; and, if this education should be universal and complete, it would do more than all things else to obliterate factitious distinctions in society. (Cremin, 1957, p. 87)

A few pages later, he sums up his argument with the famous statement, "It may be an easy thing to make a Republic; but it is a very laborious thing to make Republicans; and woe to the republic that rests upon no better foundations than ignorance, selfishness, and passion" (p. 92). In his view, then, schools are given the centrally important political task of making citizens for a republic. All other functions are subordinate to this one.

In the political rhetoric of the common school movement, we can also see some other themes with a more economic flavor that will become the centerpiece of later reform movements. One is the importance of education in reducing social differences by enhancing social opportunities for all, as shown in the earlier passage. Another is the value of education as an investment in human capital. Mann devoted part of his *Fifth Annual Report* (1841) to the latter issue.

> If it can be proved that the aggregate wealth of a town will be increased just in proportion to the increase of its appropriations for schools, the opponents of such a measure will be silenced. The tax for this purpose, which they now look upon as a burden, they will then regard as a profitable investment.... When the money expended for education shall be viewed in its true character, as seed-grain sown in a soil which is itself enriched by yielding, then the most parsimonious will not stint the sowing, lest the harvest, also, should be stinted, and, thereby, thirty, sixty, or a hundred fold, should be lost to the garners. (p. 81)

Yet his defense of the human capital rationale for schooling is backhanded at best. He was a little embarrassed to be talking about the crass economic returns on education, as he explains in his introduction to this discussion:

> This view, so far from being the highest which can be taken of the beneficent influences of education, may, perhaps, be justly regarded as the lowest. But it is a palpable view. It presents an aspect of the subject susceptible of being made intelligible to all; and, therefore, it will meet the case of thousands, who are now indifferent about the education of their offspring, because they foresee no reimbursement in kind,—no return in money, or in money's worth, for money expended. The cooperation of this numerous class is indispensable, in order to carry out the system; and if they can be induced to educate their children, even from inferior motives, the children, when educated, will feel its higher and nobler affinities. (p. 81)

Thus, economic arguments are useful in drawing needed support to the common schools, but they play merely a supporting role in the "higher and nobler" mission of supporting republican community. Only in the 20th century would such economic arguments take center stage.

EMERGING CONSUMERISM: SCHOOLS FOR SOCIAL MOBILITY

If Horace Mann and the other leaders of the common school movement were reluctant to portray education as a mechanism for promoting worldly gain, the students and parents who were consuming this new cultural commodity showed less reluctance in that regard. The need to survive and the ambition to thrive in a market economy compelled citizens to think of education as something more than a politically desirable mechanism for preserving the republic; it was also a means to upward mobility. Reading, writing, and the manipulation of numbers were essential for anyone who wanted to function effectively in the commercial life of the colonial and early national periods of American history. Individuals did not need republican theory or compulsory schooling laws to make them acquire these skills, which is why literacy was a precursor rather than an outcome of the U.S. common schools.

But this compelling rationale for education—schooling for social mobility—was not something that appeared prominently in the rhetoric of school reform until well into the 20th century. One reason for this silence was that the idea of education as a way to get ahead was a matter of common sense in a society that was founded in market relations. It was not the subject of reform rhetoric because this idea was already widely accepted. Another reason was that this self-interested motive for education was embarrassing to verbalize in the face of the selfless rationales for education that dominated public discourse in the American colonies and the early United States.

After the revolution and in the early national period, the dominant educational rhetoric focused on a political goal for schooling. Before then, during the colonial period, the dominant educational rhetoric was religious. The Massachusetts School Law of 1647 sets the rhetorical tone for religious grounding of colonial education:

> It being one chief project of that old deluder, Satan, to keep men from the knowledge of the Scriptures, as in former times by keeping them in an unknown tongue, so in these latter times by persuading from the use of tongues, that so at least the true sense and meaning of the original might be clouded by false glosses of saint seeming deceivers, that learning may not be buried in the grave of our fathers in the church and commonwealth, the Lord assisting our endeavors,—It is therefore ordered, that every township in this jurisdiction, after the Lord hath increased them to the number of fifty householders, shall then forthwith appoint one within their town to teach all such children as shall resort to him to write and read.... (Cremin, 1970, p. 181)

In the face of this rhetoric, backed by the full authority of scripture, to argue publicly that people should pursue education for reasons of commercial gain would seem not only mean-spirited but nearly heretical. But the absence of such talk did not deny the reality that commercial motives for schooling were strong.

This relative silence about an important factor shaping education resonates with an important paradox in the history of school reform identified by David Tyack and Larry Cuban (1995) in their book, *Tinkering Toward Utopia*. They note that American educational reform is often understood in two contradictory ways: Schools are continually being churned by one wave of reform after another, but at the same time schools seem to stay the same or change only slowly. The reason for this, they argue, is that reform rhetoric swirls around the surface of schools, making a lot of noise but not necessarily penetrating below the surface, while evolutionary forces of structural change may be proceeding powerfully but slowly outside of view, making substantial changes over time without ever necessarily being verbalized or becoming part of a reform agenda.

The story I am telling in this chapter is about the interaction between these two levels—the changing rhetoric of educational reform in the United States over the past 200 years and its relationship with the quiet but increasingly potent impact of market forces on American schools. In many ways, the common school movement was a Whig effort to preserve the benefits of the burgeoning market economy in the antebellum United States while ameliorating its destructive tendencies—the class differences and competing interests that threatened to destroy the civic virtue needed to sustain a fragile republic. The rhetorical shifts in subsequent educational reform movements can likewise be seen as efforts to reach an accommodation between economy and society through the institution of education, which turns increasingly critical as education itself becomes more economically salient in the late 19th and 20th centuries.

In *The Making of an American High School* (1988), I explore the way in which educational consumerism emerged as an unintended consequence of the invention of the public high school in the 19th century. Central High School was founded in Philadelphia in 1838 for the most Whiggish of reasons. Its founders liked to call it "the school of the republic," and they saw it as an effective mechanism for encouraging middle-class families to send their children to the new common schools, thus making these schools a true embodiment of the republican community. But in order to make the high school sufficiently attractive to draw students from the best private schools, they inadvertently created a highly marketable commodity—with a marble edifice, the latest scientific equipment, and a faculty of distinguished professors—which became the object of intense competition among educational consumers. It introduced a form of invidious educational distinction that was highly visible (the only school of its kind in a large city), culturally legitimate (open to anyone who could meet its academic standards), and scarce (offering a degree to only 1 in 100 of the students entering the school system). These characteristics made a Central diploma quite valuable as a way for students to distinguish themselves from competitors, even though at the time the job market was not exerting demand for the skills acquired in a secondary education. But by the 1890s, when growing clerical and managerial occupations created a defined market for high school graduates, the enormous demand for access forced the school system to expand from two high schools (Central and its female counterpart) to a whole system of community high schools throughout the city. And the new structure—organized around the model of the comprehensive community high school, which continues to characterize American secondary education—managed to preserve the exclusivity of the old Central High in the face of greater accessibility by creating a stratified curriculum, which allowed some graduates to gain greater distinction than others.

COMMITTEE OF TEN: COMMONALITY WITHOUT CITIZENSHIP

In 1893, at the same time that consumer pressure was transforming secondary education in Philadelphia, a committee presented to the National Educational Association (NEA) a proposed new structure for the high school curriculum. The Committee of Ten on Secondary School Studies was made up of six professors, three high school principals, and the U.S. Commissioner of Education; Charles W. Eliot, the president of Harvard, served as chair. The committee's report is interesting less for its impact, which was minimal, than for its iconic status in later educational debates. It occupies a transitional position, as the final attenuated expression of the common school movement, poised to be swept away by the emerging progressive movement. The progressives dismissed the report with scorn, calling it the last gasp of a discredited vision of traditional academic schooling pushed on the schools by a group of self-interested college professors. Contemporary critics of progressivism—like Diane Ravitch (2000) and David Angus and Jeffrey Mirel (Angus & Mirel, 1999)—see it as the road not taken, which would have saved us from the ravages of progressive reform and which in some ways has been resurrected and reaffirmed by the standards movement.

For our purposes, I will focus on what is usually seen as the main issue in a very long report, the committee's insistence that the high school curriculum should be quite similar in length and content for all students regardless of whether they were heading to college. There is much about this argument that is resonant with the common school reformers, but the rhetorical representation of the argument is markedly different.

> On one very important question of general policy which affects profoundly the preparation of all school programmes, the Committee of Ten and all the Conferences are absolutely unanimous. . . .

> ... The Committee of Ten unanimously agree with the Conferences. Ninety-eight teachers, intimately concerned either with the actual work of American secondary schools, or with the results of that work as they appear in students who come to college, unanimously declare that every subject which is taught at all in a secondary school should be taught in the same way and to the same extent to every pupil so long as he pursues it, no matter what the probable destination of the pupil may be, or at what point his education is to cease. Thus, for all pupils who study Latin, or history, or algebra, for example, the allotment of time and the method of instruction in a given school should be the same year by year. Not that all the pupils should pursue every subject for the same number of years; but so long as they do pursue it, they should all be treated alike. (Krug, 1961, pp. 86–87)

This proposal would resonate with Horace Mann and the other members of the common school movement because it would preserve the republican practice of education as an experience shared by the whole community. Education should supply citizens with a common set of competences needed for active political participation, and it should work to counterbalance the stratifying tendencies in the market economy with an emphasis on building a republican community. Both argue for a common curriculum. But as we have seen, in Philadelphia and elsewhere, the market was driving the high school curriculum in the other direction, stratifying curriculum choices and school experiences according to students' occupational trajectory and class origins. In many ways this report can be read—as Ravitch and Angus and Mirel do—as a cry for preserving a common education at just the point that the institution was moving sharply toward stratification.

But what a muted cry it was. Gone is the grandiloquent language of Horace Mann, the appeals to the high-level political values, the passionate vision of education as the savior of society. In a report of nearly 19,000 words, there is not a single use of terms such as "citizen," "republic," or "democracy." Replacing republican rhetoric is the cautious, circumscribed, bureaucratic language of a committee of professional educators. In the 50 years since Horace Mann wrote, the common school system he promoted had succeeded beyond his wildest dreams. It had become the standard model for American education, defining what future generations would come to see as the "grammar of schooling" (Tyack & Cuban, 1995). It had expanded from elementary to grammar to high school. And it had generated a professional corps of teachers, administrators, and college professors who saw their work as a professional practice rather than a political vocation. And so the committee uses a coolly professional rhetoric, narrowly confined to the issues at hand, sticking strictly to the business of schooling. This makes the report more appropriate to its audience in the NEA, made up of other professional educators, but it left the committee's proposals without a solid rhetorical grounding in the surrounding society.

If it is not for the benefit of building a republican community, then why should high schools have a core curriculum? The report does not really answer this question, except for a feeble wave in the direction of efficiency: "The principle laid down by the Conferences will, if logically carried out, make a great simplification in secondary school programmes" (p. 87). In the absence of solid grounding, the committee made it easy for the progressives to attribute their recommendations to a simple desire to hang on to traditional school subjects and to impose antiquated college curriculum needs on the modern high school.

ADMINISTRATIVE PROGRESSIVISM: SCHOOLS FOR SOCIAL EFFICIENCY

The progressive education movement burst on the scene in the United States at the start of the 20th century. It was a complex movement with a wide range of actors and tendencies embedded within it, but two main strands in particular stand out. Pedagogical progressives (such as John Dewey and William Kilpatrick) focused on teaching and learning in classrooms, advocating child-centered pedagogy, discovery learning, and student engagement. Administrative progressives (such as Edward Thorndike, Ellwood Cubberley, and David Snedden) focused on the structure of school governance and curriculum, advocating a mission of social efficiency for schools, which meant preparing students for their future social roles. I focus on administrative progressivism here for the simple reason that they won and the pedagogues lost in the competition over exerting an impact on American schools.[2]

In 1918, the Commission on the Reorganization of Secondary Education (chaired by David Snedden) issued a report to the NEA titled *Cardinal Principles of Secondary Education*, which spelled out the administrative progressive position on education more clearly and more consequentially than any other single document. The report announces at the very beginning that secondary schools need to change in response to changes in society:

> Within the past few decades changes have taken place in American life profoundly affecting the activities of the individual. As a citizen, he must to a greater extent and in a more direct way cope with problems of community life, State and National Governments, and international relationships. As a worker, he must adjust himself to a more complex economic order. As a relatively independent personality, he has more leisure. The problems arising from these three dominant phases of life are closely interrelated and call for a degree of intelligence and efficiency on the part of every citizen that can not be secured through elementary education alone, or even through secondary education unless the scope of that education is broadened. (p. 1)

Here we see the basic themes of the report: Schools exist to help individuals adapt to the needs of society; as society becomes more complex, schools must transform themselves accordingly; and in this way they will help citizens develop the socially needed qualities of "intelligence and efficiency."

This focus on social efficiency, however, doesn't deter the authors from drawing on political rhetoric to support their position. In fact, perhaps reacting to the Committee of Ten report, or learning from this report's failure to exert a lasting impact on schooling, the authors framed *Cardinal Principles* in explicitly political terms. In a 12,000-word report, they use the terms "democracy" or "democratic" no fewer than 40 times, an average of 1.5 usages per page; the terms "citizen" or "citizenship" appear 16 times. (The words "republic" and "republican" are nowhere to be found.)

What do they mean by democracy? They spell this out in two statements in bold-faced type in a section called "The Goal of Education in a Democracy."

> The purpose of democracy is so to organize society that each member may develop his personality primarily through activities designed for the well-being of his fellow members and of society as a whole. . . .
>
> Consequently, education in a democracy, both within and without the school, should develop in each individual the knowledge, interests, ideals, habits, and powers whereby he will find his place and use that place to shape both himself and society toward ever nobler ends. (p. 3)

So democracy is about organizing individuals for the benefit of society, and education is about readying individuals to assume their proper place in that society. This is as crisp a definition as one can find for socially efficient education.

The commission follows up on this statement of principles to spell out the implications for the high school curriculum:

> This commission, therefore, regards the following as the main objectives of education: 1. Health. 2. Command of fundamental processes. 3. Worthy home membership. 4. Vocation. 6. Citizenship. 6. Worthy use of leisure. 7. Ethical character.

What a striking array of goals for education this is. In comparison with Horace Mann's grand vision of schooling for the republic, we have a list of useful functions that schools can serve for society, only one of which focuses on citizenship. Furthermore, this list confines the rich array of liberal arts subjects, which constituted the entire curriculum proposed by the

Committee of Ten, to a single category; the authors give it the dumbed-down and dismissive title, "command of fundamental processes," and they assign it a parallel position with such mundane educational objectives as "worthy home membership" and "worthy use of leisure."

Later in the report, the commission spells out an important implication of their vision of secondary education. Not only must the curriculum be expanded radically beyond the academic confines of the Committee of Ten's vision, but it must also be sharply differentiated if it is going to meet the needs of a differentiated occupational structure:

> The work of the senior high school should be organized into differentiated curriculums. The range of such curriculums should be as wide as the school can offer effectively. The basis of differentiation should be; in the broad sense of the term, vocational, thus justifying the names commonly given, such as agricultural, business, clerical, industrial, fine-arts, and household-arts curriculums. Provision should be made also for those having distinctively academic interests and needs. (p. 16)

The commission is explaining that its call for a socially efficient education in practice means vocationalism, with the vocational skills required by the job market driving the curriculum and slicing it into segments based on the specific jobs toward which students are heading. Any leftover space in the curriculum could then be used for "those having distinctively academic interests and needs."

This report, the keystone of the administrative progressive movement, represents two major transformations in the rhetoric of the common school movement. First, whereas Mann's reports use economic arguments to support a primarily political purpose for schooling (preparing citizens with civic virtue), Snedden's report turns this upside down, using political arguments about the requirements of democracy to support a vision of schooling that was primarily economic (preparing efficient workers). The politics of the *Cardinal Principles* thus serves as a thin veneer on a structure of socially efficient education, dressing up what would otherwise be a depressingly pedestrian vision, without being specified in sufficient depth as to intrude on the newly asserted vocational function of schooling.

Second, in *Cardinal Principles*, the administrative progressives preserve the common school movement's understanding of education as a public good. There is no talk in the report about education as a kind of personal property, which offers selective benefits to the credential holder; instead, the emphasis is relentlessly on the collective benefits of education to society. What is new, however, is this: Whereas the common school men defined education as a public good in political terms, the progressives defined it in economic terms. Yes, education serves the interests of society as a whole, say the progressives, but it does so not through the production of civic virtue but through the production of human capital.

THE CIVIL RIGHTS MOVEMENT: SCHOOLS FOR EQUAL OPPORTUNITY

If the administrative progressive movement marginalized the political argument for education, using it as window-dressing for a vision of education as a mechanism for creating productive workers, the civil rights movement brought politics back to the center of the debate about schools. In the 1954 decision of the U.S. Supreme Court, *Brown v. Board of Education of Topeka* (347 U.S. 483), Chief Justice Earl Warren, speaking for a unanimous court, made a forceful political argument for the need to desegregate American schools. The question he was addressing was whether to overturn the Court's doctrine of "separate but equal," established in *Plessy v. Ferguson* in 1894, as a violation of the clause in the Fourteenth Amendment to the constitution (passed at the end of the Civil War), which guaranteed all citizens the "equal protection of the laws." In past cases, the Court was able to duck the question by ordering school systems to equalize the funding of black and white schools. But in this case, "the Negro and white schools involved have been equalized, or are being equalized, with respect to buildings, curricula, qualifications and salaries of teachers, and other "tangible" factors," which forced the Court to address the central issue:

> We come then to the question presented: Does segregation of children in public schools solely on the basis of race, even though the physical facilities and other "tangible" factors may be equal, deprive the children of the minority group of equal educational opportunities? We believe that it does.

The Court's reasoning moves through two main steps in reaching this conclusion. First, Warren argued that the social meaning of education had changed dramatically in the 90 years since the passage of the Fourteenth Amendment. In the years after the Civil War, "The curriculum was usually rudimentary; ungraded schools were common in rural areas; the school term was but three months a year in many states, and compulsory school attendance was virtually unknown." As a result, education was not seen as an essential right of any citizen, but that had now changed.

> Today, education is perhaps the most important function of state and local governments. Compulsory school attendance laws and the great expenditures for education both demonstrate our recognition of the importance of education to our democratic society. It is required in the performance of our most basic public responsibilities, even service in

the armed forces. It is the very foundation of good citizenship. Today it is a principal instrument in awakening the child to cultural values, in preparing him for later professional training, and in helping him to adjust normally to his environment. In these days, it is doubtful that any child may reasonably be expected to succeed in life if he is denied the opportunity of an education. Such an opportunity, where the state has undertaken to provide it, is a right which must be made available to all on equal terms.

This led to the second part of the argument. If education "is a right which must be made available to all on equal terms," then the question was whether segregated education could be considered to provide truly equal educational opportunity for black and white students. Here the Warren drew on social science research to argue that, "To separate [black students] from others of similar age and qualifications solely because of their race generates a feeling of inferiority as to their status in the community that may affect their hearts and minds in a way unlikely ever to be undone." He continued by quoting from a finding by a lower court in the case:

Segregation of white and colored children in public schools has a detrimental effect upon the colored children. The impact is greater when it has the sanction of the law, for the policy of separating the races is usually interpreted as denoting the inferiority of the negro group. A sense of inferiority affects the motivation of a child to learn. Segregation with the sanction of law, therefore, has a tendency to [retard] the educational and mental development of negro children and to deprive them of some of the benefits they would receive in a racial[ly] integrated school system.

In combination, these two arguments—education is an essential right and segregated education is inherently harmful—led Warren to his conclusion:

We conclude that, in the field of public education, the doctrine of "separate but equal" has no place. Separate educational facilities are inherently unequal. Therefore, we hold that the plaintiffs and others similarly situated for whom the actions have been brought are, by reason of the segregation complained of, deprived of the equal protection of the laws guaranteed by the Fourteenth Amendment. This disposition makes unnecessary any discussion whether such segregation also violates the Due Process Clause of the Fourteenth Amendment.

The argument in this decision was at heart political, asserting that education was a constitutional right of every citizen that must be granted to everyone on equal terms. In this sense, it was a striking change from the *Cardinal Principles* report, which deployed the words "democracy" and "citizenship" in support of an argument that was at heart economic. But note that the political vision in *Brown* was quite different from the political vision put forward by Mann. For the common school movement, schools were critically important in the effort to build a republic; their purpose was political. But for the civil rights movement, schools were critically important as a mechanism of social opportunity. Their purpose was to promote social mobility. Politics was just the means by which one could demand access to this attractive cultural commodity. In this sense, then, *Brown* depicted education as a private good whose benefits accrue to the degree holder and not to society as a whole. The Court's argument was not that granting access to equal education for blacks would enhance society, black and white; instead, it argued that blacks were suffering from segregation and would benefit from desegregation. Quality education was an important form of property that they had been denied, and the remedy was to provide them with access to it.

Note the language of the decision: "In these days, it is doubtful that any child may reasonably be expected to succeed in life if he is denied the opportunity of an education." Schools enable individuals to succeed in life, and politically we cannot deny them this opportunity. This was an argument that showed how much schools had come of age more than 100 years after Horace Mann. Once created to support the republic, in a time when schools were marginal to the practical business of making a living, they had become central to every citizen's ability to get a good job and get ahead socially. In the process, however, the political vision of education changed from a substantive focus on producing the citizens needed to sustain the republic to a procedural focus on providing social opportunities. The idea of education as opportunity was already visible in Mann, but it was subordinated to the political project; with Brown, educational opportunity had become the project, and politics had become the means for asserting one's right to it.

CONCLUSION

This has been a story about the changing rhetoric of American educational reform. We have seen a transition from a political vision to a market vision of education, from a focus on education as a way to create citizens for an emerging republic to a focus on education as a way to allow citizens to get ahead in a market society. During this century, however, we did not see the political argument for education disappear. Instead, we saw it become transformed from the argument that education promotes civic virtue among citizens to the argument that education promotes social mobility among consumers. In the latter form, the political vision of education retained a strong rhetorical presence in the texts of educational reform. Yet the persistence of a political argument for education came at a cost. Gone was the notion that schools exist to promote civic virtue for the preservation of a republic community; in its place was the notion that schools exist to give all consumers access to a valuable form of educational commodity. This was a political vision of a very different sort, which transformed education from a public good to a private good and from a source of political community to a source of individual opportunity.

This conclusion reinforces two major themes that run through the other studies of republicanism and education in this book. One theme is the way the republican vision of education thinned out over time, losing its initially strong political edge. In other chapters, we see that as republicanism became more universal (reaching monarchies, like Spain and Sweden, and colonies, like Argentina), its political content grew thinner. Another theme is the political and educational construction of the individual, which was central to the republican vision of education but grew more complex over time and space. Gradually, the idea of civic virtue began to look more statist, focusing on education for social efficiency and human capital production rather than the construction of republican community; and the individualism fostered by public education began to look more self-interested, focusing on consumer rights rather than citizenship roles.

NOTES

1. In the 1990s, I developed an interpretation of the history of American education as a shifting terrain defined by the relative influence at particular points in time of three major goals for public education: democratic equality (preparing competent citizens), social efficiency (preparing productive workers), and social mobility (preparing individuals to get ahead socially) (Labaree, 1997). This chapter is an attempt to complicate that earlier story, in particular by exploring the ways in which the political goal of education has itself evolved over time.
2. The terms "administrative" and "pedagogical progressives" come from David Tyack (1974). I discuss the tension between the two and the reasons for the victory of the administrative wing in *The Trouble with Ed Schools* (2004, Chapters 7 & 8).

REFERENCES

Angus, D. L. & Mirel, J. E. (1999). *The failed promise of the American high school, 1890-1995*. New York: Teachers College Press.
Brown v. Board of Education of Topeka, 347 U.S. 483 (1954).
Commission on the Reorganization of Secondary Education. (1918). *Cardinal principles of secondary education*. Washington, DC: National Education Association.
Cremin, L. A. (Ed.). (1957). *The republic and the school: Horace Mann on the education of free men*. New York: Teachers College Press.
Cremin, L. A. (1970). *American education: The colonial experience, 1607–1783*. New York: Harper & Row.

Krug, E. (Ed.). (1961). *Charles W. Eliot and popular education.* New York: Teachers College Press.

Labaree, D. F. (1988). *The making of an American high school: The credentials market and the Central High School of Philadelphia, 1838–1920.* New Haven, CT: Yale University Press.

Labaree, D. F. (1997). *How to succeed in school without really learning: The credentials race in American education.* New Haven, CT: Yale University Press.

Labaree, D. F. (2004). The trouble with ed schools. New Haven: Yale University Press.

Mann, H. (1841). *Fifth annual report to the Massachusetts Board of Education.* Boston: Board of Education.

Mann, H. (1848). *Twelfth annual report to the Massachusetts Board of Education.* Boston: Board of Education.

National Education Association. (1894). Report of the Committee of Ten on secondary school studies. New York: American Book Co.

Ravitch, D. (2000). Left back: A century of failed school reforms. New York: Simon and Schuster.

Tyack, D. (1974). The one best system. Cambridge: Harvard University.

Tyack, D., & Cuban, L. (1995). *Tinkering toward utopia: Reflections on a century of public school reform.* Cambridge, MA: Harvard University Press.

10 France—Schools in Defense of Modern Democracy
Tradition and Change in French Educational Republicanism from Condorcet to Quinet and Ferry

Fritz Osterwalder[1]

On the eve of the so-called Third, lasting French Republic's birth from among war and revolution, still in the glamorous sunset of the Empire, the young lawyer and republican delegate Jules Ferry speaks publicly on the theme "Sur l'égalité d'éducation"[2] on April 10, 1870.

Both the event and the speech are part of the republican movement's general bustle, which has already become a routine since the movement has started to reestablish itself after the devastating defeat in 1851. The speech and the presented concepts are meaningful in particular with regard to its author's future position in society. In 1879 Jules Ferry becomes the Minister of Education for the so-called "Third Republic"; until 1885 he reforms the French educational system radically as both Minister of Education and Prime Minister, and thereby gives the reforms their shape well into the 20th century; the latter continues to exist to the present day under the seal of "école républicaine."[3]

In his speech of 1870, Ferry presents a kind of programmatic blueprint for this reshaping.[4] Increasing *social* equality determines the historical progress. In order to achieve progress, namely, the establishment of a modern republic, a fundamental obstacle needs to be overcome according to him. "Avec l'inégalité d'éducation, je vous défie d'avoir jamais l'égalité des droits /. ./ et l'égalité des droits est pourtant le fond de l'essence de la démocratie" (Ferry 1870/1996, p. 63).[5]

The plan for the educational reform claims to outline the "système d'éducation normale, logique, nécessaire"[6] for the republican society. The plan had, however—says Jules Ferry—already been developed in the 18th century in the "Convention Nationale," yet without having been implemented up to then. This plan exists thanks to the secretary to the Academy of Sciences, the mathematician Marie Jean Antoine Nicolas de Caritat Marquis de Condorcet, "son prophète, son apôtre, son maître."[7] Condorcet's uncompromising dedication to the republic and its school led finally even to his death; according to Ferry, he has "ajouté à une conviction philosophique, à une valeur intellectuelle incomparable, une conviction *républicaine*, poussée jusqu'au martyre" (p. 67).[8]

Ferry refers to Condorcet's bill and its explanation of a generally accessible, meritocratic educational system, the modern republican "Instruction publique"[9] of 1792. Although the plan was discussed over and over again, it was neither implemented nor did it at least come to a formal decision,[10] even once the republic was proclaimed publically on September 21, 1792.

In his speech of 1870, Jules Ferry presents Condorcet's plan as both a prerequisite for and a constituent of establishing a future modern republic, which does undoubtedly correspond to Condorcet's concept.

For Ferry, the "école gratuite, obligatoire et laïque"[11] becomes the conditio sine qua non for the modern republic. Hence, Ferry finishes his speech about the school reform in 1870 with the appeal, "Il faut que la démocratie choisisse, sous peine de mort; il faut choisir, citoyens" (p. 75).[12]

In spite of his empathic and unreserved approval of Condorcet's project, Ferry also differs essentially from it.

Ferry not only assigns to the school the task of ensuring the same access to *rational knowledge* and sciences, and to rationally negotiated moral, for people from all different social classes, from all regions of the country, and from both sexes, in order to create a rational public. Furthermore, the republican school should generate *common ground* among the citizens, which replaces the Catholic religion within the family and public sphere and reduces the influence of the church on the latter one.

In the scientific debate on the development of republicanism in 19th-century France, frequent references are made to this development—the differences between Ferry and the founders of the third republic on this important aspect regarding Condorcet's concept of the republic and his "instruction publique," which state that these differences originate from the great influence by August Comte and the positivism 19th-century republicanism.[13]

Comte, who considered Condorcet as his most important forerunner, was, however, fundamentally opposed to the republic.[14] According to that particular thesis, a fundamentally antidemocratic element would have been built into the concept of moral and civil education in the confrontation with the religious tradition of the state school. Without wanting to refute that thesis, other lines of development shall be explored in the following, which focuses simultaneously on the continuity and political innovation within both the republicanism and its educational concept during the 19th century.

In the first part, the question is raised what political and pedagogical qualities distinguish Condorcet's republicanism from the rest, so that the former establishes itself as the point of reference for the 19th century. The second passage explores the concept of moral unity, which underlies the emotion of brotherhood, the nation, as it was being discussed in republican circles in the context of the second republic as a consequence of the preceding defeats. In the final section, Ferry's concept of the "école laïque," and in particular his "cours morale et civique,"[15] are being discussed against the background of Ferry's preoccupation with the republican tradition.

THE REPUBLICAN TRADITION AND CONDORCET'S CONCEPT OF THE "INSTRUCTION PUBLIQUE"

The First French Republic, which was proclaimed in September 1792, only to sink into Jacobinical terror shortly afterward, and to finally be buried altogether by Napoléon through the Empire, is *without any* republican past history—according to Jean-Marie Goulemot (1993). In the Ancien Régime, the republic is *politically* associated with the past rather than with a political project for the future. The traditional political party of the opposition, which was inspired by the Jansenism, was equally anti-republican in *its fundamental principles* as the last major political reform movement before the revolution of 1789, the Physiocracy and Turgot's entourage. At the center of the physocratic concepts are the individual rights to freedom and property, which are justified by natural law and secured by the corresponding reform of tax and by the reformed state administration.[16]

This does, however, neither mean that the republicanism in the Ancien Régime was totally apocryphtic nor that the one at the time of the revolution was a new creation ab ovo.

Instead, republican concepts had a different significance. They were at the center of the *historical* and *moral* interests. The republicans of Antiquity had found a particular version in order to make citizens virtuous and to educate them, which was attractive to those people, who diagnosed the moral decadence of the Ancien Régime. Accordingly, the neo-Roman republicanism hardly enters the dispute regarding the political institutions; instead, it structures the debate on education, school, and their reshaping.

This thesis can also be verified regarding the major debates during the first phase of the revolution—before the confrontation about proclaiming the republic of 1792. While in the conflict regarding the constitution and the state institutions, references to the political reforms of the Ancien Régime are being made, the neo-Roman republicanism dominates the declarations and plans concerning the reforms of education and school, in continuity with the—intense—disputes on the "éducation nationale," which have taken place ever since 1763.

Different from one another as the countless projects for the educational reform in both the Ancien Régime and the revolution debates may be, they are almost without exception very similar regarding the neo-Roman virtue discourse, to which they are all committed. By means of public, common, national education the future citizens are to be educated in *love* for the common good, for heroic bravery and self-sacrifice, both for the sake of the nation and the state. This common moral, based on emotion, can either take the form of the Gallicanic religion of conscience and introspection or of neo-Roman nationalism in the shape of love for the laws and the nation, or of a political religion such as Rousseau's social contract outlines.

Both Mirabeau's (1971/2000) "enthousiasme de l'amitié, le dévouement à la patrie" (p. 93),[17] which are being cultivated in a pedagogic manner, and Rabaut Saint-Etienne's (1792/2000) "révolution dans les têtes et les coeurs" (p. 296),[18] which is to be fostered pedagogically by the Sunday cult in the tradition of the Huguenots' church sermons; stand in this republican tradition—along with Robepierre's favorite Michel Lepeletier's plan to educate together the whole youth in public work houses, namely, "de former leur coeur & leur esprit" (Lepeletier, 1793/2000, p. 374),[19] in order to establish a nation anew (p. 351).

In this field of virtue education the republicanism of the Ancien Régime and beyond, far into the revolution, developed a noteworthy continuity.

Condorcet's plan of the "instruction publique" distinguishes itself precisely by *not* following this continuity; instead he introduces the physiocratic institutional concept of the Ancien Régime's political reform also into the dispute on virtue and education, and from there he finally attempts to modernize the institutional concept of the republic itself, too.

Already in his speech on the occasion of his admission to the Académie Française in 1782, which was dedicated to the significance of popularizing the latest findings of modern empiric sciences for the social reforms, Condorcet distanced himself polemically from the republican and religious discourses of virtue, which focus on the alleged decadence of society—against the Jansenist tradition and Rousseau. Their concept to educate the human beings to be virtuous, a virtue that will raise them above their nature, is said to be unrealistic. In this sense, he states polemically: "Le projet de rendre tous les hommes vertueux est chimérique" (Condorcet, 1782/1986, p. 185).[20] This does not, however, suggest that virtue is reserved only for the few or that society continues to be exposed to decadence. Rather it is feasible in the circumstances of a modern society "de rendre les vertus faciles" (Condorcet, 1782/1986, p. 185).[21]

The basic prerequisite for this "vertue facile" is on the one hand the increasing wealth of society and on the other the rise of sciences. Both are directly dependent on the education, and hence they both require public promotion and support. The sciences foster society's economic progress; and the knowledge about society also explains to the human beings, why, in which cases, and how individual action both for the benefit of individuals and of society as a whole can and ought to be regulated by binding rules of conduct, the laws.

Accordingly, the virtue consists only in both acquiring this knowledge and applying it for its *personal* as well as its *social* benefit. Education with the aim of the "vertue facile" means that the human beings are being introduced to this knowledge and to the rational procedure, with the help of which it can be both expanded and verified.

In the dispute on the convening of the Etats généraux, Condorcet presents anew the physiocratic concept of the administration reform as a possible alternative, which is based on the establishment of strong provincial parliaments. In this context, an educational system is being outlined for the first time, which ought to impart to the future voters the knowledge, which empowers them to be "virtuous" in the new sense and to enhance society's wealth. Without education the citizens are said to be dependent in their choice and their decisions on educated people and demagogues (Condorcet VIII., 1788/1968, p. 475).

At the height of the first crisis of the revolution—after the king's flight—on July 12, 1791, Condorcet then develops his political position, and his concept of a modern republic, by starting from this renewed concept of virtue. It is not the enthusiastic "rhethorical" appeal to heroic bravery that comes to the rescue of liberty, but instead the preparation of a rational decision making by the public, by the enlightened citizens, men and women. "Les Français n'ont plus besoin que l'éloquence les appelle à la liberté. /. ./ C'est donc à leur raison seule qu'il faut parler des moyens d'assurer à la France une liberté paisible, fortunée, digne, en un mot, d'un peuple éclairé" (Condorcet XII., 1791/1968, pp. 227–237).[22]

Hence, the concept of "instruction publique," which Condorcet presents in 1791 and 1792, is geared toward this concept of both individual liberty and virtue regarding the rational participation in the public disputes and decisions concerning the election and control of government as well as the decision of laws, the binding rules of conduct.

Accordingly, both the social rules of conduct and the procedures, which lead to them, namely, the constitution, have to be taught in general education. The "instruction publique" has to accept, however, that both these rules and any knowledge are not ever themselves absolutely valid, and that they can and ought to be improved instead. Thus, it is being stated explicitly that ethics, laws, the constitution, and procedures, which lead to them, have to be presented by the general instruction "comme un fait," rules, which were given to the republic in search for rational decisions, but which are in themselves neither made once and for all nor unchangable (Condorcet, 1791/1989, p. 67.[23] "Ni la constitution française, ni même la déclaration des droits ne seront presentées à aucune classe des citoyens comme des tables descendues du ciel qu'il faut adorer et croire" (Condorcet, 1792/1989, p. 11).[24]

Religions must be kept well away from this kind of virtue education. Not only is the choice of religion a matter of personal freedom, but religions also present unchangeable rules of virtue, which cannot be revised and corrected through rational negotiation (p. 37). Yet, it is by no means only the traditional religion, which threatens both the citizens' rational distance to the rules and their readiness to negotiate as well as improve the rules through rational disputes. The enthusiastic feeling about the republic as it is demanded by the neo-Roman republicanism—"cette habitude des idées antiques, prise dans notre jeunesse"[25] (p. 185)—leads to uncriticalness and error, to unfree individuals, to abuse of power. The enthusiasm for the new society, such as it was promoted as the main aim of the education, is likened to the traditional religions as a kind of "political religion." "C'est une espèce de réligion politique, que l'on veut créer, c'est une chaine que l'on prépare aux esprits, et on viole la liberté dans ses droits les plus sacrés, sous prétexte d'apprendre à la chérir" (Condorcet, 1791/1989, p. 68). [26]

Condorcet takes the concept of both the individual human being's natural liberty and the criticism regarding the republican education in virtue as his starting point for developing a second innovative concept, the epistemic restriction of the "instruction publique." The traditional republican education in virtue was aimed at guaranteeing the all-encompassing equality of the citizens, who participated in the republic.

The dynamics of modern society are, however, defined by the inequality of the citizens' interests and opinions; these lead also to social differences. To prevent this inequality through a uniform general education would not only rob the society of its dynamics, but it would also threaten the citizens' natural liberty to develop their own opinion and to act accordingly. "La liberté de ces opinions ne serait plus qu'illusoire, si la société s'emparait des générations naissantes pour leur dicter ce quelle doive croire" (Condorcet, 1791/1989, p. 60). [27] Hence, general education has to be restricted to the extent of protecting both the individual liberty and the conflict of opinions from undue limitation. The education is being reduced to "instruction," to imparting of that knowledge and those procedures, which lay claim to the fact that they can be continuously verified by experience, that they can be improved any time, and that they are made for these very reasons. Undoubtedly, Condorcet thus concentrates the "instruction publique" on the empiric sciences and on the technologies, which build thereupon.

Also with regard to the institutional aspect of the "instruction publique" does the historical pedagogical republicanism evolve further.

The historical republics had excluded large parts of the population from participation and had even restricted their natural liberties. In his comment on the Union-Constitution of the United States, Condorcet states that it does not only retain slavery (Condorcet VIII., 1786/1968, p. 11), but also consequently excludes women from all rights to participation in the republic (Condorcet, 1788/1989, p. 214).

Hence, the project "instruction publique" proposes that both general instruction and the access to civic and political rights are offered equally to all inhabitants, women and men alike, people from all social groups and religious backgrounds of the republic, who are capable of rational education.

Equally part of this institutional concept is the possibility that everyone has the same right to access higher levels of education, right up to the highest level, the production of science, according to his achievements and accomplishments on the lower level, and the individual willingness to advancement.

The significance of this comprehensive institution for the development of the republic and his public requires, however, also that this institution must escape the clutches of specific interests and of the state power itself.

Otherwise, the danger is both inherent and immanent that the institution itself gets abused for the retention of power (Condorcet, 1791/1989, p. 141).

Condorcet's renewed concept of public instruction aims also at achieving a modernized concept of the republic. This concept is based on the one hand on an independent institutionalized state power and on the other hand on a public, which deliberate about this state and its activities by negotiating in a rational way, legitimizing, and controlling it by intervening through veto and bills, elections and votes.

QUINET'S PEDAGOGICAL PROBLEM: CONDORCET'S PLAN AS A COMPROMISE

As it became obvious in 1849—in the aftermath of both the unsuccessful workers' uprise and the election of the adventurer by the highly symbolic name of Louis-Napoléon Bonaparte as president—that the Second French Republic would fare little better than both the first one of 1792 and the short-lived republican hopes of 1830, its few achievements and large-scale projects were dropped very quickly. The coalition of the president's followers and the church party, which was also joined by frightened former anti-clerical people of the liberal party of order, invoked "the spirit of the Catholic Restoration," which, symbolically meaningful, became first evident in educational policies.[28]

They focused not only on the hardly begun reforms of the republic but also on the regulation, which had been in place within the July Monarchy since 1833 under Guizot's liberal ministry, and which granted to the Catholic Church a safe position within the educational system. In January 1849, the law, "Loi Parieu," was passed, which further opened the path for the church to enter the sphere of elementary schools. In the "Loi Falloux" finally, which came into effect on March 15, 1850, the church was even granted the possibility of influence within the state supervision of higher education.

In the irreconcilable worsening of the conflict about the Loi Falloux, the republican opposition proposed a motion for amendment regarding the "moral and religious education," which demanded in a strikingly restrained manner that this instruction ought to be done "sans acceptation des dogmes particuliers."[29] The mover was one of the most distinguished intellectuals of the republican party, who had taught at the renowned Collège de France together with the historian Jules Michelet, before the republic had been established; his name was Edgar Quinet.[30]

Quinet's speech in parliament on the motion for amendment is less militantly "laïque" than alarmist in comparison with his earlier positions. It is primarily addressed to the liberals. Quinet highlights that the new laws fall further back than Guizot's reforms of 1833—which, in Quinet's view so far, are conciliatory with regard to the throne and the altar; he pleads for the same continued separation of church and state, "du pouvoir laïque et du pouvoir ecclésiastique, /. ./ séparation de l'école et de l'Eglise, de l'instituteur et du prêtre, de l'enseignement et du dogme" (Quinet, 1850/2001, p. 168).[31] Without this separation first, the school would be split according to different religious denominations and thereby eventually the French nation as a whole.

In 1850, on including his speech in defense of the "école laïque" in his book *L'enseignement du peuple*,[32] Quinet adds, however, that the real solution, the safeguarding of the republic, cannot be found in Condorcet's project; rather this consists of the moral link among all citizens in *one single religion*, which corresponds with the modern sciences, which can be imparted within the educational system, and which is not the Catholic faith. This solution would, however, not be possible in the France of that time. Currently—in view of the tendency toward dictatorship—Quinet urges the hesitant liberals that it is all about liberty. Clearly, this does not refer to the participative republican liberty, but instead only to the liberal freedom of conscience and individual action.

The problematic of the pedagogically imparted moral-religious unity becomes thereafter the focal point of a concept dispute on the relation of republic, liberal public, and school within the modern society. The dispute among the restricted republican circles and the few liberals, who opposed the Bonapartism, becomes the starting point of Ferry's introduction to the "école republicaine" and of his own going back to and revising of Condorcet's plan.

When Quinet, in the aftermath of the lost parliamentarian disputes about the "laïcité," published *L'enseignement du peuple* in 1850, he thought the republic already lost. The discussion is geared toward the republicans, and in particular toward breakaway liberals in view of a prospective revival of the republican movement: "il faut déjà songer à organiser une victoire inévitable" (Quinet, 1850/2001, p. 35).[33]

One of the premises of the republicanism of 1848 and its different currents from socialists to liberal republicanism was that the republic and its stability depended really on the moral unity of its people, which stands *above* the public and its rational and deliberative negotiating. The assumption is that the republic and its sovereign public can work only if led, educated, and instructed through and by a moral authority, which is accepted by all concerned.[34] In this context, it is, however, crucial for the republic, who or of what kind the moral authority is, which safeguards the school.

This question is at the center of Quinet's inquiry ever since his courses at the Collège de France in 1845; in his paper on the instruction of the people of 1850, this question forms part of his basic criticism regarding the understanding of the early modern French republicanism. His criticism is not primarily pitted against Condorcet's concept, rather, far more fundamentally against Montesquieu, who since the defeat of the First Republic had been critisized continually for his negligence of the religion in the legislation.[35] The

Catholic Church and its dogma are based on authoritarian moral principles, which in turn justify and establish the absolute monarchy.

In modern Britain and in particular in the United States, the republican, political, and social reforms were based on earlier "religious revolutions" (p. 56), which had renewed the monarchic absolutist religion and the church so much that they could allow and enhance the social and political reforms better, yet at the same time could afford the latter with moral unity.

In contrast with the above, in societies in which religious life is not developed enough to produce its own religious reforms, the attempt needs to be made to break all links between the traditional religion and the evolved society in order to reduce the religion's influence. "Le moindre lien temporel qui subsiste peut amener la ruine; car ce qui est un déclin pour une Eglise devient aisément une chute irréparable pour une nation" (p. 56).[36]

The French Revolution and its repeated republican failures are represented from these perspectives. Neither was it, according to Quinet, preceded by a religious revolution, nor was it capable of either reducing or breaking the influence of the Catholic Church on the reforms of the civil and the political life.

In his controversial lecture at the Collège de France in 1845 on "Christianity and the French Revolution," which led eventually to his suspension from teaching, Quinet presented, for the first time, by which mechanisms the Catholicism undermines the republic. Quinet not only likens the Catholic Church and the religion to the Ancien Régime's monarchy, but also to the Jacobins' terror of 1793. The Catholicism is defined as "terrorisme moral, 'unspirituel spirituel qui tient l'anathème en permanence suspendu sur les âmes des suspects" (Quinet, 1845/1857, III, p.102).[37]

Starting from this view point, Quinet enquires in his book *L'enseignement du peuple* the different positions of educational policies with regard to the place, which they are willing to accord to the Catholic Church. At the center of the criticism is not the Catholic Church itself, but the conciliatory liberals' politics, the strategy of the republican's potentially.

In his lecture of 1845, Quinet made Victor Cousin, his liberal, philosophical former master, and his openness regarding the church and the religion, downright responsible for the political instability, for the tension in the modern society. Cousin was in charge of the educational politics of the July Monarchy, together with Guizot. Quinet states that the two men had greatly opened the schools to private initiative, yet at the same time they had insisted on a state guarantee of religious education in school so as to integrate the population into an order defined by Catholicism. Indeed, with their argument "il faut un Dieu pour le people" (Quinet, 1845/1857, p. 37),[38] they had in fact opened up *moral* rifts between the educated, non-clerical upper classes and the less educated, working classes of the nation, which started to give political and moral depth to the distinction of social classes.

In Quinet's book of 1850, this criticism of liberal policies with regard to school and church is further expanded. By allowing different religions, which are recognized by the state, to instruct children in state schools in religious education, they deprive people of different religious denominations from discussing moral issues together and thus from creating a unified modern public moral, which unite them all. "Vous diminuez le domaine de la pensée publique " (Quinet, 1850/2001, p. 85).[39]

More important, it is essential that the republic or the liberal state also offer an alternative of contents to the public schools, which encompasses all existing distinctions within society in an overarching unity that is capable of "renfermer les réligions opposées" (p. 114).[40]

Without going beyond these general rules, an absolute claim, "le droit absolu,"[41] of the public school to moral unity, leadership, and to education is nonetheless deduced from these rules. The only regulation regarding the content is aimed at the "fraternité," the citizens' *affection* for one another irrespective of both their individual social standing and religious denomination (p. 139). It is in the modern industrial society not limited to the tolerance; it is also a case of "il faut encore être réciproquement d'intelligence" (p. 141).[42] The public education of the modern republic is based on an "intervention spirituelle qui ramène à la paix ceux que tout pousse à la guerre" (p. 142).[43]

It is thus all the more astonishing that Quinet finally proposes Condorcet's perspective in 1850 and starts to distance himself from the republican religion of unity.

Quinet explains this change of directions with a dilemma of the historic neo-Roman republicanism. In 1854, he published the biography on the classical republican, Marnix de Sainte Aldegonde (1538–1598) and a history of the Dutch republics. In defense of the republic, Marnix had to revolutionize Calvinism itself, the "rigorisme genevois" toward a "christianisme serein," once more by reorienting the individual's responsibility before God as an individual's responsibility before the fellow citizens' judgment (Quinet, 1854/1857, V., p. 102).[44]

After these basical position is on Protestantism, the alternatives, religious perspectives of unity of the 19th century, are being discussed next, which the republican movement itself produced in France. In allusion to the charismatic leaders, Blanqui and Proudhon, of the socialist movement, social Messiahs, "Messie social" (Quinet 1857/2001, p. 226), who proclaim any old promises of salvation with seeming mass appeal as new dogma, are dismissed as a way forward into yet another tyranny. A new social and religious unity, such as the Saint-Simonists cultivate in their productive communities, cannot be effective on a large scale within a modern, urban, industrial society. "Faire régir la société par des instituts de savants" (p. 234),[45] so as to design society and its social religion once and for all, according to any kind of scientific insights, like the positivistic circle around August Comte envisages it, is equally dismissed as deceitful and unrealistic. All perspectives of modern religions of unity, which actually exist, are thus fundamentally dismissed in the name of the individual rights of freedom.

Hence, only two real political perspectives for the battle regarding the prospective French republic still remain: Either the republic is going to fight all existing religions of society in an equally militant manner, as well as trying to edge them out of the public life by force, or the republic seeks to ally itself with everyone else, against the predominant Catholic Church, in order to break the latter's claim to the national, monarchist-absolutist unity of France.

Quinet pleads for the second solution from his exile in 1857, and thus the dilemma of the pedagogical religion of unity is resolved.

The Catholicism is not to be replaced by a new "centralisation réligieuse" (p. 249),[46] but instead by a public competition of all perspectives, "des routes diverses dans lesquelles la dignité politique peut se concilier avec la croyance,"[47] of those ideas and basic convictions, which have left pragmatic room for the freedom of choice against the Catholic Church's exclusive claim to monopoly, and thus they "ont sauvé une parcelle de la liberté" (p. 248).[48]

All religious perspectives, which deny within themselves plurality, freedom, and public disputes and claim to have the exclusive political power and validity (i.e., the Catholic religion and church), are to be excluded and *fought against* by the public and the school together.

This perspective does not, however, open a politically or pedagogically independent perspective for republicanism, at the time of the Empire, when the republican opposition ought to explain their own alternative programmatically in order to strengthen the numbers of their own followers (Furet, 1988).

In response to this challenge, the work "La Démocratie" was published in Paris in 1859, which aimed at theoretically accentuating into a clear perspective the political demands, which "have been united under the banner of democracy over the past 30 years" of republican tradition (Vacherot, 1860, p. IIX).

The author of this work, which built on the *theoretical* framework of the newer republican experiences and discussions, Etienne Vacherot (1809–1897), belonged to the generation of republicans who had only begun to form a group themselves during the disputes of the second republic and to distinguish themselves politically during the Empire mainly.[49]

Vacherot deliberately attempts to respectively strengthen and integrate the liberal positions within the republicanism, "les vrais démocrates et les vrais libéraux sont toujours amis" (Vacherot, 1860, p. XXVI).[50]

Hence, Vacherot's argumentation draws on both de Tocqueville's liberalism and Quinet's republicanism, and yet at the same time it distinguishes itself equally from both. Accordingly, Vacherot starts out with a definition of democracy as a legal regulation of the *individual* liberty. Human, civil, and political rights become part of the overarching conceptual principle of safeguarding the individual freedom; this has become a prerequisite for the *liberal* tradition within the French republicanism since Condorcet's dispute with both the traditional and the Jacobin republicanism. To counteract the political liberalism itself, the declaration is made that the individual liberty has to be constituted also as civil and political freedom (p. 6), and that it cannot be presupposed in a "Laisser faire et laisser passer"⁵¹ after the English model (p. 13), individual freedom within the democracy is articulated as a space designed by a civil, political, and legal framework.

Vacherot reduces equality to a constituent of this liberty, which defines democracy insofar as it means "égalité dans la liberté" (p. 7).⁵² All other forms of equality would be detrimental to the republic. "Fraternité," Edgar Quinet's preference for republican moral education, is excluded completely as a frame of the republic. Meaningful as this emotion is said to be for the social life, it is dismissed because liberty is based on rights, and rights cannot be legitimized through feelings but through the free citizens' rational assent. "La fraternité fait la race, le peuple, la tribu, comme elle fait la famille. C'est la justice qui fait la société politique" (p. 33).⁵³

The modern democracy's political way of life is the city, "la cité", where the individuals are rationally interlinked by a kind of contract, in contrast to the "nation" (p. 16), where they are interconnected through birth or through division of labor. In this sense, the development of the civil and political society is identical with the establishment of the democratic society itself.

For the city "communauté d'idées" (p. 29) is necessary as a forerunner of civil and political equality of the contract; this community of ideas establishes a moral equality among utterly unequal people, who are of widely differing social standing, educated in very different ways, and are employed in various professions and occupations. It is only the community of ideas that allows all these people to rationally perceive and recognize each other's liberty as equal right, and "de se rapprocher, de se comprendre, de se respecter" (p. 29).⁵⁴

Only in these conditions the human beings can create civil and political equality. This "égalité morale," moral equality, is at the core of a democracy—and thus both the preceding and overarching principle of any civil and political equality. If the social conditions of a society are designed in such a way that this moral equality is not achieved, the social differences are too big, and large parts of the population live in misery, then even civil and legal equality cannot create democracy.

Vacherot's "communauté d'idées" asks for citizens who are both able and ready to communicate with fellow citizens about creating their own society, to demand of and accord to each other rights and duties, and to participate equally in the political institutions. Thus, it is not about an emotion of natural brotherhood, not about common religious feeling, but about "le sentiment du droit et la notion raisonné de l'égalité lesquels seuls sont propre à la démocratie" (p. 40).⁵⁵

The developing theory of modern democracy explores on the one hand the social conditions and their developments and on the other hand their institutional forms. For both inquiries, the question of education and state school is crucial. "Les conditions morales d'une société démocratique se résument toutes dans un mot: éducation" (p. 42).[56] Here Vacherot argues on level of principle against Cousin's and Quinet's concepts of religion, and what Quinet understands as Condorcet's compromise program is being even more extended.

The religious unity is basically not suitable for the modern demands of the republic because it requires isolation and exclusivity, the citizen is forever subject to the religious content, whereas now he becomes an actor, who is independent of it, and who thinks rationally.

The democratic society needs a moral education, which enables every single citizen to make an effort so as to scrutinize both the democracy's content and its decisions for him– and herself, and so as to convince the other members of society to keep further improving the basic democratic concepts for the common good.

"L'unité se fera ainsi dans la société des ésprits sans contrainte et sans discipline; non plus cette unité qui ne souffre ni mouvement ni initiative individuelle, qui a besoin du silence et de la nuit, mais cette unité vivante et féconde, qui s'épanout dans la diversité, et se manifeste dans la lumière" (p. 61).[57]

The moral unity, which establishes a democratic society, can neither be justified by an individual intuition, the conscience, nor by a metaphysical system, but must be based on rules and social and individual experiences just like the empiric sciences.

Just like the democracy's industrial and social conditions are seen as part of a dynamic historical process, the democracy's moral, scientific, and pedagogical conditions ought to be seen as an equally important part of it.

Given the significance of this moral and scientific education for the democratic society, Vacherot ascribes the task of education to the central state. The state has to guarantee the scientific education of all citizens as well as the higher scientific education. This does not mean, however, that the state itself necessarily establishes and runs its own institutions.

For Vacherot, the top priorities of the central state's three institutional tasks regarding school are:

— the control that all schools are bound to democratic equality and to sciences. (p. 263)
— the guarantee that all future citizens attend general education, that school is compulsory for all without exception, and that the education is offered free of charge. (p. 262)
— the equal access to higher education for all. (p. 284)

On the other hand, Vacherot claims that the democratic state with its schools has to protect the children's liberty and equality, also against their own parents. The state is obliged to run schools which guarantee that all children are introduced to the sciences as well as to the "notions pratiques de justice et d'égalité" (p. 280).[58] As citizens the parents have the right and liberty for themselves to dismiss sciences and equality, but they do not have the right to send their own children to schools, where those are denied to them.

Finally, within any democratic society exist social and religious forces that resist democracy. The state is not allowed to spread a republican state religion against them, it can only educate the people in the rules and experiences of moral equality; the school remains nonetheless an important means of safeguarding the democratic society against its antagonists, furthering the democratic development, and fighting the opposing concepts as such. "L'école publique est le berceau de la cité. Toute démocratie qui a l'intélligence de ses vrais intérêts ne peut abandonner l'enseignement de l'Etat" (p. 286).[59]

FERRY'S CONDORCET—THE SCHOOL AT THE CENTER OF THE STRUGGLE OVER PLURALISTIC INTERESTS, AND THE REPUBLICAN MORAL

In 1866, Ferry was among the strongest defenders of Edgar Quinet's book on the revolution and his theses. He was less interested in the problem of religious revolution in France than in the clear condemnation, as a prerequisite for the republic, of the Jacobins' terror regime as a continuation of the Ancien régime's and the church's absolutism.

When he gave his keynote speech about the republican school in 1870, he was well familiar with Quinet's and Vacherot's positions and their disputes regarding Condorcet's concept. Ferry had publicly defended Quinet's thesis inside the republican movement. At the republicans' rallies, Ferry became closely acquainted with Vacherot and his theses.[60] He kept well away from the controversy, which threatened to split the republicans from the liberals, only to give much emphasis to that very position during the dispute regarding both his own reform projects and the introduction of a republican moral education.

Soon after becoming "minstre de l'instruction publique" on February 4, 1879, the outline of Ferry's reforms,[61] the future "école laïque," starts to show. Within a relatively short time span, between 1879 and 1882, the latter and its main features are established through legislation. As minister and lawyer, Ferry himself takes an active part during the crucial phase, and he also largely defines the themes for the parliamentary, public disputes, and even for their implementation within the teacher training through his concepts.

The major steps thereby are the following:

—In 1879, two laws are submitted to parliament. The first excludes all people who are not part of the educational system (i.e., in particular clerical people from the "Conseil Supérieur de l'instruction publique," the highest supervisory board of the schools). The second law dismisses the so-called "jurys mixtes," mixed examination boards of state and church representatives, and henceforth reserves the right of examination exclusively for the state. At the center of the disputes is, however, the seventh paragraph, which denies the right to work in education to any person who belongs to a church congregation that is not sanctioned by the state. Among the ones that are not authorized are the major and most common educational orders such as the Jesuits, the Dominicans, and the Marists.[62]

Yet, in the same year a third law follows. Up to then, the girls' education in both public state schools and private church schools has been exclusively entrusted to clerical teachers (Lelièvre, 1990). The new legislation now demands that women and men are trained as teachers in one state institute in each "département" and that clerical lady teachers have to acquire a teacher diploma from the state.

—In 1880, the crucial laws and decrees on primary school education are presented to parliament; they state a public primary school free of charge, compulsory, and most important they exclude of all religious themes from the curriculum.

—In 1881 and 1882, the laws and decrees come into effect, which shape the republican school, and which define the compulsory curriculum and education. First, there is the "instruction morale et civique," the moral and civic instruction, without the controversial human obligation toward God, "obligation de l'homme envers Dieu" (School Law, March 28, 1882, Art. 1); this promptly leads both to organizing a specific moral education besides the civic studies (Conseil, 1887) and to allowing also for extra focus on this theme in the teacher training—as part of the 1888 Decree by the "Conseil Supérieur de l'Instruction Publique" on the organization of teaching.

With which concepts and arguments in mind does Ferry take the different steps? Does he simply follow Condorcet herewith or to what extent does Ferry consider the arguments by Quinet and Vacherot?

In the debates on the exclusion of the congregation from the public state school on June 27, 1879, the minister emphasizes again and again that it is neither a fight against the Catholic Church nor against religion (Ferry, 1870/1996, I, p. 395), and that it is solely a question of "liberté en matière d'enseignement" (p. 391).[63] The parents' liberty regarding their children's religious education must not be restricted by the congregations' prohibition of education. Ferry states this explicitly in his public challenge of the Jesuits in his speech of Epinal on April 23, 1879. A few days later, he equally maintains that the state—the "état enseignant,"[64] as he calls it—cannot of itself define the content of the schools' curriculum (p. 406).

With regard to religious questions the school has to be neutral. "La neutralité réligieuse de l'école, au point de vue du culte positif, au point de vue confessionnel, comme on dit en d'autres pays, est un principe nécessaire qui vient . . . à son heure" (Ferry, 1880/1996, II. p. 28).[65] During the debate in the senate, when Ferry speaks out against including the expression "enseignement des devoirs de l'homme envers Dieu" in the curriculum, he becomes polemic against his own party members, who follow Quinet's concept of the republican uniform religion. In that case, the school ought to at least be given the opportunity of clarifying the question for themselves. The public has no interest in deciding on metaphysical questions "sur l'origine des choses et de leur fin" (p. 36)[66] and in including the opinion of some citizens and in respecting the one of others less by doing so.

Religion can neither be decided on by a majority vote nor can it be defined by the public without violating the rights of individuals. The assertion that the school has to be Catholic because the majority of the French belong to the Catholic Church is thus dismissed strongly. Ferry argues that the teachers' equality before the law and their freedom of conscience is otherwise called into question. All state purposes are open to any citizen irrespective of his or her religion, and it cannot be demanded of teachers to profess their faith in the name of a majority. In all these concepts, Ferry follows Condorcet's original project rather closely, which attempts to link pedagogically individual liberty, natural law of freedom, and participatory demands of the republic.

A major part of Ferry's argumentation shows, however, that he does not stop at this negative definition; quite obviously it goes well beyond and is nothing short of an actual challenge to the Catholic Church and religion.

The state has to guarantee by means of the school that the youth is not exposed to the anarchy of opinions; the state must not leave the development to chance, states the minister during the debate on the exclusion of the congregations from the schools on June 27, 1879 (Ferry, 1879/1996, I., p. 389). Ferry's main reproach against the congregations in his speech in Epinal: They have educated the youth in ignorance of and far away from the ideas, which matter to "us." Under these ideas and under this collective expression he subsumes the ideals of the French Revolution of 1789, the collective embraces those "qui révèrent 1789 comme une délivrance de la société moderne, comme un idéal" (p. 383).[67]

During the debate on the religious neutrality of school, Ferry places next to the religious indifference of education the demand to keep away those, and to fight their ideas, "qui ont des opinions séparés des notres par un si profond abîme" (Ferry, 1880/1996, II., p. 36).[68] He specifies that he means those who have declared "la Révolution française est un déicide"[69] (i.e., the Catholic Church and the Catholic religion).

Not only ideas, which are opposed to the French Revolution, are to be fought within and through the education, but equally those who misunderstand the problem of equality. In his first parliamentary debate on school, which Ferry has to face in 1879, he also draws a clear line on that side. Opinions regarding the revolution such as those that led to the socialist Commune-Uprising of 1871 must be fought equally in and through education.

In keeping with Quinet, the public state school is assigned the task of actively fighting all ideas and ties, which bind the future citizens in an authoritarian manner. The public school becomes one of the crucial means for Ferry, in Quinet's tradition, of fighting the major moral obstacles on the way to both establishing and stabilizing the republic. At the center is the historic political analysis of the French republican failures in the tradition of Quinet. The establishment of the republic thus becomes mainly a pedagogical and institutional problem or challenge.

During the debate in the senate on the congregations in teaching, the religious neutrality of schools is restricted accordingly in no small way in certain cases (i.e., even downright denied).

The state is neutral against religious doctrines, yet in cases where they contain pedagogical, moral, and political dimensions, the state is obliged to intervene. "Mais il y a deux choses dans lesquelles l'Etat enseignant et surveillant ne peut pas être indifférent: c'est la morale et c'est la politique, car en morale comme en politique, l'Etat est chez lui: c'est son domaine, et par conséquent, c'est sa responsabilité" (p. 409).[70] In this sense, in his speech in Epinal in 1879, Ferry also curtails the parents' freedom regarding the religious education of their own children by a right, an obligation even by the state to intervene. When parents send their child to a clerical school for religious education and thus delegate their own religious liberty regarding education, then the state restricts the parents' claim to education. "Ce n'est pas une liberté transmissible, et, dès que le père la délègue, l'état a le droit et le devoir d'intervenir" (p. 380).[71] Well in keeping with Vacherot, the state is given the task of protecting the child's right in education of being acquainted with the egalitarian rational moral of the city.

Ferry does, however, follow Vacherot's solution to Quinet's dilemma between the defense of the republic through moral unity on the one hand and the liberal freedom on the other hand also with regard to the pre-legal egalitarianism. Already in his speech of 1870, Ferry explains that the political, legal equality insists on the "création de moeurs vraiment démocratiques" (Ferry, 1870/1996, I., p. 64).[72] These democratic customs consist—closely following Vacherot's concept—in the fact that also socially unequal people, "maître et serviteur,"[73] recognize each other's dignity, and thus their own duties and obligations, before they can even begin to negotiate with one another. Hence, education in equality has the task to make children recognize their obligations toward any of their fellow human beings and to impart to them also the idea of the socially weaker person's dignity toward the socially stronger person and vice versa, "de lui inspirer ou rendre le sentiment de sa dignité" (p. 65).[74] An egalitarian society can only survive if it is upheld by this "esprit d'ensemble,"[75] the democratic customs, which precede politics and legislation (p. 65).[76]

Ferry answers to his opponents' objections that the "école laïque" is a school without moral, with the argument that the only true moral is the one without any reference to either God or any dogma, and that this moral alone could create a unity in the age of empiric sciences.

In that context, Ferry also refuses to describe the school's moral task as an introduction to the "devoirs envers Dieu,"[77] in the sense of a deistic or transdenominational or undogmatic religion, which republican representatives from his own camp have suggested.

How is this public moral imparted in school, which are the contents of this moral instruction? For this perspective, Ferry receives few hints from the preceding republican dispute. In contrast to the education in public morals, which Condorcet alone conceptualized, Ferry envisages a stable, unchangeable republican moral, with which to unreconcilably oppose the Catholic religion and other authoritarian traditions in sharp conflict.

In this, Ferry follows neither Quinet's democratic unitarian religion nor Auguste Comte's antidemocratic ideas of a "réligion positive" and the "culte de l'idéal," developed by himself without any reservations, fundamentally dismissed as relapse into authoritarianism by Ferry during the senate's debate of July 2, 1881 (Ferry, 1881/1996, II., p. 59).

The order of the day is not a "morale réligieuse" but a concept of morality that can serve as the basis for the different institutional and legal circumstances of republican life. Following Vacherot's concept, the "instruction morale et civique" (School Legislation of 1882) is split. It consists of an "enseignement civique," which presents the laws and the republican institutions in their demcoratic (i.e., their changeable form) thanks to public procedures of negotiating. Next to those courses, an independent instruction in morals is continuously offered to all classes throughout compulsory school, from the "section enfantine," for the 5- and 6-year-old children, through to the "école supérieure," for the 11- to 13-year-old pupils. The course subject is the republican moral as unchangeable, unified, and exclusive basis of the republic, of its social and political life.

The republic assigns the task "de fonder une éducation nationale, et de la fonder sur des notions du devoir et du droit que le législateur n'hésite pas ... à inscrire au nombres des premières vérités que nul ne peut ignorer" (Ferry, 1881/1996, II, p. 109)[78] to the school.

These unchangeable moral axioms are now introduced as consecutive teaching of social duties in the curriculum by the "Conseil supérieur de l'instruction publique," in keeping with Vachérot. The curriculum starts at the basic level with conversations and stories that illustrate the duties toward both fellow human beings and institutions. "Soins particuliers de la maîtresse à l'égard des enfants, chez lesquelles elle a observé quelque défaut ou quelque vice naissant" (Conseil supérieur de l'Instruction publique, 1887, p. 362).[79]

It is the task of this moral education to both draw clear lines against any anti-republican moral and to give a stable, unshakeable, generally binding background to the changing and freely decided republican political and social activities as well as to the variable shaping of liberal and participative freedom.

How this pedagogical moral instruction was shaped and implemented is not part of the present study. A single stanza from a little song, which was printed in the pedagogic magazine aimed at lady instructors of infants, "L'école maternelle," for moral education on the basic level, makes obvious just how close the pedagogicalized moral in defense of the republic comes to the patriotic enthusiasm, to the "réligion politique"—which Condorcet despised and which Quinet gave up after much hesitation:

> "Pour être un homme il faut savoir écrire
> Et tout petit apprendre à travailler.
> Pour la Patrie un enfant doit s'instruire
> Et dans l'école apprendre à travailler.
> L'heure a sonné, marchons au pas
> Jeunes enfants, soyons soldats." (L'école maternelle, May 1, 1882 ; cited in Ozouf, 1982, p. 112)[80]

NOTES

1. Translation by Marianne Bertsch-Junger, MA.
2. "On the Equality of Education." On Jules Ferry the still authoritative biography by M. Reclus (1947). For the circumstances of the speech in 1870 and for its public setting of the "Conférence Molé," refer to Legrand (1961).
3. "republican school"
4. About the process of reshaping classical republicanism, see Chapter 1 (this volume).
5. "With the inequality of education, I dare you, that you shall never have equality of [civic] rights/ . . . / and yet equality of [civic] rights is the foundation of the democracy's essence."
6. "the system of the normal, logical, and necessary education"
7. "his prophet, his apostle, his master/teacher." About the eschatological dimension of republicanism, Chapter 1 (this volume).
8. "Added to a philosophical conviction, and to an unparalleled intellectual value, a *republican* conviction, pushed as far as martyr."
9. "Public Instruction [in public state schools, not private schools]."
10. Refer to Baczko (2000).
11. "The compulsory and nondenominational, secular school, free of charge"
12. "It is imperative that democracy chooses, otherwise [the price is] the death sentence [for democracy itself]; one has to choose, citizens."
13. The thesis on Ferry's positivism as the basis of the confrontation between the church and religion on one hand and the moral education on the other was first presented comprehensively by Legrand (1961). Thereupon it was extended by Nicolet (1994) to a general invasion of positivism into the French republicanism.
14. On Compte's dispute regarding Condorcet's concepts, refer to Muglioni (1989) and Petit (1989).
15. "nondenominational/secular public school" . . . "courses in public moral/ ethics and in civic rights and duties"
16. About the difference between the traditional republican concept of liberty and the liberty of liberal democracy, refer to Chapter 1 (of this volume).
17. "enthusiasm for friendship, devotion for the home country"

18. "revolution in the heads and hearts"
19. "to form their hearts and their minds"
20. "The project of rendering all human beings virtuous is chimerical"
21. "make the virtues easy [to achieve]"
22. "The French are no longer in need of eloquence in order to call them to liberty./. ./It is only to their reason that one must talk about the means of safeguarding a peaceful, fortunate, dignified liberty for France, in one word, of an enlightened population."
23. "as a fact"
24. "Neither the French Constitution, nor even the Declaration of Human Rights must be presented to a single class of citizens as Tables of Law which descended from heaven and which have to be worshipped and believed"
25. "this habit of classical ideas, [an attitude] acquired in our youth"
26. "It's a kind of political religion that one wants to create, its a chain that one prepares for the minds, violating the liberty in its most sacred rights under the pretext of learning [how] to cherish it."
27. "The liberty of these opinions would by then only be illusionary, if the society would seize the coming generations as they are born, in order to dictate to them what they have to believe."
28. Both on the political swing and on the political concept of this coalition, refer to Furet (1988).
29. "without accepting any particular dogma"
30. Edgar Quinet (1803–1875) is one of the leading intellectuals in the France of the first half of the 19t[h] century, who contributed to the renewal of the republicanism, next to historian Jules Michelet. On Quinet there exist as yet no comprehensive studies besides the biography (Valès, 1936). Of importance are the Geneva Dissertation on Quinet's early development by Aeschlimann (1986), and in particular Furet's study on "La Revolution" and on the historiographic dispute within republicanism (Furet, 1986).
31. "the 'laïque' power and the eclestic power, /. ./ separation of school and church, of teacher and priest, of teaching and dogma"
32. "Teaching/Educating the Population"
33. "one already ought to think of organizing an inevitable victory"
34. P. Rosanvallon refers to the fact that this concept regarding the united moral authority of the democratic public was shared to a large extent by all French republicans in the 19th and 20th centuries (Rosanvallon, 1993).
35. Montesquieu (1748/1951, II, p. 718), De l'Esprit des Lois, Livre XXIV, Chap. V. The criticism concerning Montesquieus' concept of the generation of laws without any interference of religion is at the center of interest for the French republicans ever since the time of the Jacobin dictatorship. In 1811, Destutt de Tracy criticized Montesquieu comprehensively in a paper commissioned by Thomas Jefferson, which took a posthumous fragment by Condorcet as a starting point (Destutt/Condorcet, 1822).
36. "The least temporary link, which remains, can lead to ruin; since what is a decline for the church, becomes easily the irreparable fall for a nation"
37. "moral terrorism, a spiritual 1793 which holds the curse permanently suspended over the souls of the suspects"
38. "a/one God is needed for the people"
39. "You diminish the domain of public thoughts"
40. "to enclose opposite religions"
41. "the absolute right"
42. "furthermore an understanding of one another is required"
43. "spiritual intervention, which leads to peace those, who are pushed to war by everything"

France—Schools in Defense of Modern Democracy   213

44. So Quinet in "Marnix de Sainte Aldegonde" that he could include in his complete edition of 1857, which was published in the Paris of the Empire. The actual political conclusion, however, which is being discussed here, was not allowed to be published in Paris, as Quinet writes in his memoirs (Quinet, 1858, X., p. III).
45. "have the society governed by institutes of scholars/scientists"
46. "religious centralization"
47. "diverse routes, along which the political dignity can be reconciled with the faith"
48. "have saved a parcel of liberty"
49. On Vacherot and his work, there are no fundamental newer research papers; the older ones, dating back to the Fin de siècle, are generally heavily influenced by the political disputes of the third republic with Vacherot himself, and depending on their own positions, they either make him into a great hero or betrayer (e.g., Ollé-Laprune, 1898). Hazareesingh (1998b) offers a good overview of his life and political development.
50. "the true democrats and the true liberals are always [each other's] friends"
51. "let [them] do and let pass"
52. "equality within liberty"
53. "Brotherhood makes the race, the population, the tribe, like it creates the family. It is the justice, which establishes the political society."
54. "to approach one another, to understand each other, to respect one another"
55. "the feeling of right and the reasoned notion of equality, the only ones, which are appropriate to the democracy"
56. "The moral conditions of a democratic society can be summarized in one word: education"
57. "The unity is thus going to be created in a society of [free] minds without constraints and discipline; neither such a unity which suffers neither individual movement nor initiative, which needs silence and night, but instead this lively and fertile unity, which blooms in all its diversity, and which mainfests itself in the light."
58. "practical notions of justice and of equality"
59. "The public [not the private] school is the cradle of the city. All democracy which understands its true interests cannot abandon state education"
60. "Vacherot présidait, tu sais comment, quelle longueur et quelle amphigouris." Vacherot chaired [the meeting], you know how, at what length and with what amphigouris, wrote Ferry on April 20, 1869, to his fellow campaigner and later prime minister Gambetta (Hazareesingh, 1998a, p. 1146).
61. The republican camp was by no means uniform with regard to the aims and the procedure concerning the school. Influential representatives such as Paul Bert preferred a unified legislation in the tradition of Condorcet (on this, see Prost, 1968).
62. Refer to Ozouf (1982) for this.
63. "liberty in matters of teaching"
64. "the teaching state"
65. "The religious neutrality of the school, from the point of view of the positive worship, from the denominational point of view, as it is called in other countries, is a necessary principle whose hour has come [now]"
66. "on the origin of things and on their end"
67. "who revere 1789 as a freeing of the modern society, as an ideal"
68. "who have opinions which are separated from ours by such a profound abyss"
69. "the French Revolution is a murder of God"
70. "Yet there are two things, when the teaching and supervising state cannot be indifferent: they are the moral and the politics, since what concerns the

moral and the politics, the state is at home: they are its domain, and consequently, its responsibility."
71. "It is not a transmissible liberty, and once the father has delegated it, the state has the right to intervene."
72. "creation of truly democratic moral habits"
73. "master and servant"
74. "to inspire them with or to give to them the feeling of their dignity"
75. "spirit of togetherness"
76. Ferry opens in his concept of equality and democratic liberty and "education publique" a global perspective for human society, expressed in the future in the French politics of colonisation (see Chapter 1, this volume).
77. "obligations towards God"
78. "to found a national education, and to base it on the notions of duty and right which the legislator does not hesitate ... to inscribe among the first truths, which no one can ignore"
79. "Particular care is given by the lady teacher to children, in whom she observes a flaw or some vice about to be born"
80. "In order to be a human being, you have to know how to write/and learn how to work at a very young age./ For the sake of the home country the child must be taught/ and in school learn to work./ The hour has struck, lets march together/Young children, let's be soldiers."

REFERENCES

Aeschlimann, W. (1986). *La Pensée d'Edgar Quinet*. Paris-Genève: Georg-Anthropos.
Baczko, B. (2000): *Une Education pour la Démocratie*. Genève: Droz.
Condorcet, M. J. A. N. C. de. (1847). *Oeuvres*. A. Condorcet & M. F. Arago (Eds.). (1968). Tomes VIII & XII. Paris : Stuttgart Reprint Frommann.
Condorcet, M. J. A. N. C. de. (1986). *Sur les élections et autres écrits*. Corpus des Oeuvres de Philosophie en Langue Française. Paris : Fayard.
Condorcet, M. J. A. N. C. de. (1889). *Ecrits sur l'instruction publiques*. C. Coutel & C. Kintzler (Eds.). Vols. I & II. Paris: Edilig.
Conseil Supérieur de l'Instruction Publique. (1887). *Règlements Organiques de l'Enseignement Primaire*. Session de Décembre 1886–Janvier 1887. Paris: Imprimerie Nationale.
Destutt de Tracy, A. L. C. / Condorcet, M.-J. A. N. (1822): Commentaires sur l´ésprit des lois de Montesquieu suivi d´observations inédites de Condorcet. Paris: Desoer.
Ferry, J. (1986). Le débat sur ‚La Révolution' de Edgar Quinet dans Le Temps 1866. In F. Furet (Ed.), *La Gauche et la Révolution au XIX Siècle. Edgar Quinet et la question du jacobinisme 1865–1870 suivi de Les Pièces du Débat*. Paris: Hachette.
Ferry, J. (1996). *La République des citoyens*. (O. Rudelle, Ed.). Tomes I & II. Paris: Imprimerie Nationale.
Furet, F. (1986). *La Gauche et la Révolution au XIX Siècle. Edgar Quinet et la question du jacobinisme 1865–1870 suivi de Les Pièces du Débat*. Paris: Hachette.
Furet, F. (1988). *La Révolution*. T. 2 1814–1880. Paris: Hachette.
Furet, F., & Ozouf, M. (Eds.) (1993). *Le siècle de l'avènement républicain*. Paris: Gallimard.

Goulemot, J.-M. (1993). Du républicanisme et de l'idée républicaine au XVIIIe siècle. In F. Furet & M. Ozouf (Eds.), *Le siècle de l'avènement républicain* (pp. 287–312). Paris: Gallimard.

Hazareesingh, S. (1998a). From democratic advocate to monarchist critic of the republic: The penitent Jacobinism of Etienne Vacherot (1809–1897). *The English Historical Review, 113*(454), 1143–1179.

Hazareesingh, S. (1998b). *From subject to citizen*. Princeton: University Press.

Legrand, L. (1961). *L'influence du poitivisme dans l'oeuvre scolaire de Jules Ferry. Les origines de la laïcité*. Paris: Rivière.

Lelievre, C. (1990): Histoire des institutions scolaires (1789-1989). Paris: Nathan.

Lepeletier, M. (1793/2000). Plan d'éducation nationale, présenté par Robespierre. In B. Baczko (Ed.), *Une Education pour la Démocratie* (pp. 345–382). Genève: Droz.

Mirabeau, V. R. M. de. (1791/2000). Travail sur l'éducation publique. In B. Baczko (Ed.), *Une Education pour la Démocratie* (pp. 69–104). Genève: Droz.

Muglioni, J. (1989). Comte et Condorcet. In P. Crépel & C. Gilain (Eds.), *Condorcet, mathématicien, économiste, philosophe, homme polititique* (Colloque International) (pp. 472–479). Paris: Minerve.

Nicolet, C. (1994). *L'idée républicaine en France 1789–1924*. Paris: Gallimard.

Ollé-Laprune, L. (1898). *Etienne Vacherot*. Paris: Perrin.

Ozouf, M. (1982). *L'école, l'eglise et la république 1871–1914*. Paris: Cana.

Ozouf, M. (1993). Entre l'esprit des Lumières et la lettre positiviste: les républicains sous l'Empire. In F. Furet & M. Ozouf (Eds.), *Le siècle de l'avènement républicain* (pp. 415–440). Paris: Gallimard.

Petit, A. (1989). Condorcet ‚médité' par Auguste Comte. In P. Crépel & C. Gilain (Eds.), *Condorcet, mathématicien, économiste, philosophe, homme politique* (Colloque International) (pp. 480–495). Paris: Minerve.

Prost, A. (1968): Histoire de l´Enseignement en France 1800-1967. Paris: Armand Colin.

Quinet, E. (1845/1857). Le Christianisme et la Révolution Française. *Oeuvres Complètes, 3*. Paris: Paguerre.

Quinet, E. (1854/1857). La Fondation de la République des Provinces-Unies. Marnix de Sainte-Aldegonde. *Oeuvres Complètes, 5*. Paris: Paguerre.

Quinet, E. (1858). Histoire de mes idées. *Oeuvres Complètes, 10*. Paris: Paguerre.

Quinet, E. (1987). *La Révolution*. (C. Lefort, Ed.). Paris: Belin.

Quinet, E. (2001). *L'Enseignement du Peuple (1850) et La Révolution Religieuse au XIXe siècle (1857)*. (D. Lindenberg, Ed.). Paris: Hachette.

Rabaut Saint-Etienne, J. P. (1792/2000). Projet d'éducation nationale. In B. Baczko (Ed.), *Une Education pour la Démocratie* (pp. 295–302). Genève: Droz.

Reclus, M. (1947): Jules Ferry 1833-1893. Paris: Flammarion.

Rsanvallon, P. (1993). La république du suffrage universel. In F. Furet & M. Ozouf (Eds.), *Le siècle de l'avènement républicain* (pp. 371–390). Paris: Gallimard.

Vacherot, E. (1860). *La Démocratie*. Paris: Chamerot.

Valès, A. (1936). *Edgar Quinet, sa vie et son oeuvre*. Carrières-sous-Poissy : La cause.

Part III
Curriculum, Science, and the Fabrication of the Virtuous Citizen

11 From Virtue as the Pursuit of Happiness to Pursuing the Unvirtuous

Republicanism, Cosmopolitanism, and Reform Protestantism in American Progressive Education

Thomas S. Popkewitz

As Tröhler (2006) argues, republicanism as a cultural set of principles about civic virtue is not merely about political responsibility to a common good. It is shaped and fashioned through multiple historical trajectories that link secular and the sacred. The American republic was no exception. It assembled particular Enlightenment notions of cosmopolitan principles about reason, science, and liberty with reformed Protestant notions of redemption and salvation. The cosmopolitan concern with universal values of humanity (the inalienable Rights of Man [sic]) was ironic as the transcendent ethics of the enlightenment was initially to transcend the provincialism and localism associated with the nation-state. Change was directed to the social and individual matters found in "the city of man" no long bound by the static hierarchies of aristocracies and religious cosmologies. The American republic was narrated as a radical historical thesis of progressive human forces ordered and controlled through human reason and rationality. The moral basis of this progressivism was charged through Puritan themes of salvation brought into the secularization of government.

This chapter explores the multiple historical trajectories through which American progressive education was produced at the turn of the 20th century. That history is often told through intellectual and social traditions that assume American[1] enlightenment principles about the cosmopolitan promise of the nation.[2] The stories told, with some dissent, are about the emergence of mass schooling from Horace Mann to the different progressive education movements that either foster or hinder the realization of the American republican and democratic ideas; narratives of social, intellectual, and educational intellectual changes that coalesce into the modern school—modern in its increasing democratization of groups that participate in schooling; modern in the increasing professionalization of teachers through formal education and administration; modern through the development of the pedagogical and learning sciences; modern in educating the citizen who contributes to the economic and social purposes of the republic; and modern in the sense of bringing elite notions of the American enlightenment's cosmopolitanism into pedagogical systems that ordered the learning of the child.

This chapter goes in a different grain of writing history. It asks about the historical conditions that give intelligibility to American progressive education. I focus on American progressivism as a historical site in which particular scientific discourses become visible to order the knowledge of pedagogy and the child as an object of schooling. But to engage in such an inquiry, it is necessary to examine the historical intersections of social, cultural, and political relations, and systems of knowledge that emerge in different practices from the end of the 18th century to the first decades of the 20th century—what I will call "the long 19th century—and which come together and give intelligibility to the practices of American progressivism.

The first section explores the biblical inscriptions of Puritan narratives brought into an American enlightenment cosmopolitanism in the making of republicanism and the republic as "the light of the world."[3] The narratives about national exceptionalism,[4] as discussed in the second section, are (re)visioned in American Progressivism as cultural dialogues about science and technology providing the collective mission of the nation as "the light of the world". This "technological sublime" is inscribed in the new sociologies and psychologies of the "modern" progressive pedagogies of John Dewey, Edward L. Thorndike and the community sociologies, explored in the third section. The salvation narratives about collective belonging in science and pedagogy, however, was not only about "the light" of the nation and its "Chosen People". A comparative style of thought is discussed in the last two sections, focusing on The Social Question in which Progressive Protestant reforms gave attention to the moral disorder in the conditions and people of urban settings. In that focus is the reversal of negative to positive freedom that embodied concerns about the identity of population cast as not able to "pursues happiness", the latter picking up on the U. S. Declaration of Independence. The title of the chapter plays on this inscription of difference in Progressivism that inscribes the system of reason that juxtaposes the cosmopolitan hope of the nation with the fears of those not "virtuous" and dangerous to the envisioned future.

Republicanism and its relation to schooling are examined in the system of reason through which the objects of reflection and action in schooling are produced. The attention to rules and standards generated about "reason" and "reasonable people" is not about a philosophical notion of "pure" reason or the psychological attention to the working of the mind. How "we" think, talk and act are historical processes produced through a grid of practices whose assembly and connections govern conduct. Further, Progressivism entails historically exploring a grid of practices of the long 19th century given visibility in the various progressive reforms. I speak of the enlightenment and cosmopolitanism as epistemological principles generated with this historical grid to connect individuality to notions of community and collective "homes" (Popkewitz, 2008). Among these principles embodied in "modern" pedagogies are (a) notions of agency; that is, reason and rationality as universal rules to enable individuals to change purposely their conditions; (b) and with the notions of agency are practices to calculate the rules and standards of reason in the planning to change people as a method to change society. Cosmopolitanism, then, is an analytic to consider the system of reason as it intersects with republicanism and not a normative concept about what should be the child and society. Using this notion of history and in contrast to Pocock's (1975) argument about the United States as a classical republican, progressivism and progressive education are studied as embodying registers of social commitments to civic virtue and individual freedom that are not the sum of classical or liberal republicanism.[5]

"THE LIGHT OF THE WORLD": AMERICAN EXCEPTIONALISM, PURITAN SALVATION THEMES, AND SCHOOLING

This section explores, first, the mutation of salvation themes of the Puritans into secular narratives of the nation as the Chosen People, given divine sanction to provide "the light of the world" through its republican ideals. This national *exceptionalism* was initially about the nation as the New World that reclaimed the past moral good of Garden of Eden and serving as "the light of the world,", only to be re-visioned in the late 19th century. That revision, discussed in the second part, could no longer look to a biblical past reclaimed but to the future claimed through the knowledge of science and technology as the apotheosis of reason.

Salvation Themes and the Citizen

One can read the European and North American enlightenments written as "movements from the ideals of the Christian millennium where the proper object of study was God, to cosmopolitanisms that rejected religious morality as the basis for a common morality to mankind" (Schlereth, 1977, p. 56; see also Marx, 2003). When examined historically, the salvation themes of the Reformations and Counter Reformation were not erased with the arrival of the European and North American enlightenments. As is evident in other book chapters, the religious notions of salvation were transported and translated into redemptive themes of the secularism of new nations and its republicanism (see e.g., Lilla, 2007; Tröhler, 2006). In the United States, the idea that the cosmopolitan reason of the citizen was an individual who embodied universal characteristics of humanity that intersected with, for example, reform Protestantism in what Bellah (1975) calls a "Civil Religion."

The American Revolution is a case in point. It merged particular Calvinist salvation themes into discourses about the government enabling the individual's "pursuit of happiness" through which the notions of freedom and social progress were formed (Ferguson, 1997, p. 21). The salvation themes of the nation and its people were drawn from, in part, the sermons and prophesy founded in the calls of the New England Puritans, a Calvinist group that came to America in the 17th century to escape persecution. The Puritan gave recognition to the site of their colony as a grand historical determinism that was dialectical and rational. The founding of the colony and later of the nation told of "the unfolding of events would lead to a final Utopia on earth" (McKnight, 2003, p.19).

The land was called the *New World*, brought into political narratives about the providential character of the nation. The phrase brought religious conceptions of a Garden of Eden into the national imaginary about a people who escaped the evils of Old World traditions and its disfigurements (Jehlen, 1986; Ross, 1991). The Puritans served as God's elect to make possible "the day of God's judgment and the new reign of Christ on earth" and thus reverse the corruption of Europe (McKnight, 2003, p. 17). America signified *the Chosen People*, a phrase to signify the radical "otherness" of the nation's citizens, its place as God's chosen place, and its people as "racially elect" (Glaude, 2000).[6]

With the forming of the new nation, America was the *New World* that superseded the Old World of Europe. The New World had a double significance of a secular and a sacred place. The nation embodied a divine plan of constructing community without the old traditions that put the universality of progress in danger. That design of community contained a prophetic vision in the consecration of civil life (Bercovitch, 1978). The land was given a sacred historical mission in the American identity (McKnight, 2003). Calvin's edict about each individual entering in and participating in the world was brought into political, social, and economic narratives about the nation to fulfill the greater corporate mission. America was the "city upon a hill" (McKnight, 2003, p. 2). The saga of the nation was told of as an evangelical purity and political goodness in its land and its people. The nation was "errand in the wilderness" that served as "the terra profane 'out there' yet to be conquered, step by inevitable step, by the advancing armies of Christ" (Bercovitch, 1978, p. 26). The common good of the Republic joined "the health of the soul and the regeneration of the Christian and the virtuous citizen, exultation of the divine and the celebration of design" (Ferguson, 1997, p. 43) in planning for human improvement and "happiness."

One way to think about civic virtue associated with republicanism is through the reversal of the political doctrine of the republic about the "pursuit of happiness." Some American historians have said that the enlightenment translated the ultimate theological question of how can I be saved into the pragmatic one of "How can I be happy?" (see e.g., McMahon, 2006). Pleasure was no longer seen as a distraction for the pursuit of virtue, but virtue itself. The U.S. Declaration of Independence couples "the pursuit of happiness" with "the unalienable right" of individuals. The negative liberty inscribed enlightenment ideals into a cosmopolitan hope of liberal individualism. The founding of the republic entailed distrust that the common person could embody a cosmopolitan "reason" in the making of moral judgments necessary of the citizen. The initial task of the American republic was to control emotions and prevent excessive desire among "ordinary people" (Wood, 1999, p. 40). American progressive pedagogical reforms, particularly the pragmatism of John Dewey, provide the social technologies that brought elite notions of cosmopolitan "reason" into pedagogical practices as a way to order everyday life (Childs, 1956).

The citizen of the republic gave expression to the hopes of the American enlightenment through a biological metaphor of growth, divine providence, and the choice of light or darkness. John Adams, a signer of the Declaration of Independence, the second U.S. president (1797–1801), and a strong devotee to the republican ideal of civic duty, spoke about the need for an educated citizen. The settlement of America, Adams argued, was the "the opening of a grand scene and design in Providence for the illumination of the ignorant, and the emancipation of the slavish part of mankind all over the earth" (Wood, 1991, p. 191). Adams said, "The mind could be cultivated like a garden, with barbarous weeds eliminated and enlightened fruits raised." The cultivation of the mind would produce the common good and enable the destruction of "the savages" (Wood, 1991, p. 191). Thomas Paine, a signer of the Declaration of Independent, told of throwing off Old World prejudices through reason and rationality. "The mind once enlightened cannot again become dark" (cited in Wood, 1991, p. 191).

The cultural thesis of American exceptionalism was captured in varied cultural spaces. The novels of the nation told of heroes who had evangelical qualities given through their worldly pursuit (Furstenberg, 2006). The qualities of the new nation were embedded in the idea of Manifest Destiny. Appearing in the journal *Democratic Review* in 1837, Manifest Destiny narrated a divine quality to the territorial expansion through Puritan rhetoric in the westward development to the Pacific. It expressed the value of the nation as diverse European peoples populating the new continent to receive the divine principles of liberty and equality (Wald, 1995).

The American school of the 19th century was told as a narrative of the Manifest Destiny of the nation. The U.S. Department of Interior, Bureau of Education report on American education (U.S. Government Printing Office, 1874),[7] "Statement of the Relation of Free School to the American Commonwealth," which was prepared for a European conference, spoke of national destiny in the founding of a civilization that transformed the wildness. The history of the United States was given as "the founding [of] a civilization [in the peculiar] character in the American people" (U.S.

Government Printing Office, 1874, p. 13). The history of the nation had three evolutionary stages: (a) the settlement of new territory by pioneers and the transformation of the wilderness into an agricultural country, (b) the rise of commercial towns and the creation of transit facilities in the new regions, and (c) the development of manufacturing centers and the ascendancy of domestic commerce (U.S. Government Printing Office, 1874).

The religious idea of the Manifest Destiny and "errand in the wilderness" was woven into the frontier thesis of the westward expansion to the Pacific written by the early 20th-century historian Frederick Jackson Turner (1893/1994). "Turner wove the tale of an exceptional nation removed from the corrupting influences of Europe, a country where the frontier produced the perfect mix of abundance, individualism and equality" (Oshinsky, 2000, p. A19). The national development was imagined as the model for the advancements for all of humanity. The sense of nation as a space of belonging was, for Turner, the nation's frontier of free land, and the American westward settlement explained the particular character of the American democracy and its national "soul." The redemptive stories of the nation's exceptionalism told of freedom born in the "boundless sources of energy through which individuals discovered who they were: personality flourished only through exploration and growth" (Wiebe, 1995, p. 186).

At this point, it is possible to identify a grid through which republicanism is assembled to create a relation of the individual, the notion of common good, and the salvation theme embodied in the nation that mutates into the projects of schooling. Turner's frontier thesis gave sanction to and was given intelligibility as a way of "seeing," thinking, and acting about two overlapping registers of individuality and community. The cultural thesis was of an individual whose self-realization and freedom entail a pragmatic mode of life ordered through science and technology (for a general discussion of freedom in the American context, see e.g., Foner, 1998). The rugged individualism of Turner's frontier transformed the Puritan "errand in the wilderness" into a prophetic vision of building community and civil life through personal energy. The action-oriented and problem-oriented mode of life gave the nation its exceptionalism but also formed its image. The keys to the prophetic vision were inward and external, combining the spirituality and changes that nature's wilderness fostered. It was agrarian in one sense, but cosmopolitan in that the challenges of the frontier were ordered by universal principles of reason, rationality, and progress that enabled the national epic.

The cultural thesis of the citizen instantiated a moral universalism that differentiated those not as reasoned or without "reason"—slaves and First World people, women—as well as provided the providential purposes for territorial expansions, and, more recently in the 21st century, to assert the role of the nation and its particular ways of life in global affairs. To return to the Frederick Jackson Turner, the New World that he saw replacing the frontier was a homogenous world. It had no violence, no African slaves, no Indians, and no women to unsettle the story.

Yet the erasure of difference inscribed differences through a comparative style of thought that differentiated and divided those who belonged and those who embodied dangers to that individuality and sociality. This comparative style of thought was expressed through the universalizing that accompanied the episteme associated with the enlightenments and its notion of individuality. As I will discuss later, Reformation narratives were incorporated into the American enlightenment to juxtapose light and darkness, with the latter expressed in one context as resisting "Gothic barbarism." The Gothic barbarism was to be defeated through

> the struggle of natural science in understanding of nature, the tempering of superstition in religion in the politics of new free government—not only in the spread of science, liberty or republican government but in the spread of civilization. The civilizing was to calculate happiness. (Wood, 1991, pp. 191–192)

The civilizing was also to assume the notion of civilization as embodying rationality, science, and liberty that inscribed the nation as the light of the world in relation to its "Others." The civilizing was also cast, to continue with Wood's quote, in relation to the enlightenment expression of the capabilities and capacities that were able to "pursue happiness."

"I LIFT MY LAMP BESIDE THE GOLDEN DOOR": THE TECHNOLOGICAL SUBLIME AND THE CULTURAL THESIS OF REPUBLICANISM

An important shift occurs in the cultural narratives about the republic and its citizens toward the end of the 19th century. The epic of a lost utopian past was placed with the future in the epic told of the nation and its people. As will be discussed below, the exceptionalism of the nation, with some dissent, was in the model for creating the prosperous and equalitarian society of the future that would escape the burdens of the past. Frederick Jackson Turner, discussed earlier, made visible this new cultural vision at the end of his career. Turner lamented the closing of the frontier at the end of 19th century because of the uncertain consequences it posed for the American future.

Yet the fear of the end of the frontier and the character it gave to the individual was rearticulated as an optimism. America in contrast to Europe, Turner argued, had no history that made it possible to place its development within the course of a universal history (1893/1994). The movement from an agrarian society to an urban nation and an expanded educational system made possible a future that substituted for the mobility of the frontier west (Faragher, 1994). Concepts of that future bring into view a new temporality to the nation and its citizens. That temporarily is an irreversible process of time by which development and growth can be calculated and society and individuality planned through science and technologies. Time, however, is not only social but linked in the new sociologies and psychologies of pedagogy that ordered and classified progressive education.

Progressive education, then, brings the relation of past/present/future as a principle for the designing of the interior of the child. One can read the various works of progressive education and its sciences as inscribing an American cosmopolitan vision of the future that places science and technology in the cultural narratives of the nation. The American historian Nye (1999) calls this revision "the technological sublime." Its foundation stories of technological changes told about the marvels of the railroad, electricity, bridges, skyscrapers, as well as the natural power of the Niagara Falls and the Grand Canyon. The scientific and technological changes were placed in a cultural dialogue about the nation and the liberation of the human spirit to be realized by the republic. The America wilderness was being transformed into "a prosperous and egalitarian" cosmopolitan society whose landscape and people had a transcendent presence (Nye, 2003, p. 5). In a later section, I will explore the inscription of the technological sublime in which science and technology are made into the apotheosis of "the reason" of different progressive sciences of education and as a cultural thesis about modes of life in pedagogy. The technological sublime was given expression in literature. Mark Twain's Huckleberry Finn, for example, plays along the Mississippi River with overlapping images of the tensions of machine (the train) and the pastoral as the new landscape of the nation. The poetry of the immigrant Emma Lazarus (written in 1883), immemorialized on a plaque at the foot of the Statue of Liberty, captures the hope, sense of beautify, and awe of the sublime in the promise of the American exceptionalism. Lazarus wrote of the United States:

> "Give me your tired, your poor,
> your huddled masses yearning to breathe free,
> The wretched refuse of your teeming shore,
> Send these, the homeless, tempest-tossed, to me:
> I lift my lamp beside the golden door."

Lazarus, although a Jew, embodied the redemptive Protestant hopes of the new nation in which the constituted "wretchedness" of the Old World is shed to allow a rebirth. The land was the incarnation of the promise of the abundance and liberty that would include its newest immigrants. "The golden door" to the New World opens as the Old World's "tired" traditions are discarded. The rebirth is personal, social, and political to forge the common good: It is to enable one to "breathe free" through the enlightenment "lamp."

The new epic tale of the technological sublime worked into the social sciences that formed a part of the progressive movements. Charles Horton Cooley, an early American sociologist and progressive reformer interested in education, evoked the future and sociology as bringing the enlightenment's lamp. Cooley (1909) saw the United States as "nearer, perhaps, to the spirit of the coming order" (p. 167) that is totally different from anything before it. Evoking the American exceptionalism, Cooley wrote that "the new industrial modernity" of America was close to being the first real democracy. He asserted that the nation was "totally different from anything before it" because it places a greater emphasis on individuality and innovation in a land that "does not inherit the class culture of Europe" (cited in Ross, 1972, p. 245). The apotheosis of reason provided through the new sciences was to bring democracy and freedom to all of human kind.

The schools that became visible in progressivism joined cosmopolitan reason with the common good as a salvation narrative about a redemptive nation. Education and the family were merged, and the Puritan mission of the "errand into the wilderness" to find revelatory, spiritual fulfillment required the education of children that extended to those beyond the community of believers (McKnight, 2003, p.11). Education took Calvinist notions of salvation as a lifelong enterprise that bought together faith and reason that emerged in the Reformation (McKnight, 2003). The prophetic design of community drew on John Calvin's notion of *curriculum vitæ or* "a course of life." Education was the persistent preparation for a conversion experience. Rational thought combined with that of the Reformation's faith and conversion experience (McKnight, 2003). Family discipline was to produce the consciousness of the child whose inner voice served external authority. Community was part of this course of life or one's *curriculum vitæ* that joins the individual's freedom as indivisible from the shared cultural world that gave a unity to human kind (McKnight, 2003).

Progressivism as the redemptive future of the republic was told as the story of the public (mass) school. In a speech given at the National Education Association meeting of educational leaders, Martin (1895) asserted that history is "crystallized in our American notion of patriotism, five hundred years of passionate struggles for liberty, of breaking chains and abolishing formulas." That culmination of history of the American nation is expressed in its national anthem and "The Rights of Man" (Martin, 1895, p.134). "America is a sweet land of liberty; land where our fathers' died; Columbia's heroes fought and bled in freedom's cause; in the rockets' red glare, and with bombs bursting in air, the star-spangled banner waves o'er the land of the free and the home of the brave" (Martin, 1895, p. 134). The heroes of Cromwell, Lafayette, Touissant, Bolivar, and Garibaldi meet their finality in the American Revolution and George Washington.

The new patriotism, Martin argues, is not the old theology of building monuments and hanging flags at school, nor is it an unyielding obedience to authority and social inequities. The new patriotism, he continues, is in the inscription of the character and dispositions that tell the good from the evil. Drawing on a notion of civic virtue, education is the march of the Republic

> to develop common standards and "a common weld" in which personal interest are set aside for public ends. The civilizing of the child is to combine social and personal obligation. The past, present and future are joined as education civilizes by bringing back new patriotism . . . to penetrate this system and bring back personal responsibility and social harmony that combines social and personal obligations. (Martin, 1895, p. 138)

The (re)visioning of American exceptionalism was looked on as the cosmopolitan model for others to bring forth enlightenment principles in state formations as well as for the search for re-creating human conditions that were to embody universal values. The turn of the 20th-century educators traveled from Europe and South America to the 1904 St. Louis World Fair and the 1915 San Francisco World Fairs to bring back progressive notions of schooling to modernize society through its educational practices (Sobe, 2002; Sobe & Rackers, 2009). The writings as well of prominence intellectuals, such as the German sociologist Max Weber and the Italian Marxist Antonio Gramsci, with some hesitations and modification, looked to the U.S. as a paradigm of the future of society.

PROGRESSIVE SCIENCES AS CIVILIZING PROCESSES: "THE SOCIAL QUESTION" AND URBAN REFORMS

Progressive reforms to change American society consecrated the prophetic visions in the knowledge of science and technology. Progressivism was cast in narratives of a struggle between darkness and light and "the civilizing mission" of the nation. The evangelistic hope of exceptionalism was to bring the Christian gospel to Christians and non-Protestant Christians alike in order to produce civic virtue as principles of everyday life. The fears were expressed as double gestures—as a need to provide legislation and conditions to enable immigrants and others to embody the sensitivities and dispositions articulated as civic virtue in American exceptionalism, and fears of the qualities and characteristics of the life of the immigrant that stood as dangers to the realization of the cosmopolitanism of the nation. A book for missionaries who worked with different immigrant groups in New York began with "How long will American Christianity allow this process of degeneracy to go on, before realizing the peril of it, and providing the counteracting agencies of good?" (Grose, 1906, p. 224).

Progressive political reforms established civil service in government, for example, to reestablish notions of civic virtue by countering corruption in government (e.g., New York's Tammany Hall) and the dehumanizing

From Virtue as the Pursuit of Happiness to Pursuing the Unvirtuous 229

"soullessness of modern life." In addition was legislation to fight against exploitations of the workplace, child labor, and efforts to alter the living and working conditions of the city through public transportation systems, garbage collection, sewage systems, and plumbing brought into housing. The development of public education for the lower classes, immigrants, and racial groups were constructed, with a new school being built every day for almost a decade around the turn of the century.

By the first decades of the 20th century, the sciences became more empirically oriented and disciplinary. The convergence of policy and science embodied the belief that The Social Question "should be based on extensive, systematic, and empirical analysis of the underlying social problems" (Wittrock, Wagner, & Wollmann, 1991, p. 33). The Social Question, a cross-Atlantic movement, was ordered through a Protestant reformist notion of the darkness, perceived moral disorder of the city, and the cosmopolitan hope of its redemption. Cross-Atlantic Protestant movements of American progressive reforms, the British Fabian Society, the German Evangelical Social Congress, the French Musée Social, and the Settlement House movements that focused on the environmental conditions in multiple countries gave attention to the conditions and modes of living of the new urban poor, immigrants, and racial groups (Rodgers, 1998).[8] The reforms had "an intense preoccupation with the social problems of industrial society, whether in the literacy form of Dickens, the aesthetically and reform-oriented writings of Ruskin and Morris, the romantic historical work of Carlyle, the activities of the emerging labour movement, or in the connections with government activities proper" (Wittrock, Wagner, & Wollmann, 1991, p. 33). The Social Question recognized distinct populations for inclusion yet, I will argue in the next section, categorized as different and living in spaces outside of its boundaries of "reason" and reasonable people.

The different social, political, education, and cultural changes urbanized previous agrarian populism into an urban problem to change the social conditions given expression in The Social Question and counter the threat and dangers to "the common weld." Jane Addams, a leader of the Settlement Movement in Chicago's Hull House and close colleague to John Dewey, searched for ways "to transform social relations and establish patterns of thinking so that increasing numbers of people, from increasing numbers of cultural traditions, could live together in crowded, urban conditions and still maintain a sense of harmony, order, beauty, and progress" (Lagemann, 2000, p. 55). Addams thought that the influx of foreigners brought people who were "densely ignorant" of American customs and institutions (cited in Lybarger, 1987, p. 181).

My interest, however, is less in these institutional developments but in the system of reason that becomes visible to change society by changing people. The redemptive enlightenment's "lamp" of freedom was embodied in the emergence of the social sciences that overlapped historically with European and North American reform movements directed to the conditions of urban populations. The human sciences were directed to assisting the state in policies and programs concerned with urban poverty. At first a loose association of elites, the American Social Science Association (1865) formed to assist the state in planning to alleviate the conditions of poverty after the American Civil War.[9] The Association entailed diverse membership and embraced "the notion that the social scientist was a model citizen helping to improve the life of the community, not a professional, disinterested, disciplinary research" (Wittrock, Wagner, & Wollmann, 1991, p. 38).

The belief in practices to socially intervene entailed a new expertise that joined policy with the emergence of empirically oriented social and education sciences. The sciences "were meant to contribute to the amelioration of social evils and provide a basis for the rational and enlightened ordering of societal affairs" (Wagner, Weiss, Wittrock, & Wollmann, 1991, p. 2).

Science was an attitude as well as a set of practices for undermining established traditions and the harmful effects of modernity. It enunciated particular cultural practices about how judgments are made, conclusions drawn, rectification proposed, and the fields of existence made manageable and predictable. The different theories and conceptual principles carried the optimism of American exceptionalism about the opening up of a more progressive and democratic society. Dewey's pedagogical creed was to install methods of science into daily life to shed the traditions that prevented progress and salvation. Dewey wrote of William James in 1929 that he was "well within the bounds of moderation when he said that looking forward instead of backward, looking to what the world and life might become instead of to what they have been, is an alteration in the 'seat of authority' " (cited in Diggins, 1994, p. 39). Action directs thought and participation in a future unencumbered by the past. That future was to be without an authoritarian system of religion, as well as without fixed classes and ancient institutions. "The old culture is doomed for us because it was built upon an alliance of political and spiritual powers, an equilibrium of governing and leisure classes, which no longer exists" (Dewey, 1916/1929, pp. 501–502).

In historically reviewing American sociological traditions, Levine (1995) argues that its distinctively empirical character was bound to particular Protestant reform movements. One was from the secularized Unitarianism of Emerson and New England Transcendentalists who bring Christian ethics into daily life to respond to the excessive individualism embodied in turn-of-the-century industrialists such as Carnegie, Rockefeller, Morgan, and others called "Robber Barons." The other element was from The Social Gospel, a late 19th-century movement of a reconstituted Puritanism for "promoting good works through canvassing social woes" (p. 251). The latter, a minority of clergy and reformers, brought the belief that the ethics of Jesus Christ could resolve the contractions of progress and poverty in progressive reform movements. The calls for social justice were given as the appeal of shouting "in the wilderness," a phrase that echoed the Puritan imagery discussed earlier (Reese, 2002, p. 73).

The new human sciences had two trajectories related to the forming of the citizen. The theories and methodologies of the sciences were to calculate and administer social and personal affairs. The new urban planning and the psychological studies of children are two examples of this function of science. The second trajectory was to view science as a mode of living. The school sciences of pedagogy, for example, embodied cultural theses about life as ordered "rational" processes that guided thought and action. Notions of problem solving, learning, and "action" were to form experiences as processes that ordered the development of life in regularized sequences of time. The two trajectories of science were inscribed in the grid of social, political, and cultural practices through which individuality and sociality were given intelligibility.

REVERSING THE SUBJECT: FROM THE PURSUIT OF HAPPINESS TO PLANNING "THE UNHAPPY"

The progressive enlightenment hopes of creating the heavenly world in the city of man [sic], to paraphrase the title from Carl Becker (1932) book about the 18th-century philosophers, gave recognition to redemptive themes of the nation in confronting the issues posed by urbanization in The Social Question. The recognition that gave identity to immigrant and racial populations inscribed a comparative style of thought and, ironically, difference. Particular populations were classified, given conceptualization, and differentiated as living in spaces outside those characterized with qualities of civic virtue. The identities assigned to the problem of The Social Question made as the starting point of equality as inequality and difference as having an ontological basis. Counter-intuitively, progressivism makes visible the reversal of the American enlightenment principle of the "pursuit of happiness" of the negative freedom of laissez faire in the early 19th-century republic. The inscription of difference was part of the large social, political, and education movements about positive freedom that today is called the welfare state. The particular professional expertise generated through the new human sciences embodied principles about the modes of living of those populations classified as different.

This reversal that recognized difference by making difference can be sociologically considered as a change in social thought and action that directed attention to the "unhappy populations" who are different and cast in unlivable spaces (Popkewitz, 2008). My use of the "unhappy" is not to suggest any psychological/pathological distinction, but to the principles that represented, ordered, and divided given identities—principles that comprised the unvirtuous who are unable to pursue happiness. The new scientific psychologies of childhood and the sociological theories of community embodied a comparative style of thought about the hope of the future envisioned through the technological sublime. And with that hope was the simultaneous double gesture of fears of the dangers and dangerous populations to the envisioned future of the republic.

My focus on the inscription of a comparative style of thought is historical, to draw attention to different practices assembled in the long 19th century through which human difference was given recognition and identity. It is not that comparative ways of reason were not possible earlier. If I briefly take an excursus, elements of the enlightenments' "humanizing" qualities morphed into the cultural practices that formed the modern nation, republicanism, and schooling. The emergence of the philosophy of consciousness, for example, inscribed the idea of independence of the mind and human agency with notions of representations (see e.g., Deleuze, 1964/1994). Changes in aesthetics and art, theories of biology, and technologies of the camera, and a notion of irreversible secular time, enabled a new "observer" to see, think, and feel about individuals as having analytically and differentiated elements that functioned in systems (Crary, 1999). The comparative style made possible the invention of modern medicine and science. It opened up the interior of the mind as having discrete qualities, capabilities, perceptions, and motivations that could be identified and administrated through science. It also made possible new hopes about social life through differentiating the characteristics of systems of "civilizations" as placed in hierarchies and a continuum of values. And the joining of social, scientific, and moral criteria became evident in its extremes in eugenics and the colonialism by the 19th century, two social examples of such comparative thought in a quasi-scientific language.

The comparative style of thought is evident in the notion of poverty undertaken in the new human science of the city. Poverty, at least in Protestant England and the United States in the early 19th century, was seen as the fault of the individual's sinfulness and idleness. By the end of the century, poverty was no longer tied only to inner moral qualities of the person but located in the social conditions that made sinfulness possible. This notion of poverty makes it possible to think of the intervention and planning of urban life to change the conditions and people who constitute poverty. Sin, however, was also a secular notion of saving the soul who did not embody the norm and values of the common good and pursue freedom through pursuing happiness, an important purpose of American republicanism. The changes, on the surface, make possible progressivism's attention to those groups that have suffered from industrialization and urbanization, and institutions related to the welfare policies of the State and the formation of the modern school.

Further, focus on the conditions of those who could not pursue happiness made possible the journalist "muckrakers" and settlement house movements. The muckraking traditions in American newspapers, for example, were to uncover the evils produced in the new city landscape of labor, and

From Virtue as the Pursuit of Happiness to Pursuing the Unvirtuous 233

housing, and designing welfare systems. Some of these journalists became part of the new Chicago sociology and social work that mapped urban conditions, providing census materials and ethnographies of tenement life to highlight the conditions of the city's poor and the need for a humanized moral order in the processes of industrialization.

Progressive reforms in schooling embodied double gestures of American enlightenment's hope of reason and science of the "enlightened" that coincided with attention to the "unhappy" populations defined, for example, in The Social Question. The epic of the people's "errand in the wilderness" implied fears of populations who did not have the capabilities and capacities to "reason" as the citizen and to act with the norms of civil virtue. Schools were urban institutions to teach American moral behavior and conduct and to aid society by preventing disease, vice, or future crime (Bloch, 1987). Thomas Jesse Jones, instrumental in forming social studies as a curriculum subject, was interested in the transformation (social evolution) of the immigrant to embody "the Anglo-Saxon ideal" (Lybarger, 1987, p. 185). Jones had been involved with the Settlement House Movement in New York before moving to the Hampton Institute. He talked about the educational needs of Italians to be less impulsive and more cautious and deliberate and the "need" of educational experiences for Jewish children to make them more impulsive and less cautions and deliberate (in Lybarger, 1987). The notion of "need" was "the social judgment . . . about what ideals and traits ought to be inculcated in the weak by the strong through instruction in the social studies" (Lybarger, 1987, p.187).

The sciences of pedagogy were for the educational psychologist Edward L. Thorndike (1909/1962) to change the individual so as to enable the "pursuit of happiness" and promote the civil virtues of the democratic processes of the Republic.

> To change men's wants for the better, we must heed what conditions originally satisfy and annoy them since the only way to create an interest is by grafting it onto one of the original satisfiers. To enable men to satisfy their wants more fully, the crude curiosity, manipulation, experimentation and irrational interplay of fear, anger, rivalry, mastery, submission, cruelty and kindliness must be modified into useful, verified thought and equitable acts. (Thorndike, 1912/1962, p. 76)

The ridding of "the irrational," fear, and anger was coded in the psychology to signified particular urban populations and women. The science of psychology was to identify *the nature* of the individual that pedagogy could develop in *finding happiness and decreasing human discomfort*. "Education as a whole should make human beings wish each other well, should increase the sum of human energy and happiness and decrease the sum of discomfort of the human beings that are or will be, and should foster the higher, impersonal pleasures" (Thorndike, 1909/1962, p. 47). Education is to move the individual from mere instinctual habits "to more complex, capacity, predispositions that grow into thought, speech, music" that embodies, as cited above, "the capacity for reasoning" that will "satisfy one's wants" (Thorndike, 1912/1962, p. 76).

Thorndike's psychology assumed cosmopolitan purposes of teaching in a differentiated society. That differentiation was in Thorndike's laws of psychology directed to undo the irrational, emotional, and unlettered qualities of immigrant populations in urban and industrial America. The psychological principles of pedagogy were to nurture the "good" wants that are natural to the child and to suppress that which is not productive to the pursuit of happiness.

The psychological qualities of Thorndike's individual were homologous to the exceptionalism in the frontier thesis of the rugged individual of Fredrick Jackson Turner. Making a more precise and accurate knowledge about individual behaviors was to improve the nation's human resources by enabling the fittest, who would profit the most from schooling. The studies of human variations in abilities gave sanction to the liberal theories about individual freedom and self-actualization through the teacher's discovering "where the child stands and lead him from there" (Joncich, 1968, p. 21). The connectionism of Thorndike's psychology to "pursue happiness" was to change the child and "prevent ... each new generation from stagnating in brutish ignorance, folly and pain. But far better education is needed to reduce the still appalling sum of error, injustice, misery and stupidity" (Thorndike, 1912/1962, p. 72). Education, in this context, was not only to prepare children for adult life but also to adapt childhood to the eventual position to hold as an adult. Training "may improve in estimating others from various causes," and training might also give ideas as to how to estimate most successfully habits of making the judgments in better ways, making allowance for constant errors, and avoiding certain prejudices (Thorndike & Woodworth, 1901/1962, pp. 52–53).

The double gestures of hope and fears instantiated a continuum of values in the different progressive sciences and The Social Question. Lester Frank Ward (1883), another founder of American sociology, spoke about moving the immigrant family of the settlement house away from the habits of the savage and the barbarian. Ward's *Dynamic Sociology* argued that education needs an "absolute universality" that was intended "to neutralize the *non-civilized* or it will lower all of society." The inscription of reason was to stand as a universal principle that made visible the civilized child who "can act as desired" with liberty. Methods in socialization in education were to take "the lesser of a civilization," "the savage and used by stagnant people" (Ward, 1883, pp. 159–160) in order "to raise the *uncivilized* classes up toward its level" (Ward, 1883, p. 595; italics original).

The pragmatism of Dewey's "habits of the mind" brought a cultural thesis of the mode of life into everyday life as the hope of countering the debilitating effects of modern conditions and its modes of living. "The existence of scientific method protects us also from a danger that attends the operation of men of unusual power; dangers of slavish imitation partisanship, and such jealous devotion to them and their work as to get in the way of further progress" (Dewey, 1929, p. 11). But at the same time there were fears that traveled with that hope. The systematic training in "thinking" was to prevent "the evil of the wrong kind of development [that] is even greater . . . the power of thought . . . [as it] frees us from servile subjection to instinct, appetite, and routines" (p. 23).

The "unhappy" populations who embodied capabilities and qualities that were outside the spaces of the norms of the common good were spoken about as individual and psychological characteristics that were related to the family and social conditions. The comparativeness was embedded in the systems of reason through which identities were ascribed and differences inscribed to make inequality as equality and thus reinscribe difference itself.

REDEMPTION AND THE ABJECTIONS IN MAKING CIVIC VIRTUE: SOME CONCLUDING THOUGHTS

In writing this chapter, its interpretive strategy goes against the grain of writing educational history of American progressive education. It focuses on the system of reason that historically ordered and classified what is seen, talked about, and acted on. It explores the grid of practices produced in the long 19th century that becomes visible and gives intelligibility to American progressive education, its notions of republicanism, and in particular enlightenment values about individuality and the citizen.

The assumption of the analysis is that the citizen is not born but made. And schooling is central to that process, particularly with the modern nation where republican principles of individual responsibility and participation were necessary for government. To historicize the principles generated to govern conduct is to approach the grid of historical practices that emerge in the long 19th century and become visible as the "reason" and reasonable people of schooling. Reason, then, is generated within a historical grid that connects individuality to principles of collective belonging that included the cultural instantiation of religion, social movements, science, and political patterns. Among these in American progressive education were the new psychologies and sociologies that assembled and connected elements of the American enlightenment cosmopolitanism with Protestant reformism to signify common belonging of the national exceptionalism. Further and as important, the pedagogical projects and its sciences embodied the double gestures that were not only of pedagogy. The Social Question inscribed ordering and classifying principles about modes of living that differentiated and divided the qualities encased as civic virtues of "the chosen people" from those different and casting out in other, unlivable spaces.

My argument about inclusion/exclusion, however, is not about the intent of policy or the sciences but about the epistemological principles historically generated and its double gestures. The very inclusive principles that ordered the sciences of education and pedagogical practices entailed inequality through the divisions that characterized and distinguished the qualities of individuality. The focus is on reason as a practice to be scrutinized historically; not an argument against reason or rationality. Rather it is a diagnosis of the limits of the particular historical instantiations of the rules and standards that organize "thought," and the principles generated about who the child is, should be, and is not.

NOTES

1. I am using "America" as the noun given historically to the nation and not to claim its appropriateness as a generic term for the nation that occupies only a part of the Americas.
2. American historical traditions tend to leave unscrutinized the relation of the idea of schooling and its principles of children's learning to reason and be a "reasonable" person to its historical inscription in enlightenment movements or the assumption the normative claims of the enlightenment child/citizen in its narratives.
3. See Popkewitz (2008).
4. Exceptionalism is used to understand the cultural narrative of the nation. It is not a normative argument about the nation as exceptionalism. When viewed comparatively, my reading of the different national stories of its foundations and promise evokes continually narratives of exceptionalism or believing of the future to be achieved, from Sweden, Russia, China, and Japan. The United States is not an exception except in the way it tells of its exceptionalism.
5. Pocock's argument is interesting in the sense of this chapter because it moves between an intellectual history that classifies in its singular and speaks of the radicalism of the American revolution through its reassembly and connections of different historical movements of which republicanism is one and which the outcome is not merely the sum of its parts.
6. Of course, the chosen did not include all of the people inhabiting the nation. When the phrase of the American race was used to differentiate the nation from others, it embodied particular distinctions about the manner and capabilities of those who occupied the spaces of "the elect."
7. The report was prepared for a meeting of state superintendents in order to send representation to a conference in Vienna to talk about conditions of education in the United States. The statement was signed by Superintendents Doty of Detroit and William Torrey Harris of St. Louis, the latter who was an influential member of the American Herbartian Society and later head of the federal Bureau of Education.
8. The differentiations and divisions were not stable and changed over time. In the 18th and early 19th centuries, the British are the "other" in relation to the German and the French; and other times, the relations move to other axes, such as the post-Civil War, World War I, and World War II.
9. The British Social Science Association was formed in 1832 and the American Social Science Association in the 1865 as groups to assist the state in dealing with problems of welfare. They were men of the gentry and professional

classes, dilettantes with no specific training except the concern with issues of poverty and the city.

REFERENCES

Becker, C. (1932). *The heavenly city of the eighteenth-century philosophers.* New Haven: Yale University Press.
Bellah, R. (1975). *The broken covenant: American civil religion in time of trial.* Chicago: University of Chicago Press.
Bercovitch, S. (1978). *The American Jeremiad.* Madison: University of Wisconsin Press.
Bloch, M. (1987). Becoming scientific and professional: An historical perspective on the aims and effects of early education. In T. S. Popkewitz (Ed.), *The formation of the school subjects. The struggle for creating an American institution* (pp. 25–62). New York: Falmer Press.
Childs, J. L. (1956). *American pragmatism and education: An interpretation and criticism.* New York: Henry Holt.
Cooley, C. H. (1909). *Social organization: A study of the larger mind.* New York: Charles Scribner's Sons.
Crary, J. (1999). *Suspensions of perception: Attention, spectacle, and modern culture.* Cambridge, MA: MIT Press.
Deleuze, G. (1968/1994). *Difference and repetition* (P. Patton, Trans.). New York: Athlone Press of Columbia University.
Dewey, J. (1916/1929). American education and culture. In J. Ratner (Ed.), *Character and events: Popular essays in social and political philosophy* (Vol. II, pp. 498–503). New York: Henry Holt and Co.
Dewey, J. (1929). *The sources of a science of education.* New York: Horace Liveright.
Diggins, J. P. (1994). *The promise of pragmatism: Modernism and the crisis of knowledge and authority.* Chicago: University of Chicago Press.
Faragher, J. M. (1994). Introduction: "A nation thrown back upon itself": Frederick Jackson Turner and the frontier. In J. M. Faragher (Ed.), *Rereading Frederick Jackson Turner* (pp. 1–11). New Haven, CT: Yale University Press.
Ferguson, R. A. (1997). *The American enlightenment, 1750–1820.* Cambridge, MA: Harvard University Press.
Foner, E. (1998). *The story of American freedom.* New York: W. W. Norton & Company.
Furstenberg, F. (2006, July 4). Spinning the revolution. *The New York Times*, p. A17.
Glaude, E. (2000). *Exodus! Religion, race, and nation in early nineteenth-century Black America.* Chicago: University of Chicago Press.
Grose, H. (1906). *Alien or Americans? Forward mission study courses, edited under the auspices of the Young People's Missionary Movement.* New York: Easton & Mains.
Jehlen, M. (1986). *American incarnation: The individua , the nation, and the continent.* Cambridge, MA, and London, England: Harvard University Press.
Joncich, G. M. (1962). Science: Touchstone for a new age in education. In G. M. Joncich (Ed.), *Psychology and the science of education.* Selected writings of Edward L. Thorndike (pp. 1-26). New York: Bureau of Publications, Teachers College, Columbia University.
Lagemann, E. C. (2000). *An elusive science: The troubling history of education research.* Chicago: University of Chicago Press.
Levine, D. (1995). *Visions of the sociological tradition.* Chicago: University of Chicago Press.

Lilla, M. (2007). The politics of God. *The New York Times Magazine*, pp. 28–35, 50, 54–55.

Lybarger, M. (1987). Need as ideology: Social workers, social settlements, and the social studies. In T. Popkewitz (Ed.), *The formation of the school subjects: The struggles for creating an American Institution* (pp. 176–189). New York: Falmer Press.

Martin, G. H. (1895). *New standards of patriotic citizenship*. Paper presented at the National Educational Association, St. Paul, MN.

Marx, A. (2003). *Faith in nation: Exclusionary origins of nationalism*. New York: Oxford University Press.

McKnight, D. (2003). *Schooling, the Puritan imperative, and the molding of an American national identity. Education's "errand into the wilderness."* Mahwah, NJ: Lawrence Erlbaum Associates.

McMahon, D. (2006). *Happiness: A history*. New York: Atlantic Monthly Press.

Nye, D. E. (1999). *American technological sublime*. Cambridge, MA: MIT Press.

Nye, D. E. (2003). *America as second creation: Technology and narratives of new beginnings*. Cambridge, MA: MIT Press.

Oshinsky, D. (2000, August 26). The Humpty Dumpty of scholarship: American history has broken in pieces. Can it be put together again? *The New York Times*, pp. A17, A19.

Pocock, J. G. A. (1975). *Machiavellian moment: Florentine political thought and the Atlantic republican tradition*. Princeton, NJ: Princeton University Press.

Popkewitz, T. (2008). *Cosmopolitanism and the age of school reform: Science, education, and making society by making the child*. New York: Routledge.

Reese, W. (2002). *Power and the promise of school reform: Grassroots movements during the Progressive Era*. New York: Teachers College Press.

Rodgers, D. T. (1998). *Atlantic crossings: Social politics in a progressive age*. Cambridge, MA: Belknap Press of Harvard University Press.

Ross, D. (1972). *G. Stanley Hall: The psychologist as prophet*. Chicago: The University of Chicago Press.

Ross, D. (1991). *The origins of American social science*. New York: Cambridge University Press.

Schlereth, T. (1977). *The cosmopolitan idea in enlightenment thought*. Notre Dame, IN: Notre Dame Press.

Sobe, N. W. (2002). Travel, social science and the making of nations in early 19th century comparative education. In M. Caruso & H.-E. Tenorth (Eds.), *Internationalisation: comparing educational systems and semantics* (pp. 141–166). Frankfurt am Main: Peter Lang.

Sobe, N. W., & Rackers, C. (2009). Fashioning writing machines: Typewriting and handwriting exhibits at US world's Fairs, 1893-1915. In M. Lawn (Ed.), *Modeling the future exhibitions and the materiality of education* (pp. 87-105). London: Symposium Books.

Thorndike, E., & Woodworth, R. (1901/1962). Education as science. In G. M. Joncich (Ed.), *Psychology and the science of education. Selected writings of Edward L. Thorndike* (pp. 48–69). New York: Bureau of Publications, Teachers College, Columbia University.

Thorndike, E. (1912/1962). Education. A first book. In G. M. Joncich (Ed.), *Psychology and the science of education. Selected writings of Edward L. Thorndike* (pp. 69–83, 141–147). New York: Bureau of Publications, Teachers College, Columbia University.

Thorndike, E. L. (1909/1962). Darwin's contribution to psychology. In G. M. Joncich (Ed.), *Psychology and the science of education: Selected writings of Edward L. Thorndike* (pp. 37–47). New York: Bureau of Publications, Teachers College, Columbia University.

Tröhler, D. (2006). Max Weber und die protestantische Ethik in Amerika [Max Weber and the Protestant ethic in America]. In J. Oelkers, R. Casale, & R. Horlacher (Eds.), *Rationalisierung und Bildung bei Max Weber: Beiträge zur Historischen Bildungsforschung* (pp. 111–134). Bad Heilbrunn: Klinkhardt

Turner, F. J. (1893/1994). The significance of the frontier in American history. In J. M. Faragher (Ed.), *Rereading Frederick Jackson Turner* (pp. 31–60). New Haven, CT: Yale University Press.

U.S. Government Printing Office. (1874). *A statement of the theory of education in the United States of America as approved by many leading educators*. Washington, DC: Author.

Wagner, P., Weiss, C., Wittrock, B., & Wollmann, H. (1991). The policy orientation: Legacy and promise. In P. Wagner, C. Hirschon Weiss, B. Wittrock, & H. Wollmann (Eds.), *Social sciences and modern states. National experiences and theoretical crossroads* (pp. 2–27). Cambridge, UK: Cambridge University Press.

Wald, P. (1995). *Constituting Americans: Cultural anxiety and narrative form*. Durham, NC: Duke University Press.

Ward, L. F. (1883). *Dynamic sociology, or applied social science, as based upon statistical sociology and the less complex sciences*. New York: D. Appleton and Co.

Wiebe, R. H. (1995). *Self-rule: A cultural history of American democracy*. Chicago, IL: University of Chicago Press.

Wittrock, B., Wagner, P., & Wollmann, H. (1991). The policy orientation: Legacy and promise. In P. Wagner, C. Hirschon Weiss, B. Wittrock, & H. Wollmann (Eds.), *Social sciences and modern states. National experiences and theoretical crossroads* (pp. 28–84). Cambridge, UK: Cambridge University Press.

Wood, G. (1999). The American love boat. *The New York Review of Books*, 56(15), 40–42.

Wood, G. S. (1991). *The radicalism of the American Revolution*. New York: Vintage Books.

12 Literacy, Nation, Schooling
Reading (in) Australia

Bill Green and Phillip Cormack

> [K]knowledge about the nation depends so much on reading.
> (Atkinson, 2002, p. 32)

It is relatively commonplace now to point to the long cusp between the 19th and 20th centuries as a crucial turning-point in many aspects of education and society worldwide. This is clearly the case with Australia, with 1901 being the now iconic date when a new nation was constitutionally formed out of what was previously a set of British colonies, all located in a single landmass, a vast island-continent. Just three decades previously, in an important landmark for what would later be described as "this great British nation in the south" (Browne, 1927, p. xxi), a series of Education Acts had been passed in different colonies, effectively establishing a national system of essentially secular (primary) schooling. That first decade of the 20th century was particularly significant, however, educationally as well as politically—a second revolution, in effect—in that it saw the installation of what was to be a newly revitalized and rapidly consolidating apparatus of public schooling, with the first major moves toward the extension of its remit beyond the primary sector to embrace secondary education. This was a heady period of educational development and change, all the more remarkable because it was observed (albeit somewhat unevenly) right across the newly formed nation, notwithstanding the fact that Federation itself had no explicit or formal educational charter. A sharp distinction was drawn at the outset between those aspects to come under the legislative authority and auspices of the federal government and those remaining firmly the responsibility of the states. Accordingly, it could be said quite emphatically soon after that "[t]he Federal Government takes no part in Education, which is entirely under the control of the States" (Browne, 1927, p. xviii). Yet it was also the case that public schooling came to exert considerable influence on the shaping of national identity, in all its complexity and ambivalence. As one commentator has observed, "The first half of the twentieth century witnessed great changes in Australian society, and formal education played an increasingly influential role in fostering and shaping these changes" (Turney 1983, p. 1). Among the questions that might be asked are these: In what ways has education and schooling been influential in the formation of national culture and identity? What is distinctive in this regard in the Australian experience? How best to understand this so-called turning-point in history? How illustrative is this in its own way of the distinctive work of national formation, "republican" sentiment and educational development characteristic of what is described in the Introduction of this book as "the long 19th century"? And finally, what are its traces in the present and its significance for the future, in the first decades of the 21st century and a new era of (post)modernization, globalization, and nation re-building?

In this chapter we focus specifically on reading pedagogy, and more broadly on English teaching and the English subjects, or mother-tongue education, as a significant cultural technology in the formation of subjectivity and the production of a distinctive national imaginary.[1] We are especially concerned here with issues of citizenship and civic identity, and more specifically with what is described in the Introduction as political culture and civic education. This is because, for us, reading and writing, literacy and literature ("texts"), which lie at the very heart not simply of English teaching but also education and schooling, matter in much more than utilitarian ways and indeed are always-already profoundly social practices. As such, they have an inescapable political dimension. English teaching has not commonly been linked with citizenship discourses and debates (Meredyth, 1994). More commonly it is either subject history or social studies to which reference is made in this context perhaps because they might seem to overtly thematize such concerns within the disciplinary field of the social sciences. However, it can be argued that what the subject of English has to offer in this regard is quite distinctive and often overlooked.

The chapter builds on the work of a curriculum-historical project studying English teaching, teacher education, and public schooling in Australia, in the period from 1901 to 1938 (e.g., Green & Cormack, 2008), and further studies of literacy, adolescence, and schooling from the late 19th century through the first few decades of the 20th century (Cormack, 2004). The first section considers the centrality of communications and, specifically, print culture in the formation of modern nation-states. We discuss how this was particularly the case in Australia, faced as it was with distinctive challenges of colonial identity, isolation, and geography. In the second section, we consider the ways in which the print apparatus more generally and literacy in particular are central to modern schooling and more broadly to the project of modernity. Understood within the larger context of the history of Australian schooling and English curriculum practice, the primary school subject of reading was characteristically deployed as a specific technology for "reading" the nation, and reading materials form a rich source of data about the emergent "imagined community" of the nation. In the particular case of Australia, this involved both nation-building and also the formation of Australian citizens as members of a British Empire conceived in both racial and economic terms. The third part of the chapter considers reading curriculum and pedagogy around the period of Federation, with specific reference to "School Papers"—sets of materials for the primary-school reading lesson produced by the education departments of the colonies/states of Australia. These materials were produced as a supplement to reading primers typically imported from the United Kingdom. One of the aims of the School Papers was that they would address the needs of Australian children and focus on local issues. We look, in particular, at one such School Paper—*The Children's Hour*—produced by the South Australian Education Department, which featured stories, historical tales, reports of current events, regular columns, and songs, among other texts. It is argued that young readers reading in and about Australia, in the context of both a reinvented and reinvigorated public schooling system and a newly established nation, were engaged in a particular kind of identity-work, marked by all the contradictions and ambivalence of what was to be played out as 20th-century Australian modernity. In this way, the quite specific literacy project of the public school, distinctively organized in terms of nation and empire within a changing world order, was profoundly implicated in the discursive construction of Australian identity.

Australia was formally created as a nation in 1901 in a constitutional event thereafter known as Federation. One hundred years later, in 2001, this was a matter of some considerable celebratory and sometimes controversial attention, discussion, and debate, *including* renewed focus on the question of republicanism. Although "[t]he history of republicanism in Australia has revolved around two focal points—constitutional reform and national identity, both of them underpinned by the notion of inevitability," as McKenna (1996, p. 256) writes, it needs to be noted that Australia was and indeed remains a constitutional monarchy, albeit with a rich history of interest and involvement in debates concerning republicanism, liberalism, and democracy. The immediate pre-millennial period saw a national referendum on the topic of an Australian republic, at which time the proposal was defeated, in the end quite decisively. That "Federation" and the "republic" should be linked in this fashion and at this time is, however, worth further consideration here. This is because, although for some their association is quite understandable and even predictable, for others it is much less so. Something that did feature heavily in the period leading up to the centennial celebrations was a heightened awareness among politicians, journalists, and others that there was little in the way of an explicit civic identity in the Australian people, at best a patchy historical imagination and, in particular, an attenuated sense of political heritage. "Federation means little to most Australians," as Birrell (2001, p. 1) asserted quite bluntly. Moreover, just as Federation itself was much more than simply the one event—"both a beginning and an end," as Irving (1999, p. 1) put it—so too was the centennial year. Gathering momentum from the latter part of the 1980s on, there was considerable debate about Australia's re-positioning in a changing global geopolitical context and concomitant anxieties over national identity. Comparisons were made in this regard with the situation in other countries, notably the United States, and a growing consensus emerged that what was needed, as at least part of the solution, was a more knowledgeable and politically attuned populace, to be realized in and through a systematic school program in civics and citizenship. This might be understood as a matter of articulating reason and emotion (or "passion"), within what is at least notionally the logic(s) of republicanism, as adumbrated in this book. At issue here more broadly is the question of what the Australian historian Alan Atkinson (1997) describes as "Australian political culture," which he glosses as "methods of thinking about self and authority at all levels" (pp. ix–x). This needs to be explored and explicated here. We begin, however, with a brief historical account of Australian education and society, with specific reference to post-Federation developments in English teaching, teacher education, and public schooling.

David Hamilton (1989) has proposed that educational history—the history of educational practice—"lies at the intersection of economic history and the history of ideas" (p. 5). Although this certainly needs to be extended to take in social and, in particular, cultural history, nonetheless it is revealing in considering the Australian case. What made the late 19th- and early 20th-century period so dynamic in the forging of a new national formation in terms of culture and economy alike and a strong and distinctive nation-state? Something worth noting from an economic perspective is that the overall period in question has been described as a *second* Industrial Revolution or as one of two distinct but related Industrial Revolutions, "the first start[ing] in the last third of the eighteenth century . . . the second one, about 100 years later" (Castells, 1996, p. 34):

> The historical ascent of the so-called West, in fact limited to Britain and a handful of nations in Western Europe as well as to their North American and Australian offspring, is fundamentally linked to the technological superiority achieved during the two Industrial Revolutions. (Castells, 1996, p. 35)

What is significant about this is its contextualization in an account of what is called "the information technology revolution," or informational capitalism, as a distinctively new era and the next decisive phase in what became a thoroughly globalized ("networked") social organization.[2] But it is also important to note that it coincided with the emergence of Australia on the world scene. Economic historian Christopher Lloyd (2003) argues that:

> [u]nlike almost all other parts of what became the industrialised world of the early to mid-twentieth century, and in comparison with other former settler economies in the Americas, Australia was founded

within and was an integral part of the world economy from the very beginning. (p. 404)

This was directly related to its historical linkages with British colonialism and imperialism, and the fact that Australia was "born as a *modern* component or offshoot of the British state" (Lloyd, 2003, p. 404; italics original). He points to a long period of development from the early to mid-19th century onward, with Australia becoming by the 1830s "of major importance to Britain in both penal and economic senses" and somewhat racially and culturally exclusivist "[i]deas of liberalism, democracy and socialism [taking] root" from early in the second half of the 19th century (Lloyd, 2003, p. 405). A new state-regulatory economic and industrial "settlement" was put in place, along with an attempt to "create a new kind of democratic society":

> What has recently been called the Australian "compromise" or "settlement", in which the state was so central, emerged from the experience of a century of development up to the late nineteenth century and became a nation-building ideology and project in the early twentieth. (Lloyd, 2003, p. 405)

This formation remained intact and in place until the 1960s, and a new phase of political-economic negotiation emerged from the 1970s onward. The significance of the Federation period was that it marked for Australia a phase of active nation-building based in part on the principle of "laborist-protectionism" and its associated conceptual-ideological baggage. How was the nation to be represented? As Lloyd (2003) observes:

> The national sentiment that helped give rise to federation was not radical republicanism of American or Irish sorts although there was a republican current. Rather it was predominantly a nationalism of racial and cultural feeling about Britishness, egalitarianism and democratic social solidarity among the majority rural and urban working population. (p. 412)

Moreover, it is important to realize that for much of the first half of the 20th century, Australia's population was remarkably homogenous. Writing in 1927, the curriculum scholar George Browne observed of Australia and what he described as its unique "educational problem" that "[h]ere was a whole continent as large as the United States and nearly as large as Europe" and "[a]s yet it contains only six million people . . . *almost entirely of British stock*" (p. xviii; italics added). As Miriam Dixson (1999) writes: "At its highest point, in 1947, 'the British component of the population was over 90 per cent, of which the vast majority was born in Australia' " (p. 35; citing James Jupp). Dixson is concerned to assert the importance of what she calls the Anglo-Celtic tradition in Australian history and society and urges its re-assessment and revaluation in the face of the manifest challenges of ethnic, linguistic, and cultural diversity in post-World War II Australia. She emphasizes the profound relationship between social cohesion and what she terms (not at all unproblematically, it must be said) "core culture," contending that "over a period of transition and consolidation, the Anglo-Celtic core culture must continue to function as a 'holding' centre for an emerging and newly diverse Australia" (Dixson, 1999, p. 7). As she argues, "a revitalized Australian civic identity, with its citizenship protocols, its institutional practices and rhetoric, is indeed essential. *But civic identity must be deeply rooted in the core culture*" (Dixson, 1999, p. 8; italics added). The implications of such a view for schooling, curriculum, and literacy in a post-9/11 world are quite profound and certainly so for a now undeniably multicultural Australia.

Another historian, Alan Atkinson, while sharing this sense of the significance of the Anglo-Celtic tradition, broadens the terms of reference to include a critique of republicanism (and, correspondingly, a defense of the monarchy) as well as an explicit engagement with various discourses of exclusion in Australian history and society. Insisting on the need for a better appreciation and more informed understanding of the 18th century as a rich (re)source for Australian history, his work among other things connects readily with certain aspects of the history of political thought associated with the so-called Cambridge School of historical research (e.g., Pocock, 1993). This is particularly so in his focus on literacy, and on language more generally, and on the significance of the interface between technology and communication, from print culture to more recent electronic forms and practices—although, interestingly enough, he might be seen as similarly underplaying or glossing over the place of formal education in this regard. Although our more specific thesis is that there are important similarities between the historical moment of Federation and the present, from the late 20th century to the early 21st, his work encourages us to take account of a much broader historical perspective. He reaches back to the 18th century not simply in relation to "Australia's political culture" but also to emphasize Australia's essential "modernity" and its characteristic forms of collective belonging and indeed nationalism, colonial and otherwise. Where we see links between the (post-) Federation period in educational history and the contemporary moment, he takes a longer view. As he observes, "[t]he late twentieth century has certain things in common with the eighteenth":

> The idea of "progress" is as problematic now as it was then. The three-way relationship of ethnicity, politics and social feeling troubles us as much as it troubles men and women two hundred years ago, though ethnicity now is less complicated by questions of rank. Theirs was an age—especially the period from the 1760s to the 1780s—which ended in cataclysmic revolution, affecting everything from forms of

government to sense of self. Thanks to recent revolutions we are now said to be passing beyond the "modern" era which was their creation. (Atkinson, 1997, p. xiv)

This is a typically measured, careful acknowledgment of the movement into "postmodernity" that is arguably the present.

At issue here is how Australia is represented—that is, the *image* that is produced in and by historical writing, in working on and with available archives (documentary traces of various kinds). For Atkinson, Australia is to be understood as very distinctly a democracy, although not wholly so or at all unproblematically, from the very beginning of its European phase. He also notes "the inventive character of the Federation period, the boldness and originality of the years up to World War One, when Australian social reform set the pace, in some respects, for the rest of the world" (Atkinson, 2002, p. 127). This latter point is often remarked on by commentators, as we have seen (e.g., Lloyd, 2003), although always with various caveats and provisos—for example, as Atkinson (2002) himself observes, "democracy, as originally conceived in Australia, was monocultural" (p. 81), to say the least. Further to this, Australia has always been deeply linked to Britain not just economically and politically but also *culturally*, and hence it is important to take due account of the dialogue between "nation" and "empire," something that has indeed featured heavily in our own investigations into English curriculum history in the early to mid-20th century. This dialogue is strikingly realized in the movement from "subject" to "citizen" that Davidson (1997) charts in his study of Australian citizenship discourses and debates. How to be at once an imperial "subject"—that is, subject to the British Crown—and yet a "citizen" of Australia, as a newly defined, distinctive nation: That was precisely the challenge of the post-Federation period, in particular. In this regard, Atkinson's stated aim to address what he calls "the subjectivity of subjects" is worth noting, given that the period he is concerned with at the time of writing is quite specifically pre-Federation. The "subjects" he is referring to here are those colonial "Australians" who, to varying degrees, still identified as British and were still governed by British laws and values, something that in fact continued to be the case for many well into the 20th century. Although it is not explicitly acknowledged, "subjectivity" refers more or less directly to the poststructuralist formulation of the double sense of "subjection-subjectification," thereby evoking the nexus of power, discourse, and identity that is fundamental to our argument in this chapter.

A further point to consider is Atkinson's evocation of the uniqueness and specificity of Australia, geo-politically, as a nation-continent characterized by vast distances and expanses, internal and external, and an inevitably sparse population. Not only did this give rise to distinctive issues of managing time and space, but the question arose also of finding appropriate and effective ways of governing and coordinating territories and populations.

This presented specific challenges in terms of the relationship of geography and governmentality, which in turn indicates the historical significance of communication—overall, a theme we have introduced elsewhere, with reference to curriculum inquiry in Australia (Green, 2003a).

Atkinson's interest in communication is crucially apposite here and indeed a recurring theme in his work. As he writes in the Foreword to the second volume of his monumental history of the Europeans in Australia: "This volume, even more than Volume 1, is concerned with a revolution in communications, a little like the one that transformed the world during the last years of the twentieth century" (Atkinson, 2004, p. xiv). He is referring to a new intensity in literate culture and commerce: "By the 1840s attitudes that might be called global had started to emerge as a result of massive quantities of books (fact and fiction), pamphlets, and newspapers, and as a result of the unprecedented speed with which these, plus letters of all kinds, now moved around the world" (Atkinson, 2004, p. xiv). Elsewhere he points to the special significance of the postal system and, later, the telegraph and the telephone. Newspapers are also crucial, as he argues, a means of negotiation between the local and the global, between particular places in all their specificity and their diversity and what would later come to be formalized as the *nation*-continent. Literacy and the power of "writing (print and hand-writing)" (Atkinson, 2002, p. 24) are fundamental to his account. Describing the 19th century as "a turning point in the history of writing," he observes: "From that time, when print was adapted to a mass market, we have been a truly literate culture" (Atkinson, 2002, p. 23). He draws on Benedict Anderson's work on "imagined communities" and print capitalism to explore issues of nation-hood and nationalism, linking these matters explicitly to literacy, to "literate habits of thought" (Atkinson, 2002, p. xi). As he writes: "It can easily be argued that the history of Australia, maybe more so than any other country in the world, is a story about literacy, about writing, its facility, its virtuosity, its extraordinary power" (Atkinson, 2002, p. 1). He moves readily to the concept and indeed the problematic of the nation, observing that "the idea of the nation itself grew out of writing and reading" (Atkinson, 2002, p. 6) and, further, pointing to "the ways nations, including Australia, were formed as imagined communities by the power of print" (Atkinson, 2002, p. 59). Here he is drawing on Anderson's thesis that "nationality, or ... nation-ness, as well as nationalism, are cultural artefacts of a particular kind" (Anderson, 1991, p. 4). This is to highlight the role and significance of "culture," of language and imagination, and more broadly of *discourse*, in nation-hood and nation-building—and, by extension and implication, in national schooling. "Nations are imagined things," Atkinson (2002, p. 22) writes; "[t]hey are real and imagined," and "[t]hey have to be read about—and, once read, spoken about—in order to take a substantial life." It is worth recalling that Anderson isolates the novel and the newspaper, "two forms of imagining which first flowered in Europe in the eighteenth century," as providing "the technical means for 're-presenting' the *kind* of imagined community that is the nation" (Anderson, 1991, p. 25). In Atkinson's account, both the novel and the newspaper are key cultural technologies of colonial and federal nationalism in Australia, as well as being directly formative in the "real"-ization of the nation. Whether in novels or newspapers, fact or fiction, "shared stories, printed for mass circulation, in some sense tell us who we are and where we are" (Atkinson, 2002, p. 23).

At this point, it is useful to draw in the notion of the *national imaginary*, not simply in relation to Australia, as "played out in curriculum work and public education," but more broadly with reference to "an ever-expanding range of countries and their respective educational circumstances and trajectories" (Green, 2003b, p. 18). For Popkewitz (2001a), the concept enables due consideration of "how certain global discourses overlay national educational practices to produce narratives and images of the individual who acts and participates" (p. 262), as a problem of modern government. Civic participation and citizenship are not to be simply assumed; rather, they must be actively and ongoingly *produced*, as attributes of the citizen-subject. Schooling is profoundly implicated in this, having "historically played a pivotal role in the construction of national representations and the principles through which individuals construct subjectivities" (Popkewitz, 2001a, p. 266). Importantly, "[t]his is not simply a matter of personal identity," although it is certainly that, but also of national identity, "and indeed the material and symbolic relationship between the person and the nation" (Green, 2003b, p. 18). As Popkewitz (2001a) puts it, schooling "constructs national imaginaries" (pp. 264–265), narratives and images of the nation (partly in contradistinction with other nations and other people), in "constructing systems of collective 'belonging' and the accompanying anxieties as individuals imagine themselves as citizens with obligations and responsibilities" (Popkewitz, 2001a, p. 265). He emphasizes that this production of narratives and images is always heterogeneous, achieved "through an amalgamation of technologies, ideas and social practices" (Popkewitz, 2001a, pp. 267–268). Moreover, national imaginaries are to be understood from the outset as "hybrids" rather than as "unified images of a nation or individuality" and as specific articulations of culture and power (Popkewitz, 2001a, p. 271). In the case of Australia, certainly in the early 20th century but arguably still evident today, this is to be understood in terms of what has been called the Bush Myth, the symbolic value of the Outback and the play of various (inland) rural imaginaries, stories of pioneers and bushrangers, convicts and pastoralists, stoic heroism and laconic egalitarianism, and the strange persistence of a Frontier sensibility that is at odds with the fact that Australia is now one of the most urbanized countries in the world, with the bulk of the population located on the coastal fringe (Gill, 2005; Green & Letts, 2007). What is interesting in this regard is that, notwithstanding Popkewitz's refusal of geography or perhaps simply its elision in his argument (Popkewitz, 2001a, p. 267; see also Popkewitz, 1998), geography clearly matters in the case of Australian national imaginaries, as indeed it seems to do for certain other countries (e.g., Canada), which might have a significant bearing on how best to engage contemporary discourses of globalization and cosmopolitanism.

At this point, we want to turn our attention more directly to issues of literacy and schooling, modernity and governmentality. We want to work from the premise that a fundamental relationship exists between language and literacy, on the one hand, and curriculum and schooling, on the other hand. This is to argue for the centrality of language and literacy in the constitution of the school—what has been described as "the insistence of the letter in curriculum and schooling" (Green, 1993a, p. 1). Furthermore, Green (1993a) argues for particular attention to "written language and its associated cultural politics, social relations and epistemological effects" (p. 1). This argument posits an institutional and historical connection between literacy and modern(ist) schooling. In a related way, Popkewitz's (2001b) argues that curriculum itself also needs to be understood as "an invention of modernity" (p. 159), and indeed in and of itself "a literate concept" (W. Reid, 1993, p. 15).

What is at issue here, in particular, is the concept of the *print apparatus*. Drawn from film theory and referring in part to the technocultural complex of the printing and publishing industries—linking therefore to what Anderson (1991) has described as "print-capitalism"—this concept extends to the nexus between subjectivity and a specific institutional practice, namely, that associated with literacy and schooling. As Gregory Ulmer (1989) writes, apropos of what he sees as a decisive contemporary shift in "the apparatus of culture," this involves "change not only in technology but in institutional practices and the ideology of the subject as well" (p. xii). His immediate point of reference is what he terms "the academic apparatus," which we can understand here as more specifically the system of school knowledge:

> In terms of the academic apparatus, we would relate the technology of print and alphabetic literacy with the ideology of the individual, autonomous subject of knowledge, self-conscious, capable of rational decisions free from the influences of prejudice and emotion; and to the practice of criticism, manifested in the treatise, and even the essay, assuming the articulation of subject/object, objective distance, seriousness and rigor, and a clear and simple style. (Ulmer, 1989, p. 4)

Thus, the system of school knowledge involves bringing together the print-publishing complex with a certain hegemonic subject-form and what might be called *school literacy* or perhaps (as it has been otherwise described) "print-essayistic literacy." Importantly, this involves a distinctive form of rationality (and an associated mind-set) that might be characterized as (phal)logocentric, linear rationality. This normative way of thinking/

believing is one of the most important of "the effects of print culture and the significance of 'essayistic literacy' in the formation of human attributes, within the culture of modernity" (Green, 1993b, p. 211), which is so crucially part of the legacy of the Enlightenment.

All this can now be grasped more historically. Anderson's (1991) account of print-capitalism and nation-hood—"the discontinuity-in-connectedness of print-languages, national consciousness, and nation-states" (p. 46)—indicates very clearly that changed linguistic conditions were at once decisive and symptomatic with regard to the emergence of national(ist) sentiment, post-Reformation. He points specifically to "unified fields of exchange and communication below Latin and above the spoken vernaculars," "a new fixity to language," and new "languages-of-power" (Anderson, 1991, pp. 44–45), noting moreover "the explosive interaction between capitalism, technology, and human linguistic diversity" (Anderson, 1991, p. 45). Nations as "imagined communities" were formed out of new dynamics of inclusion and exclusion, identity and difference, Self and Other. Within this momentous social and political change, an important role was played out in the emergence of distinctive reading communities, notably those associated with the new cultural technologies of the novel and the newspaper. It is noteworthy, finally, that Anderson's later discussion of the "official nationalism" of the 19th century has an explicit educational dimension: involving increasing state interest and intervention in education, along with the emergence of a distinctive English (literary) educational practice and associated forms of cultural policy.

Also relevant to this connection is work on print culture, early modernity, and the history of political thought, represented perhaps most notably by the historical scholarship of J. G. A. Pocock. This work is, among other things, addressed to the relationship between republicanism and the Enlightenment. Importantly, a particular role is assigned to the emergence and consolidation of a new phase in what is explicitly described as "print culture" as an "element of central significance to the early modern era and to the understanding of its political discourse" (Pocock, 1993, p. 2). Largely based in London, this early modern print culture is linked with the following:

> the advent of a humanist discourse and a print medium capable of conveying it; the explosion of unlicensed printing at the outset of the mid-seventeenth-century internal wars; the growth of journalism and another explosion of printed matter in the troubled late seventeenth century; the appearance of the novel and essay in the early eighteenth century; and the further expansion of the reading market throughout that century. (Pocock, 1993, p. 2)

Further to this, a particular significance is assigned to "literature," understood in the broadest sense, and to "literacy." This "literature" embraced not simply "the genres of political literature . . . the broadsheet, the pamphlet, the newsletter, the journal, and the essay, treatise or learned folio seen as interacting with all of these" and with "great works of jurisprudence, divinity, philosophy and history ... read in the context of an occasional, polemical and public literature with which they in fact interacted," but also "the major printed genres—poetry, drama, the novel—for which the term 'literature' is conventionally reserved" (Pocock, 1993, p. 3). What is important to register here is, first, that such an expanded, expansive view of literacy and literature is quite at odds with how these come to be understood within the history of English teaching and the English subjects, and with the early 20th-century installation of "English" at the heart of the public school curriculum; and second, the centrality of politics and of political culture in such circumstances, linked decisively to notions of rhetoric and textuality. Although it is necessary to point out that this was far from being a popular phenomenon, socially and educationally, nonetheless it is of immense historical significance, with ramifications and resonances for the much wider reach of what was to later become the British Empire and for the West more generally. In particular, it speaks to the emergence of a distinctive political subjectivity as a crucial marker of modernity.

We have already seen that a strong case exists for the significance of literacy and the power of writing in Australian history, and also for Australian political culture. We return now to the immediate post-Federation period in Australian educational history. We do so in order to explore the particular relationship between curriculum and literacy, with reference to the politics *and* poetics of nation and empire. It is pertinent to note that this was a period of great energy and innovation, particularly from the early years of the century through to the Great War, described by various commentators as "an educational awakening" (Turney, 1983, p. 1) and a "renaissance" (Spaull, 1925; cited in Campbell and Sherington, 2006, p. 193). As Campbell and Sherington (2006) observe, "it was a period of intensive educational reform discourse and activity" (p. 193), moreover "clearly associated with the New Education movement" (Baker, 2001; Selleck, 1968). This in turn needs to be understood as an important reference point for English curriculum history and for the emergence of "English" as a distinctive school subject, especially in Australia (Green & Cormack, 2008; Green, Cormack, & Reid, 2000). Although commonly regarded now as a feature of the comprehensive secondary school, English was newly installed in 1905 as the "hub" of the primary school curriculum, as its organizing, authorizing center, the "cornerstone" (Green & Reid, 2002; Patterson, 2002). Moreover, literature figured heavily in this officially sponsored version of English, thoroughly filtered through Arnoldian and Wordsworthian perspectives on language, culture, and race. This meant, in turn, a programmatic focus on *reading*, on gaining access to the literary Heritage, all "sweetness and light." In learning to read, children acquire the capacity to participate in literary culture more generally—provided, of course, that they (and their teachers, too, in their own training) are provided opportunities and invitations to engage with "good literature" as a crucial resource in their identity-work, active "in refining and elevating character" (Tate, 1893). There are parallels with developments in countries such as France, where curriculum innovation in the mother-tongue over the same general period saw French authors increasingly incorporated into primary teaching programs for reasons that were at once "literary," "national and French," and "moral" (Chartier & Hébrard, 2001, p. 279). Although admittedly just one among a range of English subjects, then, "reading" was nonetheless critical, especially in the early 20th-century Australian primary school.

Looking at reading pedagogy in the post-Federation period, in the first few decades of the 20th century, is revealing. What were children asked to read, and how did they go about doing so? Indeed, how did they learn to read, and, having done so, what was the relationship between learning to read thus and reading thereafter, throughout their schooling and beyond? This last is an important question because it raises the issue of the extent to which curriculum, literacy, and schooling connects organically, if never causally, with citizenship. To what extent is reading pedagogy implicated in the production of political subjectivity? Such inquiry links usefully to available cultural histories of reading and, more broadly, to what has been called the history of the book (Febvre & Martin, 1976; Lyons & Arnold [eds], 2001). Lyons (1992) distinguishes among "texts," "books," and "readers" as foci for cultural history, and it is pertinent to note that although English teaching characteristically has attended to texts and readers, in various ways and in varying degrees, it has tended to gloss over the materiality of the book, including the socioeconomic practices and conditions of its production, distribution, and consumption. At the same time, it is by no means clear-cut what constructions of text and reading have been mobilized in the historical record, certainly at the level of practice, although there is some information regarding this in the available curriculum prescriptions, in what Lyons (1992) calls "the normative sources—that is, the texts which tell readers what they should and should not read, as well as how they ought to respond to their reading" (p. 8). He points to the actual artifacts, the "books themselves as material objects," and also "the autobiographies of individual readers" as further important sources.

Lyons' particular interest is in readers and reading, albeit within a resolutely materialist cultural-historical frame (e.g., Lyons & Taksa, 1992). Elsewhere, in an account of reading practices in Australia in the first half of the 20th century, he writes:

> Any account of reading practices which attempts to identify what was individual about the Australian reader must acknowledge all the ambiguities of a colonial society, the characteristics it shared with the rest of the western world, together with its local peculiarities. (Lyons, 2001a, p. 335)

This is consistent with his observation of "the schizophrenic nationalism of the period, in which there was little perceived contradiction between imperial and Australian loyalties" (Lyons, 2001b, p. xviii–xix). From our perspective, what is notable about his work and that of his associates on "the history of the Australian reader" (Lyons, 1992, p. 14) is a curious underplaying of the role and significance of formal education, of schooling and reading pedagogy. This is perhaps because of a sense of disjunction, registered more generally, between the child and the citizen as generationally distinct subjects, and a failure to recognize and appreciate the work of becoming, of formation—of *bildung* (Whitson, 2009). It is not that Lyons ignores schooling; for instance, it is clear from the account he and Taksa provide of "the generation of 1914," the so-called "poetry generation," that the effects of choral reading practices and of recitation are long-lasting, with specific reference to "choric learning by collective repetition or chanting" as "a standard pedagogical technique" (Lyons & Taksa, 1992, p. 69). He also refers to "[t]he Anglophilism of Australian reading practices," which he sees as reinforced by "the traditional emphases of the school curriculum on the classics of English literature and history" (Lyons, 2001a, p. 339). Yet there is a sense in which education is indeed backgrounded, perhaps understandably so, which further suggests the value of attending more closely to what goes on in classrooms and schools, in curriculum prescriptions *and* enactments, or as much as the latter is possible, historiographically.

What did the reading curriculum of post-Federation primary schools consist of? What did it look like? Although there are now various accounts available (Cormack, 2006; Reeves, 1996; Reid & Green, 2004), these are mainly of a preliminary or exploratory nature. A distinction is to be made between the syllabus materials as such, which were prescribed, with reference to both content ("texts") and pedagogy, and various support materials, such as the School Paper, all of which were produced by the state education departments. In addition, there was a considerable educational publishing industry, producing a range of textbooks and other print-based resources. In what follows, we examine some of the features of the primary reading curriculum, understanding this within the terms of reference of "English" as a distinctive, newly emergent school subject. This is to be seen, moreover, as a cultural technology, a practice producing subjectivity on the level of both the individual and the population. As such, it participates within more generalized practices and programs of governmentality, as "a new relation between state governing practices and individual behaviors and dispositions" (Popkewitz, 2001b, p. 160). The reading lesson is therefore to be conceived as a particular, orchestrated performance of the self in relation to authority, as the becoming-subject of the reader and the citizen.

The first point to be made is that literature figured heavily; moreover, this was firmly understood to be "*English* literature," "*good* literature," with nationality ("Englishness") thus coming together inexorably with predetermined notions of moral and aesthetic quality. It was asserted time and time again that the principles of selection were to be grounded in judgment, in a considered assessment of what was worthy of being included in the curriculum, and hence what was worth teaching. Morgan's (1990) reference to "the 'Englishness' of English teaching" is entirely apposite here and a continuing theme in English curriculum history, although arguably with particular resonance for those Anglophone countries with constitutional and other links to the (former) British Empire. This was certainly the case for post-Federation Australia. Reading in this light was seen as "the means of unlocking for us the noble thoughts of the past, so that the great ideas that genius has created throughout the ages become our own" (*English—Course of Instruction*, South Australia, 1921; cited in Cormack, 2006, p. 122). It is worth noting that although previously statements such as this would have referred to what was specifically called the "English subjects" (History, Geography, Literature),[3] by the 1920s, "English" was reserved for those categories and activities that are now recognizably and conventionally part of English teaching per se (poetry, writing, reading, spelling, etc). Reading books, or Readers, remained, however, largely "literary" in nature or orientation, or at least significantly so.

An important part of the reading curriculum was the so-called School Paper. Indeed Musgrave (1994a) observes, apropos of elementary/primary schools in Victoria, that "[f]rom 1896 to 1930 the prescribed material for reading in these schools . . . was *The School Paper*, a monthly newspaper published by the State Education Department" (p. 1). The equivalent text in New South Wales was the *Commonwealth School Paper*, "published monthly from 1904 to 1915 as an official 'supplementary reader' for public schools" (Firth, 1970, p. 128), whereas in South Australia it was *The Children's Hour*, "the first such paper in Australia, introduced by the South Australian Department in March 1889" (Musgrave, 1994a, p. 1). Furthermore, School Papers and the like were "for many children the only material which they could, and did[,] read," and therefore they "take on considerable importance in understanding the values of society to which children were exposed" (Townsend, 1989, p. 148).[4] Clearly texts such as these are an important resource for understanding reading in Australia in the early 20th century, which makes their omission from Lyons and Arnold's (2001) edited history of the book in Australia (1891–1945) all the more striking. Firth (1970) remarks of the NSW School Paper that "[a]s an officially edited magazine designed to provide children with ideas rather than mere practice in reading, it is especially good evidence of public school values" (p. 128)—including, presumably, those associated with books and reading. However, rather than address the full substance of these "public school values," we shall concentrate here on the issue of political subjectivity, and on the textual work bearing more directly on social identity formation and on nation-building, and hence on notions of patriotism and national(ist) sentiment.

In this regard, Musgrave (1994b) looks specifically in the Victorian School Paper at "the nature of the invitations presented to young Australians to assume the Australian identity" (p. 12). He traces these "invitations" through the manner in which Australia was represented as a "place," in terms of its physical and human (and also its "patriotic" [p. 13]) geography, and also with regard to its historical heritage and political culture. In the latter case, "[t]he legacy of the mother country was—and was thought to be—crucial," with "British, or more exactly English, history ... seen as the source of democratic freedom" (Musgave, 1994b, p. 13). Concerned overall with the question of education for citizenship, he traces the way in which subtle negotiations were required between sometimes conflicting, sometimes complementary national ("Australian") and imperial ("British") identifications, observing, however, a gradual but inexorable shift from the latter to the former:

> Education for citizenship was seen up to perhaps the 1930s as historical in nature, and the relevant history was British. But the longer Australia was an independent nation the more it felt the need for its national identity to be rooted in the Australian, rather than the British, heritage. (Musgrave, 1994a, p. 14)

Elsewhere he traces the somewhat chequered curriculum history of Civics as a school subject over the same period, drawing on the same historical material (Musgrave, 1996). What is pertinent here, however, is that reading is clearly conceived as a crucial technology in the "making" of Australians. As such, it serves an important function in the so-called "moral curriculum" of the Australian school. Curiously, Musgrave arguably misrecognizes the significance of the relationship between language and morality in public education, and hence the particular relevance of the English subjects; in that regard, it is worth noting that he had some time earlier observed that "[t]he native tongue is the primary vehicle for carrying the moral assumptions of a nation" (Musgrave, 1979, p. 120).

Firth's account of the situation in New South Wales is equally illustrative. Public education saw as its clear mandate the inculcation of social and moral values: "The public school pupil was to be presented with the assumptions of a particular kind of colonial patriotism, politically conservative and socially respectable, which remained public school orthodoxy until World War 1." Hence: "Despite Federation, public school children continued to be taught loyalty equally to England and to Australia" (Firth, 1970, p. 132). The active, mediating role of the editors of these School Papers is a significant one: S. H. Smith in New South Wales, for instance, later Director-General of Education,[5] and also Charles Long in Victoria, heavily involved in the Victorian Department's educational publishing program. The NSW Commonwealth School Paper (CSP) was insistent in its patriotic moralism, with "[p]oems ... chosen for the lessons they were expected to teach" and "[n]ot merely poetry but literature in general . . . judged by its moral content" (Firth, 1970, p. 134). Furthermore: "Accordingly to the CSP, there were two patriotisms which the children were to hold: 'patriotism which is concerned solely with the country in which we live' and 'that wider patriotism which embraces the whole Empire' " (Firth, 1970, p. 136). This was not conceived as a matter of "divided loyalty," moreover, rather as entirely complementary and mutually reinforcing.

With South Australia's *The Children's Hour*, it is possible to trace a somewhat more detailed and textured picture of identity-work and nation-building in the early decades of the 20th century in Australia.[6] What emerges from this study is a complex sense of citizenship, linked decisively to constructions of race and ethnicity and socio-symbolic dynamics of inclusion and exclusion. "Whiteness" is both assumed and asserted. Indigenous people are largely disregarded or else categorized among the natural phenomena of the country. Interestingly, and in contrast to Musgrave's (1994b) analysis, *The Children's Hour* does not simply focus on English stories, history, and geography. Indeed, readers are deliberately introduced to "children of the world," including a range of East Asian, South Asian, African, and European lands. Much work was done to locate these places in relation to Australia and the Empire, of course, with military conflict, trade, and imperial concerns often used as markers of those relations. This text showed that children were being formed not only as local or national subjects but as connected also into more global economies and politics.

The "Australian" is typically a white settler and a loyal British subject of the Empire. (This is notwithstanding the fact that, in South Australia, a certain proportion of the early settlers were German.) "He" is textually constructed as a certain type of individual, with qualities or attributes that have enabled him, and many like him, to successfully make the often difficult transition from the old country to a new land. Stories of explorers dominate in this regard, painting the continent's interior as unknown and as presenting formidable barriers to the settlers, but also possibly representing unknown possibilities for agricultural expansion. One contemporary commentator on children's reading in South Australia noted the importance of "adventure" stories, "[f]or boys of a certain age [such as t]hose dealing with the contact of civilized with savage life, as in exploring or in settling a new country" (1907 *Education Gazette*, p. 79). Thus, the subject of the stories could, in some cases, be seen as the ideal subject of nation and empire, exploring and settling, and civilizing "his" own place.

A further dimension of such comparative work is the assertion in these various School Papers of a distinctive colonial and later state-specific identity in addition to those associated with nation and empire. Hence, in 1904, one article begins: "It will help us to understand more clearly 'Our Own Country' if we first consider it as part of the great island continent of Australia. It will further assist us if we can also consider Australia in its true relation to much older known parts of the world" (CH, No. 170, Vol. XVl, p. 22 [Class lV]). Here, the reader is invited to move through varying scales of locality and identity.

Importantly, the very form of *The Children's Hour* is revealing. As a curriculum artifact, it is marked by intertextuality and heteroglossia. It contained a rich variety of material ranging from short stories, fairy tales, and verse through to regular and special columns and feature articles, news reports, and puzzles. It thus brought together a multiplicity of voices and discourses, and hence of reader and subject positions, across a diverse, fragmentary, and often contradictory body of texts and images. One effect of this multi-voicedness is that it disrupts any notion that nation-building and citizen formation were ever stable, unified, coherent discursive projects in Australian public schools in the period at issue here. However, what does emerge is a strong sense of the discursive field, its regularity and its complexity, and the fact that it was so consistent and more or less exclusively a feature of everyday classroom life, over such a long time, suggests that it may well have been significant in organizing and regulating the production of children's subjectivity, in accordance with a richly textured, hybridized national imaginary. A distinctive "story" emerges, powerful and persuasive, and yet somewhat ambivalent, shared, "printed for mass circulation, [which] in some sense tells us who we are and where we live" (Atkinson, 2002, p. 23). Indeed, there is evidence that the reach of the School Papers extended far beyond the classroom, with a number of educators at the time noting that the *Children's Hour* was an important source of reading and pleasure in the isolated country homes from which many children came to school. The *Children's Hour* also featured letters from children in other Australian states and from North America, demonstrating that this text circulated widely and rapidly enough for such correspondence to occur.

The School Papers were part of a larger program of reading pedagogy in Australia from the late 19th to the early to mid-20th centuries, which was itself a new phase in a longer history of Antipodean modernity—arguably a classic, albeit distinctive, manifestation of the programmatic articulation of education and citizenship internationally in the context of what has been identified here as "the long 19th century" (see Introduction). An initiative of the recently consolidated educational bureaucracies, these School Papers need to be understood as putative solutions to the problems of governmentality that confronted public educators and social reformers alike, in accordance with new challenges of geography, demography, and democracy. The question was how best to manage these problems and challenges in such a way as to foster and sustain collective forms of belonging and identification amenable to the emergence of a new and distinctive national identity. Recent debates on Federation and the republic are symptomatic not simply of a changing political culture but also of an emergent structure of feeling in Australia, a renewed sense of historical possibility *and* constraint. Today, as we enter into a quite different world order, it is clear that it is not only the case that a rearticulated and renewed political imagination is urgently required but also that this needs to be thoroughly informed by and alert to the lessons of history, in all their recalcitrance and their complexity.

NOTES

1. The subject-disciplinary space at issue here is presumably akin to that of fields such as "Spanish" or "Russian" in other national educational systems—that is, broadly concerned with language and literature, and at various levels, teaching reading and writing.
2. This has relevance to the situation at the turn of the 21st century given the significance of the epochal shift from "print" to "digital electronics" that has been observed in relation to contemporary developments in literacy studies.
3. In South Australia, for example, up until 1900 at the University designed examinations for schools the label "English" stood for the study of "(a) Outlines of the History of England; (b) English Literature: Coleridge's Ancient Mariner . . . [and] (c) Outlines of geography, especially the Geography of Australia" (1900 Public Examinations Board, Adelaide). By 1902, English became "English Literature" and included only the study of Shakespeare and other authors, poetry, and "grammar and prosody," taking up the form that was to be stable for decades (Cormack, 2004).
4. Moreover, as Townsend (1989) also notes: "State production of school newspapers was unique to Australia" (p. 148). This is a point worth following up if indeed it is the case. Presumably she is referring specifically to countries within or associated with the former British Commonwealth, although it would be of interest to see what the situation was beyond the Commonwealth.
5. Smith was in fact the editor of various "magazines" and "papers" of this kind in the period in question, from the *Children's Newspaper* through the *Australian School Paper* and the *Commonwealth School Paper* to the *School Magazine for Boys and Girls*, later simply the *School Magazine*, which began in 1916 (Townsend, 1982).
6. We acknowledge the work and invaluable assistance of Melissa Stevenson in researching this text and its associated materials.

REFERENCES

Anderson, B. (1991). *Imagined communities: Reflections on the origin and spread of nationalism* (rev. ed.). London: Verso.

Atkinson, A. (1997). *The Europeans in Australia: A history* (Vol. 1). Oxford: Oxford University Press.

Atkinson, A. (2002). *The Commonwealth of speech: An argument about Australia's past, present, and future*. Melbourne: Australian Scholarly Publishing.

Atkinson, A. (2004). *The Europeans in Australia: A history* (Vol. 2). South Melbourne: Oxford University Press.

Baker, B. M. (2001). *In perpetual motion: Theories of power, educational history, and the child*. New York: Peter Lang.

Birrell, B. (2001). *Federation: The secret story.* Sydney: Duffy & Snellgrove.
Browne, G.S. (1927). Introduction. In G. S. Browne (Ed.), *Education in Australia: A comparative study of the educational systems of the six Australian states* (pp. xvii–xxi). London: Macmillan.
Campbell, C., & Sherington, G. (2006). A Genealogy of the Australian System of Comprehensive High Schools: The Contribution of Educational Progressivism to the One Best Form of Universal Secondary Education. *Paedagogica Historica,* 42(1&2), p. 191–210.
Castells, M. (1996). *The rise of the network society.* Oxford: Blackwell.
Chartier, A.-M., & Hébrard, J. (2001). Literacy and schooling from a cultural historian's point of view. In T. S. Popkewitz, B. M. Franklin, & M. G. Pereyra (Eds.), *Cultural history and education: Critical essays on knowledge and schooling* (pp. 265–288). New York and London: RoutledgeFalmer.
Cormack, P. (2004). *Adolescence, schooling, and English/literacy: Formations of a problem in early twentieth century South Australia.* Unpublished doctoral dissertation, University of South Australia.
Cormack, P. (2006). Reading and the primary English curriculum: An historical account. *Australian Journal of Language and Literacy,* 29(2), 115–131.
Davidson, A. (1997). *From subject to citizen: Australian citizenship in the twentieth century.* Cambridge: Cambridge University Press.
Dixson, M. (1999). *The imaginary Australian: Anglo-Celts and identity—1788 to the present.* Sydney: University of New South Wales Press.
Febvre, L., & Martin, H-J. (1976). *The coming of the book: The impact of printing 1450–1800.* London: New Left Books.
Firth, S. G. (1970). Social values in the New South Wales primary school, 1880–1914: An analysis of school texts. In *Melbourne studies in education* (pp. 123–159). Melbourne: Melbourne University Press.
Gill, N. (2005). Life and death in Australian "heartlands": Pastoralism, ecology, and rethinking the putback. *Journal of Rural Studies,* 21, 39–53.
Green, B. (1993a). Introduction. In B. Green (Ed.), *The insistence of the letter: Literacy studies and curriculum theorizing* (pp. 1–12). London: The Falmer Press.
Green, B. (1993b). Literacy studies and curriculum theorizing, or, The insistence of the letter. In B. Green (Ed.), *The insistence of the letter: Literacy studies and curriculum theorizing* (pp. 195–225). London: The Falmer Press.
Green, B. (2003a). Curriculum inquiry in Australia: Towards a local genealogy of the curriculum field. In W. F. Pinar (Ed.), *Handbook of international curriculum research* (pp. 123–141). Mahwah, NJ: Lawrence Erlbaum Associates.
Green, B. (2003b). Curriculum, public education, and the national imaginary: Re-schooling Australia? In A. Reid & P. Thomson (Eds.), *Rethinking public education: Towards a public curriculum* (pp. 17–32). Flaxton, Qld: Post Pressed & the Australian Curriculum Studies Association.
Green, B., & Cormack, P. (2008). Curriculum history, "English" and the new education; or, Installing the Empire of English? *Pedagogy, Culture and Society,* 16(3), 253–267.
Green, B., Cormack, P., & Reid, J.-A. (2000). Putting our past to work. *English in Australia,* 127–8, 111–119.
Green, B., & Letts, W. (2007). Space, equity, and rural education: A trialectical account. In K. N. Gulson & C. Symes (Eds.), *Spatial theories of education: Policy and geography matters* (pp. 57–76). London & New York: Routledge.
Green, B., & Reid, J.-A. (2002). Constructing the teacher and schooling the nation. *History of Education Review,* 31(1), 30–44.
Hamilton, D. (1989). *Towards a theory of schooling.* London, New York, & Philadelphia: The Falmer Press.

Irving, H. (1999). *To constitute a nation: A cultural history of Australia's constitution.* Cambridge: Cambridge University Press.

Lloyd, C. (2003). Economic policy and Australian state building: From labourist-protectionism to globalisation. In A. Teichova & H. Matis (Eds.), *Nation, state, and the economy in history* (pp. 404–423). Cambridge: Cambridge University Press.

Lyons, M. (1992). Texts, books, and readers: Which kinds of cultural history? *Australian Cultural History, 11,* 1–15.

Lyons, M. (2001a). Reading practices in Australia. In M. Lyons & J. Arnold (Eds.), *A history of the book in Australia 1891–1945: A national culture in a colonised market* (pp. 335–354). St. Lucia, Qld: University of Queensland Press.

Lyons, M. (2001b). Introduction. In M. Lyons & J. Arnold (Eds.), *A history of the book in Australia 1891–1945: A national culture in a colonised market* (pp. xiii–xix). St. Lucia, Qld: University of Queensland Press.

Lyons, M., & Arnold, J. (Eds.). (2001). *A history of the book in Australia 1891–1945: A national culture in a colonised market.* St. Lucia, Qld: University of Queensland Press.

Lyons, M., & Taksa, L. (1992). *Australian readers remember: An oral history of reading 1890–1930.* Oxford: Oxford University Press.

McKenna, M. (1996). *The captive republic: A history of republicanism in Australia, 1788–1996.* New York: Cambridge University Press.

Meredyth, D. (1994). English, civics, and ethical competence. *Interpretations, 27*(3), 70–95.

Morgan, R. (1990). The "Englishness" of English teaching. In I. Goodson & P. Medway (Eds.), *Bringing English to order: The history and politics of a school subject* (pp. 197–241). London, New York, & Philadelphia: The Falmer Press.

Musgrave, P.W. (1979). *Society and the curriculum in Australia.* Sydney: George Allen & Unwin.

Musgrave, P. W. (1994a). Readers in Victoria, 1896, 1: The school paper and children's world. *Paradigm, 15,* 1–10.

Musgrave, P. W. (1994b). How should we make Australians? *Curriculum Perspectives, 14*(3), 11–18.

Musgrave, P. W. (1996). Becoming a subject? *Curriculum Perspectives, 16*(3), 1–9.

Patterson, A. (2002). Installing English at the "hub" of early twentieth-century school curricula in Australia. *History of Education Review, 31*(2), 45–57.

Pocock, J. G. A. (1993). Editorial Introduction. In J. G. A. Pocock (Ed.), *The varieties of British political ghought, 1500–1800* (pp. 1–10). Cambridge: Cambridge University Press.

Popkewitz, T. S. (1998). *Struggling for the soul: The politics of schooling and the construction of the teacher.* New York and London: Teachers College Press.

Popkewitz, T. S. (2001a). National imaginaries, the indigenous foreigner, and power: Comparative educational research. In J. Schriewer (Ed.), *Discourse formation in comparative education* (pp. 261–293). Frankfurt: Peter Lang.

Popkewitz, T. S. (2001b). The production of reason and power: Curriculum history and intellectual traditions. In T. S. Popkewitz, B. M. Franklin, & M. G. Pereyra (Eds.), *Cultural history and education: Critical essays on knowledge and schooling* (pp. 151–183). New York and London: RoutledgeFalmer.

Reeves, N. (1996). Reading in Australia: A history of primary reading education 1790–1945. In B. Green & C. Beavis (Eds.), *Teaching the English subjects: Essays in English curriculum history and Australian schooling* (pp. 170–203). Geelong, Victoria: Deakin University Press.

Reid, J.-A., & Green, B. (2004). Displacing method(s)? Historical perspective in the teaching of reading. *Australian Journal of Language and Literacy, 27*(1), 12–26.

Reid, W. (1993). Literacy, orality, and the functions of curriculum. In B. Green (Ed.), *The insistence of the letter: Literacy studies and curriculum theorizing* (pp. 13–26). London: The Falmer Press.
Selleck, R. J. W. (1968). *The new education: The English background 1870–1914.* Melbourne: Pitman & Sons Ltd.
Tate, F. (1893). *Literature as a study for the teacher: A lecture, presented as the first of the monthly lectures inaugurated by the State School Teachers' Literary Society.* Melbourne: Patterson & Henderson.
Townsend, N. (1982). Philosophy of history in the school magazine of New South Wales, 1916–1922. *Journal of Australian Studies, 11,* 36–53.
Townsend, N. (1989). Moulding minds: The school paper in Queensland, 1905 to 1920. *Journal of the Royal Australian Historical Society, 75*(Part 11), 147–157.
Turney, C. (1983). Introduction. In C. Turney (Ed.), *Pioneers of Australian education: Vol. 3. Studies of the development of education in Australia (1900–1950).* Sydney: Sydney University Press.
Ulmer, G. (1989). *Teletheory: Grammatology in the age of video.* New York & London: Routledge.
Whitson, J. A. (2009) *Is there no outside to curriculum-as-text?* In E. Ropo & A. Tero (eds.), International Conversations on Curriculum Studies: Subject, Society and Curriculum, Rotterdam: Sense Publishers, pp. 340-354.

13 *Historia Magistra Civis*
Citizenship Education and Notions of Republicanism in Dutch History Textbooks Around 1800

Willeke Los

THE BATAVIAN SCHOOL REFORM (1801–1806) AND CITIZENSHIP EDUCATION

From a republican perspective the Dutch Republic experienced its finest hour in the decade around 1800. The French invasion following the French Revolution enabled the Dutch patriots to seize power and create a new republic, which was soon acknowledged by the French government. The Batavian Republic put an end to the reign of stadholder William V, who fled to England, and enabled a more democratic form of government. It was also responsible for the first Dutch constitution, issued in 1798. One of the most important achievements of the Batavian Republic was a reform of education, known as the Batavian school reform.

Shortly after its installation in 1795, the National Assembly set up a committee to design a plan for national education. For this purpose, the committee consulted the Maatschappij tot Nut van 't Algemeen (Society for the Common Good; the "Nut" in short) that from its very start in 1784 had published profusely on educational reform. Already in 1796, the Nut presented a substantial report that owed a lot to former publications of the Nut and several societies of science. In its report the Nut held the national government responsible for a reform of education because, according to her, it is the government's obligation to inform all its members of their duties toward society. Echoing one of the main arguments from the discussion on educational reform in the preceding decades, the Nut stated that all children, regardless of gender or class, should be educated toward virtuous and useful members of society (Boekholt & de Booy, 1987; Dodde, 1971; Los, 2005).

In accordance with its policy of national unification and reconciliation, the Batavian government adopted this inclusive ideal of civil or moral citizenship instead of a civic notion of citizenship, which stressed martial virtues connected with the willingness to protect one's native town or country that had been popular among the patriots in the previous decade.[1] Thus, the *Ontwerp van Staatsregeling voor het Bataafsche Volk* (Plan of Constitution for the Batavian people, 1798) states:

The people of the Netherlands require that the education in all moral and civil virtues, arts, sciences and other necessary and useful knowledge, be made available and made accessible to all. (Van Hoorn, 1907, p. 2)

To achieve this aim, the *Ontwerp van Staatsregeling* formulated a program of school reform in a number of successive articles. To begin with, an adequate amount of schools were to be provided for to educate children in reading, writing, arithmetic, "and all subsequent knowledge to best further the circumstances of the free citizen (in observance of local conditions)"(Van Hoorn, 1907, p. 2). Although the new republican government acknowledged the existence of a Supreme Being, it also ruled that religious dogma, which until then had constituted an important part of the curriculum of many primary schools, was to be kept outside the school walls (Van Hoorn, 1907). Additionally, schoolteachers were to become statutory appointees and would be required to have the requisite skills and hold the appropriate certifications. Furthermore, a new corpus of textbooks would be made available to serve the goal of proper national education, namely, education toward becoming an able and virtuous citizen (Van Hoorn, 1907). Finally, a system of inspection and supervision was to be established to guarantee the implementation of the proposed measures for school reform. For the elaboration and implementation of this program, the government installed a Ministry of National Education (Agentschap van Nationale Opvoeding) and appointed J. H. van der Palm (1763–1840) professor in Eastern languages and one of the former revolutionaries as its minister. Van der Palm was explicitly instructed to stimulate patriotic feelings and republican virtues through a list of appropriate schoolbooks (Van Hoorn, 1907).

Due to political instability in the wake of developments in France (the early years of the 19th century saw three changes of government in the Batavian Republic), the 1801 law on education was twice revised (in 1803 and 1806). Although these acts are differently formulated and also differ in their methods of organization and financing of the school system, they share a common spirit with regard to the aim and content of primary education: the development of the rational and moral faculties of children and their commitment to society. In the words of the 1806 act on education:

> All education should be organised in such a way, that through the learning of appropriate and useful knowledge, the mental faculties of children will be developed and they will be educated towards all civil and Christian virtues. (Van Hoorn, 1907, p. 225)

Like the *Ontwerp van Staatsregeling*, the 1806 act on education forbids the teaching of religious dogma by schoolteachers, but—as the quote above shows—it still prescribes Christian education in a general sense. This approach to religion would prove fatal in later years, as explained by Dekker (Chapter 3, this volume). With respect to the use of textbooks, however, the 1806 act on education takes a stricter view by obliging teachers to limit themselves to the textbooks named on a list to be drawn up by the Secretary of State for Internal Affairs (Van Hoorn, 1907).

Although the 1806 act on education proved successful (lasting until 1857), the same cannot be said for the Batavian Republic itself. In the year in which that law on education was enacted, the Batavian Republic, through the machinations of Napoleon Bonaparte, was remodelled into a monarchy with the emperor's brother, Louis Napoleon, as its sovereign king. This change of government did not, however, affect the legislation of school education. The order for a required book list for primary education was upheld. In 1810, the *Algemeene Boekenlijst* was published, the same year in which Louis Napoleon was forced to abdicate his Dutch throne and the Netherlands were incorporated in the French empire. Five years later (1815), the list was revised due to another, this time final, change of government: the return of the House of Orange to the Netherlands after the fall of Napoleon Bonaparte. William, son of stadholder William V, who had fled the Netherlands in 1795, was inaugurated in 1813, not as stadholder, like his father, but as sovereign king, and in this role he became known as William I (1772–1843). The new king accepted his sovereignty on the condition that the Liberty of the Dutch people should be guaranteed by a written constitution, and so the Dutch kingdom became a constitutional monarchy (Kossmann, 1984).

These political developments present an interesting paradox: Enacted by the three successive governments of the Batavian Republic, the Batavian school reform was implemented by the three non-republican governments succeeding the Batavian Republic. How could this political discontinuity coexist with a continuity in educational policy? Or was this continuity only of a formal or superficial nature? Differently put: To what extent did this change of government affect the implementation of republican notions and ideals laid down in the 1806 act on education and the educational discussion that preceded it? Did school education uphold republican values or did they diverge from them as a result of the changed political climate?

To answer these questions we have to pay attention to two different aspects. First, the notion of citizenship that was at the heart of the Batavian school reform: Was this notion upheld or modified during the implementation of the school reform in the first decades of the nineteenth century? Second, the valuation of Dutch republicanism in the early 19th century: How did the new Dutch monarchy reflect on its own identity in relation to its republican history? Did it perceive its new form of government as a radical breach with the past?

Primary education textbooks on national history are an interesting source to study these problems in their interdependency. For not only do they by their very nature provide an account of the history of the Dutch Republic and Dutch republicanism, history as a primary education teaching subject—even though it only became compulsory in 1857—was the subject par excellence that combined the intellectual and moral education of children, the educational goal that laid the foundation of the 1806 law on education. Furthermore, primary education was the most accessible type of education and therefore the most important means toward citizenship education.

As a starting point for my analysis I take the compulsory list of schoolbooks for primary education of 1810 and 1815, following two lines of inquiry: first, notions of citizenship in relation to the propagation or rejection of republican values; and second, implicit and explicit republican connotations (or the lack thereof) in the representation and evaluation of the history of the Dutch Republic. To provide a context for this analysis, I start with a paragraph on Wagenaar's (1759) *Vaderlandsche Historie* (National History). Wagenaar's *Historie* was not only the most important and influential national history dating from the 18th century, it was also written from a republican point of view. The reactions to his work provide insight in the historical issues that were at stake between state-minded republican readings of history and Orangist interpretations.

THE BIRTH OF MODERN DUTCH NATIONAL HISTORIOGRAPHY

With his 21-volume masterpiece *Vaderlandsche Historie* (National History), published between 1749 and 1759, the self-taught historian Jan Wagenaar (1709–1773) laid the foundation for modern Dutch national history.[2] Although Wagenaar stood outside the university tradition, he was a pioneer in more than one way. Not only did his *Vaderlandsche Historie* further the development of national history as an independent subdivision within Dutch universities, it also presented a new model for writing history because Wagenaar aspired to overcome the traditional dualism between the politically oriented *historia* and the more culturally oriented *antiquitates* (Blaas, 1999; for a more detailed account of Wagenaar, see Wessels, 1997).

By using the term "vaderlandsche historie" (national history/history of the fatherland) Wagenaar indicated that his account addressed all the seven provinces that constituted the Dutch Republic and that he intended to write a history of the Dutch people, instead of a history of princes. Moreover, it expressed a new perspective on history, that is, a political, republican, viewpoint. As Wagenaar stated in the introduction to the first volume of his *Vaderlandsche Historie*, he aimed to give an account of the way Liberty had triumphed over its many attacks: "Our national history [...] can thus be seen as a history of the provoked, oppressed, revived and victorious Liberty of our Fatherland."[3]

Despite this republican viewpoint, Wagenaar did not advocate or even condone a partial account of the past. According to him, impartiality should be the main characteristic of the historian. This impartiality not only consisted of the use of reliable sources, but also meant that history should not be written to legitimize actual political constellations or prerogatives. Thus, Wagenaar's choice for Liberty as the basic theme ("Leitmotiv") of his history was not chosen a priori, but had followed a posteriori as a result from his research. Wagenaar tried his best to abstain from all prevailing prejudices. For this reason, he denounced a more philosophical or theoretical perspective on history, as had been used by Hume or Voltaire (Wessels, 1997). In two more ways Wagenaar distanced himself from existing historiographical traditions: He broke with the theistic tradition of history writing as well as with the Ciceronian, humanistic saying *historia magistra vitae*. Instead he focused on the past relationship between religious and secular powers and studied history first and foremost for its own sake. In trying to establish the impartial truth, while abstaining from moral judgment, Wagenaar hoped to make a contribution that would be of value for all political parties (Wessels, 1997).

Wagenaar's aim to render an impartial account of the history of the Dutch Republic notwithstanding, several of his volumes gave rise to criticisms to the contrary. The publication of volume X (1754), dealing with the quarrel between orthodox protestants and Remonstrants in which the stadholder Maurits chose the side of the orthodox protestants, which finally led to the conviction and the execution of the state pensionary Johan van Oldenbarneveld in 1619, was criticized by the orthodox protestants as biased and too much in favor of the Remonstrants' point of view. The publication of volumes XIII and XIV, dealing with the murder of the state-minded De Witt brothers in 1672, even gave rise to a paper war, openly accusing its author of partiality in favor of the De Witt brothers (Wessels, 1997).

Of a more fundamental nature was the criticism expressed by the Dutch publicist Elie Luzac (1721–1796)—who had also taken part in the De Witt war—in his four-volume Dutch history: *Hollands rijkdom* (Holland's wealth) published in 1780–1783. Luzac, a firm defender of the Dutch stadholderate and a representative of the Dutch conservative Enlightenment, accused Wagenaar of neglecting economic factors, especially Dutch commerce, in favor of politics and statecraft. Contrary to Wagenaar's state-minded republican point of view that true liberty only occurred during the stadholderless periods in which the General States ruled, Luzac did not consider the stadholder as a threat to but as a safeguard for liberty (Blaas, 1999; Velema, 1993; Wessels, 1997).

These criticisms did not prevent Wagenaar from becoming the most popular Dutch historian ever. His *Vaderlandsche Historie* was enormously successful. It was acclaimed in academic as well as in political—namely, patriotic (state-minded republican)—circles and was reprinted twice in the 18th century. Wagenaar's *Vaderlandsche Historie* inspired fellow historians to publish comments, appendixes, and sequels. Well into the 19th century it set the tone for other accounts of the history of the Dutch Republic, like *De opkomst en bloei van de Republiek der Vereenigde Nederlanden* (1774) by Simon Stijl (Blaas, 1999; Wessels, 1997). Wagenaar's *Vaderlandsche Historie* not only laid the foundation for academic national historiography, it also proved to be a role model for schoolbooks. In his last volume Wagenaar had added an abridged version of his *Vaderlandsche Historie* for the use of children: *Vaderlandsche Historie verkort*. This version was also very successful. During the 18th century it was printed and reprinted by five different publishers in at least five cities, while several printings went through more than one edition.[4] Next to Wagenaar's own abridged version other adaptations for children were published during the 18th and early 19th centuries while it served many—state-minded republicans as well as Organists—as an example and source of information.[5] In an extended, new edition, Wagenaar's abridged national history was one of the titles on the compulsory list of history textbooks.

HISTORY TEXTBOOKS ON THE BOOK LISTS OF 1810 AND 1815

The book list was one of many measures prescribed by law to reform primary education.[6] It took the government 4 years to finish this selection. According to the Inspector-General of Education, Adriaan van den Ende, who also had drafted the final law of 1806, this delay was not only caused by the large amount of work involved, but was also the result of a strategy to allow schoolteachers to get used to all the innovations. The government was aware that a thorough reform of primary education could only be successful if schoolteachers were allowed the time needed to master the new ideals regarding intellectual and moral education (Van den Ende, 1810). Besides, the government wanted to give booksellers whose list mainly consisted of old schoolbooks the opportunity to get rid of their old stock. During the period in which the primary education book list was drafted, booksellers and all other interested parties were invited to send in titles for the selection. To this end notices were published repeatedly in the *Koninklijke Courant* (Royal Newspaper) and the *Bijdragen*, the most important educational journal, supervised by the state (*Bijdragen*, 1806, VI. Stuk, p. 34 and 1807, X. Stuk, pp. 75–76).

The government intended to draft a book list that would be exhaustive and of general use. For this reason the book list did not restrict itself to all useful primary education textbooks but also listed reading books for children and special literature for teachers (Van den Ende, 1810). After its publication in 1810 all interested parties again were invited to send in titles they missed on this list.

The primary education book list defined content and structure of the curriculum: It prescribed the teaching subjects for the three successive levels of primary education as well as the books that should be used at each level.

Also, the book list was instrumental in adopting class teaching because all children within one class were obliged to use the same textbook (Van den Ende, 1810). The textbooks on the list were not ordered at random, but in order of usefulness or quality, starting with the most simple ones (Van den Ende, 1810).

According to the book list, history should only be taught in the third class or highest level of elementary school. However, it was not a compulsory teaching subject, but belonged to the so-called "useful skills." Nevertheless, history in general and national history in particular were regarded as important teaching subjects. This was made very clear by Van den Ende himself in an address to all schoolteachers, published in the *Bijdragen* to celebrate the inauguration of William I as constitutional monarch of the Netherlands. Van den Ende presents national history as the very subject to instil patriotism and to help restore the unity and welfare of the fatherland.[7]

The 1810 list of schoolbooks contains six titles for the teaching of history in the third or final year of elementary school. The 1815 list of schoolbooks adds another four titles. The change of government did not lead to any titles of the former list being removed; in some cases, however, the list referred to a later, updated edition. The table at page 269 gives the titles of the 1810 and 1815 book lists in their order of preference and provides data on their first editions and 19th-century reprints.

From this table we can draw the following conclusions. First, the titles on the 1810 book list prevail after 1815: Of the titles added in that year, only one seems to have been successful (no. 2 on the 1815 list). Second, the 1810 book list did not draw on new history textbooks, but selected a small number of titles already in use, half of which dated from the second half of the 18th century. Although the 1810/1815 book list contains three successful titles that were first published after 1800, continuity does seem to have been an important feature of the history textbooks used in primary education. To what extent these textbooks contain republican notions and meet the ideal of citizenship laid down in the 1806 law on education can only be established by a comparative analysis of the titles involved. This analysis is presented according to political content and affiliation of the author.

LISTED NATIONAL HISTORY TEXTBOOKS BY REPUBLICAN AUTHORS

Three of the history textbooks on the book list were written by authors known for their republican sympathies: the historian Jan Wagenaar, the minister of the Church and writer Johannes Florentius Martinet (1729–1795), and the primary school teacher Hendrik Wester (1752–1821), who became a school inspector in 1801.

Table 13.1 Titles of the 1810 and 1815 Book Lists in Their Order of Preference

No. on list 1810	No. on list 1815	Titles Book List 1815	Ed. Book-list 1810	Ed. Book-list 1815	First ed.	Number of eds. 1810–1850[8]	Last 19th-C. ed.
1	1	A. van der Swan, *Allereerste beginselen der Geschiedenis onzes Vaderlands voor de scholen*. (First principles of our native history [history of our fatherland] for schools)	1810	1810	1810	11	1855
–	2	*Vaderlandsche Geschiedenis in twee-en vijftig lessen, voor de Nederlandsche Jeugd en Scholen* (National History in fifty-two lessons, for Dutch youth and schools).		1814		14	1851
2	3	H. Wester, *Schoolboek der geschiedenissen van ons Vaderland* (Textbook of the histories of our fatherland)	5th ed. 1810	6th ed. 1815	1801	11	1847
3	4	*Kort begrip der Geschiedenissen van het Koningrijk Holland, in vragen en antwoorden, geschikt ten gebruike der Scholen* (Synopsis of the histories of the Dutch Monarchy, in questions and answers suitable for schools)	4th revised and expanded ed. 1808	5th revised and expanded ed. 1810	Unknown[9]	Unknown[10]	
4	5	Wagenaar's *verkorte Vaderlandsche Historie, in vragen en antwoorden, voortgezet na den vrede van Tilsit* (Wagenaar's abridged National History, in questions and answers, continued after the peace of Tilsit)	New ed. 1808	1808	1759	3	1833

(continued)

Table 13.1 (continued)

No. on list 1810	No. on list 1815	Titles Book List 1815	Ed. Book-list 1810	Ed. Book-list 1815	First ed.	Number of eds. 1810–1850	Last 19th-C. ed.
5	6	J.F. Martinet, *Het vereenigd Nederland verkort, ten gebruike der Scholen* (The United Netherlands abridged, for schools)	3rd ed. 1808	3rd ed. 1808	1790	0	
6	7	[Arend Fokke Simonsz] *De Vaderlandsche Historie in Themata* [...] (National history, in subjects)	5th ed. 1801	5th ed. 1801	1783	7	1825
--	8	T. Van Swinderen, *Over de verdiensten der vorsten van Oranje-Nassau jegens het Vaderland, een Leesboek voor de Nederlandsche Jeugd* (On the merits of het kings of Oranje-Naussau regarding the Fatherland, a reading-book for Dutch youth).		2nd ed. 1814		3	1818
--	9-	W. van den Hoonaard, *Geschiedenissen van ons Vaderland sedert het begin der omwenteling in November 1813 (in Zamenspraken)* (Histories of our Fatherland from the beginning of the revolution of November 1813, in dialogues)		1814		2	1816
--	10	*Staatkundige verlossing van de Vereenigde Nederlanden in den jare 1813. In gesprekken voor de aankomende jeugd.* (Constitutional deliverance of the United Netherlands in the year 1813. In dialogues for Young people).		1814		0	

Wagenaar's republicanism shows clearly in the way he connects the teaching of history with civic education in the preface to his *Verkorte Vaderlandsche Historie*. He judges national history to be the second-most important subject, reserving the position of prime importance to biblical history because "we are all born as members of the commonwealth and share, from our first youth, in the prosperity and adversity of our State" (Wagenaar, 1759, Preface). Therefore, the fortunes of the state should be a serious subject of study "for the children of all honest citizens, however humble their place in society" (Wagenaar, 1759, Preface) and should not be restricted to upper class children who need to be prepared for their future governing roles because the power of the state lies to a large extent in the masses of honest citizens. Wagenaar's view on the importance of history education for all children foreshadows the later school reformer's stress on primary education as a prerequisite for citizenship.

According to Wagenaar, his *Verkorte Vaderlandsche Historie* distinguishes itself from other history textbooks because of its impartiality, something that Wagenaar deems very important with regard to the education of citizens because:

> ... nothing is more harmful to civil society than that the minds of children be filled with a partial understanding of its national history; by contrast, nothing can better further the peace and unity among a nation's citizens than that each of them, from childhood on, learns to think temperately and truthfully about the great changes that have come to pass in one's fatherland. (Wagenaar, 1759, Preface)

Wagenaar's plea for impartiality proves to be more than a rhetorical device. This becomes evident when we take a look at the way he presents the two episodes in which the political struggle between the party of the stadholder (the Orangists) and the state-minded republicans (*staatsgezinden*) reached a climax: the execution of the Advocate of Holland, Johan van Oldenbarneveld (1547–1619), and the murder of the Pensionary of Holland Johan de Witt (1625–1672) and his brother Cornelis (1623–1672), regent of Dordrecht. In both cases Wagenaar restricts himself to the bare facts without passing moral judgment or revealing emotion, but upon close reading we can discern where his sympathies lie. In the case of Oldenbarneveld, for instance, Wagenaar states that Oldenbarneveld's death sentence would not have been possible had Maurits not changed the government of the cities beforehand (Wagenaar, 1808, pp. 94–95).

After Wagenaar's death his *Verkorte Vaderlandsche Historie* was expanded twice: once to include the period after the peace of Tilsit (1808) and again to cover the institution of the Dutch monarchy (1820). The first expanded version continues Wagenaar's factual account. The patriotic revolt in the 1780s is described without moral judgment, whereas the history of the Batavian Revolution is written with particular focus on its constitutional aspects. The second expanded edition exhibits a moderate Organist viewpoint, presenting the Prince Royal as a brave warrior and King William I as an engaged ruler very concerned with the trials and tribulations of his people (Wagenaar, 1820, 1833).

In contrast with Wagenaar's *Verkorte Historie*, Martinet's (1790) *Het Vereenigd Nederland verkort* is written from a theistic perspective.[11] In the first of the nine conversations that make up this textbook, Martinet argues that national history is a very pleasant and useful means to learn how God through a thousand good offices, benefactions, and salvations has made the fatherland into its present state (Martinet, 1790). According to Martinet, the most important event of Dutch history is that idol-worship, savagery, and servitude have been replaced by the gospel, civilization, and liberty (Martinet, 1790).

Martinet's account of Dutch history, then, is not based on the single notion of liberty—as is the case with Wagenaar's *Vaderlandsche Historie*—but on two central notions: religion and liberty. These Martinet calls "the two most important pledges" of the fatherland (Martinet, 1790, pp. 186–187). Their interconnectedness comes to the fore in Martinet's account of the Dutch Revolt against King Philip II of Spain. According to him the Dutch owed it to Divine intervention, that they had the courage to pick up their arms and fight the Duke of Alba, Philip II's representative who was sent to the Netherlands to break the Dutch resistance against Philip. Martinet argues that this revolt was legitimate because Philip abused his power in violating the privileges of the Dutch aristocracy (Martinet, 1790). His republican sympathies are clearly expressed in his evaluation of this episode. According to Martinet, all violent political oppression against free people carries the seed of its own destruction; sovereignty can only last when it is founded in justice (Martinet, 1790).

Martinet's republicanism, however, is of a moderate kind. Although he clearly prefers a republican form of government, he is careful enough to state that history has abundantly shown that the stadholder is "most useful" to the Dutch Republic (Martinet, 1790, p. 171); a strategic remark considering that his textbook was published 3 years after the suppression of the patriotic revolt against stadholder William V. The same carefulness characterizes his account of this episode, which he mentions only very briefly with the excuse that one would have to write a number of books to relate the many things that happened in this period (Martinet, 1790). Another example of Martinet's moderate stance is the way in which he represents patriotic virtues as pertaining to the character of the Dutch people—a representation that became popular in Dutch historiography from the 1780s onward (Blaas, 1999). Thus, with reference to history, Martinet states that the Dutch by nature are very patriotic, lovers of liberty, courageous, brave, industrious, unwavering, generous, modest, sociable and easy to live with, honest, and so on (Martinet, 1790).

Wester's (1801) *Schoolboek der geschiedenissen van ons Vaderland* is the only one in this group that was written after the Batavian Revolution.

It was the winning entry to a 1799 contest held by the *Maatschappij tot Nut van 't Algemeen*. Just as Wagenaar, Wester's intent was to make his account of Dutch history as impartial as possible, but his narrative is more distinctly republican in character. This shows in the way in which Wester presents the major conflicts in the history of the Netherlands as results of the violation of the political and religious liberties of the Dutch nobility and citizenry. Thus, the Dutch Revolt is depicted as a legitimate resistance movement against Philip II, who abused his power as a sovereign by denying the Dutch nobility their political rights and the Dutch citizens their freedom of religion. Elsewhere, the conflict between Oldenbarneveld and the stadholder Maurits is explained not as a primarily religious conflict, but one also revolving around the issue of the lawful power of the stadholder. This state-minded republican argument is also found in Wester's account of the 18th-century patriotic revolt and his presentation of the Batavian Revolution as the restoration of the rights of Dutch citizens (Wester, 1801).

Wester connects the emphasis on the political and religious rights of the Dutch citizens with an ideal of active citizenship, in which citizens take part in the revolt against the violation of their rights. This ideal of citizenship clearly shows in Wester's accounts of the many courageous acts of citizens during the Dutch Revolt (such as the conquest of Den Briel by the Sea-Beggars or the siege and liberation of the cities of Haarlem and Leiden) and in his account of the establishment of debating societies in the 1780s in an effort to restore the rights and Liberties of Dutch citizens (Wester, 1801). In comparison to Wagenaar and Martinet, Wester pays more attention to the courageous behavior of heroes like Kenau Simons Hasselaar, Maarten Harpertsz Tromp, and Michiel Adriaansz De Ruiter. That their courage and patriotism should be an example to Dutch children can be inferred from Wester's reference to the biographical sketches of Hasselaar and De Ruiter published by the *Maatschappij tot Nut van 't Algemeen (Stukken het Schoolwezen betreffende*, vol. 2, 1793–1796 and vol. 4, 1797–1801). Like Martinet, Wester's republicanism was of a non-militant, Christian nature. He repeatedly stressed the importance of unity within the Dutch nation and the hand of God in the events of history. Fully in keeping with the general Christian ideology of the *Maatschappij tot Nut van 't Algemeen*, he argued that an internalized faith should be the basis of a virtuous and useful life. This notion agrees very well with the post-revolutionary climate of de-politization in which the patriotic ideal of civic citizenship was replaced by a notion of civil or moral citizenship akin to the concept of citizenship developed in the 1760s.

In the fifth and sixth edition prescribed by the booklists of 1810 and 1815, Wester adapts his account of the Batavian Revolution and the reign of Napoleon Bonaparte in view of the changes of government. Thus, in the fifth edition of 1810, Wester exchanges his careful optimistic evaluation of the new republican government for a paragraph on the sufferings of the Dutch people due to the revolution (Cf. Wester, 1801, p. 117 and idem, 1810, p. 117). In the sixth edition of 1815, Wester renders a very critical account of the French Revolution that was the cause of the Batavian Revolution (Wester, 1815, pp. 120–121). His description of the Batavian Revolution also becomes less positive, and he is clearly critical of the French influence during the reign of Napoleon Bonaparte (Wester, 1815, pp. 123–124 and 131–137). Wester presents the return of the Prince of Orange and his inauguration as sovereign king as a God-given deliverance from the French occupation. However, Wester's state-minded republicanism does not disappear completely, but still shows in his account of historic events further removed in the past. Thus, in the case of Oldenbarneveld, Wester ads a paragraph in which he praises them as one of the greatest men of state of their time, to whom the Netherlands owe a great debt (Wester, 1810, p. 63 and Wester, 1815, p. 69).

LISTED NATIONAL HISTORY TEXTBOOKS IN BETWEEN REPUBLICANISM AND ORANGISM

The *Allereerste Beginselen der Geschiedenis onzes Vaderlands* written by the schoolmaster A. Van der Swan (1810) and the *Vaderlandsche Historie in Themata*, attributed to the publisher and man of letters Arend Fokke Simonsz (1755–1812),[12] take up a position in between republicanism and Orangism.

Van der Swan's booklet is a very short summary of the main events of the history of the Netherlands. As the author indicates in his Preface, this synopsis, presented in questions and answers, should be expanded on by the schoolmaster himself in lectures to be written down by his pupils. Although this formula is probably the reason for its success, it also makes it difficult to deduce the author's political affiliations, the more so because the author seems to take a neutral position, praising both parties for their merits. Despite its brevity, Van der Swan also draws attention to the cultural history of the Netherlands by referring for instance to Huygens' invention of the pendulum clock and listing the names of important writers, painters, and scientists like Hooft, Cats, Vondel, Rubens, Rembrandt, Van Leeuwenhoek, and Boerhaaven. For this Van der Swan was praised in a review in the *Bijdragen ter bevordering van het onderwijs en opvoeding* (Vol. 1, 1810, p. 231). The reviewer states that the country whose history no longer consists of revolutions, war, and destruction but of honorable, useful, and humane endeavors will be truly happy.

The political affiliations of *De Vaderlandsche Historie in Themata* are also difficult to detect. Like Wagenaar, Fokke Simonsz states in the Preface of the first edition that his is a truthful and impartial account. In the second edition of 1788, one year after the patriotic revolt, he again stresses the importance of impartiality, pointing out that it would be harmful for children to teach them the political quarrels of the past because children are by nature easily influenced. According to the author, the most important lesson children should learn is to love God above all and love thy neighbor as thy self because this is the only way to mitigate resentment and make way for the civil peace on which the welfare of society depends.[13] In his accounts of politically sensitive events, he pays attention to both sides of the story. Nevertheless, *De Vaderlandsche Historie in Themata* seems to be in favour of the Orangist point of view. This can be deduced from the fact that the sympathy the author expresses with the unfortunate deaths of Oldenbarneveld and the De Witt brothers restricts itself to a human level and does not extend to their political role ([Fokke Simonsz.], 1801, p. 58 and 71). The political affiliations of the author are more clearly expressed in his critical account of the patriotic revolt. The patriots are called 'degenerate minds' ('ontaarte gemoederen') and Van der Capellen tot den Pol's anonymously published famous patriotic pamphlet *Aan het Volk van Nederland* (To the people of the Netherlands) (1781) is referred to as 'a certain rebellious booklet'([Fokke Simonsz.], 1801, p. 116). Despite his critical evaluation of the patriotic revolt, the author does not render a one-sided account of the Batavian Revolution. He relates for instance that the returning patriotic refugees were given a cheerful reception, while the French troops, through their discipline and courage, earned the respect of all Dutchmen, whatever their own sympathies ([Fokke Simonsz.], 1801, pp. 166–167).

As with Wagenaar and Wester, the lifetime of Fokke Simonsz's history textbook extended beyond that of its author. Although Fokke Simonsz's political opinion was ambivalent, or at least unclear, the Preface of the first printing published after his death left little room for doubt with regard to its political affiliations. To start with, the anonymous author of this Preface mentions that the censorship during the Batavian Republic had made a new printing of the *Historie in Themata* impossible, which is remarkable because this censorship did not prevent its being put on the list of obligatory schoolbooks. Second, he openly denounces the Batavian Revolution and the corrupting influence of the French while stating that, with the return of the Prince of Orange as king, true liberty had been restored to the Dutch. According to this author, historically the Netherlands had always been most peaceful and prosperous while ruled by a stadholder from the House of Orange. For this reason, this edition revises and expands Fokke Simonsz's original text in several places to allow for a more extensive account of the merits of the House of Orange ("Voorberigt" to Fokke A. Simonsz, 1816).

LISTED NATIONAL HISTORY TEXTBOOKS IN PRAISE OF THE HOUSE OF ORANGE

The remaining group of history textbooks was published after the installation of William I as sovereign king. As can be expected from this fact, they all clearly express a pro-Orangist point of view. Apart from this shift in interpretation, they also formulate a different notion of patriotism and citizenship to support the new-born constitutional monarchy.

The anonymously published *Vaderlandsche Geschiedenis in twee-en vijftig lessen* (1814) is the only one of this group that provides a comprehensive account of Dutch history. Like its predecessors, the author of this textbook claims to be impartial. And indeed, notwithstanding his anti-revolutionary, pro-Orangist point of view, he gives a fairly balanced account of the deaths of Oldenbarneveld and the De Witt brothers. The execution of the "honourable" Oldenbarneveld is presented as the result of "fatal conflicts," and the murder of the De Witt brothers is depicted as cruel and horrible (*Vaderlandsche Geschiedenis*, 1814). It is also notable that for supplemental information, the author refers in his Preface to Wagenaar and Martinet, who were known for their republican affiliations (*Vaderlandsche Geschiedenis*, 1814, "Voorberigt"). Like Martinet, the author of the *Vaderlandsche Geschiedenissen in twee-en vijftig lessen* attributes an important role to Divine intervention in the history of the Netherlands. However, he advocates a different kind of patriotism than Martinet and his fellow republicans by mixing it with "the purest and most tender love for the illustrious House of Orange" (*Vaderlandsche Geschiedenis*, 1814, "Voorberigt").

Van Swinderen's (1814) tale of the merits of the House of Orange and Van Den Hoonaard's (1816) and the anonymous account of the liberation of the Netherlands from Napoleon are written as additions to the existing textbooks of Dutch national history. Van Swinderen explicitly presents his textbook as a supplement to Wester's textbook. This is remarkable because Van Swinderen writes from a different political perspective. As he states in his Preface, Van Swinderen considers himself most useful to his country by inspiring the Dutch youth with love for the king and his dynasty because this love is of the utmost importance in a hereditary monarchy: Love for the king and his dynasty furthers social harmony and makes the citizens content with the government (Van Swinderen, 1814, "Voorberigt"). This royalist stance with its stress on obedience to a monarch seems a far cry from Wester's republican notion of active citizenship. This also applies to Van Swinderen's partial account of the role of the House of Orange in the history of the Dutch Republic. He stresses the courage, expertise, and self-sacrifice of the stadholders while downplaying their mistakes and neglecting the role of the General States, thus presenting a version of history that identifies the House of Orange as the main party in the struggle for Dutch Liberty. Van Swinderen's biased account of history and honoration of the House of Orange provides what Ernest Renan in later years would describe as the indispensable foundation for nation building: "Un passé héroique, des grands hommes, de la gloire [...] voilà le capital social sur lequel on assied une idée nationale."[14]

Van den Hoonaard's textbook and the anonymous account of the liberation of the Netherlands from Napoleonic rule share Van Swinderen's Orangist version of history while elaborating on the inherent notion of citizenship, using an interesting blend of republican rhetoric and royalist ideals. Van den Hoonaard for instance appeals to the republican notion of active citizenship by repeatedly stressing the role citizens played in the liberation of the cities occupied by French troops while presenting King William I as the lawful heir to the Dutch throne and the commander of the liberation of the Netherlands (Van den Hoonaard, 1816). It is also noteworthy that Van den Hoonaard stresses the constitutional character of the new Dutch monarchy, although he also presents this as the natural and legitimate succession to the Dutch stadholderate (Van den Hoonaard, 1816). Van den Hoonaard appeals to the martial dimension of republican citizenship by recommending military service as a patriotic duty (Van den Hoonaard, 1816).[15] At the same time he applauds the outstanding courage, patriotism, and leadership of the Prince Royal in the war with the French (Van den Hoonaard, 1816).

The author of the *Staatkundige Verlossing van de Vereenigde Nederlanden* (1814) shares Van den Hoonaard's notion that it is the duty of every citizen to contribute to the defense of his country in times of need. But now that peace is restored, contentedness with one's lot is the main duty of every citizen because it will take years to overcome the disasters that befell the Netherlands during the reign of Napoleon. For this reason every citizen should support the present government and refrain from all partisanship. Instead, citizens should help each other to bear the burden in unison and be prepared to sacrifice their own interest to the greater good. Within their own walk of life, it is the duty of every citizen to contribute to the restoration of society by industriousness and good morals like thrift, honesty, philanthropy, and impartiality. Obedience to the Sovereign who has the general interest at heart is the last but not the least duty this author lists for citizenship education in the Dutch constitutional monarchy (*Staatkundige Verlossing*, 1814).

CONCLUSION

From the analysis presented we can draw the following conclusions. To begin, the successive changes of government that took place after 1795 did not result in a clean break with the past. The book lists of 1810 and 1815 contain national history textbooks written before 1795, which represent different political affiliations. Although in 1815 four new titles of a distinct Orangist point of view were added, textbooks by republican authors remained on the list and, with the exception of Martinet, were reprinted several times during the first decades of the 19th century. This can be explained by the quality of the historical narrative as well as the moderate variety of republicanism expressed by the authors. These qualities very well fitted the policy of unification and nation building started after the Batavian Revolution and continued after the inauguration of William I as constitutional King. From 1815 onward, the Orangist element intensified through new publications as well as through the adaptation of previously published textbooks. However, this did not mean that republican notions altogether ceased to be of any importance in history textbooks. Although the historical narrative was adapted to accommodate recent events, there were authors like Hendrik Wester, who voiced state-minded republican views in the interpretation of historic events further removed in history.

Second, the majority of the history textbooks expresses a theistic notion of history that is closely connected with the Ciceronian, humanistic view that history is the teacher of life. Although Wagenaar's *Vaderlandsche Historie* and its abridged textbook version served as important works of reference, his professional notion to value history for its own sake has not been of much influence on the perspective used in the majority of the listed textbooks. This is probably closely connected with the background of the authors involved. Wagenaar was the only professional historian among them. At least four were schoolmasters and/or school inspectors (Van der Swan, Wester, Van Swinderen, and Van den Hoonaard), one was a minister of the church (Martinet), and one was a man of letters (Simonsz), while the authorship of the remaining three is uncertain. Wagenaar's conviction that history should not be written to legitimize actual political constellations or prerogatives was also not followed by the authors of the textbooks added on the 1815 booklist. Their textbooks clearly served a propagandist purpose.

Third, the increasing influence of the Orangist element not only resulted in a reinterpretation of history, it also resulted in a changing notion of citizenship, stressing obedience to the King and contentedness with the government. However, citizens were not supposed to become completely passive subjects. They were required to be patriotic in a general kind of sense and to contribute to the restoration of society by industriousness and good morals like thrift, honesty, philanthropy, and impartiality—virtues that had also been propagated by republican authors during the 18th century. Thus, the new notion of citizenship not only fitted the new political constellation, it was also in harmony with the educational aims laid down in the law of 1806.

NOTES

1. On the process of post-revolutionary unification and reconciliation, see Van Sas (2005). One of the main representatives of this civic notion of citizenship is J. H. Swildens. See the entry "Burger" in his famous *Vaderlandsche A-B Boek voor de Nederlandsche jeugd* (1781). In his *Republykynsche Katechismus* (1795), Swildens provided a catalogue of republican virtues that, to a large extent, overlap with Christian virtues, thus showing the indissoluble connection between Dutch republicanism and a general notion of Christianity. On the patriotic notion of civic citizenship and civic society, see also Van Sas (2005).
2. [Jan Wagenaar], *Vaderlandsche Historie, vervattende de Geschiedenissen der nu Vereenigde Nederlanden, in zonderheid die van Holland, van de vroegste tijden af* (Amsterdam: Isaak Tirion, 1749–1759).

3. 'Onze Vaderlandsche Historie [...] kan dus als eene *Historie der getergde, verdrukte, herleevende en zegepraalende Vryheid des Vaderlands* aangemerkt worden.' Jan Wagenaar, *Vaderlandsche historie*, I, viii, cited from Blaas (1999, p. 371).
4. Buijnsters & Buijnsters-Smets (1997) mentions four different editions (1758, 1759, 1770, 1782), some of which were issued more than once.
5. Buijnsters & Buijnsters-Smets (1997) mentions two abridgements of Wagenaar's *Vaderlandsche Historie*. See for an example of a continuation of Wagenaar's *Vaderlandsche Historie Verkort*, Ibidem (p. 154).
6. The *Bijdragen* bear witness to all the innovations realized: the opening of new and the renovation of old school buildings, the growing amount of teachers (male and female) who passed their teaching exams, the foundation of societies for schoolteachers to further their knowledge, the results of school inspections, and the exams taken by pupils. See also Boekholt and de Booy (1987).
7. "Aan de Schoolhouders in de Vereenigde Nederlanden" in: *Bijdragen ter Bevordering*, vol. 4 (1813), pp. 121–132, especially pp. 129–130. For similar remarks: "Voorberigt" in Ibidem, vol. 5 (1814) pp. 1–8. Although history as a primary education teaching subject only became compulsory in 1857, the frequent reviews of history textbooks and articles on didactics of history teaching in the *Bijdragen* show an increasing awareness of the general importance of this subject from 1814 onward.
8. The number of editions listed is based on Huiskamp (2000) and the PiCarta database.
9. Not mentioned in Huiskamp or PiCarta.
10. Idem.
11. Martinet was an advocate of Leibniz's notion of theodicy (De Haas & Paasman, 1987). *Het vereenigd Nederland verkort* is an abridged version of J. F. Martinet, *Het Vaderland en het Vereenigd Nederland* (1788) in six volumes (Amsterdam: Johannes Allart) and is dedicated to "two young lady friends" because Martinet considered national history also very important for girls.
12. Arend Fokke Simonsz was a son of the engraver Simon Fokke, who made the engravings for Wagenaar's 21-volume *Vaderlandsche Historie* and his *Verkorte Vaderlandsche Historie*. Although the bibliographies by Buijnsters (1987) and Huiskamp (2000) attribute *De Vaderlandsche Historie in Themata* to Arend Fokke Simmons, biographical lemma's don't mention his authorship of this book. See for instance Marco de Niet, "De zonderlinge talenten van Arend Fokke Simonsz" and *H. Frijlink* (1884).
13. "Voorbericht voor den tweeden druk" [1788] cited in: *Vaderlandsche Historie in Themata* (4th revised and expanded printing, 1796).
14. Ernest Renan (1882), 'Qu'est-ce qu'une nation?' (cited in Van Sas, 2005).
15. This notion is shared by the anonymous author of the *Staatkundige Verlossing* (1814).

REFERENCES

Algemeene Boekenlijst ten dienste der Lagere Scholen in Holland.[...] (1810). Leyden: D. du Mortier en Zoon.
Algemeene Boekenlijst ten dienste der Lagere Scholen in de Noordelijke Provincien van het Koningrijk der Nederlanden.[...] (1815). 's Gravenhage: Algemeene Landsdrukkerij.

Bijdragen betrekkelijk den staat en de verbetering van het schoolwezen in het Bataafsche Gemeenebest, Vols. 1–5 (1801–1805). Leyden: D. Du Mortier en Zoon.
Bijdragen betrekkelijk den staat en de verbetering van het schoolwezen in het Koningrijk Holland, Vols. 6–9 (1806–1809). Leyden: D. Du Mortier en Zoon.
Bijdragen ter bevordering van het onderwijs en de opvoeding, voornamelijk met betrekking tot de lagere scholen in Holland, Vols. 1–5 (1810–1814). Leyden: D. Du Mortier en Zoon. From 1812–1814: Haarlem: Joh. Enschedé en Zoonen.
From 1815 continued as: *Nieuwe Bijdragen ter bevordering van het onderwijs en de opvoeding voornamelijk met betrekking tot de lagere scholen in de Vereenigde Nederlanden (1815–1829)*. Leyden: D. Du Mortier en Zoon.
Blaas, P. B. M. (1999). 'Het karakter van het vaderland. Vaderlandse geschiedenis tussen Wagenaar en Fruin, 1780–1840'. In N. C. F. van Sas (Ed.), *Vaderland. Een geschiedenis van de vijftiende eeuw tot 1940* (pp. 365–389). Amsterdam: Amsterdam University Press.
Boekholt, P. Th. F. M., & de Booy, E. P. (1987), *Geschiedenis van de school in Nederland vanaf de middeleeuwen tot aan de huidige tijd*. Assen/Maastricht: Van Gorcum.
Buijnsters, P. J., & Buijnsters-Smets, L. (1997), *Bibliografie van Nederlandse school- en kinderboeken 1700–1800*. Zwolle: Waanders.
De Haas, F., & Paasman, B. (1987). *J .F. Martinet en de Achttiende Eeuw. In ijver en onverzadelijken lust om te leeren*. Zutphen: De Walburg Pers.
De Niet, M. (s.a.). *De zonderlinge talenten van Arend Fokke Simonsz (1755–1812)*. Retrieved January 2, 2007, from http://www.home.zonnet.nl/neasden/fokkebio.htm.
Dodde, N. L. (1971). *Een onderwijsrapport. Een historisch-pedagogisch onderzoek naar de invloed van een onderwijsrapport voor onderwijsverbetering en –vernieuwing op de onderwijswetgeving na 1801.*'s-Hertogenbosch: L.C.G. Malmberg.
Fokke Simonsz, A. (1796). *Vaderlandsche Historie in Themata* (4th rev. expanded printing). Amsterdam: A. B. Saakes.
Fokke Simonsz, A. (1816). *Vaderlandsche Historie in Themata* (6th rev. expanded printing). Amsterdam: A. B. Saakes.
Frijlink, H. (1884). *Arend Fokke Simonsz. Zijn leven, denken en werken, uit echte bronnen verzameld en uitgegeven*. Amsterdam: Ten Brink en De Vries.
Huiskamp, F. (2000). *Naar de vatbaarheid der jeugd. Nederlandstalige kinder- en jeugdboeken 1800–1840. Een bibliografische catalogus*. Leiden: Primavera Pers.
Kossmann, E. H. (1984). *De Lage Landen 1780–1940. Anderhalve eeuw Nederland en België*. Amsterdam/Brussel: Elsevier.
Los, W. (2005). *Opvoeding tot mens en burger. Pedagogiek als Cultuurkritiek in Nederland in de 18^e eeuw*. Hilversum: Verloren.
Martinet, J. F. (1790). *Het Vereenigd Nederland, verkort, ten gebruike der scholen*. Amsterdam: Johannes Allart.
Staatkundige Verlossing van de Vereenigde Nederlanden, in den jare 1813. [...] (1814). 's Gravenhage: Johannes Allart.
Stukken het Schoolwezen betreffende, uitgegeeven door de Maatschappij tot Nut van 't Algemeen, Vol. 2 (1793–1796) and Vol. 4 (1797–1801). Leyden: D. Du Mortier en Zoon.
Swildens, J. H. (1781). *Vaderlandsch A-B Boek voor de Nederlandsche jeugd*. Amsterdam: W. Holtrop.
Swildens, J. H. (1795). *Republykynsche Katechismus, en Eerste Grondregelen van Republykynsche Zedekunde, voor de opvoeding der jeugd van beiderlei geslacht, in de huisgezinnen en in de schoolen*. Amsterdam: W. Holtrop.

Vaderlandsche Geschiedenis in twee-envijftig lessen voor de Nederlandsche Jeugd en Scholen. (1814). Zutphen: H.C.A. Thieme.
Van den Ende, A. (1810). Ophelderende aanmerkingen betrekkelijk de algemeene boekenlijst ten dienste der lagere scholen binnen Holland. [...] In *Algemeene Boekenlijst* [...] (pp. 1-32). Leyden: D. Du Mortier en Zoon.
Van den Hoonaard, W. (1816). *Geschiedenissen van ons Vaderland, voorgevallen van het begin der omwenteling in november 1813 tot de vestiging van den vrede te Parijs den 20 november 1815.* Amsterdam: Schalkamp en v.d. Grampel.
Van der Swan, A. (1810). *Allereerste Beginselen der Geschiedenis onzes Vaderlands voor de scholen.* Haarlem: François Bohn.
Van Hoorn, I. (1907). *De Nederlandsche schoolwetgeving voor het lager onderwijs 1796-1907.* Groningen: P. Noordhof.
Van Sas, N. C. F. (2005), *De metamorfose van Nederland. Van oude orde naar moderniteit 1750-1900.* Amsterdam: Amsterdam University Press.
Van Swinderen, Th. (1814). *Over de verdiensten der Vorsten van Oranje-Nassau jegens het Vaderland.* [...] Groningen: J. Oomkens.
Velema, W. R. E. (1993). *Enlightenment and conservatism in the Dutch Republic. The political thought of Elie Luzac (1721-1796).* Assen/Maastricht: Van Gorcum.
Wagenaar, J. (1759). *Vaderlandsche Historie Verkort; en bij vraagen en antwoorden voorgesteld.* Amsterdam: Isaak Tirion.
Wagenaar's verkorte Vaderlandsche Historie in vragen en antwoorden, voortgezet tot na den landvrede van Tilsit, [...] ten dienste der jeugd in de scholen en huisgezinnen (1808), Amsterdam: opvolgers van I. Tirion.
Wagenaar's verkorte Vaderlandsche Historie in vragen en antwoorden, voortgezet tot na de oprigting van het koningrijk der Nederlanden, ten dienste der jeugd in de scholen en huisgezinnen (1820). Dordrecht: Blussé en Van Braam.
Wagenaar's verkorte Vaderlandsche Historie in vragen en antwoorden, voortgezet tot na de oprigting van het koningrijk der Nederlanden, ten dienste der jeugd in de scholen en huisgezinnen (1833). Dordrecht: Blussé en Van Braam.
Wessels, L. H. M. (1997). *Bron, waarheid en de verandering der tijden. Jan Wagenaar (1709-1773), een historiografische studie.* Den Haag: Stichting Hollandse Historische Reeks.
Wester, H. (1801). *Schoolboek der geschiedenissen van ons Vaderland, uitgegeeven door de Bataafsche Maatschappij: Tot Nut van 't Algemeen.* Leyden: D. du Mortier en Zoon; Deventer: J.H. de Lange and Utrecht: G.T. Paddenburg en Zoon.
Wester, H. (1810). *Schoolboek der geschiedenissen van ons vaderland, uitgegeeven door de Bataafsche Maatschappij: Tot Nut van 't Algemeen.* Vijfde druk. Leyden: D. Du Mortier en Zoon; Deventer: J.H. de Lange en Groningen: J. Oomkens.
Wester, H. (1815). *Schoolboek der geschiedenissen van ons vaderland, uitgegeeven door de Bataafsche Maatschappij: Tot Nut van 't Algemeen.* Zesde druk. Leiden: D. Du Mortier en Zoon; Deventer: J.H. de Lange en Groningen: J. Oomkens.

14 The Masters of Republicanism?
Teachers and Schools in Rural and Urban Zurich in the 18th and the Long 19th Centuries

Andrea De Vincenti and Norbert Grube

The Republic of Zurich was an aristocratic republic in the concepts of Montesquieu.[1] The surrounding countryside of the city of Zurich was a subject territory.[2] According to Barbara Weinmann (2002), two different principles characterized the city-state as a whole—that is, the actual republic and the territory subject to it: for one, autonomy of the rural communes (*Gemeinde*) and, for another, republicanism of the city (Weinmann, 2002). The present contribution examines the republican and non-republican imaginations and practices with regard to schools in both the city republic and in the rural areas subject to the republic. By examining the issue in these two very different lights—the elementary school in the countryside in the 18th century and the secondary school (high school) in the city in the 19th century—we aim to plumb the depths of the conference topic as completely as possible and, through this, generate broader support for the findings.

SCHOOLS IN RURAL ZURICH AT THE END OF THE 18TH CENTURY

The first aim is to throw light on the schools outside of the actual republic in the rural areas subject to Zurich. The question is what characterized these schools: the official and thus city-republican laws, local practice in the communes, or a combination of these or other factors. To put the question another way: Did the rural schools in the territory subject to the Republic of Zurich reflect republican or non-republican imaginations and practices?

In a brief introductory first section, we will place the school within constitutional history. We then examine normative goals and purposes of the schools and educational practices. In a third section we analyze the election of the schoolmasters with regard to power relations between the city authorities and the rural communes. And in the fourth and final section, the findings on the countryside schools of Zurich will be closely examined in connection and in comparison with the concept of republicanism.

Positioning the Rural School Within Constitutional History

In the Ancient Regime the school fell under church matters, but political lines of demarcation still played a role, as the areas of responsibility of the state and church in post-Reformation Zurich could no longer be clearly disentangled. For the Christian state, there was no independent church but only the church as an area of state administration; in reverse, there was no secular state restricted to secular purposes but rather authorities by the grace of God, who had the God-given duty to tend as much to the salvation of their subjects as to their physical well-being and to perform the functions of guarding over and punishing violations of the first tablet *and* the second tablet of the Ten Commandments (Wernle, 1923). This means that *Bürgermeister* (mayor) and *Rat* (council) issued all of the church rules and commands; gave official validity to denominations, catechisms, and hymn books; and through state organs monitored the church's carrying out of its duties as well as church service attendance. In return, the authorities acted consciously as Christian authorities, and they were supervised and advised by the clergy. In addition to fulfilling their ecclesiastical duties, the clergy also took over administrative tasks, such as, for example, supervision of the schools, so that in the countryside, they were seen as representatives of the government (Ziegler, 1978). The school regulations were therefore issued by the city government, but they were claimed valid for the entire domain of the Zurich church—that is, also outside of the countryside areas under the political control of the city.[3]

The Rural Schools of Zurich: Normative Goals and Educational Practice

The normative goals for the rural schools are found laid down in the school regulations, for one, and in the instructions to the schoolmasters, for another. In all of these documents, the key word is moral discipline (*Anleitung für die Landschulmeister*, 1771; *Erneuerte Schul- und Lehrordnung*, 1778; *Satzungen den Land-Schulen*, 1744). Through this, the glory of God as well as the prosperity of the people was to be promoted. Here, the schoolmasters, who were usually citizens of the commune, played an important role.[4] They were to act as a role model of good manners, cleanliness, purity, and—altogether—fear of God. A schoolmaster was also to be particularly peaceable, get along well with everyone, and keep his distance from all quarrels in the community (*Anleitung für die Landschulmeister*, 1771). But in what manner was moral discipline taught in the school lessons? What did the schoolmasters teach? What were their teaching materials?

Reading, learning by heart, writing, and singing were the main school subjects. Sometimes arithmetic was also offered, but it was never a required subject for all pupils. In the main, teaching materials with religious contents were used. There was not one commune in the countryside of Zurich that did not use the Catechism.[5] Other widely used teaching materials were the psalm book, a little book of prayers by Weiss, and the *Namenbüchlein*, which was used to teach the children the alphabet. To teach the reading of handwriting—which was achieved by not all of the boys by far and by even fewer girls—schoolmasters often used bills of sale or borrower's notes. This indicates that for practical reasons, for the school subject of reading handwriting, viewed as not so important, simply anything at hand was used. Still, it can be clearly stated that the largest part of teaching and learning (especially reading and learning by heart, which were viewed as important subjects) took place using teaching materials with a religious and moral orientation. We also know that in the school communes in Zurich the lessons began and ended with a prayer. This provided the appropriate frame for the working with the religious contents. The goal was to educate the pupils as Christians and not republicans. Moral discipline and the fear of God as an educational goal remind more of Montesquieu's "laws of education" in a despotic state.[6] But further down in this chapter we will discuss discrepancies between such imaginations and local practices, and we will throw light on the fact that, even though imaginations or educational goals might seem despotic at first glance, everyday practices in school administration can show some republican features.

In order to prepare this discussion we have to ask some preliminary questions: How do the normative goals and purposes of moral discipline stand with regard to the religious contents through which the teaching actually takes place? Is the goal realized using this material? Whose interests does a school of this makeup represent? Were they the interests of the church, the clergy, the city authorities, the schoolmaster, the commune, or of others? These questions must be clarified in order to be able to decide who took part in shaping the rural schools, in what way—who established and supported its contents. Were these the authorities who laid down the school laws in which we could find the educational goals discussed before or were these the people who locally realized school in everyday practices?

It was Bernd Hamm (1992) with his concept of the *normative Zentrierung* (normative centering) who taught us how closely related religious beliefs and societal or political behavior are. The assumption is that the Reformation did not bring about secularization but that instead religion and society became more closely related to one another, more aligned— that is, normatively centered. Hamm describes this as having led to a more intensive fusion of *politia* and *ecclesia*. According to Hamm, there was no longer a separate, fenced-off sacredness contrasted to a profanity; the Reformation brought about a sacralization of the world. The "whole world . . . becomes the field of activity for sanctification" (Hamm, 2004, p. 281); all areas of life became part of service to God, all believers became priests (Hamm, 2004). This fusion of *politia* and *ecclesia* made also moral discipline a matter for all believers in a community, and there was also collective responsibility for the sins of the individual. Each member of the commune was encouraged to keep the Eucharist community pure (Leith, 1990). To the same degree, it was also the authorities who had to answer to God for the deeds of their subjects (Schmidt, 1995). As far as moral discipline is concerned, the interests of the authorities, the pastors especially, and the communes must overlap. Safeguarding moral discipline is not the carrying out of orders by the authorities but instead a matter of central concern of each commune. It is this that explains—in the face of the low penetration of the authorities in the subject territory—the moral and religious character of the school practice and the all-pervasive realization of a religiously based rural school. By using religiously saturated teaching materials, the aim was not to teach theological dogma but to raise the morality of the children and young people in order to make them good members also of the political commune. The educational goals discussed above as despotic therefore are at the same time to some extent republican goals as far as they stress the importance of virtue (morality) and community understood not only as an abstract Eucharist community but also as the community where daily life takes place. A look at teaching practice, therefore, confirms the defined normative purpose of school learning in moral discipline and supports the assumption that the schools were shaped by the overlapping interests of the authorities and the communes. This was possible because of the two very different aspects of education: on the one hand the rather despotic education to the fear of God and on the other hand the more practical aspect of a morally correct conduct of life. Thus, it is worth examining the relationship of the interests of the city and the communes.

How Schoolmasters Were Elected

School is not only teaching and learning. It is very informative in our connection to look at the school as a political-societal phenomenon. Who has the say in the school? In whose hands, in fact, are the rural schools? According to the school regulations, school is held by the schoolmaster and supervised by the local pastor. The pastor was meant to be the local school authority. He was a citizen of the city, was elected in the city to a sinecure, and was assigned to monitor the carrying out of the school regulations. The balance of power of communal and city interests can be demonstrated by the very choice of the schoolmasters. How is a schoolmaster put into office? Who elects or decides on him?

The election of the schoolmaster is stipulated in the school regulations. The right to elect the schoolmaster is held exclusively by the *Examinatorenkonvent* (Examiners Committee), made up of 12 clergymen and several members of the government. In the three *Pfarrkapiteln* (chapters)—Frauenfeld, Steckborn, and Oberthurgau—that is, in 3 of the 10 administrative districts of the church—the responsible pastors were asked about the course of events in electing a schoolmaster and about the legal basis of the election procedures. The aim of the questions was to find out who claimed the right to elect the schoolmaster in the various locations and on the basis of what kind of law. For the latter, the pastors were given three possible choices: on the basis of misuse, practice (established or customary right), or a written law.[7] A second question asked the pastors to state whether the schoolmaster was elected again each year.[8]

The result of the inquiry is astonishing, considering the normative documents: Almost all of the pastors report that the right to elect the schoolmaster was held by the commune. This means that electing the schoolmaster was not handled as foreseen by the school regulations. Many of the pastors' responses show that the pastors have no idea of the legal situation. Many of them, such as in the cases of Wigoldingen and Rapperswil, appear to have made a futile search for written laws and given up completely. There are repeated complaints from the pastors that they were powerless against the practice of the communes, that the communes did not allow anyone to tell them how it should be done, and that the communes asserted that they had always possessed the right to elect the schoolmaster.

In the commune of Wellhausen a dispute developed between the commune and the pastor in the matter of the election of the schoolmaster. It is apparent that the pastor, Johannes Hug, was gnashing his teeth as he answered the first question in the School Inquiry as to what the legal basis of the right to elect the schoolmaster was. Pastor Hug says that in his commune, the pastor had likely never been invited to the commune assembly at which the schoolmaster was elected. His city-person ignorance of the local law is readily apparent. He has to admit that he does not know what the legal basis is and also that he has not been able to find out. Because the members of the commune who would be honest enough could not give an answer because they did not know. And Pastor Hug says that he does not want to ask the people who do know because he knows that they would not tell him. He believes, however, that the right to elect claimed by the commune was purely customary. In an effort to attain his right himself, Pastor Hug concocts a plan. He plans to appear unannounced at the commune assembly and to put the commune in its place. When the time comes, however, he does not dare to take this step due to another dispute that has already broken out with his flock—and this even though the most senior official has assured him that he most certainly could demand his right to participate that was being ignored by the commune.[9] Pastor Hug waits patiently for a full year, and again he is not invited to the meeting. Now he decides to put his plan into action and to appear at the next meeting. But he is not able to reserve the right to have anything more than the role of an extra. New is that he now may attend the meeting but only for the purpose of asking the commune each year whether they have any complaints to bring forward about the school and to, finally, formally declare that the schoolmaster would retain office. Pastor Hug most certainly is aware of his continuing weak position. He says that since he began attending the meetings, no new schoolmaster had been elected but that the commune with certainty would claim the right to do so. He concludes his report with the ejaculation that the commune was pushing it too far with their freedoms and that one wished ardently that there were school regulations from the higher authorities—much to his regret, he did not know that school regulations already existed that nobody was able to push through.

In the village of Kirchberg, Pastor Fries also complains about the greater strength of the communes. He reports that like all persons in office, the schoolmaster always has to take care to protect himself from being removed from office and therefore gets into unbelievable dependency on the commune. When it then in fact comes to that, and a schoolmaster is to be removed from office, Pastor Fries decides to take sides with the commune so as not to get into difficulties himself (Tröhler & Schwab, 2006). This he had learned from his own experience when he had himself decided that the congregation would no longer, as was customary, sing all of the verses of Psalm 38. Some mostly older members of the community immediately began to grumble and threatened to "make a bigger noise about this." The intimidated pastor gave up in resignation and notes only that, "I now let it be sung. And say thank you, too. I must have deaf ears, etc., etc." (Tröhler & Schwab, 2006, p. 8).

It was not only in the election of the schoolmaster but also in other matters that the communes made their influence felt vehemently. The next example shows clearly that the pastors received little support from Zurich even when they requested it.

In Wila, in the *Pfarrkapitel* (chapter) of Elgg at the end of the 18th century, the mountain school is divided into two: For the first half of the winter, school is held in Ottenhub and in the second half in Mentzenhub. This is a thorn in the side of the pastor, who wants to have as many of the children schooled as possible throughout the entire winter and to this purpose wants to move the school to a new location that can be reached by both school locations. He therefore asks the responsible *Examinatorenkonvent* (Examiners Committee) for help. The committee—even though it basically agrees with the pastor—refuses the request for their support. The explanation for their refusal is that the proposed move of the school is not possible without a unanimous decision by the citizens of the commune, and this would never come about because they would use their old freedoms as an excuse and thus reject the proposal (Tröhler & Schwab, 2006).

These reports give us a new picture of the shaping of the local school. What we discover is not the strictly hierarchically organized (church)-state but instead an enormous variety of very self-confident communes as a very influential factor. They defend their rights with great emphasis, including the right to elect the schoolmaster, who in their eyes holds an office in the commune just as the other office holders do. The communes insist on exercising their rights and reject any interference from outside.

The Rural Schools of Zurich and Republicanism

In view of the many, very disparate definitions of republicanism, it is difficult to specify what republicanism actually is. We therefore attempted to distill something like the smallest common denominator.[10] An important point is certainly the rejection of any domination by others, whether from the outside or from within. Within a group of citizens, this means making it impossible by means of the written or unwritten constitution of the commune for one citizen to dominate another. The totality of the citizenry makes its laws at least in part by itself or through elected representatives. All public officials are elected, with elections held periodically. The misuse of power that a citizen accumulates with his election to office is prevented by virtue. Here the goal is to keep the commune in working order and to guarantee the general orientation to peace and the common good.

It is at first surprising that all of these features of republicanism are found also in the school reality described above in the countryside not belonging to the republic. The practice of electing the schoolmaster shows the self-organization of the communes; the schoolmaster is understood to be a public official of the commune and is therefore elected by the communal assembly. In addition, the communes act very self-confidently and reject any domination by Zurich by referring to the tradition of the customary right. If it is a communal item of business—and the selection of the public officials is definitely that—then the communes defend their autonomy.[11] Let's remember the core business of the rural schools in the 18th century. Education in moral discipline, education to be good Christians is meant to secure the children's salvation but also—within the canon of values of the communes themselves—to educate them to become useful members of the political commune. The aim is definitely to transmit certain virtues, which will keep the commune well able to function. And the schoolmaster, as was shown above, was to act as a role model not only for morality, hygiene, and equality but also to represent the principle of peaceful coexistence or peace in the commune. All of this serves the ultimate goal of the well-being of the commune, the common good.

How can this strong affinity to republicanism be explained? The rural areas examined here are not a part of the republic, and according to their political, judicial, and ecclesiastical structure, their relationship with Zurich is one of complicated dependence. For this reason, the apparent features of republicanism described above—defense against domination, (in part) sovereign citizenry, political and judicial structures, shared values at least in part, and peace and the common good as *telos*—cannot be interpreted as republicanism. To explain the appearance of these features also outside of the republic, republicanism must rather be interpreted as a subset of a similar but broader phenomenon. The common ground of the non-republican countryside with the Republic of Zurich lies in the common communal culture or in a communal practice that is shared by all constituted communes, whether a town or village.¹² In this way, as proposed by Blickle (1986)—republicanism can be seen as communalism raised to a form of state government. Both are based on the same underlying principle, which can be subsumed relatively well under the features listed above: defense against domination, (in part) sovereign citizenry, political and judicial structures, shared values at least in part, and peace and the common good as *telos*. In this way, the occurrence of the apparently republican features in the rural communes of Zurich can be explained without losing track of the differences between the countryside and the Republic of Zurich.

THE SECONDARY SCHOOL OF ZURICH 1832–1930

When we turn from the rural schools of Zurich of the 18th century to the urban secondary school of the 19th and 20th centuries, we expect to find at least a more intensive use of republican language. This language will be analyzed in a first section referring to the founding context of the cantonal secondary schools in Aarau and Zurich in 1802 and 1833. At the same time, we will touch on the question of school self-administration. The second section will throw light on how the school subject of German, with its raised status in the *Kantonsschule*, the High School of the Canton of Zurich, from 1833 to 1930, contributed to the transmission and realization of republican virtues. Here we will focus on teacher hiring practice and the production, contents, and use of textbooks based on quantitative evaluation of the school programs that were published annually. In a final and third section, we will take up the use of elements of republican language and their refashioning through nationalistic views in the first third of the 20th century.

Legitimation of the Founding of Cantonal Secondary Schools 1802/1833: Borrowing from the Republican Language

The founding of the *Kantonsschule* in Zurich and in Aarau at the beginning of the 19th century was legitimized rhetorically by its proponents and initiators using republican language elements (Tröhler, 2006). In a work on reorganizing schools in Zurich titled *Paedagogische Ansichten über äußere Trennung und geistige Einheit* (Pedagogical Views on External Separation and Spiritual/Mental Unity), school reformers Johann Caspar von Orelli (1787–1848) and Leonhard Usteri (1769–1853) stated in 1831 that realistic-technical, humanistic-higher, and elementary educational institutions should be separated. However, they remarked, caste divisions in a republic are out of the question, so that all three of the institutions were bound within a higher unity through three ideas: religion, morality, and fatherland (Orelli & Usteri, 1831). These three guiding principles were to serve in the High School of the Canton—with its integrative organization of natural sciences-mathematics, modern languages *Industrieschule*, and humanistic-classical languages *Gymnasium*—as socialization maxims and thus provide for social coherence in the virtuous Christian community. The school was to enable the individual, in terms of character and performance, to serve the fatherland, as Orelli already demanded in 1808: "Whoever has a fatherland is obliged to act for same, even if this action, if he has to limit it, consists only in writing" (Orelli, 1808/1891). A similar purpose was defined for the *Kantonsschule* by the education council of the Canton of Zurich in 1834. It was to educate young men in order to both promote patriotic interests in the state, church, and health and safeguard and increase industrial prosperity for the common good (Hunziker, 1933). Here, commerce and republicanism no longer appear as in the 18th century as opposites (Pocock, 1993) but instead together determine the welfare of the fatherland—especially with a view to competition with other countries. At this time also, the director of the Aarau Seminary and member of the canton government, Augustin Keller, argued for an all-round integral education of the true republican citizen (Brändli, Landolt, & Wertli, 1998).

But the chosen conception of a socially integrative higher school system without "caste division" was not only limited to republican Zurich. It also marked the organization and policy of the urban school in German lands around 1800 before the separation of *Realschule* (junior high school) and classical languages *Gymnasium* (high school) gained acceptance as a selection mechanism for university studies (Kuhlemann, 1992; Müller, 1977). In Zurich, too, Orelli's notion of a school institution of integral design, with cross-admission among the school types being highly open, was soon overhauled. The *Kantonsschule* became more and more differentiated up to the beginning of the 20th century. Here, as also in the secondary school in the Catholic Canton of Lucerne, the *Industrieschule* branched into the *Handelsschule* and the *Oberrealschule*, which became practically independent educational institutions. Even the Literary Gymnasium and the Real Gymnasium remained only loosely connected, as "higher preparatory schools" in the law on education of Zurich of 1872 (*Gesetz betreffend das gesammte Unterrichtswesen des Kantons Zürich*, 1872, Art. 67). This differentiation was due, among other things, to innovations in science and technology and to the associated expectations of the school in qualifying pupils. It is true that the law on education of 1859 planned for the *Industrieschule* "the realization of a more general and coherent education (...) as a counterbalance against just specialized studies" (*Gesetz über das gesammte Unterrichtswesen des Kantons Zürich*, 1859: p. 57, Art. 181). But at the same time, the school duration was shortened by 6 months in order to allow immediate entrance (without a break) to studies at the Federal Institute of Technology (ETH), which had been founded in 1854.[13] In the mid-century, the education councilor and entrepreneur Alfred Escher (1819–1882), among others, supported the priority of "efficiency," which Kliebard (2004)[14] identifies as the dominant ideal in the making of the curriculum since the end of the 19th century. Did not "efficiency" successively replace not only the classical languages schooling (Greek) but also republican thought patterns and expectations? This reorganization of secondary schools in Zurich can be seen as an indication of the competition of the classical and modern type of republicanism as they are outlined in the Introduction of this book.

In 1832 the education authorities in Zurich still defined the Canton School in the sense that Orelli did, as an important agent of political socialization for making the young generation good representatives of the liberal community (Hunziker, 1933). The function of the school was described similarly in a brochure on the opening of the Canton School of Aarau in 1801; its aim was "to teach the pupils, who are to become someday useful members of a free state, the rights and duties of the person and the citizen (...), and, through convictions and feelings, to build their republican character for both" (Staehelin, 2002, p. 19). The Canton School of Aarau was at first the result of the initiative of business people and educated citizens. They formed the basis of the 107 subscribers who financed the school with their donations. The institution was at first to a considerable extent self-administered. The meeting of donors, the funders, elected the directorate of the school, the highest institution of the Canton School. Respected entrepreneurs and physicians taught free of charge the subjects of botany, physics, chemistry, and anthropology. Citizens' part ownership and participation in the school, however, soon met with the first restrictions, when Head of School Ernst August Evers (1779–1823) from the Hannover Electorate was given broader authority with regard to the hiring of teachers and the organization of the school. The efforts to centralize that are apparent here were taken up by, of all things, the supposed liberal Aargau Party, starting in 1807. Administration, finance, and control of the Canton School were finally put under the government in 1813. In Zurich, too, the extent of government control of the high school was disputed. Orelli had defined the school system as a government matter. At first, the newly formed *Schulsynode*, which was an assembly of all teachers in Zurich that was promoted by Konrad Melchior Hirzel (1793–1843), claimed pre-eminence over the cantonal education authorities in 1834. They were also permitted to nominate two of their members for election to the education authorities. However, to do so, they needed the consent of the Large Council, which also authorized the annual report of the education authorities, a copy of which was merely sent to the *Schulsynode* for their information (*Gesetz über das gesammte Unterrichtswesen*, 1859; Hunziker, 1948). Although this did not make the teachers' ambitions for participation completely impossible, it certainly limited them—a burden for the "masters of republicanism."

There were also setbacks to the realization of republican-based educational goals at the Canton School of Zurich. The school subjects of German and History were particularly suitable for transmitting important virtues for future political participation: love of the fatherland, public spirit, freedom by reference to historical and literary heroes, both of these converging in the figures of Wilhelm Tell and Winkelried (De Captani, 2000; Tröhler,

2000). The teaching of history was the more successful in vitalization and conceptualization. History lessons were increased to 5 hours per week at the *Gymnasium* in Zurich, whereas in the *Industrieschule*, French, mathematics, and the natural sciences dominated. But German literature, as opposed to classical languages, had a hard time gaining acceptance. Orelli, who was a classical scholar, deemed Greek and Latin literature morally valuable for the development of political convictions in young Swiss people, whereas in German lessons, the students were to be given merely "a passing acquaintance with recognized classical works of the German nation," such as with Herder's *Cid* and Schiller's *Tell* (Orelli, 1831, p. 44).

German and History in the Service of Republican Socialization and Knowledge Transmission? On Teachers' Origins and the Genesis of Textbooks

For the teaching of German, which had improved in status somewhat but was still considered to be an inferior school subject, there was a lack of qualified Swiss-German teachers and a lack of teaching materials. Due to the lack of suitable candidates, Ludwig Ettmüller (1802–1877), a Germanist from Jena, was offered a position at the Zurich Canton School (Grube, 2007). He was followed by others from Germany. By the end of the 1860s, two fifths of the German teachers at the *Industrieschule* and three fourths of the German teachers at the *Gymnasium* were from Germany. At the new Canton School of Aarau, as many as four of the initial seven full-time teachers were German emigrants. This tendency became firmly established up to the mid-19th century, when many political refugees from monarchist Germany, who had to flee because of their involvement in the national movement, found shelter at the Canton School of Aarau. These teachers left their mark on teaching for some decades, also as editors of German readers. The complaint of many Swiss teachers, that poetry, except for Schiller's *Tell*, granted the poetic heroic figures of old Switzerland practically no good word, prevailed on the German emigrant August Adolf Ludwig Follen (1794–1855) to publish in 1828 *Bildersaal deutscher Dichtung*, containing his own epics from the history of Switzerland that he wrote himself (Follen, 1828).[15] The production of readers for the elementary school was also oriented to Prussian models of training for faithful obedience to the authorities; for example, the *Schweizerische Kinderfreund* published in 1808–1809 was based on Friedrich Wilmsen's *Kinderfreund* of 1801 (Fuchs, 2001).

On the background of the unsatisfactory situation in Germany, the German teachers from Germany often idealized nation romanticizing supposed origins of ancient Teutonic freedom and of German splendor of the Middle Ages in their teaching and in their textbooks. Also in Switzerland, historical references to medieval heroes and myths, such as the Middle High German *Nibelungenlied*, served the in part ritualized identification with the Swiss

Confederation. Accordingly, countless festival productions in the 19th century recalled the medieval origins of Swiss freedom and Confederation unity (Ferrari, 2000; Hettling et al, 1998; Orelli, 1817). But when German teachers from Germany like Follen or Ettmüller took on chivalrous or even monarchistic habits and clothing, this practice ran counter to the republican intentions of the high school reformers. The circle of friends around the German teacher Follen, who was called *Burschenkaiser* (emperor of the boys), included German exiled writers such as Georg Herwegh (1817–1875) and Hoffmann von Fallersleben (1798–1874) and at times also the republican-minded *Industrieschule* teacher and future diplomat under Bismarck, Julius Fröbel (1805–1893). This circle was not much about brotherly equality; it was more about male society loyalty under the patriarchal dominance of the individual. There were also differences between the Swiss-German teachers and their German colleagues with regard to their understanding of freedom, fatherland, and readiness to defend, which in Aarau caused numerous conflicts. The pupil associations founded in the 1820s in Aarau with the support of German teachers were based on the German model of nationalistic students' dueling associations and gymnastics clubs. As happened also in monarchist Germany, the Swiss cantonal authorities quickly banned or regulated them due to escalating alcohol abuse and rampaging among the youth. But these associations certainly in part conformed to republican ideas, and even in the Helvetic Society at the end of the 18th century there developed a cult of fraternal friendship in drinking bouts (Hunziker, 1933; Staehelin, 2002; Tröhler, 2006). In the 20th century, the school regulations of Zurich granted pupils freedoms to belong to associations, but the school of republican Switzerland possessed no "students'" republic with student self-government, in which they could have practiced political ownership and participation. Tentative attempts at the Canton School around 1910 to establish "British-American student organizations" in the form of class groups, student council, or student government failed (Hunziker, 1933; *Jahresbericht der Zürcher Industrieschule*, 1913/1914).

In addition to the differences between German and Swiss-German teachers referred to above, there was also, however, considerable intersection—but mainly at the level of negation. Teachers from Germany, especially the refugees, were to a great part anti-Prussian, anti-French, anti-materialist, and anti-modernist and in this way served the resistance—inherent to classical republicanism—against other countries and against economic growth under the sign of increasing personal profit (Markwart, 1908). Going along with this, as mentioned above, both German and Swiss-German teachers referred back to origins of medieval freedom and unity. In the teaching of German at the Canton School of Zurich up to 1860/1870, this led to extensive reading of Old High German and Middle High German literature. However, quantitative evaluations of the annually published school programs show that it was not republican-Swiss confederate but instead German heroes who served as backdrop for the transmission of chivalrous bravery, piety, and most of all courage as the basis of all male virtues. In addition to that, the reading of the classics predominated—Goethe, Schiller, Lessing, and, into the first decade of the 20th century, the German patriotic odes of Klopstock and works by Herder. At least Friedrich Gottlieb Klopstock (1724–1803), with his republican-liberal praise of the American War of Independence and the French Revolution in his ode "Sie und nicht wir," could serve as a source of identification for the high school pupils in Zurich, and as late as 1902 he was named in a lecture before the *Schulsynode* by the Swiss professor of German studies, Julius Stiefel (1847–1908) (ETH Zurich), as a warrantor of supposedly exemplary unchauvanistic Germany (Stiefel, 1902; Winter, 1989).

This and German-speaking Switzerland's orientation to Germany around 1900 explain why German could succeed at the Canton School of Zurich for many decades up to the beginning of the 20th century. At the same time, it becomes plausible that in German readers the educated German-speaking Swiss youth were confronted with manifold German works—despite the revaluation of Swiss German literature. Besides Goethe, Schiller, or Lessing, the readers contained *Lied der Deutschen* by Hofmann von Fallersleben of the national movement, Johann Gottlieb Fichte's speeches to the German nation, and works by the Lutheran theologian Friedrich Schleiermacher.

The Teaching of German Between Republican and National Expectations

Just prior to 1900, with the final establishment of civics as a school subject and in the context of Swiss national festivals, there was an increasing politicization of higher schooling altogether and also of German as a school subject. Knowledge of Swiss-German literature was to contribute to Swiss identity and integration within the cantonal diversity, or even inner conflict, demanded Jakob Bächtold (1848–1897) in his dissertation as early as 1870 (Bächtold, 1899). Bächtold, who taught at the Canton School of Zurich and was also culture editor at the *Neue Zürcher Zeitung*, was named professor of German studies at the University of Zurich in 1888, and to this purpose he published a much used reader for higher German teaching and learning. In 1888 the members of the Zurich *Schulsynode* were greeted with the express request to declare belief in the Confederation: *Wer den Schweizersohn will führen/In der Freiheit Land hinein,/Soll ein selbstbewusster Kämpfer,/Muss ein freier Bürger sein* (He who will guide the sons of Switzerland into the land of freedom must be a self-confident warrior, a free citizen) (*Bericht über die Verhandlungen der Zürcherischen Schulsynode*, 1888, p. 136). With the aim to revitalize the republican-national pathos taken up by the members of the *Schulsynode*, the education authorities and the canton government, starting in the 1870s and 1880s, promoted the hiring of Swiss-German German teachers and professors of German studies, who were to be given preference over the German colleagues (Hunziker, 1948). Complementary to this, the German readers published by German emigrants were revised so that German classes at the Canton School of Zurich should deal with Swiss history and Swiss dialect poetry using patriotic songs, among others by Abraham Emanuel Fröhlich (1796–1865), and deal with the Alps as a national integrative symbol of Switzerland (Elias Canetti), republican convictions like "virtue and bravery (...), self-denial, and love of the fatherland" (Schnorf, 1900, p. V; see also Canetti, 2003; De Capitani, 2000). The reading of Gottfried Keller's novel *Martin Salander* or his short novels *Frau Regel Amrein* and *Das Fähnlein der sieben Aufrechten*, a short novel about the Swiss national shooting festival (*Schützenfest*), were to serve this purpose, despite Keller's ambivalent view of the fatherland (Böhler, 1996; Clauss, 1955). Literary works by Keller or Jeremias Gotthelf ascended in the Swiss-German school reading canon up to 1930 and replaced the Old High German literature and the works of Klopstock and Herder.

However, the teaching of German at the Canton School of Zurich was seen in the first third of the 20th century not only as an instrument of republican education but also decisively as resistance and protection against rapid technological, economic, and social changes (Steiger, 1930).[16] In this rather cultural pessimistic and nationalistic perspective, Otto von Greyerz (1863–1940), professor of German studies in Bern, Emil Ermatinger (1873–1853), von Greyerz's antipode in Zurich, and other representatives of traditional native country culture rejected contemporary literature as culturally uprooted, lacking values, and hedonistic (Jost, 1983). They wanted German as a school subject to serve as a "route to national education." In a book of that title credo on methods of teaching German, Greyerz—2 years after the Treaty of Versailles—demanded using national community diction (*Volksgemeinschaftsduktus*) of all teachers of German that "felt a deep inner connection with the German cultural community" to "educate students to German feeling and thinking" (Bächtold, 1921, p. V; Greyerz, 1921).

Nationalistic reshaping of the republican language can be found as early as around 1900. The Zurich professor of German studies, Julius Stiefel, in his lecture before the Zurich Schulsynode in 1902 that was mentioned above and was titled "Poesie und Schule," criticized Gottfried Keller's poem "An mein Vaterland," which as one of the first Keller works was used in German readers early on. Stiefel called it as universal as it was and thus not a binding love poem to the native country. It would arouse the same national feelings in a Serbian pupil at the *Industrieschule* as in a Swiss young person. Keller's poems on the native country depicted "in simple strains of songs" the "honest reality of republicanism" (Stiefel, 1902, p. 85f.). Against that, stated Stiefel, it was only in his "Prolog zur Schillerfeier in Bern 1859" that Keller captured the all-encompassing national feeling of the whole nation and expressed, like Conrad Ferdinand Meyer in the poem

"Schutzgeister" or Jakob Frey in "Lied vom Vaterland," the national will of "all classes of the people" in a way that was more than merely republican (Stiefel, 1902, p. 86).

Around 1900 republican-based assignments of function to the teaching of German in Zurich appeared increasingly in the form of rhetoric of crisis and lament, with anti-modern, anti-capitalist elements of resistance (Weinmann, 2002). In their perception of the social, economic, and cultural changes as dangerous decadent tendencies, Swiss-German Germanists reshaped the republic orientation to the common good with accents of nationalism and national community (*Volksgemeinschaft*). The discourse of virtue stood more and more in the service of a "national integration and mobilization ideology" (Münkler, 1991, p. 403). What had also contributed to this was the reception of the neighboring German Empire, which was viewed by many as a role model. Had national competition eroded republican traditions here?

CONCLUSION

Examining the republican and non-republican imaginations and practices in two different lights revealed various discrepancies.

For one, a discrepancy was revealed between the republican rhetoric and the attempts undertaken mainly by city and cantonal government organs to stem the right to self-administration or participation. These rights were established in the countryside in accordance with common law (customary practice) particularly for the election of the schoolmasters, which collided with the city's claim to rule. In the city, in contrast, the cantonal government restricted the executive authority claimed by the *Schulsynode*, whereas student associations were regulated and self-governing committees were supported only half-heartedly. The republican government of Zurich thus did not show the expected affirmative stance toward self-administration and participation, and thus the attempts on the part of the government to restrict these are surprising, although one must keep in mind the difference between republicanism and democracy (see Introduction).

For another, there is a great discrepancy between citizens and non-citizens. The republicanism is exclusive; it includes in the republic only men with citizenship in Zurich, whereas both urban residents without citizenship and also the entire countryside as the subject territory remains excluded.

Discrepancies are also found between republican-based notions of integral school organization and function and the actual differentiation into independent school types, from the different branches of the university preparatory high school (*Gymnasium*) to vocational school (*Industrieschule*) and junior high school (*Realschule*). Also, practice in the teaching of German as a school subject for many decades was only conditionally in accord with republican suppositions. For teachers from Germany, who had a monarchist bent and at the same time were also national and liberal-minded, taught the adolescents growing up in Zurich over many decades and dominated the production of textbooks. In Zurich republican-grounded textbooks were not produced by the German-speaking Swiss until the end of the 19th century.

Besides, self-administrative practices in the school, such as the election of the schoolmaster by the commune, are not necessarily bound to a republican system.

The school comes to realization within this field of tension of norms and practices. To ensure that we do not take up just some individual aspects from this field of tension, it is necessary to examine language use—in our case, for example, the republican language—in the social cultural and political contexts in which it is used. Is the republican language reshaped or deformed, particularly as it is frequently revitalized at times when there is a perception of crisis? Does the language become watered down in school and education competition with non-republic neighboring states like Germany? Does the language stand in contrast to a very differently accented practice? Only if questions like these can be explained can we avoid confusing constructions from differing functional rhetoric with the school reality. And besides, it seems sensible to only very cautiously invoke individual, apparently republican elements as a guarantor of the existence of republicanism because such elements also can be found outside of republics.

Finally, the question as to whether teachers and pupils prove to masters of republicanism can hardly be answered. If they did, from our point of view a republican constitution would be an important framework condition in order to be able to speak of republicanism. However, this was not the case in the countryside around Zurich. But even in the city Republic of Zurich, republican language elements compete with demands for the school to impart qualifications that are usable toward economic success or with monarchistic, nationalistic notions from the neighboring countries. If language is an expression of mentality and culture, then republican language mixes with increased mobility and increasing exchange among countryside, city, and individual nations that assign different cultural meanings. Assumedly republican attitudes were in danger of becoming watered down so that the revitalization attempts for the teaching of German can also be seen as worry on the part of school policymakers or teachers that they would erode—or as a symptom of a resistant stance against internationality. Here, republican assignments to teachers and the school are in danger of becoming a construction that teachers and schools cannot fulfill.

NOTES

1. See the Introduction of this book.
2. For a good overview of the constitution and the administration of the city-state, see Weibel, T. (1996). An older but still valuable account is provided in

Guyer, P. (1943). On the relation of the city to the countryside, see in particular p. 78f.

3. Because the responsibility for the entire rural school system (school regulations, hiring and dismissals of the schoolmaster) lay with the *Examinatorenkonvent* (Examiners Committee), the highest church administrative council, it also extended to the schools in Thurgau and Rheintal (see here Wernle, 1923). The validity of the Zurich school regulations for the areas of the *Gemeine Herrschaft* (areas under the control of more than one canton) is confirmed also by Angelus Hux (2002) in his study on the secondary school in Frauenfeld. For this source, we thank Carla Aubry.

4. Parents, of course, were also decisively involved in their children's moral education. However, the opinion that parents themselves are not capable of leading a moral life was widespread among village pastors, so that in their eyes, the school had an important compensatory role to fulfill.

5. This information is taken from responses to the School Inquiry (*Schul-Umfrage*) conducted in all of the school communes in the Canton of Zurich in 1771–1772. This material is located in the Staatsarchiv Zürich under the classification numbers (=StAZH) EI 21. 2–21. 9, StAZH EII 163, StAZH EII 164, StAZH A 313. The data have also been published in the form of a CD-ROM (Tröhler & Schwab, 2006).

6. See Introduction of this book.

7. "1. ma #quæstio: 1. quæst[io] Bey wem stehet die wahl der schulmeister an jedem ort? Worauf gründet sich das recht? Auf missbrauch? Auf üebung oder auf ein würkliches gesez?" See here: Felben, Anhang zu den Schul-Fragen, p. 15 on the CD-ROM (Tröhler & Schwab, 2006).

8. "II. da quæstio. 2. #quæst[io] #Was #ist #bey #der #jährlichen #bestellung #der #schul #für #eine #üebung? #Wird #um #den #schulmeister #gemehret?" See here Felben, Anhang zu den Schul-Fragen, p. 16 on the CD-ROM (Tröhler & Schwab, 2006).

9. This shows clearly once again how overlooked the norms set down in the school regulations remained. Even the representatives of the authorities, the pastor and the most senior official, were apparently satisfied with having the pastor assist with the selection and did not even attempt to push through the *Examinatorenkonvent*'s right to select the schoolmaster.

10. On what republicanism actually is, there is no uniform opinion. Various discussion circles follow differing interpretations. A very comprehensive overview that supports this impression is provided by Wolfgang Mager (1984). In *The Stanford Encyclopedia of Philosophy*, Philip Pettit (2003) integrates the diffuseness directly into his definition of republicanism: "If you understand the experience of exposure and vulnerability to another—the experience of domination—and if you can see what is awful about it, then you are well on your way to understanding republicanism" (p. 1). Republicanism is about avoiding domination: "Whether in classical Rome, renaissance Italy, seventeenth century England or eighteenth century America, all republicans saw domination as the great evil to be avoided in organising a community and a polity" (Petit, 2003, p. 2). It is about resistance to foreign domination as well as resistance to domination within the citizenry, which is to be avoided by means of a corresponding constitution. That is why the central concept is "the common good." Frank Lovett (2006) substantively revised Petit's (2003) entry in *The Stanford Encyclopedia of Philosophy*, and his entry on republicanism emphasizes the distinction between civic humanists and civic republicans, linking this to their differing concepts of freedom. Although civic republicans start out from a negative concept of freedom and active political participation,

civic virtues, and so on are for them also important values, they are viewed as instruments for maintaining freedom and not as intrinsically valuable components of human flourishing (Lovett, 2006). On this background, a selection of some basic aspects of republicanism seems fairly justified. Especially for the distinction between republicanism and liberalism, see also Introduction of this book.

11. In order to describe the self-organizing communities as a type, the concept of communalism has been proposed. It essentially assumes that the sovereignty resides in the communal assembly, which exercises that sovereignty at least for certain areas of responsibility and for the right to elections by issuing statutes and punishing their violations. The concept does not attribute the communes with democratic character, nor does it postulate the complete absence of domination or the complete rejection of law-giving by higher government authorities. Peter Blickle (2000), who coined the term communalism, puts it this way: "*Der Kommunalismus erträgt also Herrschaft, aber er leitet sich nicht von Herrschaft ab*" (p. 69).
12. Citing this similarity, the research concept of communalism does not preclude differences between city and village but instead points out that these are more gradual than principle differences. Especially when examining their constitution, city and village show strong similarities (Blickle, 2000). The gradual difference between communalism and republicanism then lies in the acceptance of a higher authority and, with this, sovereignty only in certain areas in communalism as opposed to the perception of full sovereignty in republicanism.
13. Riedweg (2000) sees in Orelli's integrated school concept continuity up to the debate today on combined schools. On the differentiation of the high school system in Zurich, compare Kronbichler (1983).
14. Foucault (2004) sees the replacement of the principle of legitimation by the categories efficiency, success, and effectiveness as hallmarks of the liberal political economy.
15. Some examples of further readers and literary histories written by German exiles are Mager, K. (1843) and Lüning and Sartori (1861).
16. For an interpretation of the dialect movement as protection of cultural heritage, see Helbling (1994).

REFERENCES

Anleitung für die Landschulmeister. (1771). Zürich: Orell, Gessner, Fuesslin und Compagnie.
Bächtold, J. (1899). Vorrede zur Inauguraldissertation: Der Lanzelet des Ulrich von Zatzikhoven. In T. Vetter (Ed.), *Jakob Bächtold. Kleine Schriften. Mit einem Lebensbilde von W. von Arx* (pp. 57–60). Frauenfeld: Huber.
Bächtold, J. (1921). *Deutsches Lesebuch für höhere Lehranstalten der Schweiz* (O. von Greyerz, Ed.) (10th ed.). Frauenfeld: Huber.
Bericht über die Verhandlungen der Zürcherischen Schulsynode von (1888). Zürich: [s.n.].
Blickle, P. (1986). Kommunalismus, Parlamentarismus, Republikanismus. *Historische Zeitschrift, 242*, 529–556.
Blickle, P. (2000). *Kommunalismus. Skizzen einer gesellschaftlichen Organisationsform* (Vols. 1 and 2). Munich: R. Oldenbourg.
Böhler, M. (1996). Nationalisierungsprozesse von Literatur im deutschsprachigen Raum: Verwerfungen und Brüche—vom Rande betrachtet. In M. Huber &

G. Lauer (Eds.), *Bildung und Konfession. Politik, Religion und literarische Identitätsbildung 1850–1918* (pp. 21–38). Tübingen: Niemeyer.

Brändli, S., Landolt, P., & Wertli, P. (1998). *Die Bildung des wahren republikanischen Bürgers. Der aargauische Erziehungsrat 1798–1998*. Aarau: Erziehungsdepartement des Kantons Aargau.

Canetti, E. (2003). *Masse und Macht* (29th ed.). Frankfurt am Main: Fischer.

Clauss, W. (1955). Prof. Dr. August Steiger 1874–1954. In *Jahresbericht des kantonalen Literargymnasiums Zürich: [s.n.] 1954/55* (pp. 21–24).

De Capitani, F. (2000). Die Schweiz. Bild und Inszenierung einer Republik. In M. Böhler, E. Hofmann, P. H. Reill, & S. Zurbuchen (Eds.), *Republikanische Tugend. Ausbildung eines Schweizer Nationalbewusstseins und Erziehung eines neuen Bürgers* (Travaux sur la Suisse des Lumières, 2) (pp. 19–32). Geneva: Editions Slatkine.

Erneuerte Schul- und Lehr-Ordnung für die Schulen der Landschaft Zürich. (1778). Zürich: [s.n.].

Ferrari, M. C. (2000). Johann Caspar von Orelli und das Mittelalter. In M. C. Ferrari (Ed.), *Gegen Unwissenheit und Finsternis* (pp. 157–189). Zurich: Chronos.

Follen, A. A. L. (1828). *Bildersaal deutscher Dichtung. Zunächst für Übung in mündlichem und schriftlichem Erzählen, im Deklamieren und in ästhetischer Kritik. Geordnete Stoffsammlung zum Behuf einer allgemeinen, poetischen und ästhetischen Schulbildung. Nebst einer Übersicht der deutschen Srach= und Literatur=Geschichte. Erster Theil: Epos und episch=lyrische Dichtung*. Winterthur: Steiner.

Foucault, M. (2004). *Geschichte der Gouvernementalität II. Die Geburt der Biopolitik*. Frankfurt am Main: Suhrkamp.

Fuchs, M. (2001). *Dies Buch ist mein Acker. Der Kanton Aargau und seine Volksschullesebücher im 19. Jahrhundert*. Aarau: Sauerläder.

Gesetz über das gesammte Unterrichtswesen des Kantons Zürich. (1859). Zürich: [s.n.].

Gesetz betreffend das gesammte Unterrichtswesen des Kantons Zürich. (1872). Zürich: [s.n.].

Greyerz, O. von (1921). *Der Deutschunterricht als Weg zur nationalen Erziehung. Eine Einführung für junge Lehrer*. 2. Auflage. Leipzig: Julius Klinkhardt.

Grube, N. (2007). Dichten auf dem Pferdpauschen: Germanisches Mittelalter in der Entstehung des Deutschunterrichts im Kanton Zürich nach 1833. *Zeitschrift für pädagogische Historiographie, 13*(1), 48–56.

Guyer, P. (1943). *Verfassungszustände der Stadt Zürich im 16., 17. und 18. Jahrhundert unter der Einwirkung der sozialen Umschichtung der Bevölkerung*. Unpublished doctoral dissertation, University of Zurich, Zurich.

Hamm, B. (1992). Reformation als normative Zentrierung von Religion und Gesellschaft. *Jahrbuch für Biblische Theologie, 7*, 241–259.

Hamm, B. (2004). *The Reformation of faith in the context of late medieval theology and piety: Essays by Berndt Hamm* (Studies in the history of Christian thought) (R. J. Bast, Ed.). Leiden: Brill Academic Publishers.

Helbling, B. (1994). *Eine Schweiz für die Schule. Nationale Identität und kulturelle Vielfalt in den Schweizer Lesebüchern seit 1900*. Zürich: Chronos.

Hettling, M., König, M., Schaffner, M., Suter, A., & Tanner, J. (1998). *Eine kleine Geschichte der Schweiz. Der Bundesstaat und seine Traditionen*. Frankfurt am Main: Edition Suhrkamp.

Hunziker, F. (1933). *Die Mittelschulen in Zürich und Winterthur 1833–1933*. Festschrift zur Jahrhundertfeier. Zürich: Erziehungsrat des Kantons Zürich.

Hunziker, F. (1948). *Der Erziehungsrat des Kantons Zürich*. Zürich: Erziehungsdirektion des Kantons Zürich.

Hux, A. (2002). *Von der Lateinschule zur Oberstufe. Geschichte der Sekundarschule Frauenfeld im Rahmen des Frauenfelder Schulwesens*. Frauenfeld: Huber.
Jahresbericht der Zürcher Industrieschule. (1913/1914). In Programm der Kantonsschule Zürich, 1915.
Jost, H. U. (1983). Bedrohung und Enge (1914–1945). In *Geschichte der Schweiz— und der Schweizer* (Vol. 3). Basel, Frankfurt am Main: Schwabe.
Kliebard, H. M. (2004). *The struggle for the American curriculum 1893–1958* (3rd ed.). New York, London: Routledge.
Kronbichler, W. (1983). *Die zürcherischen Kantonsschulen 1833–1983. Festschrift zur 150-Jahr-Feier der staatlichen Mittelschulen des Kantons Zürich*. Zürich: Erziehungsdirektion des Kantons Zürich.
Kuhlemann, F.-M. (1992). *Modernisierung und Disziplinierung. Sozialgeschichte des preußischen Volksschulwesens 1794–1872*. Göttingen: Vandenhoeck & Ruprecht.
Leith, J. H. (1990). Kirchenzucht. *Theologische Realenzyklopädie*, 9. Berlin: W. de Gruyter, p. 173–176.
Lovett, F. (2006). *Republicanism. The Stanford Encyclopedia of Philosophy*. Retrieved January 19, 2007, from http://plato.stanford.edu/entries/republicanism.
Lüning, H., & Sartori, I. (1861). *Deutsches Lesebuch für die unteren und mittleren Klassen höherer Schulen (Gymnasien, Industrieschulen u.s.w.)*. Erster Theil. Zweiter Theil. Zurich: Druck und Verlag Friedrich Schulthess.
Mager, K. (1843). *Deutsches Elementarwerk. Lese- und Lehrbuch für Gymnasien und h.[öhere] Bürger = (Real=)schulen, Cadettenhäuser, Institute und Privatunterricht*. Neue Auflage. Stuttgart; Siebente Auflage Stuttgart und Augsburg 1857.
Mager, W. (1984). Republik. *Geschichtliche Grundbegriffe, Historisches Lexikon zur politisch-sozialen Sprache in Deutschland*, 5, 549–651.
Markwart, O. (1908). Prof. Heinrich Motz. Ein Lebensbild. In *Programm der Kantonsschule in Zürich*/Beilage: [s.n.] (pp. 1–25).
Müller, D. K. (1977). *Sozialstruktur und Schulsystem. Aspekte zum Strukturwandel des Schulwesens im 19. Jahrhundert*. Göttingen: Vandenhoeck & Ruprecht.
Münkler, H. (1991). Die Idee der Tugend. Ein politischer Leitbegriff im vorrevolutionären Europa. *Archiv für Kulturgeschichte*, 73, 370–403.
Orelli, J. C. (1808/1891). *Wahrheiten für ein Gymnasium allenthalben*. Ein Jugendbrief J. C. Orelli's (1808). Sonderabdruck aus dem Jahresheft des Vereins Schweizerischer Gymnasiallehrer, 22, without page numbers.
Orelli, J. C. von. (1817). Bericht über die Lesung des Nibelungenliedes. In *Wöchentliche Nachrichten für Freunde der Geschichte, Kunst und Gelahrtheit des Mittelalters*, 4, 36–41.
Orelli, J. K., & Usteri, L. (1831). *Pädagogische Ansichten über äussere Trennung und geistige Einheit der wissenschaftlichen und technischen Schulen: nebst einem Bruchstücke aus dem Zürcherischen Schulplane von 1830 und einem Vorschlage für die neue Organisation des Unterrichtswesens im Kanton Zürich*. Zürich: Orell Füssli.
Pettit, P. (2003, Spring). *Republicanism. The Stanford Encyclopedia of Philosophy*. Retrieved January 19, 2007, from http://plato.stanford.edu/archives/ spr2003/ entries/republicanism.
Pocock, J. G. A. (1993). *Die andere Bürgergesellschaft. Zur Dialektik von Tugend und Korruption*. Frankfurt/Main, New York: Campus Verlag.
Riedweg, C. (2000). Bildungspolitik im frühen 19. und am Ende des 20. Jahrhunderts. Zu den bildungspolitischen Leitideen Johann Caspar von Orellis. In M. C. Ferrari (Ed.), *Gegen Unwissenheit und Finsternis. Johann Caspar von Orelli (1787–1849) und die Kultur seiner Zeit* (pp. 327–354). Zürich: Chronos.

Satzungen den Land-Schulen von den obersten Schulherren der Stadt Zürich fürgeschriben. (1744). Zürich: Heidegger.

Schmidt, H. R. (1995). *Dorf und Religion. Reformierte Sittenzucht in Berner Landgemeinden der Frühen Neuzeit (Quellen und Forschungen zur Agrargeschichte, 41).* Stuttgart: Gustav Fischer.

Schnorf, K. (1900). *Deutsches Lesebuch für die untern und mittlern Klassen höherer Lehranstalten der Schweiz (Gymnasien, Industrieschulen u.s.w.).* Erster Teil Zweite Auflage (Vierte Auflage des Lesebuches von Lüning und Sartori). Zürich: Druck und Verlag von Schulthess & Co.

Staehelin, H. (2002). *Die alte Kantonsschule Aarau 1802–2002. 200 Jahre aargauische Mittelschule.* Aarau: AT Verlag AZ Fachverlage.

Steiger, A. (1930). *Sprachlicher Heimatschutz in der deutschen Schweiz.* Erlenbach bei Zürich: Rentsch (*Volksbücher des deutschschweizerischen Sprachvereins*, 12).

Stiefel, J. (1902). Poesie und Schule. Vortrag an der außerordentlichen Synode vom 9. Juni. In *Berichte über Verhandlungen der Zürcher Schulsynoden 1898–1902* Zürich: [s.n.] (pp. 73–102).

Tröhler, D. (2000). Republikanismus als Erziehungsprogramm: Die Rolle von Geschichte und Freundschaft in den Konzepten eidgenössischer Bürgerbildung der Helvetischen Gesellschaft. In M. Böhler, E. Hofmann, P. H. Reill, & S. Zurbuchen (Eds.), *Republikanische Tugend. Ausbildung eines Schweizer Nationalbewusstseins und Erziehung eines neuen Bürgers (Travaux sur la Suisse des Lumières, 2)* (pp. 401–421). Geneva: Editions Slatkine.

Tröhler, D. (2006). *Republikanismus und Pädagogik. Pestalozzi im historischen Kontext.* Bad Heilbrunn: Klinkhardt.

Tröhler, D., & Schwab, A. (Eds.). (2006). *Volksschule im 18. Jahrhundert. Die Schulumfrage auf der Zürcher Landschaft 1771/72: Quellen und Studien.* Bd. 1. Bad Heilbrunn: Klinkhardt.

Weibel, T. (1996). Der zürcherische Stadtstaat. In N. Flüeler & M. Flüeler-Grauwiler (Eds.), *Geschichte des Kantons Zürich* (pp. 16–65). Bd. 2. Frühe Neuzeit–16. bis 18. Jahrhundert, Zurich: Werdverlag.

Weinmann, B. (2002). *Eine andere Bürgergesellschaft. Klassischer Republikanismus und Kommunalismus im Kanton Zürich im späten 18. und 19. Jahrhundert.* Göttingen: Vandenhoeck & Ruprecht.

Wernle, P. (1923). *Der schweizerische Protestantismus im XVIII. Jahrhundert.* Bd. 1: Das reformierte Staatskirchentum und seine Ausläufer (Pietismus und vernünftige Orthodoxie). Tübingen: J.C.B. Mohr.

Winter, H.-G. (1989). Klopstocks Revolutionsoden. In A. Herzig, I. Stephan, & H.-G. Winter (Eds.), *"Sie, und nicht wir." Die Französische Revolution und ihre Wirkung auf Norddeutschland* (Vol. 1, pp. 131–151). Hamburg: Dölling und Galitz.

Ziegler, P. (1978). *Zürcher Sittenmandate.* Zurich: Orell Füssli.

Contributors

Phillip Cormack is Associate-Professor of Education in the School of Education at the University of South Australia, Australia. His research interests include the history of adolescence, and contemporary and historical perspectives on literacy policy, curriculum and pedagogy.

Jeroen J. H. Dekker is professor of history and theory at the University of Groningen in the Netherlands. He was a visiting professor at the European University Institute in Florence in 1998 and 2005, and in 2010 at the European Institute of Columbia University in New York. A former president of ISCHE, he is Co-Editor–in-Chief of *Paedagogica Historica*. His research interest is social and cultural history of education and childhood. His most recent book is *Educational Ambitions in History* (2010).

Andrea De Vincenti is Research Associate in the research group "School in a Social context"at the Zurich School of Education (PHZH) with special interests in the history of schooling in the 18th century, interaction between institutionalized education and society, institutional change, citizenship education and social theory.

Inés Dussel is researcher and professor at the Latin American School for the Social Sciences (FLACSO/Argentina). Her main research areas are the history of education and pedagogy and educational policies. Her recent work includes a reflection on the intersection among visual studies, history, and pedagogy.

Bill Green is Professor of Education at Charles Stuart University, New South Wales, Australia. His research interests are in literacy studies and curriculum inquiry, with a particular focus on curriculum history and English curriculum studies.

Norbert Grube is research associate at the "Pestalozzianum Research Library" at the Zurich School of Education (PHZH) with special interests in school reform discourse and implementation around 1800, history of mentality and perceptions, new cultural history of politics, political planning, and consultation (contemporary history).

David Hamilton retired from a chair of education at Umeå University (Sweden) in 2005. During the 1970s, he extended an interest in classroom life into the history of schooling, a diversion that yielded *Towards a Theory of Schooling* (London: Falmer, 1989) and *Learning about Education: An unfinished curriculum* (Buckingham: Open University Press, 1990).

David F. Labaree is a professor and associate dean for student affairs in the Stanford University School of Education (USA). His research focuses on the history of American education. He was president of the History of Education Society (USA) in 2004–2005 and vice-president for Division F (history of education) of the American Educational Research Association (2003–2006). His books include *The Making of an American High School* (1988), *How to Succeed in School Without Really Learning* (1997), and *The Trouble with Ed Schools* (2003).

Daniel Lindmark, PhD, is Professor of History and History Didactics at Umeå University, Sweden, and Associate Professor of Church History at Åbo Akademi University, Finland. His research interests include literacy studies, religious studies, emigration studies, Saami studies, and various aspects of educational history, preferably primary and secondary education in Sweden before 1850.

Willeke Los is lecturer in the history of humanism at the University of Humanistics in Utrecht, the Netherlands. Her main field of interest is the history of education in the Netherlands in the 18th century.

Jorge Ramos do Ó is Professor of History of Education and discourse analysis at the University of Lisbon and invited professor at the University of Sáo Paolo, Brazil. He has written about political history, history of culture and mentalities during the authoritarian period in Portugal (1926–1974), and also about history of education and modern pedagogy (19th and 20th centuries).

Fritz Osterwalder is Professor at the University of Bern, Switzerland. His main fields of research in the History of Education are the research on the developments of modern mass-schooling in the context of religious, political, and economical conceptions. Recent publications include co-editions of *Pädagogische Modernisierung. Säkularität und Sakralität in der modernen Pädagogik, Forum Bildung und Beschäftigung* (1), *Das verdrängte Erbe. Pädagogik im Kontext von Religion und Theologie*.

Thomas S. Popkewitz is Professor and former Chair in the Department of Curriculum and Instruction, The University of Wisconsin-Madison, Madison, Wisconsin. His studies in the United States and comparatively are concerned with the systems of reason that govern educational reforms and research in teaching, teacher education, and the sciences of education. His most recent books include *Cosmopolitanism and the Study of School Reform* (2008) and *Globalization and the Study of Education* (2009, with F. Rizvi, eds.).

Daniel Tröhler is Professor and Director of the Research Unit "Language, Culture, Media, and Identities" at the University of Luxembourg. He has written *Languages of Education. Protestant Legacies, National Identities, and Global Aspirations* (in press, 2011). He is editor and annotator of the critical edition of the complete letters written to Pestalozzi and chief editor of the journal *Bildungsgeschichte/International Journal for the historiography of education*. His research interests include the analysis of educational and political languages, republicanism, pragmatism, and methodological problems of historiography.

Antonio Viñao is professor of Theory and History of Education at the University of Murcia (Spain). Ex-member of the Executive Committee of the International Standing Conference for the History of Education (1996–2000) and ex-chair of the Spanish Society of History of Education (2001–2005), his main fields of research are history of literacy (reading and writing as cultural practices) and history of curriculum (school space and time, school subjects), as well as the relationships between school cultures and educational reforms.

Index

A
Adão, Áurea, 76, 77
Addams, Jane, 229
Administrative progressivism, 185
Alcalà Galiano, Vicente, 99
Alfonso X the Wise, 106
American enlightenment, 221
American exceptionalism, 221, 223, 226–228, 230
Ancien Régime, 99, 100, 106, 134, 153–155, 158, 162, 195, 196, 201, 206
Anderson, Benedict, 247–250
Argüelles, Augustín, 101, 108
Atkinson, Alan, 240, 243, 245–248, 257
Australia, 1, 18, 22, 24, 240–249, 251–258

B
Bacon, Francis, 125
Baker, Bernadette, 251
Basedow, Johann Bernard, 51, 52
Batavian Republic, 24, 51, 53, 57, 59, 60, 63, 64, 262–264, 275
Bentham, Jeremy, 106
Binet, Alfred, 85
Boece, Hector, 118
Bonaparte, Joseph, 97, 101,
Bonaparte, Louis-Napoleon, 23, 24, 199, 264, 273, 274
Bosch, Bernardus, 56
British Empire, 241, 251, 253
Brugghen, J.J.L.van der, 62
Buchanan, George, 117
Buijs, Jacobus, 53
Bullinger, Heinrich, 170
Burmann, Gottlob Wilhelm, 53

C
Cabarrús, Domingo de, 96, 98, 107
Calvin, Jean, 20, 112, 222
Calvinism, 153, 202
Campe, Joachim Heinrich, 51, 52, 64
Campomanes, 95, 96, 99, 109
Campos, Ramón, 99
Capellen tot den Pol, Joan Derk van der, 51, 275
Castiglione, Baldassare, 115
Catechism(s), 16, 17, 20, 34, 35, 37–39, 41- 46, 62, 97, 98, 101–104, 107, 109, 120, 137, 149, 159, 283
Catholic, catholics, 12, 16, 20, 24, 56–64, 99, 100, 102, 104, 107, 108, 114, 148, 155, 162, 168, 173, 208
Catholic church, 16, 20, 95, 96, 102, 106, 108, 148, 168, 169, 194, 199, 201, 203, 207, 208
Catholic Enlightenment, 98, 102, 106,
Catholic immigrants, 168
Catholic religion, catholicism, 8, 96, 101, 104, 109, 153, 201, 203, 208, 210
Cats, Jacob, 53, 56, 274
Charles IV, 101
Christian, 16, 17, 21, 22, 29, 41, 43, 44, 46, 50, 54, 56, 58–61, 95, 97, 104, 113, 136, 155, 159, 162, 168, 169, 221, 222, 228, 230, 263, 273, 278, 283, 284, 288, 290
Church, 16, 32, 33–35, 40, 41, 47, 58, 62, 74, 81, 96, 98, 108, 109, 112, 117, 120, 153, 155, 157–161, 168–170, 181, 194, 199–201, 206, 211, 212, 268, 278, 283, 284, 287, 298
Chydenius, Anders, 44, 45
Cicero, Marcus Tullius, 115

Citizen, 1–10, 12–22, 31, 32, 34, 46, 47, 50, 52–59, 63, 64, 70, 71, 74, 75, 78, 80–83, 94, 95–107, 109, 113, 116, 126, 134, 141, 145, 154–157, 163–167, 170–172, 177–181, 184–191, 194, 197, 198, 200, 202, 204, 205, 208, 211, 212, 217, 220–226, 230, 231, 233, 235, 236, 241, 246, 248, 253, 257, 263, 271, 273, 276–278, 283, 285, 287, 288, 290, 291, 294, 296
Citizenship, 2, 3, 6, 12–17, 20, 23, 50, 51–53, 55, 63, 64, 70, 71, 73, 74, 91, 94, 98, 100, 102, 105, 107, 117, 135, 136, 138, 142, 146, 147, 183, 186, 189–191, 241, 243, 245, 246, 248, 252, 255, 256, 257, 262, 264, 265, 268, 271, 273, 275–278, 296
civic virtue, 12, 15, 17, 18, 23, 31, 43–47, 71, 81, 82, 91, 94–96, 106, 109, 177, 178, 182, 187, 188, 190, 191, 219, 221, 222, 228, 231, 235
Civil rights movement, 178, 188, 190
Class, 31, 57, 58, 70, 71, 73, 78, 84–87, 89, 90, 114, 119, 124, 125, 140, 143, 179–180, 182, 184, 229, 230, 262, 268, 296
Coelho, Adolfo, 73, 74
Comenius, Johan Amos, 114
Common school movement, 178–183, 187, 190
Comparative style of thought, 18, 19, 220, 225, 231, 232
Comte, Augusto, 82, 194, 202, 210
Condorcet, Marie Jean Antoine Nicolas de Caritat Marquis de, 9, 158, 193–202, 203, 205–208, 210–213
Condado, Manuel Joaquín de, 99
Condillac, Étienne Bonnot de, 23
Constitution, 13, 16, 21, 23, 24, 51, 53, 57, 59, 60, 62, 73, 91, 94, 97, 98, 100–109, 132, 135, 138, 139, 153–155, 158, 159–164, 166, 167, 169, 170, 188, 195, 197, 249, 262, 264, 288, 297–299
Consumerism, 181, 182
Cooley, Charles Horton, 227
Cortes, Hernán, 94, 96, 100–103, 105, 106, 107, 109

Cosmopolitan self, 142
Costa, Isaac da, 62
culture of oneself, 72
curriculum, 3, 5, 17, 21, 22, 32, 33, 34, 35, 36, 46, 47, 59, 60, 64, 71, 72, 75, 78, 81–84, 86, 89–91, 98, 114, 118, 141, 150, 159, 164, 166, 170, 183, 184, 185, 186, 187, 188, 207, 210, 217, 233, 242, 244, 245, 247, 248, 249, 251, 252–255, 257, 263, 267, 290

D

De Witt (brothers), 266, 275, 276
Deken, Aagje, 54, 55, 63
Dekker, Jeroen J. H., 14, 16, 22, 50, 52, 53, 56, 60, 62, 263
Democracy, 2, 10, 11, 15, 18, 24, 80, 91, 121, 122, 153, 158, 163, 167, 169, 170, 184, 186, 187, 189, 193, 203–205, 211, 213, 224, 227, 242, 244, 246, 257, 296
Descartes, René, 123
Destutt de Tracy, Antoine-Louis-Claude, 106, 212
Dewey, John, 5, 185, 220, 223, 229, 230, 234, 235,
Dialectic, 113, 122, 123, 125, 222
didactic style, 123
Direct democracy, 24, 153, 163, 169, 171
Discipline, 15, 74, 82, 83, 86, 98, 99, 102, 105, 143, 205, 213, 275
Dixson, Miriam, 244, 245
Dutch Enlightenment, 16, 50, 51, 53–56, 63
Dutch Monarchy, 50, 62–64, 264, 269, 271, 277
Dutch Revolt, 272, 273
Duties, 16, 17, 31, 32, 41–48, 83, 94, 95, 98, 103, 105, 106, 107, 126, 159, 204, 209, 210, 262, 283, 291

E

Ecole laïque, 194, 200, 206, 209
Economic societies, 95, 99, 109
Effen, Justus van, 54, 56, 63
elites, 18, 73, 135, 230,
eloquence, 113, 116, 118–120, 197, 212
Ende, Adriaan van den, 60, 61, 267, 268
English teaching, 241, 243, 251, 252, 254
Englund, Tomas, 33, 34, 46

Erasmus, Desiderius von Rotterdam, 115, 118, 169
Escoiquiz, Juan de, 97
Estate, 35, 40–43, 45, 47, 95, 106, 108, 163
Ettmüller, Ludwig, 292, 293
Eurocentrism, 132
European and North, 221, 229
Exam, 76, 78, 86, 87, 89
experimental education, 75, 82, 83

F

family, 14, 23, 41, 42, 52, 53, 74, 101, 115, 145, 194, 213, 227, 235
fatherland, 4, 7, 9, 20, 33, 96, 135, 145, 162, 164, 166, 171, 172, 265, 268–272, 289, 291–293, 295
Federation, 240, 242–246, 255, 257
Fernando VII of Borbon, 100, 101, 104, 108
Ferry, Jules, 193, 194, 200, 206, 207, 208, 209, 210, 211, 213, 214
Floridablanca, José Moñino y Redondo de, 96
Foucault, Michel, 86, 142, 299
French Revolution, 8–11, 15, 99, 107, 154, 157, 170, 201, 208, 213, 262, 274, 294
Fusely, John Henry, 157

G

Galicanism, 96
Garden of Eden, 113, 117, 221, 222
Garelli, Nicolás Mª, 115
General states, 266, 276
Génestet, Petrus de, 54
Glasgow University, 111, 122, 124
Gomila, Juan Piconelly, 97
Governmentality, 247, 249, 253, 257
Groen van Prinsterer, Guillaume, 62

H

Hamelsveld, IJsbrand van, 56
Hamilton, David, 14, 16, 20, 22, 111, 113, 243
Herculano, Alexandre, 70, 71, 73, 77–80, 87, 91
Hjortsberg, Magnus, 43
Hoonaard, Will C. van den, 270, 276, 277, 278
House of Orange, 264, 275, 276
Hull, Willem van den, 54
Human capital, 23, 177, 178, 180, 188, 191

Humanism, 14, 16, 112–114, 116, 117, 121, 169
Hunziker, Frei Gustav, 159, 165, 171, 290, 291, 293, 295

I

Ideas "out-of-place", 132
Instruction publique, 194–198, 206, 207, 210,

J

Jardine, George, 111, 124, 125
Jesuit, 16, 22, 72, 79, 99, 112, 114, 116, 207

K

Kant, Immanuel, 11, 125, 126
Kneppelhout, Johannes, 52
Knox, John, 20, 112
Knudsen, Tim, 31, 32, 46, 47
Kooi, Willem Bartel van der, 55, 56, 63

L

Labaree, David, 14, 15, 19, 22, 131, 191
Lavater, Johann Casper, 157
Lepeletier, Michel, 196
Liberalism, 9, 19, 70, 74, 94, 108, 131, 132, 138, 144, 148, 203, 242, 299
Liberty, 8, 9, 13, 14, 74, 90, 117, 178, 197, 200, 204, 205, 211–214, 219, 225–227, 234, 264–266, 272, 275, 276
Lipsius, Justus, 114
Literacy, 20, 118, 121, 135, 136, 179, 181, 229, 240–242, 245, 247, 249, 250, 252, 258
Lloyd, Christopher, 243, 244, 246
Locke, John, 23, 51, 103, 104
Loyola, Ignatius of 20, 112
Lundgren, Ulf P., 33
Luther, Martin, 17, 31, 32, 34, 35, 40, 42, 44
Lutheranism, 31, 32, 153
Luzac, Elie, 266
Lyons, Martin, 252–254

M

Maatschappij tot Nut van't Algemeen, 51, 262, 273
Machado, Bernardino, 70, 71, 73, 77, 84–86, 91
Marín y Mendoza, Joaquín, 99

Market, 178, 183, 184
Marquis of Pombal, 72
Martinet, Johannes Florentius, 53, 56, 268, 270, 272, 273, 276–279
Marx, Karl, 15, 100, 221
Maurits, Cornelis Escher, 266, 271, 273
Mayans, Gregorio, 99, 109
McKnight, Duncan, 222, 227
Militia army, 162, 165
Mirabeau, Honoré-Gabriel de, 196
Modern republicanism, 9–11, 24, 50–53, 135, 146
Modernization, 16, 21, 50, 70, 71, 86, 90, 115, 121, 144, 241
Moens, Petronella, 55
Moniz, Jaime, 70, 72, 87, 88, 89, 90
Montesquieu, Charles-Louis de, 6–8, 11, 12, 96, 96, 98, 99, 100, 200, 212, 282, 284
Moral Philosophy, 17, 41, 43–47, 105, 122
Moral unity, 19, 194, 200–202, 205, 209

N
Nation, 1, 6, 12, 14, 16, 18–21, 50, 51, 53, 56, 63, 64, 74, 80, 100–102, 105, 107, 109, 131–135, 139, 142–145, 147, 149, 194, 195, 201, 204, 212, 219–228, 231, 236, 240–244, 246–248, 250, 251, 255, 256, 276, 277, 296, 297
national identity, 3, 12, 111, 117–119, 124, 126, 240, 242, 243, 248, 255, 257,
National symbols, 3, 143
nation-state, 1, 4, 5, 70, 125, 143, 146, 219, 241, 243, 250
Natural Law, 9, 11, 17, 33, 41, 46, 47, 99, 104–107, 157, 161, 162, 195, 208
Neutrality of the school, 213
New Education, 53, 82, 167, 251
New England Puritans, 222
Newton, Isaac, 123
Nieuwenhuijzen, Jan, 56
Nóvoa, António, 71, 73, 74, 77

O
Oldenbarneveld, Johan van, 266, 271, 273–276
Orangists, 271
Orelli, Johann Caspar von, 289

Ortigão, Ramalho, 70, 71, 73, 77, 79–84, 87, 91

P
Palm, Johannes Hendrik van der, 60, 63, 263
Palti, Elías José, 131–133, 147, 148
Passos, Manuel, 74–76, 78, 87, 88, 89
Patriarchalism, 40, 42–47
Patriotic Catechism, 136, 137, 145, 146
Patriotic revolt, 271–275
Patriotism, 14, 16, 51, 52, 95, 98, 107, 109, 149, 156, 163, 166, 169, 172, 227, 228, 254–256, 268, 273, 275–277
Patriots, 51, 52, 64, 262, 275
Pedagogy of statues, 144
Pestalozzi, Johann Heinrich, 157, 162, 171, 172
philanthropic society, 51, 52, 56, 57
Philo-Jansenism, 96, 102
Pleijel, Hilding, 35, 36, 39
Pocock, John Greville Agard, 10, 221, 236, 245, 250, 251, 290
political subjectivation, 72
Popkewitz, S. Thomas, 5, 6, 14, 16–18, 20, 22, 89, 131, 169, 219, 221, 231, 236, 248, 249, 253
Pothmann, Mor Kasim, 43
Private good, 177, 190, 191
Progressive movement, 178, 183, 187, 188, 237
Protestant, 8, 12, 16, 17, 50, 62, 114, 121, 162, 226,
Public good, 177, 187, 191
Public school, 60, 126, 153, 154, 155, 162–168, 178, 179, 188, 189, 202, 208, 211, 242, 251, 254, 255, 257
public schooling, 240–243
Puffendorf, Samuel Freiherr von, 109
Puritan, 14, 16, 170, 219–224, 227, 231

Q
Quinet, Edgar, 193, 199, 200–213
Quintana, Manuel José, 102, 103, 105, Quintilian, Marcus Fabius, 78, 115

R
reading pedagogy, 241, 252, 253, 257
reciprocity, 42, 47
Reformation, 15, 20, 112, 113, 117, 168, 169, 221, 225, 227, 284

Reformed Protestant, 24, 155, 167, 168, 169, 219
Reformed Protestantism, 8, 153, 155, 156, 160, 168
relationships, 23, 41, 42, 43, 44, 45, 54, 94, 106, 137, 185, 305
Religion, 8, 15, 16, 32, 44, 45, 56, 59, 60, 63, 64, 96, 97, 98, 101, 107, 119, 122, 155, 156, 159, 168, 197, 198, 200, 201, 205, 207, 208, 211, 212, 225, 230, 235, 263, 272, 273, 284, 289
Renan, Ernest, 149, 276, 279
Representative democracy, 153, 158, 163, 169, 170
Republic
Republic of Zurich, 15, 17, 153, 154, 155, 168, 282, 288, 289, 297
Republican, 2, 13–15, 70, 71, 86, 96, 121, 140, 155, 163, 164, 167, 169, 180, 185, 200, 203, 206, 284
Republican city-state, 155
Republican community, 94, 177–180, 182, 184, 185, 191
Republican language, 8, 20, 146, 162–164, 289, 295, 297
Republicanism, 1, 7–11, 15–18, 20, 21, 24, 70, 77, 94, 95, 100, 102, 106, 111–113, 118, 121, 125, 126, 131–134, 138, 139, 141, 142, 144, 146–148, 153, 155, 162, 164–167, 169, 171, 191, 194–196, 203, 204, 211, 212, 219, 220–222, 224, 225, 232, 235, 236, 242, 243, 245, 250, 262, 274, 277, 282, 288–291, 295–299
Republicanism, classical 8–11, 21, 24, 98, 135, 153–155, 157, 162, 163, 164, 167, 171, 211, 293,
rights, 16, 17, 59, 95, 98, 99, 101–105, 109, 124, 132, 139, 154, 155, 158, 159, 163, 164, 191, 198, 204, 208, 219, 273, 287, 291, 296
Ritual, 143
Ross, Alexander, 188, 222, 227
Rousseau, Jean-Jacques, 9, 16, 20, 51, 52, 56, 64, 95, 98, 99, 133, 135, 146, 148, 171, 195, 196

S
Saint-Etienne, Rabaut, 196

Salas, Ramón de, 106
Salzmann, Christian Gotthilf, 51, 52
Sarmiento, Domingo Faustino, 96, 133, 138, 139, 140–142, 144–146, 149
School, 1, 2, 4, 5, 10, 12, 14–22, 32, 33, 56–60, 62–64, 72, 76, 79–81, 85, 91, 96, 97, 103, 119, 120, 121, 124, 126, 135, 138, 141, 144–147, 153–173, 178–191, 193–195, 200–203, 205–214, 227, 229, 233, 249, 251–254, 257, 258, 263, 269, 270, 282–295, 297, 298
school acts, 53, 57, 60, 61
school battalions, 145, 150
school board, 158–161, 163, 164
School Papers, 242, 254–257
Schoolmasters, 57, 58, 60, 118, 278, 282–285, 296
Scottish Enlightenment, 14, 111, 112, 117, 118, 122
Self-government, 16, 113, 136, 140, 153–155, 159, 160, 161, 163, 167, 168, 172, 293,
Simonsz, Arend Fokke, 274, 275, 278, 279
Smith, Adam, 11, 99, 118, 122, 123, 125
Social mobility, 177, 181, 190, 191
Sousa, Marnoco e 73
Spanish enlightenment, 95, 109
Spanish liberalism, 96
State, 3, 4, 6, 15, 23, 40, 41, 50, 51, 57, 58, 60, 62–64, 71, 74, 75, 80, 81, 83, 89, 98, 101, 102, 108, 109, 126, 140, 143, 153, 158–160, 163, 164, 166, 167, 169, 185, 188, 189, 195, 200, 202, 204–209, 230, 232, 236, 240, 244, 267, 271, 283, 290
State Education, 74, 75, 77–80, 109, 213, 253, 254
State-Minded republicans, 267, 271
Statists, 76
Stiefel, Julius, 294–296
Swinderen, Bruno van, 270, 276, 278
Switzerland, 4, 7–9, 11, 13, 14, 20, 22, 24, 153, 157, 162–165, 169, 171, 172, 292, 293–295

T
Table of Duties, 17, 31, 32, 34–47
Technological sublime, 225–227, 232

Textbook(s), 15, 34, 35, 41–44, 46, 115, 116, 120, 136, 143–145, 147, 149, 155, 161, 162, 164, 165, 166, 171, 172, 253, 262, 263, 264, 267, 268, 269, 271, 272, 274–279, 289, 292, 297
The social Gospel, 230
The social question, 17, 19, 220, 228, 229, 231, 233, 234, 235
Thorbecke, Johan Rudolph, 62
Thorndike, Edward L., 185, 220, 233, 234
Tröhler, Daniel, 5, 6, 8, 14, 15, 17, 19, 20, 22, 23, 24, 157, 162, 169, 170, 171, 298
Turner, Frederick Jackson, 224, 225, 234

U
universalism, 31, 32, 33, 34, 47
U.S. Constitution, 13, 154

V
Vacherot, Etienne, 203–207, 209, 210, 213
Valbuena, Manuel de, 103
Vallejo, César, 95–99
Vatebender, Gerrit C.C., 53, 57
Virtue education, 196, 197, 228
virtues, 9, 15, 23, 45, 46, 52, 53, 57, 61, 154, 165, 212, 288, 291
Vives, Juan-Luis, 115, 136

W
Wagenaar, Jan, 265–269, 271–276, 278–279
War, 51, 100, 101, 107, 138, 139, 149, 169, 193, 212, 250, 274, 277
War of Independence, 97, 101, 104, 137, 138
Ward, Lester Frank, 234
Weisse, Christian Felix, 53
Wester, Hendrik, 268, 269, 272–276, 278
Wigelius, Samuel, 41, 42, 46
William I, 264, 168, 272, 275, 277
William V, 262, 264, 272
Wolff, Betje, 54, 55, 63
Woodworth, Robert, 234

Z
Zárate, Gil de, 108, 109
Zurich, 7, 12, 15, 17, 20, 22, 153–160, 163, 164, 167–171, 173, 282–284, 287–299
Zwingli, Huldrych, 155, 160, 169, 170
Zwinglian, Zwinglianism 15, 24, 153, 154, 155, 159, 161, 162, 170